PITT SERIES IN

Policy and Institutional Studies

THATCHER REAGAN MULRONEY

IN SEARCH OF A NEW
BUREAUCRACY

Donald J. Savoie

University of Pittsburgh Press
Pittsburgh and London

135587

Published by the University of Pittsburgh Press, Pittsburgh, Pa., 15260
Copyright © 1994, University of Pittsburgh Press
All rights reserved
Manufactured in the United States of America
Printed on acid-free paper

Library of Congress Cataloging-in-Publication Data

Savoie, Donald J.
    Thatcher, Reagan, Mulroney : in search of a new bureaucracy /
Donald J. Savoie.
        p.   cm. — (Pitt series in policy and institutional studies)
    Includes index.
    ISBN 0-8229-3775-1. — ISBN 0-8229-5519-9 (pbk.)
    1. Civil service reform—United States.   2. Reagan, Ronald.
3. Civil service reform—Great Britain.   4. Thatcher, Margaret.
5. Civil service reform—Canada.   6. Mulroney, Brian.   I. Title.
II. Series.
JK692.S28   1994
351.6—dc20   93-24373
                                                                        CIP

A CIP catalogue record for this book is available from the British Library.
Eurospan, London

To Linda, Julien, and Margaux
for their patience

Contents

Preface

THIS BOOK was born of a desire to understand the impact on the civil services in three countries that elected right-of-center politicians to power in the 1980s. Bureaucracy has few friends, even in the best of times. To many observers, the word *bureaucracy* itself suggests bad public administration. Margaret Thatcher, Ronald Reagan, and Brian Mulroney came to office convinced not only that their bureaucracies were inefficient but also that the bureaucracies were responsible for much of the economic woe that gripped their respective countries. To be sure, all three leaders were antigovernment, but they were even more antibureaucracy. And all three set out to reform their civil service.

Career civil servants, meanwhile, take great pride in their ability to work with politicians of all persuasions and ideologies. Their purpose is not to hold firmly to specific policy positions but rather to assist the politicians in power to define their policy preferences and then to implement them. However, a large body of literature argues that career civil servants intuitively favor the status quo and that many of them have developed a well-honed capacity to give the appearance of change while, in fact, moving very slowly or even standing still. One can, of course, understand that civil servants will resist measures that threaten their interests or the well-being of their institutions. Civil servants are also human. In Thatcher, Reagan, and Mulroney, the civil service in three countries came face-to-face with a political leadership bent on smashing the status quo. In reporting on their efforts, this book also assesses the legacies that the three leaders have left behind.

All writers are more in debt to friends, colleagues, and others than is commonly known. I owe a great deal to all those who traveled the territory before me, and I acknowledge many intellectual debts in the notes. Others, however, are not so formally acknowledged.

I must first thank present and former government officials in Britain, the United States, and Canada who gave so generously of their time and dealt with all my questions. This book would have not been possible without their assistance and insights. A number of them also made important new data available. In consultations with academic colleagues in London and Washington and with several government officials in the three countries, I made a list of people I wanted to interview. There were only two on the list I was not able to interview. Both were former senior officials: one I was not able to track down and the other simply refused, saying that he had decided not to grant any interviews about his work while in government.

A number of respondents went out of their way to be helpful. They led me to explore several avenues and issues that I had not—and would not have—identified. Although in my request to meet with them, I had asked for no more than one hour of their time, a good number, at their initiative, gave me more than an hour.

I owe a special word of thanks to Peter Hennessy and Colin Campbell who assisted me in identifying some of the officials I interviewed in London and Washington. The Canadian Centre for Management Development (CCMD) provided inestimable help in opening doors in London, Washington, and Ottawa.

A number of scholars and practitioners read the first draft of the book and made important suggestions to improve the study. I owe a special thanks to Peter Aucoin, Colin Campbell, John Chenier, Ben and Jean Higgins, B. Guy Peters, Paul Thomas, Doug and Cynthia Williams, and Walter Williams. Their comments led me to undertake a substantial rewrite of two chapters. I also owe a debt to Joan Harcourt who read the manuscript and made many editorial suggestions. The book is greatly improved as a result. Ginette Benoit typed and retyped these pages and to her my exceptional word of thanks. But all the defects of the book are mine.

As always, my family gave me the encouragement, affection, and above all, the patience I needed throughout the time I was researching and writing this book. I dedicate this book to Linda and our children, Julien and Margaux.

THATCHER
REAGAN
MULRONEY

1

Introduction

Historians will look to the 1980s as a watershed period in the development of Western bureaucracies.[1] By the early 1980s, public bureaucracies stood accused of being many things: bloated, cumbersome, uncreative, lethargic, and insensitive.[2] This widely negative perception could be found in many countries. A keen and respected observer of American politics remarked that

> two thirds of the public believe that the federal government employs too many people and that they do not work as hard as those who hold private sector jobs. These attitudes are not held only by the uninformed; opinion polls consistently show that respect for government servants steadily dwindles as one moves up the scale of education and income. Indeed, among the more affluent and better educated, one of the few things that unites the left and the right is their common disdain for bureaucrats.[3]

In Britain, a number of journalists and observers by the late 1970s began to write about the scale, cost, and efficiency of the state and "what was thought to be the privilege of officialdom."[4] Canadians told public opinion surveys throughout the 1980s that "they had less confidence in the public service than in any other institution, save for the trade union movement, politicians and more recently the tobacco industry."[5] A royal commission on Canada's economic future warned in 1985 that "The reach of the state has in many ways outrun both our administrative and technical capacities, and our capacity to ensure democratic accountability."[6] Alan Cairns summed it up well when he observed that "The binge of post World War II state worship . . . has ended, and a reassessment of state, market and state society is underway."[7]

Certainly many politicians were quick to express frustration with their public services. Ronald Reagan, on assuming office, wasted no

3

time in making his own views known about bureaucracy. He declared on his inaugural day that he had come to Washington "to drain the swamp."[8] In Great Britain, shortly after coming to office, Margaret Thatcher made literature on public choice theory required reading for senior public servants. In Canada, Prime Minister Mulroney said in his election campaign speeches that once in office he would hand out "pink slips and running shoes to bureaucrats."[9]

It would be wrong, however, to assume that only the political right has strong reservations about public bureaucracies. John K. Galbraith, himself a leading proponent of the twentieth century for a greater role for government in society, recently observed that bureaucracy has given government a bad name. Galbraith argues that "It's more than the liberal task to defend the system. It is far more important now to improve the operation than enlarge and increase its scope. This must be the direction of our major effort."[10] Christopher Pollitt reports that, by 1984, both Republican and Democratic parties had come to include elements strongly critical of the bureaucracy. The president of the American Society for Public Administration spoke of the "snow-blanket of citizen suspicions of governmental institutions" and be-wailed the way in which "public debate of the issue has shrunk down to ankle-height." And Aaron Wildavsky remarked that "the most se-nior bureaucracy now is only for the brave."[11]

British left-wing politicians have also not hesitated to contribute to the mounting criticism. Tony Benn argued that "the power, role, in-fluence and authority of the senior levels of the Civil Service in Britain . . . have grown to such an extent as to create the embryo of a corporate state."[12] Even centrist politicians who had worked well with public servants while in office became openly critical of them once they were out of power in the 1980s. Shirley Williams, for example, wrote that "My impression of the British Civil Service is that it is a beauti-fully designed and effective braking mechanism. It produces a hundred well argued answers against initiative and change."[13]

But it was the right-of-center politicians who, in the 1980s, arrived in office armed with a firm agenda for reforming their respective public services. These politicians came to office with preconceived notions of how things actually worked or, better yet, how they did not work inside government. And they did not hesitate to introduce important reforms:

Reagan set up the Grace Commission to investigate the operations of the U.S. government, and he subsequently introduced changes; like Reagan, Thatcher looked to outside advice to revamp the British public service and then put in place a host of new measures; Mulroney served notice that making the public service more responsive and more efficient was at the top of his political agenda, and he, too, introduced wide-ranging changes to the Canadian public service.

The purpose of this book is to examine how three governments sought to modernize their bureaucracies. I set out to answer a number of questions: What forces led to these changes? How sweeping have they been? Have they resulted in traditional concerns of public administration being pushed aside? What role has political ideology played in the attempts to reshape public bureaucracies? How do the various changes square with established theories of public administration? What implications do they hold for our public services as institutions? What are the similarities or differences in the various reforms when looked at from a comparative perspective? What lessons have we learned about what works and what does not? Where do we go from here?

In this book I look at the reforms in the United States, Great Britain, and Canada because we can learn a great deal more about the impact of change even to a specific public service by comparing the experiences of different countries rather than by focusing exclusively on one. Ferrel Heady argues that we can "enrich general public administration by widening the horizon of interest in such a way that understanding of one's own national system of administration will be enhanced by placing it in a cross-cultural setting."[14] Unfortunately, the study of comparative public administration appears to be in decline. Guy Peters wrote,

> This field of inquiry in political science once displayed great promise and for some time made great strides. It is now the concern of relatively few scholars, however, and has become mired in endless descriptive studies of rather minute aspects of administrative structure or behavior in single countries, with little theoretical and conceptual development. . . . The vast majority of the work in this field rather dully describes relatively minor elements of an administrative system in some country or makes predictable normative arguments about the virtues of development administra-

tion by those who stand to profit from more funding for it. The real intellectual fire appears to have gone from the field.[15]

It is my hope that this book will not only make a modest contribution to the study but also encourage others to tackle public administration from a comparative perspective.

Peters is not alone in lamenting the lack of a comparative perspective. Robert Dahl wrote in 1947 that "the comparative aspects of public administration have largely been ignored; and as long as the study of public administration is not comparative, claims for a science of public administration sound rather hollow." More recently, Lee Sigelman concluded that the comparative public administration field is "floundering at a time when other social scientists have finally come to appreciate the central role bureaucracy plays in the political process."[16]

It is relatively easy to agree that studies in comparative public administration are thin on the ground.[17] It is quite another matter to deal with the many pitfalls involved in a systematic comparison of substantial administrative reforms in several governments. Some valiant attempts have been made to define key concepts and construct broad theoretical frameworks.[18] However, most of these have concerned developing countries, and all have been found wanting. Peter Savage, for example, reports that comparative public administration "started with no paradigm of its own and has developed none."[19] He adds that we have, thus far, seen more fantasies than theories. Yet we have also heard warnings against the search for the Holy Grail. Lee Sigelman argues that "the seemingly never-ending quest for an all-inclusive analytic framework is positively perverse" and endorses Jorgen Rasmussen's supplication "O Lord deliver us from further conceptualization and lead us not into new approaches." Sigelman concludes that students "have spent so much time and energy debating issues of comparison, putting forth general analytic frameworks and sketching out the environment of administration that we have been diverted from the study of administration itself."[20]

We also know that no comprehensive theory of bureaucratic behavior, transcending place and time, has been developed. James Q. Wilson reports that he has grave doubts that any such theory will exist: "Theories will exist but they will usually be so abstract or general as to explain rather little."[21] I take these warnings to heart, and I do not in this study seek to put forward another general analytical framework or a new all-encompassing theory. My goals are much more modest. I look at bureaucracy as a common institution in three governments, and I seek to cast the far-reaching changes their leaders attempted in the 1980s in a broad comparative perspective and to answer the questions outlined above.

The world of public bureaucracies has long been considered a creature of routine, deliberately resistant to change and largely incapable of dealing with new challenges.[22] Yet the 1980s proved to be a particularly tumultuous decade for the bureaucracies of the three countries under review. Thus, I hope this comparative study will be welcomed both by students of government and by practitioners. Students will be interested in how the various reforms were introduced, how reforms square with long-established views about how bureaucracies work, and how bureaucracies are held accountable. Practitioners will be interested in the implications of the various reforms for their own institution and how the public services in the other countries are coping. They may also welcome the effort to document and review the various reforms since, all too often, governments tend to reinvent the wheel when they set out to reform their public service. The memory of politicians and even public servants themselves is amazingly short in this respect. I hope this review in a comparative setting will prove useful for a government planning to announce it intends to reform its public service, an announcement that will surely come sooner or later. If the past thirty years or so have taught us anything, it is that when it comes to reforms and reorganizations, governments tend to rediscover old solutions—whether those solutions are their own or someone else's.[23]

THE SETTING

Why did I choose to study the United States, Great Britain, and Canada? There are several reasons. All three countries elected right-of-center governments for the 1980s, each replacing left-of-center governments. As well, they all pointed to a reform of the bureaucracy as a key item on their respective agendas. But there are other similarities. The United States and Canada have a federal form of government;

both their public services were strongly influenced by the British experience; Great Britain and Canada have a parliamentary system; and all three countries have their public servants accountable to democratically elected political authority. In short, the three countries have common institutional roots, which "facilitates a comparative approach."[24]

There are also, of course, important differences. While Great Britain and Canada claim to have a nonpartisan public service with senior appointments based on merit, in the American public service a large number of these are political appointments and incumbents enjoy tenure only while their political party (or even the president who appointed them) holds office. There are significant differences in the political and bureaucratic cultures of the three countries: unlike Britain and Canada, the United States has no major political party of the left, for example. There are also major differences in their political and administrative institutions. As Joel Aberbach and Bert Rockman argue,

> Ten Downing Street is not 1600 Pennsylvania Avenue in appearance or in staffing. The former lacks an extensive non cabinet apparatus analogous to the Executive Office of the President. . . .
> The American parallel to the British television show "Yes Minister" would be "Yes Congressman," denoting which set of officials in each country the senior civil servants find most important.[25]

Important differences in the machinery of government between Britain, Canada, and the United States stem from basic differences in the structure of government. The strength of Congress and of interest groups in the United States provides for a more open government and exposes the "president to many more assaults from outside the executive-bureaucratic community." For these reasons, and others, U.S. presidents invariably have a much stronger in-house capacity for partisan advice than have British or Canadian prime ministers. The term *cabinet government* means something quite different in an American context than it does in a British or Canadian context. Executive authority in the United States lies with one person, the president. It is the president who ultimately "shoulders responsibility individually for the executive decisions of his administration."[26] In Britain and Canada, the cabinet is collectively responsible for the executive decisions of the government.

Notwithstanding the similarities and differences, it remains that Reagan, Thatcher, and Mulroney shared a strong commitment to reducing both the scope of government in society and the size of the public service and to increasing the efficiency of government. By the end of the 1980s, numerous government operations had been privatized in all three countries, and new public management concepts and approaches to public service had been introduced. The changes were such that in the case of Great Britain one observer labeled them "the biggest story of the 20th century, bigger even than the collapse of Keynesianism."[27]

Why study Thatcher, Reagan, and Mulroney? It was Thatcher's 1979 election victory that signaled a break with the past. She had scarcely been in office a few months before observers began to write about the Thatcher revolution. She brought to office ideologically driven programs of privatization, deregulation, contracting out, and trade union reforms.[28] For Thatcher, "positive government" had run its course and in the process had brought Britain low. She repeatedly pointed out that, during the 1960s and 1970s, public spending had grown faster than national income with the consequence that general government expenditure as a proportion of GDP rose from around 35 percent in the early 1960s to around 46 percent in the early 1980s. When the Conservative party came to power in 1979, its manifesto declared "the State takes too much of the nation's income, its share must be steadily reduced." Once in office, Thatcher's strong views were immediately apparent, as she set out to widen the area of the economy that was subject to competition and consumer choice.

Observers in the United States also began to write about the Reagan revolution in the early 1980s. Reagan himself, early in his first mandate, spoke of a new beginning, frequently claiming that it was "Morning in America." Like Thatcher, Reagan regarded government as an important part of the problem he was setting out to fix, rather than as part of the solution. He, too, wanted to cut government down to size. The high point of the Reagan revolution was in 1981 when Congress approved massive spending and tax cuts.[29] Reagan and his most senior advisors "detested" government and felt that they had a mandate to "smash government programs that had created the welfare state."[30] The Reagan presidency left little doubt that it would challenge the civil service. Walter Williams explains that the "attitude of detesting government and of not really being a part of *it*—recognizing *it* means *them* the bureaucrats—marked Reagan's two terms."[31] Like Thatcher, Reagan was intent on making the public sector behave more like the private sector.

Mulroney repeatedly claimed, even in his final months in office, that he had inherited a mess from the Trudeau government. Although arguably not as ideological in thinking as Thatcher's and Reagan's, Mulroney's policy agenda had a striking resemblance to theirs. There is little doubt that when Mulroney came to office in 1984, he looked to these two conservative soul mates for inspiration. Canadians were by then well aware of Thatcherism and Reaganomics. Mulroney's claim that government spending was out of control and that there were far too many government programs working at cross purposes rang true with many Canadians.[32] Mulroney also took dead aim at the civil service, arguing that it had become unresponsive, costly, and largely ineffective. Like Thatcher and Reagan, Mulroney wanted a public sector that emulated the private sector.

Thus Thatcher, Reagan, and Mulroney held similar views not only on what was wrong with government but also on how to make things right. Cutting government down to size and eliminating government programs constituted only parts of the solution. Equally important was to see bureaucracy behave more like private firms. In this book I examine how measures to reform the civil service in one country can influence or shape efforts in another country. We know that Thatcher led the way on many fronts, in part because she was the first of the three to be elected to power. We also know that Thatcher had a strong influence on both Reagan and Mulroney. Advisors to both men report as much, revealing that Thatcher personally briefed the other two on her efforts to reshape the British civil service, at G7 meetings or during bilateral meetings, and that she urged them to introduce similar measures in their countries.[33]

Thatcher, Reagan, and Mulroney were apostles of the new right. Although there is much debate on the merits of their long-term legacies, there is no denying that the three (Thatcher, in particular) had a profound impact on government operations at home and abroad. Thatcher's new definition of privatization has been tried and adopted in over a hundred countries throughout the developed and developing worlds. Leading international specialists are now reporting on the "triumph" of the neoconservative agenda in all corners of the world.[34] Ronald Reagan argued at a major conference on global development in Cancun, Mexico, in 1981, that the magic of the market could do its work in all settings, including the developing world. Thus, it is important for students of government to return to the source and to study the measures introduced by the leading proponents of the neoconservative agenda to reform the civil service.

It would be wrong to assume, however, that Thatcher, Reagan, and Mulroney were the first politicians to attempt the reform of bureaucracy. Reforms of one kind or another had been tried throughout the 1960s and 1970s. Jimmy Carter, it will be recalled, won his presidential election campaigning against Washington, and he did introduce several important changes to the public service. Pierre E. Trudeau also made a number of attempts to reform the Canadian public service, and there were "earlier attempts at administrative revolution in Whitehall."[35] Many of these attempts failed, however, and the great majority of the changes that were introduced certainly did not live up to expectations. In Britain by the late 1970s, there was widespread disillusionment with administrative reform, with "countless high quality reports concerning public sector management remaining ignored and unimplemented because the British civil service resisted radical revision of its structure, process, and traditional attitudes." In the United States, meanwhile, the changes were "seldom followed by systematic efforts to assess their effect. . . . They seem to be a source of frustration and ridicule and become regular and unlamented casualties of experience with trying to achieve significant reform."[36]

In many ways these earlier failures served to strengthen the resolve of the new political leaders. This was certainly true of Margaret Thatcher. The failures also confirmed what right-of-center politicians had suspected all along: bureaucracies are all too often self-serving, wedded to the status quo, and incapable of introducing lasting change that would make their institutions more efficient. Accordingly, in their attempts to introduce reform, the three leaders looked to outside help both for advice and, in some instances, for implementing the recommended changes. A pattern is easily seen emerging in the 1980s, in the three countries surveyed, which suggests that their governments were no longer entirely prepared to trust public servants with the task of reforming their own bureaucracies. To be sure, there had been instances before when governments sought outside expertise to revamp bureaucracy—whether it took the form of a royal commission or an independent task force or commission. This time, however, outside expertise was brought on board not solely to identify new approaches but also to implement the changes or to look for new ways of doing things. The objective here clearly was to avoid the "Yes, Minister" syndrome where public servants allegedly take hold of the agenda and direct the scope and pace of change—often giving the appearance of activity while, in fact, standing still.

THE APPROACH

This study suggests that the reforms introduced by Thatcher, Mulroney, and Reagan will have far-reaching consequences for bureaucracy. Indeed, some of these may well fly in the face of what the political leaders sought to accomplish. In this study, I also argue that efforts to reshape bureaucracy could hold important implications for democracy or for the ability of politicians to direct the work of permanent officials.

Specifically, the study rests upon two hypotheses. (1) Although the three governments surveyed have strong distinguishing characteristics and each operates within its own endogenous rules and constraints, there are common threads linking the various reforms introduced by Thatcher, Reagan, and Mulroney. (2) The three leaders, albeit unwittingly, caused us to return to the origins of the public administration discipline and to revisit the politics-administration dichotomy. I write "unwittingly" because I would not want to suggest that this was part of a well-thought-out grand design to reshape bureaucracy. We are not dealing with philosopher kings or queens here. Still, the onslaught of the new right against bureaucracy was not limited to cutting government down to size. Convinced that permanent officials wielded too much influence over policy, the political leadership built its strategy of containment around the notion that only politicians should define and move the political and policy agenda. Leadership sought to redefine the role of bureaucracy so that senior civil servants would be managers rather than policy advisors or administrators. In brief, the 1980s saw an attempt to apply the politics-administration dichotomy to government operations, with management replacing administration. To substitute management for administration is no insignificant matter; indeed, it has serious implications for public administration. The idea of management carries with it such concepts as "empowerment," which challenge some of the fundamental principles of bureaucracy, notably hierarchy. If successfully implemented, the reforms would hold far-reaching consequences: for the relationships between public servants and elected officials and the general public, for the emphasis on due process, and for the systems of controls and accountability traditionally found in government. Although the measures introduced were cast entirely as a set of management reforms, some go further and raise fundamental questions about where power should lie in government.

ORGANIZATION OF THE APPROACH

This study consists of three parts. The first part reviews briefly some of the most important writings that have shaped our understanding of how public bureaucracies operate and theories of executive leadership. All too often students and, in particular, practitioners tend to overlook the key role our most important writings have played in shaping our public services. At the risk of stating the obvious (to the serious student), I must note that seminal works on public administration do matter. A review of the most important essays on governance will thus enable us to go beyond the various reforms on a case-by-case basis and assess those of the 1980s from a broad perspective. The first part also looks at key events and forces that have shaped the three public services. We will look at several important historical milestones in the development of the three public services. This will enable us to gain a greater appreciation of the forces that helped shape the reforms of the 1980s and then allow us to view them from a historical perspective.

My own experience in government reveals that many practitioners are often unaware of what the seminal essays on governance have to say about their work, and even of the important historical developments and events that have shaped their institution. There are, no doubt, a variety of reasons for this. For one thing, only a minority of career government officials have received formal training in public administration or political science. There is a great variety in the educational background of career officials, ranging from engineering, economics, and business, to law.[37] One can even complete a university degree program in these subjects without encountering, for example, Woodrow Wilson's classic, "The Study of Administration." Once in a government position, officials invariably become too busy with day-to-day decisions to step back and review even the most important studies of their institutions.

In the second part of this study, I look at the rhetoric of the new political leadership and at how reforms were planned, introduced, and implemented. I also look at the transition to power and how the governments set out to work with their public services, as well as the role played by the private sector in shaping and implementing the various reforms. The three governments looked to privatization, to the contracting out of some of their activities to private firms, and to the importing of private sector management practices to government operations. They also announced new measures, to restructure their machinery of government, to strengthen their hold on the bureaucracy, and to facilitate the implementation of their "management" agenda. In addition, at least two of the three governments surveyed announced new measures to restructure some of their operations in a fundamental fashion. Again, they looked to the business community for inspiration. These developments led to new challenges and requirements, notably equipping public managers with new knowledge and new skills. The study examines how the three governments sought to deal with these developments.

In the third part, I seek to understand how the reforms fit into the historical development of public administration in the three countries. I argue that, whether desired or predicted or not, the reforms all had far-reaching consequences for our bureaucracies. The reforms are redefining what governments do, and who does it. The reforms are also redefining the relationships public servants have with elected officials and the public. I also argue that the reforms overlooked problems that now need fixing and sought to fix things that were not broken.

Information for this study comes from a number of sources, including published and unpublished government documents. Between September 1991 and August 1992, I also interviewed seventy-two officials from the governments of Great Britain, Canada, and the United States. I interviewed present and former cabinet ministers, present and former senior-level government officials from both the appointed and careerist camps, and middle- as well as lower-level career officials. Almost all (seventy) were in the executive branch. I decided to do off-the-record interviews to elicit the most candid comments. In any event, numerous respondents insisted on speaking off-the-record. The interviews lasted on average just over one hour, but several lasted nearly two hours, and I took notes during all the interviews.

I made no attempt to draw a representative sample, which would have been impractical for the purpose of the study. I interviewed people who had occupied or were occupying major policy and advisory positions, those who manage government programs, those who work on the front line delivering programs or services, and those who perform audit or evaluation functions of one kind or another. I had developed a list of potential respondents by consulting scholars and senior government officials I knew in London and Washington. Ottawa was no problem because I had served as a senior official with the Treasury Board in the government of Canada in the late 1980s and I knew the public service well. My main concern was to strike a proper balance between central agencies (about 25 percent) and line departments (75 percent) and between the various functions: policy (20 percent), program administration (65 percent), and audit and evaluation (15 percent). I maintained the same balance in Washington and London. I held twenty-five interviews in Britain, twenty-seven in the United States, and twenty in Canada. I also contacted another twenty-one officials in the three countries, by telephone or fax, to secure factual information on the implementation of various management-reform measures.

The interviews were unstructured, and each was tailored to the position of the respective respondents. The interviews had two main goals. The first was to determine how the reforms were planned and how they were implemented. The second was to gain an understanding of the respondents' attitudes toward the reforms and to hear firsthand how they saw the reforms fitting into the development of the public services.[38] Accordingly, I did not put a series of common questions to all respondents. I did, however, invite all respondents, toward the end of the interviews, to reflect on the evolution of the civil service in the 1980s. The participants responded to the call with heartfelt observations. The reader will note that I made full use of some of these observations in reviewing the various reforms of the 1980s from the perspective of career officials.

PART 1
THE SETTING

2

The Underpinnings

Many practitioners dismiss out of hand any search for a theoretical understanding of how public bureaucracies work. Robert B. Denhardt reports, "The works of the classical theorist do not seem to comprehend or to explain the experiences of practitioners."[1] Practitioners point out that theories depend on generalizations, and (they insist), when it comes to understanding how public bureaucracies work, to generalize is to oversimplify. Decision making in government departments is much too untidy a business for generalizations. The theories available, they invariably report, exude an aura of otherworldliness and hardly apply to the give-and-take that actually occurs. There is little doubt that there is some truth to this, and it may well be that we should not attempt to run before we learn how to walk.[2]

Still, there are clear advantages to examining some of the major essays in the field of public administration. They emphasize a wide agenda and point to the more important issues. They also go to the heart of the matter and deal with the central questions facing public administrators. Practitioners inevitably are caught up with the day-to-day issues, the looming crises, and the clients who need attention. Practitioners no doubt look upon each situation as unique, each located in its own set of variables that cannot be scientifically explained. However, in dismissing out of hand any search for a definitive theory or the merits of any existing theory, they may well be shortchanging themselves. Lord Keynes's warning that "practical men, who believe themselves to be quite exempt from any intellectual influences, are usually the slaves of some defunct theories" holds a ring of truth that can be applied here. I also believe that Denhardt was right in suggesting that "Many practitioners today are experiencing discouragement, frustration and exhaustion, part of which is due to the lack of theoretical development."[3]

In this chapter, I look briefly at some of the most important studies

19

of public administration, to put in perspective recent public service reforms and to gain a greater understanding of their scope and objectives. There is, of course, a risk in doing this. The specialist will invariably be more familiar than others are with issues raised here, and some readers will likely ask why I do not deal, for example, with the works of the scientific management school, Herbert Simon's "pure science of administration," various organizational theories, the new public administration, and the neoinstitutional approaches. For one thing, it is impossible in one chapter to review all the relevant major works. For another, we already have some comprehensive reviews of the most important theories of public administration and management.[4] In this chapter, I look briefly at the politics-administration dichotomy, the work of Max Weber, public choice theory, the similarities between public and private sector management, accountability in government operations, and leadership in government. I chose to review these issues simply because they are central to the purpose of this book. Indeed, I return to them time and again.

THE POLITICS-ADMINISTRATION DICHOTOMY

Woodrow Wilson wrote over a hundred years ago about the indifference to public administration evinced by scholars of politics and government. "Up to our own day," he reported,

> all the political writers whom we now read had thought, argued, dogmatized only about the constitution of government, about the nature of the state, the essence and seat of sovereignty, popular power and kingly prerogative. . . . The question was always: Who shall make law, and what shall that law be? The other question, how law should be administered . . . was put aside as practical detail.[5]

As every student of public administration knows, Wilson set out to define a "science of administration which shall seek to strengthen the paths of government, to make its business less unbusinesslike, to strengthen and purify its organization, and to crown its duties and dutifulness." The key building block for such a science, he maintained, was an apolitical public administration. Politicians should establish policies and administrators be left free to administer government programs. He went on to argue at some length that the "administration lies outside the proper sphere of politics. Administrative questions are not political questions. Although politics sets the tasks for administration, it should not be suffered to manipulate its offices."[6] The dichotomy was important, he felt, not simply for establishing efficient administration but also for strengthening democracy itself. To separate politics and policy from administration would constitute an important counterweight to "centrifugal" democracy.[7]

This is not to suggest that Wilson favored dispersing administrative authority throughout the organization. He felt that administrative efficiency and responsibility would be strengthened through the establishment of single centers of power directing hierarchical structures. He explained, "there is no danger in power, if only it be not irresponsible . . . if it be centred in heads of the services, and in heads of branches of the service, it is easily watched and brought to book." He insisted that "businesslike principles should guide the operations of government" and that the "field of administration is a field of business."[8]

Wilson was not alone in arguing that "politics" and "administration" should be exclusive or near exclusive categories. For example, Frank Goodnow's *Politics and Administration*, published in 1900, picked up the theme of an administration based on isolation and separation.[9] There is no doubt the push was on to build a public administration that would borrow from experiences in the "military," from "abroad," from "business," and that would clearly favor hierarchy. Indeed, it is impossible to overstate the importance of this development and of its impact on government. Dwight Waldo, for one, wrote, "by the eve of the First World War the synthesis was complete, books and journals confidently proclaimed the new philosophy, and a revolutionary change had been effected in the meaning of democracy for administration."[10] He added that, "The means and measurements of efficiency . . . were the same for all administration: democracy, if it were to survive, could not afford to ignore the lessons of centralization, hierarchy, and discipline."[11] There is no doubt, as Waldo reports, that the Wilson school carried the day in the early 1900s. Howard McCurdy summed it up well when he wrote that the Wilson politics-administration dichotomy became "the holy writ of American public administration."[12]

The criticism directed at the principles of this dichotomy has been varied and sustained, however. We now know that "as the 1930s advanced, doubt and dissent increased. In the 1940s refutation and repudiation came to the fore. By the 1950s, it had become fashionable to refer to the politics-administration dichotomy as an outworn if not ludicrous creed."[13] A good number of informed students began to argue that it is not always possible to separate policy and administration. Luther Gulick, among others, argued that "every act of public servants is a seamless web of discretion and action" and that discretion can be found at all levels of the organization. The degree of discretion is more pronounced in "badly organized and poorly directed administrative units."[14] Paul H. Appleby went further, stating that "public administration is policy making," and argued that "administrators are continually laying down rules for the future, and administrators are continually determining what the law is, what it means in terms of action."[15] Others have insisted that it is not possible to import into public administration practices commonly found in business or even in foreign governments. A country's own constitution, history, and endogenous political developments all have an important impact on how the government works. In short (the argument goes), Wilson's politics-administration dichotomy may be appropriate in the private sector, where the goals of a firm can be made clear to everyone, but the same is not true in government, with all the various checks and balances at play and with political leaders holding varied and often changing goals.

David Levitan rejects the distinction between politics and administration on democratic grounds. He claims that policy is made at all levels of administration, and he makes a plea for bringing democracy into administration. "Democratic government," he wrote, "means democracy in administration, as well as in the original legislation. It is of supreme importance that the administrative machinery established for the execution of legislation be permeated with democratic spirit and ideology." Edward C. Page picks up the same theme, that officials are in reality far from being the passive administrators described in the classical model, merely carrying out "the will of the elected politicians." They are in fact, he argues, "involved in policy making: moreover, they know they are involved and actually enjoy being involved. The problem with such an approach is that it is doubtful whether many significant analyses of bureaucracy have ever been based upon the belief or assertion that this is the case, and thus it is hardly illuminating to reveal that such a classical model is inaccurate."[16]

Although there are now precious few students of public administration who still adhere to the politics-administration dichotomy to explain how the real world of government actually works, the principle still haunts many public services and individual government officials. Government bureaus everywhere cling to the difference between policy decisions and policy execution in describing their work: decisions flow from politics and execution from administration, they insist. Two Canadian students of public administration recently laid out a Westminster-style model outlining the meaning of political neutrality. And the first tenet of their model was "politics and policy are separated from administration; thus politicians make policy decisions, public servants execute these decisions."[17] Robert B. Denhardt summed up the debate best when he wrote,

> as a theory, the politics-administration dichotomy was soon dead, although it is perhaps more accurate to say that it had never been alive. As a practical matter, however, because writers wished to direct their works to the practical problems of a specific audience— administrative personnel—the politics-administration dichotomy lived on in an institutional definition of public administration. And, to the extent that public administration is still defined in institutional terms, the dichotomy survives.[18]

Some leading students of public administration have recently argued that the myth of the politics-administration dichotomy survives in part because politicians are now turning to it to preserve and justify the powers of the political executive.[19] Wilson, Weber, and Goodnow, however, wrote about the dichotomy in terms of protecting administration from the excesses of politicians, notably the "machine" politics found in all levels of government in the United States.

Other students have sought to modernize the dichotomy by breaking it down into four distinct images: the first looks to the politics-administration dichotomy as both an ideal and an empirical reality; the second explains that public servants are indeed involved in policy-making but deliberately limit their involvement to the providing of knowledge and facts; the third suggests that public servants are involved in policy-making to a greater degree than the mere providing of knowledge and facts, since the very providing requires some political calculation. The fourth image goes much further and suggests that the involvement of public servants in all facets of policy-making is strong and at times barely distinguishable in intensity from that of the politicians they serve.[20]

MAX WEBER

It is one thing to suggest that a line, however blurred, should exist to separate politics and administration, but it is quite another matter to explain how an efficient bureaucracy should function. The works of Max Weber, the German sociologist, have had considerable impact on this front. Weber's main contribution was not so much that he defined a single theory of bureaucracy as that he brought forward an intelligent discussion about the kind of historical conditions that give rise to the development of bureaucratic government, about what was specific to bureaucracy as a form of social and political organization, and about the potential challenges that this organization poses for the exercise of political leadership. He approved of bureaucratic organization because, in his view, it constituted the most efficient approach to coordinate and control the work of large numbers of people pursuing stated goals. He explained, "Experience tends universally to show that the purely bureaucratic type of administration is, from a purely technical point of view, capable of attaining the highest degree of efficiency and is in this sense formally the most rational known means of carrying out imperative control over human beings."[21]

He saw no alternative to bureaucratic organizations, where clear structures of authority can be laid out to give directions and commands and to establish a sense of the possible results. Indeed, he felt that bureaucratic organization would expand to cover nongovernment fields of activity. He was so certain that a bureaucratic form of organization was superior to any other type that he boldly declared, "The future belongs to bureaucratization."[22] It is difficult to imagine anyone, even the most ardent supporter of the public service as an institution, making such a statement today and expecting to have any chance of making it stick. Weber explained that, as activities grow increasingly complex and diverse, it becomes essential that clear authority and direction be established through hierarchical structures.

He wrote, "Bureaucratic administration is, other things being equal, always from a formal, technical point of view, the most rational type. For the needs of mass administration today, it is completely indispensable. The choice is only that between bureaucracy and dilettantism in the field of administration."[23] Weber sought to define in specific terms how the bureaucratic organization should function, and he outlined its central characteristics. It is worth repeating his views here:

1. Officials are personally free and are subject to authority only with respect to their impersonal official obligations.

2. They are organized in a clearly defined hierarchy of offices.

3. Each office has a clearly defined sphere of competence, in the legal sense.

4. The office is filled by a free contractual relationship. Thus, in principle, there is free selection.

5. Candidates are selected on the basis of technical qualifications. In the most rational case, these qualifications are tested by examination, guaranteed by diplomas certifying technical training, or both. Candidates are appointed, not elected.

6. They are remunerated by fixed salaries in money, for the most part with a right to pensions. Only under certain circumstances does the employing authority, especially in private organizations, have a right to terminate the appointment, but in addition to this criterion, the responsibility of the position and the requirements of the incumbent's social status may be taken into account.

7. The office is treated as the sole, or at least the primary, occupation of the incumbent.

8. The office constitutes a career. Promotion is based on seniority, achievement, or both, and depends on the judgment of superiors.

9. Officials work entirely separated from ownership of the means of administration and without appropriation of their positions.

10. They are subject to strict and systematic discipline and control in the conduct of the office.[24]

Weber's view of bureaucracy strongly emphasized that the power of the organization was in the hands of those officials with the necessary technical skills. Weber's bureaucracy operates on the basis of office hierarchy where there are clear lines of authority and subordination. Hierarchy and technical skills are considered important for a host of reasons. For one thing, it is important to define the necessary technical skills, not only to ensure an efficient organization but also to insulate them from "dilution by influences from outside and corruption from within the organization."[25] Hierarchy is required to provide clear lines of authority, through which commands can be transmitted, and to allow a "calculability of results" for those in positions of authority.[26] Moreover, a hierarchical division of responsibility and authority ensures that the higher office does not take over the work of the lower office and also provides for the "governed" a clear line for appealing "the decision of a lower office to the corresponding superior authority."[27] In Weber's view, this and the central characteristics outlined above give bureaucratic organization a clear edge over any other type of organization. Weber explained why:

> the decisive reason for the advances of bureaucratic organization has always been its purely technical superiority over any other form of organization. The fully developed bureaucratic apparatus compares with other organizations exactly as does the machine with the non-mechanical modes of production. Precision, speed, unambiguity, knowledge of the files, continuity, discretion, unity, strict subordination, reduction of friction and of material and personal costs—these are raised to the optimum point in the strictly bureaucratic administration, and especially in its monocratic form.[28]

Weber, however, accepted that bureaucratic organization would be challenged on a number of fronts. He asked whether bureaucracy would wield too much power, and he did not dismiss the possibility out of hand but said that, in bureaucracy, there was an element at the top of the organization "which is at least not purely bureaucratic."[29] What was important, in his view, was to ensure that the people selected to fill top political positions were chosen through open parliamentary struggle. He had little doubt that permanent officials would fail as politicians and explained,

> officialdom has been brilliant whenever it had to prove its sense of duty, its impartiality and mastery of organizational problems in the face of official, clearly formulated tasks of a specialized nature. But here we are concerned with political, not bureaucratic achievements, and the facts themselves provoke the recognition which

nobody can truthfully deny. That bureaucracy failed completely whenever it was expected to deal with political problems. This is no accident, rather, it would be astonishing if capabilities inherently so alien to one another would emerge within the same political structures.[30]

Weber was also clear about the kind of relationship permanent officials should have with their political leaders:

> An official who receives a directive which he considers wrong can and is supposed to object to it. If his superior insists on its execution, it is his duty and even his honour to carry it out as if it corresponded to his innermost conviction, and to demonstrate in this fashion that his sense of duty stands above his personal preference.[31]

He also insisted that an ideal type of bureaucracy required a strong parliament: "Only a working, not merely speech making parliament, can provide the ground for the growth and selective ascent of genuine leaders, not merely demagogic talents. A working parliament supervises the administration by continuously showing its work."[32] For Weber, a strong working parliament has three distinct roles: it controls the power of bureaucracy, it generates political leadership that directs bureaucratic activities, and it holds that leadership accountable.

Weber's views have become the classic entry point into the study of bureaucracy.[33] Scholars and practitioners alike turn to Weber time and again to gain a better appreciation of bureaucracy and how it could be made to work better. Anthony Downs, for one, argues that Weber greatly influenced the introduction of formalized rules as a key characteristic of bureaucracy and as a "widely accepted . . . inherent trait of (government) bureaux."[34]

PUBLIC CHOICE

We have seen in more recent years the rise of the public choice school, a school that Thatcher publicly applauded. Its adherents took dead aim at the organic views of organizations that look to individuals in terms of their functional contributions to the fulfillment of the organization's goals and needs. A leading advocate of the public choice school, Vincent Ostrom argues that there is an intellectual crisis in American public administration:

> the mainstream of public administration theory from Wilson through at least Simon has been too concerned with the efficiency of the administrative process, efficiency generally sought through mechanism of centralization and control. . . . Theorists and practitioners lack both a clear sense of identity and the confidence to deal with the increasingly difficult problems they now face.[35]

For Ostrom and for a number of others, public choice best explains how government works and the behavior of individual public servants.

The public choice school starts with the premise that the individual is the basic unit of analysis. To be specific, individual choice is the basis for organizational or collective action so that what is usually thought of as collective action is, in reality, the aggregation of individual choices. The individual decision maker is much like the classical economic man and is, as a result, self-interested, rational, and always seeking to maximize his own utilities. Dennis Mueller defined public choice theory succinctly as "the economic study of non-market decision-making, or simply as the application of economics to political science."[36]

Public choice theory holds obvious implications for how governments should organize their activities. Public choice theorists claim that different types of organization and of decision-making structures will have varying impact on the behavior of individuals who are always seeking ways to maximize their own interests. Vincent Ostrom, for example, argues that "no single form of organization is presumed to be good for all circumstances."[37] He disagrees with Woodrow Wilson and others who argue that in all governments there must be a single center and source of power. Ostrom favors a multiorganizational arrangement that, he argues, can stimulate healthy competition among agencies. He is highly critical of bureaucracy as the principal mode of public organization and insists that: The very large bureaucracy will

> (1) become increasingly undiscriminating in its response to diverse demands, (2) impose increasingly high social costs upon those who are presumed to be the beneficiaries, (3) fail to proportion supply and demand, (4) allow public goods to erode by failing to take actions to prevent one use from impairing other uses, (5) become

increasingly error prone and uncontrollable to the point where public actions deviate radically from rhetoric about public purposes and objectives, and (6) eventually lead to a circumstance where remedial actions exacerbate rather than ameliorate problems.[38]

There is no denying that the application of the public choice theory to explain the behavior of public servants has gained considerable popularity in recent years, and many social scientists believe it to be the most likely explanation for the growth in government spending. One, for example, recently went so far as to suggest that "government bureaucrats, like any other bureaucrat (or indeed, any other people), are quick to seize on new program possibilities that promise general advancement—again, virtually without regard to likely results. Unless we try massive lobotomies, we are unlikely to change behaviour so rooted in human nature."[39]

Although the work of public choice theorists has had considerable impact both on students and practitioners of public administration, it is not without its opponents. Norton Long, for one, wrote that public choice theorists "argue with elegant and impeccable logic about unicorns."[40] He and a number of others argue that these theorists take much too narrow a view of the world when they hinge much of their work on a narrowly defined concept of the rational self-interested individual. By ignoring the social character of human action, the intuitive and emotional aspects of decisions, the public choice school is running off (the argument goes) in a much too narrow world to explain all or even most of what is important about organizing an organization. Many practitioners also dismiss the school out of hand not simply because it is highly critical of bureaucracy but also because, in their opinion, it offers no practical solutions to correct the shortcomings of government departments and agencies. When reading public choice theorists, some critics are no doubt reminded of Jean Renoir's film *The Rules of the Game* where "the house party sallies forth from La Colinière, on a Sunday morning and shoots every bird and rabbit in sight for miles around. The carnage is incredible. Bang! Bang! Bang! go the pointed criticisms and down they crash. Before long the landscape is littered with the corpses" of earlier works of public administration and modes of government organizations.[41] Little, however, is recommended of any practical value to replace what has been shot down.

PUBLIC AND PRIVATE SECTOR MANAGEMENT

Students of public administration have debated over the years to what extent public and private sector managements are alike or different. Wallace Sayre wrote, over sixty years ago, an often quoted paper in which he argued that public and private managements are "fundamentally alike in all unimportant ways." Most public sector managers would agree. This is not to suggest that they believe public sector management is superior to that in the private sector. Indeed, the opposite is likely true. Graham Allison, for example, makes the point that "the perception that government performance lags behind private business performance is . . . correct. But the notion that there is any significant body of private management practices and skills that can be transferred directly to public management tasks in a way that produces significant improvements is wrong."[42]

To be sure, some private sector management experience can benefit government operations, particularly in the areas of human and financial resources. Graham Allison points to many such areas. He looks to Luther Gulick's work to support his claim. Gulick sought to strike a proper balance between specialization and the division of labor and to put in place a structure of authority to ensure coordination. He developed his now famous acronym PODSCRB (Planning, Organizing, Directing, Staffing, Coordinating, Reporting, Budgeting). He also divided the work that needs to be done along line and staff groupings. Staff people, he insisted, should devote their time exclusively to "knowing, thinking and planning." They should not have administrative responsibilities. In his view, they can only achieve results through their "authority of ideas" and their powers of persuasion. Allison maintains that at "one level of abstraction" much of Gulick's PODSCRB activities applies to both the public and private sectors. Both need to achieve a proper division of labor and to put in place means of coordination and control. What is true of staff people in the private sector is also true for the public sector. Allison goes on to outline his own composite lists of "major functions that are identified for general managers, whether public or private" (see table 1).[43]

TABLE 1
Functions of General Management

STRATEGY

1. Establishing objectives and priorities for the organization (on the basis of forecasts of the external environment and the organization's capacities).
2. Devising operational plans to achieve these objectives.

MANAGING INTERNAL COMPONENTS

3. Organizing and staffing:
   In organizing, the manager establishes structure (units and positions with assigned authority and responsibilities) and procedures (for coordinating activity and taking action); in staffing, he tries to find the right persons for the key jobs.
4. Directing personnel and the personnel management system:
   The capacity of the organization is embodied primarily in its members and their skills and knowledge; the personnel-management system recruits, selects, socializes, trains, rewards, and exits the organization's human capital, which constitutes the organization's capacity to act to achieve its goals and to respond to specific directions from management.
5. Controlling performance:
   Various management information systems—including operation and capital budgets, accounts, reports and statistical systems, performance appraisals, and product evaluation—assist management in making decisions and in measuring progress toward objectives.

MANAGING EXTERNAL CONSTITUENCIES

6. Dealing with "external" units of the organization subject to some common authority:
   Most general managers must deal with general managers of other units within the larger organization—above, laterally, and below—to achieve their unit's objectives.
7. Dealing with independent organizations:
   Agencies from other branches or levels of government, interest groups, and private enterprises that can affect the organization's ability to achieve its objectives.
8. Dealing with the press and public whose action or approval or acquiescence is required.

Source: Allison, "Public and Private Management," p. 526.

Still the differences between the public and private sectors remain great. Allison presents a veritable who's who in corporate America of people who have managed in both sectors and who unanimously report that public management is different from private and that it is "harder." Several other authors have also pointed to numerous key differences, including (1) *time perspective*, that is, public managers have shorter time horizons because of key political imperatives; (2) the need for more *persuasion and direction* in government to accommodate various pressures to arrive at a solution; (3) the lack of a clear *bottom line* in government; and (4) the *legislative requirements* of reviewing the work of public managers.[44] Indeed, public managers are dependent upon political bodies both for their authority and their budgets, and they are subject to far greater public scrutiny of their actions. They are directly accountable to their political masters, and no matter what form of government organization is in place it can only enjoy legitimacy through the political process. Although it can take various forms, governments must have an accountability process to make the exercise of power responsible.

ACCOUNTABILITY

We know that parliamentary government imposes its own rules on bureaucracy and that responsible government in Britain and Canada is based on the individual and collective responsibilities of ministers to Parliament. In a parliamentary system, the ministers are constitutionally responsible for the conduct of the government in power and, accordingly, responsibility is concentrated in the hands of ministers. In addition, the system of government is not compartmentalized between Parliament and government, in that the executive is composed of members of Parliament and, thus, is not separate from Parliament.

Ministerial responsibility requires that ministers be personally responsible for the activities carried out by their departments, and "this concept is fundamental to the long struggle to impose responsibility on the exercise of power." Ministers are assailable on a daily basis (notably in Question Period in Parliament) for their actions and for the actions of their officials. Officials, however, are not. Nor may they be held constitutionally responsible by Parliament. Indeed, "the traditions of civil service anonymity built up in England during the later part of the

19th century and the creation in Canada of the Civil Service Commission in 1908 to ensure that public servants would be non-partisan, reinforced this principle." The convention is that public servants serve with strict loyalty all governments, of whatever political persuasion, and that they are accountable to ministers. Permanent secretaries in Britain and deputy ministers in Canada are thus responsible to their respective ministers and "their appointment by the prime minister reinforces their commitment to ensure the successful functioning of ministerial government."[45] Although appointed by the prime minister and not by an independent civil service commission, it is assumed that a change in government or in prime minister does not necessitate a change in permanent secretaries or deputy ministers. Public servants, at all levels, enjoy permanent status during good behavior and are accountable to the government of the day. In short, the power in a parliamentary system of government flows from the crown and is exercised in turn by the executive (or the cabinet) in a responsible fashion before Parliament.

These fundamental principles hold far-reaching implications for the day-to-day work of public servants. In the case of parliamentary forms of government, the principle of ministerial accountability has given rise to centralized controls and standardized systems. Although few still expect ministers to accept responsibility for the individual, and perhaps unauthorized, actions of public servants, some observers insist that ministers can still be held accountable for the system of rules, procedures, and controls guiding the work of permanent officials. But even here there is some disagreement. Some now argue that the principle of ministerial responsibility is a myth. They point out that ministers no longer resign even when a "serious" departmental error is committed—nor should they.

One can only assume, then, that if ministers cannot be held responsible for departmental actions, the burden of responsibility must shift to permanent officials. Yet, the parliamentary system of government offers very limited possibilities to hold public servants accountable. Changing this would require a substantial redefinition of the relationship between ministers and their officials. Although one could easily put in place reforms to make officials more accountable to Parliament on administrative matters, it is quite a different story to see officials accountable to Parliament on policy matters. This, the argument goes, would very likely compromise the doctrine of public service anonymity and neutrality, since public servants owe their loyalty to the government of the day but not to the party in power. Accordingly, public servants should not be held accountable to Parliament on policy issues because they would be forced to state their policy preferences. The British have long held that a politically neutral public service is key to the efficient operation of their government. The Masterman Committee reported, over forty years ago, that the political neutrality of the civil service was "a fundamental feature of British democratic government and is essential for its efficient operation. It must be maintained even at the cost of some loss of political liberty by certain of those who elect to enter the Service."[46] It remains today that "fewer posts in Whitehall are affected by party-political changes than in most other major government bureaucracies."[47]

Traditional thinking here is that, in return for loyally and impartially serving the government of the day, public servants enjoy security of tenure—hence the reference to the "permanent" government. It is also expected that public servants perform their duties in an anonymous fashion. In turn, ministers are expected to take full credit—or, conversely, public blame—for the departmental actions. By remaining anonymous, it is held that public servants can more freely provide frank and impartial advice to ministers. It is important to note that a good part of the responsibility for remaining anonymous lies with public servants themselves. A former secretary to the Canadian cabinet explained:

> anonymity . . . involves a substantial act of self-denial. It means an unwillingness to hint at influential association with policies or decisions; refusal to give the private briefing of a journalist that can lead to a benevolent and admiring story; avoidance of photographs with the great; and, within reasonable limits, eschewing the physical trappings of status that are demonstrations to the beholder of unspoken power and importance.[48]

Few would deny that the traditions and requirements of responsible government have in the past served Canada and Britain well. Indeed, many insist that they still serve these countries well, by offering

> a timeless focal point for legal, political and administrative responsiveness. Though governments may be repudiated, ministers may die or leave cabinet, and civil servants enjoy the right of employ-

ment mobility, none of this matters because the current minister of a department is responsible retrospectively through the history of state activity in the policy area. . . . Thus the doctrine offers democratic control over bureaucratic administration, past and future.[49]

In short, to the purists, the constitutional principle of ministerial responsibility should still apply today.

Nevertheless, many now insist that the doctrine "has mostly outlived its applicability to modern political life."[50] The thinking is that the doctrine of ministerial accountability undermines the potential for genuine accountability on the part of the person who ought to be accountable—the senior permanent official of the department. Some observers argue that the principle may well have been overtaken by an enormous growth in government activities in the modern world, and by the behavior of British and Canadian cabinet ministers in recent years. The principle was defined in preindustrial Britain, in an era when the government functioned "in a very narrow context of limited governmental expenditure, limited government activity, limited liberal democracy and a limited administrative structure."[51] Nobody could have predicted it would be necessary to enlarge the need for accountability that would go beyond legal and financial accuracy, or that governments would be involved in (among many other things) regional development, space exploration, and promoting research and development in numerous areas. The size of the British government in the 1890s, compared with in the 1980s, brings the point home. Between those dates, the "number of persons employed in the public sector expanded from approximately 3.5 percent of the working population to approximately 30 percent."[52] By sticking to the principle, we run the risk of having no one ultimately accountable in the vast machinery of government and of having permanent officials who may not be "necessarily obliged to reveal why they do what they do."[53] Meanwhile, cabinet ministers—who are expected to know and to be accountable for everything that happens in their departments—are "really ignorant prisoners in the hands of the appointed bureaucratic experts who are not directly responsible to any body. . . . The total picture is one of irresponsible power and non-accountable financial management."[54] Lord Hunt, former secretary to the cabinet in Britain, summed up the problems with the principle of ministerial responsibility when he observed, "the concept that because somebody whom the Minister has never heard of has made a mistake means that the Minister should resign is out of date, and rightly so."[55]

Although many are convinced that the principle is out of date, no government has moved to deal with the problem head-on. Yet, it has become widely accepted that ministers, if only because of their ignorance of much of the work that occurs in their departments, no longer resign over departmental mistakes. As a result, both Canada and Great Britain have introduced some measures, however inadequate, to hold public servants more directly accountable. In Canada, a special House of Commons committee was established in 1985 to review the role of parliamentary committees and to create a more important role for backbenchers in Parliament. It also sought to identify ways to make permanent officials more visible and accountable before House committees. Now, officials can be instructed to appear for review before a committee of Parliament before being appointed deputy ministers.

Although absolutely no action has been taken, we also hear more and more in Canada about the need to define a new doctrine to hold permanent officials more accountable for their actions. Such a doctrine would presumably set out the obligations of senior public servants and call on officials to testify on a regular basis before parliamentary committees. In addition, it is felt that a new doctrine should encourage regular open contact between the senior public service and members of Parliament and that this would "lead to a more realistic understanding of administrative practices and more precise pinpointing of accountability."[56]

In Britain, the Commons established in 1979 an elaborate system of select committees designed to strengthen the capacity of the legislature to oversee the work of departments. The committees have the power "to examine the expenditure and policy of Government departments . . . and to send for persons, papers and records."[57] Because public servants can be called before committees, there were originally fears that the conventions of anonymity and the confidentiality of advice to ministers could well be compromised. The Civil Service Department sought to deal with this danger by circulating a memorandum, commonly known as the Osmotherly Memorandum, that "gives civil servants some guidance on what could and could not be revealed to or discussed with select committees. In consequence, civil servants' participation in these committees has been less responsive than might be desired by those seeking to promote more responsible and open government."[58]

In the United States, the accountability of permanent officials is tied to the checks and balances of the political system. The Constitution makes it clear that the executive power is vested in the president but that power "flows from the people." The emphasis is less on controlling power by making politics and administration accountable and more on limiting power and countervailing its operation through checks and balances. This is not to suggest for a moment that officials are never held accountable for their activities before committees of Congress. They are. But power is formally divided between the legislature, the executive, and the judiciary. Once the more senior officials are appointed by the president and confirmed by Congress, however, "members of the executive are formally accountable only to the president who . . . except in the extreme (i.e. impeachment) case is accountable not to the congress but to the people."[59] Also, a number of senior officials in the United States are politically appointed, have no pretension of being politically neutral, and accordingly do not enjoy permanent status.

The president has several means to hold the bureaucracy and officials accountable. He holds the power to appoint and remove some 2,700 senior officials who occupy key positions in the executive branch. Congress has also delegated to the president the authority "to formulate the rules and regulations under which the bureaucracy functions."[60] Congress, meanwhile, also has the power to hold officials accountable—notably, the "power of the purse." It has created its own office to scrutinize the budgets of government agencies. Committees of Congress can hold hearings on appropriation and launch special investigations. The Senate, meanwhile, has the authority to confirm many presidential appointments. And government agencies are legally accountable to the courts for the "administrative observance of statutes and constitutionally granted rights and liberties."[61]

LEADERSHIP

Students of government have developed a variety of conceptual frameworks to study leadership in government. Getting elected is one thing. Being able to exert strong leadership to implement a political agenda once in power is quite another. We know intuitively that Winston

Churchill, David Lloyd George, and Franklin D. Roosevelt provided a vastly different type of leadership than did Edward Heath or Jimmy Carter. Why? Is it a matter of personality or style? Is it a matter of circumstances, given that Lloyd George, Churchill, and Roosevelt led their nations in times of deep crisis? How important is the machinery of government in facilitating strong leadership? Colin Campbell, for example, suggests that American presidents rely much less on cabinet and bureaucratic organization than do prime ministers "even in times of impending calamity."[62]

A number of factors have been identified that influence political leadership. Some observers argue that recent trends in the political environment have reduced the power that presidents and prime ministers can exercise, while at the same time adding substantially to their daily work load.[63] Factionalism, centrifugal forces at play both inside and outside government, the proliferation of interest groups, the discipline being imposed by the global economy, and the need for fiscal restraint have all chipped away at the powers of a political leader. At the very least, these forces have made it more difficult for political leaders to implement substantial policy changes. Other observers argue that timing is important and that a successful political leader must know when to push the right button and pull the right lever. Thomas Cronin makes the point that the longer a president is in office the less he is liked.[64] Others have sought to break down in some detail the various phases a political leader will experience while in office, ranging from the honeymoon period when he or she is first elected, to a period of decompression when the difficulties of working with other branches of government or the bureaucracy become apparent, to planning a reelection campaign.

Still others suggest that an "overload" problem confronts all modern-day political leaders. As before, leaders have to contend with the demands of their political supporters, the legislative branch, and foreign affairs. The post-Watergate media has become more demanding, domestic policies require far more attention than they did twenty or thirty years ago, and the growth in government bureaucracies has not made the task easier for political leaders—if anything, it has generated more paperwork and more administrative-type decisions.[65] Some observers insist that the more an organization grows (and governments have grown substantially over the past thirty years), the less efficient and the less politically responsive it becomes.[66] Some students of American politics were suggesting, as far back as fifteen years ago, that presidential responsibilities were such that one person alone could no longer cope.[67] The argument is increasingly being made that successful political leaders must carefully pick and choose a limited number of issues that are extremely important to them and then focus their efforts.

Leadership style is also important, a point I stress throughout this study. Some students of government have sought to define personality types in political leaders.[68] Others have gone further and presented a typology of leadership styles. A survey of political leaders will reveal that some will want to rule with a firm hand and draw as many key policy decisions to their office as the policy and institutional environments will permit. Others will be content to "hit the high points" and give plenty of decision-making room to ministers or political staff. Still others will seek to promote countervailing forces—competing policy positions or bureaus—in the system itself, to ensure that all sides of a policy issue are fully debated before decisions are made. One student of comparative government lays down four basic leadership styles:

1. Broker politics: decisions are made in the periphery, through negotiations between competing authorities, and tracked by central agencies

2. Administrative politics: decisions largely occur in the periphery so that departments and agencies obtain near hegemony over segments of program management

3. Planning-and-priorities: political leaders challenge departments to come up with imaginative and crosscutting policy alternatives, at the same time expecting central agencies to bring these alternatives together in a comprehensive strategy

4. The politics of survival: an administration or a government will attempt to secure control by sharply reducing the number of countervailing units and bringing to the center many matters previously decided in the periphery.[69]

I discuss at some length in this study both the leadership styles and the personalities of Thatcher, Reagan, and Mulroney. There is no doubt that these factors had an important impact on the success of the various measures introduced to reform the three civil services.

Suffice to say that Thatcher had a forceful and disciplined personality. Colin Campbell wrote that "one of the least endearing qualities of Britain's iron lady is her determination."[70] Thatcher came to office certain about what needed to be done, and she saw little merit in a planning-and-priorities style of leadership. Together with a handful of key advisors and a handful of senior ministers, she established the broad policy framework and pushed many administrative decisions down to ministers and their departments. She wanted her ministers to act as chief executive officers of their departments and to take charge. As a result, one should describe Thatcher's leadership style as administrative politics, and the label fits to a large extent. As we shall see, however, she never hesitated to get involved in administrative-type issues whenever she felt it necessary to ensure the success of her political agenda.

Ronald Reagan also adopted an administrative-politics leadership style. Like Thatcher, Reagan had a clearly articulated agenda when he came to office. He did not want a planning-and-priorities style that would rely on the bureaucracy to generate ideas as to what should be done. In pursuing an administrative-politics style, however, Reagan never demonstrated the same degree of hands-on or follow-through activity on issues as Thatcher did. Indeed, Reagan displayed a nonchalance "about the details of government."[71] Bert Rockman, for example, described Reagan's leadership style as "an active presidency without a highly active and involved president."[72]

Mulroney's political agenda was also clear when he came to office, although he was less committed to the neoconservative agenda than were Thatcher and Reagan. He and his closest advisors were deeply suspicious of the permanent bureaucracy. Thus, the planning-and-priorities style had no chance of appealing to Mulroney. One student of Canadian politics, Peter Aucoin, describes Mulroney's style as "brokerage politics." He explains that Mulroney viewed political leadership as the need to accommodate interests and not as the interplay of ideas. He adds that Mulroney attached "a high priority to consensus as an end in itself."[73] "Uncertainty" appears to have been an important part of Mulroney's leadership style. Of the four styles outlined above, it is a combination of administrative politics and the politics of survival that best describes Mulroney's leadership style. He—together with his most senior advisors and trusted ministers—

reacted to many emerging issues in a crisislike atmosphere and would quickly bring matters under his direct control.

CONCLUSION

This chapter suggests that there is no clear and agreed-upon theory of public administration and government organization. Also, a good number of studies in public administration report that, for every theory or approach developed, we have seen a wave of criticism shooting it down. The only issue in which there seems to be some amount of agreement is that public sector management is different from private sector management. It should come as no surprise that we have numerous theories or conflicting approaches to the study of public administration. As every student of politics and government knows full well, this comes with the territory. What is different in this context is that senior researchers in the field admit that considerable uncertainty exists about where we go from here. The public choice school, one of the most powerful bodies of literature in recent years, has been useful in explaining growth in government. It has been of limited use, however, in providing direction for the future. Even Vincent Ostrom— who is certainly less rigid and narrow-minded than the other public choice theorists and whose theory of democratic administration holds some practical application—spends more time explaining what does not work than what would.

Some efforts have been made, particularly in the United States, to rescue the field from "a kind of wondering relevance to students, practitioners and the future."[74] The Minnowbrook conferences, one held in 1968 and the other in 1988, did have some influence in the research agenda and, some argue, in the practice of American public administration. This is particularly true of the first conference. The themes emerging from this conference pointed to the importance of policy issues rather than to a strict concern with management. Social equity emerged as an issue, in addition to efficiency and an economic justification for policy decisions. A new emphasis was placed on ethics and responsibility in government and on encouraging citizen participation in decision making.[75] In many ways the first conference challenged participants to become proactive on social issues. The conference reflected the times. Positive government had come of age, and scholars and practitioners were convinced that, working together, they could solve many of the country's socioeconomic ills.

The second Minnowbrook conference picked up many of the same themes as the first but came to different conclusions. It also added new themes—notably, leadership in government—and urged a new emphasis be placed on constitutional and legal perspectives and technology.[76] It too reflected its times. There was much less enthusiasm and confidence that public organizations could "solve" the country's socioeconomic problems. Expectations about what public administration could accomplish were considerably lower than at the first conference. The discipline was in retreat. It was certainly not immune to the challenges of the new right and Ronald Reagan. One student explained, "Reagan's public philosophy made many in public administration increasingly nervous and defensive, and with good reason." He went on to argue that the field was caught "awkwardly in the middle of the onslaught . . . finding itself in an intellectual swamp with only a modicum of theoretical legitimacy."[77] A more recent review of the state of public administration discipline in the United States hardly gives reason to be optimistic. Aaron Wildavsky sums it up in this way:

> Perry and Kraemer tell us our research fails to cumulate into greater understanding . . . and is little valued professionally. Rainey refers to a widely perceived insufficiency in relevant research. Studies of public administration, Caiden advises, are fragmented. Worse still, efforts to unify the discipline through public choice theory could well lead to environmental degradation and social disintegration. . . . Although viable alternatives exist . . . the schizoid character of opinion on administration, which results in contradictory recommendations, makes progress difficult.[78]

The fact that there has been an ongoing intellectual crisis in the study of public administration is of little comfort to practitioners who themselves are confronting a crisis situation. We hear that, in the United States, "it will take years to rebuild morale and motivation within the civil service."[79] The situation is no better in Canada, where recent surveys of senior federal public servants reveal that a "serious morale problem" exists and that the problem is, if anything, "getting progressively worse."[80] Similarly, numerous reports in the British press in recent years suggest that the "Whitehall revolution" has taken its toll on morale in the public service. This also comes at a time when some fundamental traditions establishing the parameters of accountability of public servants to cabinet ministers and Parliament are increasingly being challenged.

Meanwhile, Thatcher, Reagan, and Mulroney came to office with no interest in the planning-and-priorities style of leadership. They also held strong views about what their civil services had to offer on the policy front and they had little interest in it. Rather, they would look to their political ideology and partisan advisors on how to make things right. Before we can look at how they sought to deal with some of these problems, it is important to review key historical milestones in the development of the three public services.

3

Getting There

Pᴇᴛᴇʀ Hᴇɴɴᴇssʏ wrote that "the history of Whitehall is a story of long periods of routine punctuated by occasional orgies of reform when the system broke down or, as in the greatest reform of all in the mid-nineteenth century, when scandal and outraged public opinion moved those in authority . . . to inquire and then to act."[1] By and large, the same can be said for the history of the American and Canadian public services. However, it is not uncommon for ambitious and high-profile reforms to be unveiled, endorsed, and publicly applauded, only to die on the vine within a few years.

One can also easily see similarities in the types of reforms attempted in the three public services. For example, the Canadian public service has over the years borrowed from both British and American experience. In turn, the Americans have on some occasions looked to the British to shape their public service, as when American reformers sought to introduce the principles of merit and expertise to their public service. Similarly, British officials looked to American experience when they attempted to introduce a more performance-based expenditure budget system. In short, developments in one public service have often led the others to attempt similar reforms.[2]

GREAT BRITAIN

There are many important milestones in the historical development of the three institutions. One in Great Britain was the damning Northcote-Trevelyan report of the 1850s that uncovered numerous shortcomings in the British civil service. Brief and to the point, the report argued:

> Admission into the Civil Service is eagerly sought after, but it is
> for the unambitious, and the indolent or incapable that it is highly

44

desired. Those whose abilities do not warrant an expectation that they will succeed in the open professions, where they must encounter the competition of their contemporaries, and those whom indolence of temperament, or physical infirmities unfit for active exertion, are placed in the Civil Service, where they may obtain an honourable livelihood with little labour, and with no risk.[3]

Those bright and ambitious people who happened to stumble into the civil service were quickly reduced to performing simple and repetitive tasks, unrelated to their talents or potential. Promotions were inevitably based on length of service or patronage, rather than on merit.

The Northcote-Trevelyan report proposed four key reforms: (1) entry into the civil service should be through open competition and examination; (2) promotion should be on merit, based on proper assessments prepared by superiors; (3) a distinction should be established between intellectual and mechanical labor; and (4) measures should be put in place to unify the civil service, including a common basis of recruiting. It took some time for Northcote-Trevelyan to be fully implemented—according to some, not until the end of World War I. And to be sure, there was some resistance to the Northcote-Trevelyan report. The Whitehall barons obviously favored the status quo. Some British politicians felt that the report constituted the first step toward republicanism and toward placing talent before character and loyalty. It is reported that Queen Victoria herself had serious reservations about opening the civil service to public competition, fearing that this would open up high office to low people without the breeding or the feelings of gentlemen.[4] It is true that a civil service commission was established in 1855, but for several years, its work and authority fell far short of what Northcote-Trevelyan envisaged.

Still, the reformers pressed on—and they had some powerful political allies, including William Gladstone who had initially launched the study. He was firmly of the view that while "the seventeenth century had been an age of rule by prerogative, and the eighteenth by patronage, the nineteenth would become a rule by virtue." This could be accomplished, he felt, through a liberal education that "attempted, above all, to produce citizens who were morally good and such it was that would succeed in examination."[5]

The reformers were also assisted by scandals and the inability of the system of government and the military to support war efforts abroad.

Peter Kellner and Lord Crowther-Hunt explain: "The reformers received a well-timed if unpleasant boost in October 1854." The British army fighting in the Crimea suffered from patronage and incompetence such as Northcote and Trevelyan had found in the civil service, one consequence of which was the disastrous charge of the Light Brigade: "the incoming government though by no means radical by inclination, felt that expediency demanded action on both Army and Civil Service reform."[6] The public, including key business people and journalists, began to clamor for change and for measures to modernize the government machine. With first Palmerston and later Gladstone occupying No. 10 Downing Street and a keen reformer, Robert Lowe, serving as the Chancellor of the Exchequer, by the late 1860s there was no looking back. Although initially the Civil Service Commission (CSC) lacked the authority and scope that Northcote-Trevelyan envisaged, it was able slowly but surely to establish itself as a relevant agency. By the early 1870s, a system of open competition was firmly in place as the proper means to secure employment with large government departments.

The reformers also secured the support of influential members of Oxford and Cambridge universities. Indeed, many argue that both universities were accomplices in the reform movement. Cambridge had long argued that the great majority of its fellowships were open to free competition, which had in itself given the university a high moral elevation. As well, the heads of some Oxford colleges made clear their willingness to revise their curricula to support the proposed reforms, which were seen as providing an opportunity to "open up a new field of knowledge and a new root striking into a new soil in society." They believed that the reforms "would probably do more to guide the progress of their Universities than any legislative measures that could be adopted."[7]

The Northcote-Trevelyan scheme sought through education and open competition to create a unifying culture or a "bond of unity" among civil servants. The report set the stage for a civil service that would clearly favor young recruits with a "proper" education and subsequently see to it that promotions to more senior levels would be from within the service. The report asked "whether it is better to train young men for the discharge of the duties which they will afterwards have to perform, or to take men of mature age, who have already acquired experience in other walks of life?" and it quickly provided the answer:

> It is decidedly best to train young men. Without laying too much stress on the experience which a long official life necessarily brings with it, we cannot but regard it as an advantage of some importance. In many offices, moreover, it is found that the superior docility of young men renders it much easier to make valuable public servants of them, than of those more advanced in life.[8]

Entrance to the civil service would be through examinations, and success at these would be ensured through the study of classics, mathematics, and modern languages. The examinations would take place for vacancies at two levels: senior positions would be open to applicants between the ages of nineteen and twenty-five, and junior positions would be open to applicants between the ages of seventeen and twenty-one. It was the recruitment process that would serve to give the civil service a unifying force linking the various departments through the bond of having "entered by the same gate and of being of the same vintage, or perhaps a year more or less in battle than Smith of the Department across the road." Once in government, young recruits could only secure promotion through establishing their competence and demonstrating superior skills, in short, "according to their deserts."[9]

In time, the civil service developed a distinct "corporate" culture and its own road map to the top. It would become highly centralized, its values shaped by a humanistic education, and it would seek to detach itself from the objectives of the government of the day. Individual civil servants increasingly saw their role as essentially one of balancing and adapting the environment and government activities to support political goals. The civil servants' objective was to serve their political masters well, but in a detached manner, never publicly identifying themselves directly with the politicians or their policies. An education provided an entry ticket, but once in, one learned by observing, by doing, and by acquiring new techniques or knowledge from within. Some observers have commented that an attitude of "effortless superiority" or "gifted amateurs" was being promoted.[10]

The Northcote-Trevelyan reforms had a profound impact on the relationship between elected and permanent officials, between senior civil servants and their ministers in particular. Previously, the loyalty of senior civil servants had been to ministers, often to the ministers who had secured their appointment. Political patronage had been the key to both employment and promotion. Open competition now brought with it less attachment to a particular minister and more "loyalty to the Service."[11] In addition, a nonpartisan civil service advising government on policy meant that a good part of the work of the service would become anonymous to those outside government and that advice would be put forward under the cloak of secrecy.

It is hardly possible to overstate the importance of Northcote-Trevelyan in shaping the British civil service. Indeed, the 1968 Fulton review observed in its opening line that the "Home Civil Service is still fundamentally the product of the nineteenth-century philosophy of the Northcote-Trevelyan Report."[12] Writing in the late 1980s, Peter Hennessy stated that Northcote-Trevelyan

> created the country's first true meritocracy, a genuine aristocracy
> of talent. Its bone structure is clearly visible in the higher civil
> service of today—despite two world wars, the complete extension
> of the franchise, a social revolution or two, the rise and fall of the
> British empire and the decline of the country as the world's lead-
> ing manufacturer and exporter. . . . For the Northcote-Trevelyan
> reforms and their gradual implementation over half a century *were*
> the greatest single transformation the British Civil Service has
> ever undergone, and, in their day, they were wholly beneficial.[13]

Some further reforms were carried out during the 1910s, but these were not nearly as sweeping. In many ways, they simply served to complete the implementation of the Northcote-Trevelyan report. World War I provided the impetus to centralize decision making further, particularly personnel management. The permanent secretary of the Treasury was formally recognized as head of the civil service, and promotions to the most senior levels would be decided at the center rather than in the ministries. Measures were put in place to break down the isolation between departments. One such measure was the decree in 1919 that the prime minister would, on the advice of the head of the civil service, hold full authority to accept or reject all appointments to the top positions in all departments. The prime minister and his advisors would in turn reserve the prerogative to survey all departments and the whole civil service to identify the most promising candidates for the position of permanent secretary.

THE UNITED STATES

The Northcote-Trevelyan reforms were soon felt across the Atlantic also. Frederick C. Mosher points to England, France, and Germany "in approximately that historical order" to explain the development of the American public service.[14] He explains that early Americans were by and large transplanted Englishmen who carried to the new country their values and the kind of institutions they were familiar with. The French provided the technical knowledge, notably in engineering, while the Germans provided new thinking in education and public administration.

It was, however, the Progressives and later the scientific-management movement that promoted administrative reforms in the United States. The progressive reform movement, which was particularly strong at the turn of the century, applauded the notion of a politically neutral bureaucracy, pushed for greater control and efficiency in government operations, and called for an end to political graft and corruption. Meanwhile, scientific-management became a fad, and "efficiency" a cult, early in the century. The business committee embraced scientific management principles, and later even universities and churches established efficiency committees. Frederick Taylor's book *Scientific Management* became required reading in many business and government circles, and government operations became a testing ground for Taylorism. Taylor believed that every act of every worker could be reduced to a science, and he proposed to look at all the components of work in a scientific manner and in so doing improve efficiency.[15]

A milestone in the development of the American civil service was the 1883 Pendleton Act, which stands out as a landmark in the development of the political and civil service history. To celebrate its centenary, Paul P. Van Riper wrote,

> The Pendleton Act is deservedly recognized as a landmark in our political and administrative history for several reasons. It created a public personnel system compatible with American life and unique

in the world. It signalled the birth of our modern administrative state by providing that foundation of merit and expertise which was increasingly to be required. And it foreshadowed the transformation of our political party system by commencing to remove from political warfare one of its principal armaments, patronage. Moreover, though the Civil Service Reform Act of 1978 effectively superseded the Pendleton Act, the essence of the latter is still very much in place.[16]

There is little doubt that the Northcote-Trevelyan reforms in Britain influenced the passage of the Pendleton Act. Van Riper explains, "A fairly complete and firm legislative foundation for the development of a civil service based on examinations and merit in the English manner has existed in the United States since the passage of the Pendleton Act in 1883." The Pendleton Act was the "Americanizing of a foreign invention."[17]

The Pendleton Act was the result of a hard-fought campaign to clean up the spoils system. Political patronage was far more prevalent in the United States than in Great Britain, in the latter half of the nineteenth century. Accordingly, the driving force behind the American reform movement was, first and foremost, to eradicate patronage—or the evil—in government and not necessarily to ensure a more efficient service. Again, Van Riper suggests that efficiency in government operations was a secondary consideration "and not a very close second at that." The reform movement was thus negative, in that it wanted above all to stop something—political patronage. One reformer, quoted by Van Riper, explained, "There is no political reform which would tend so much to the relief of so many evils as a rigorous diminution of patronage." Another student of the movement, Lionel Murphy, concluded, "These reformers regarded their demand as a second emancipation."[18]

The Pendleton legislation gave rise to a lengthy and at times heated debate in Congress, particularly in the Senate. The debate canvased a host of issues, including the impact the proposed legislation would have on the constitutional position of the president and Congress, on the civil service, and on the American people. The proposed legislation, as tabled by Senator Pendleton, essentially provided for the adoption of the British civil service model in the United States and the Senate debate is full of references to the British experience. Still, by the time the legislation was finally approved, it provided for a very different system from the British.

The Pendleton Act did put in place a politically neutral civil service based on competitive examinations and security of tenure, but it is different from the British reforms on several fronts. For one thing, the American Senate saw little merit in an academic-type essay for gaining entry to the civil service. The American tradition values more practical knowledge and capacity and explains the Senate's going to great lengths to define the requirements of positions and to classify them. Practical examinations could then be more easily tailored to the knowledge and skills required of a position. The Senate also rejected the British notion that one should gain entry at the lowest grade, and any notion that the civil service would be closed at all levels to outsiders. They made provisions for entry at all levels. The Senate also stressed that the American tradition of democracy in public office and in a representative bureaucracy was a fundamental tenet of a democratic state. Accordingly, "the authors of the legislation of 1883 and their political supporters, knowingly or unknowingly, were taking as few chances as possible that the American civil service might not be representative as a whole, in terms of geography, mobility, ideas, and outlook."[19] The importance of a representative bureaucracy also no doubt inhibited any strong links developing between a few universities and the entrance system of the kind that had developed between the British civil service and Oxford and Cambridge.

The American legislation provided for some delay in implementing the act, and certainly things did not change overnight. Indeed, the legislation itself was for the most part "permissive rather than mandatory."[20] That is, only about 10 percent of the positions in the civil service under the merit system were designed to form the classified service. The rest of the service was left unclassified, only to be brought in when the president so decided. In short, the act gave the president full discretion to move as slowly as he chose. To be sure, a sudden attempt to classify all positions and bring them under the merit system would have fallen flat on its face. But clearly there were also political reasons for delay. The permissive aspect of the legislation enabled politicians to claim credit for sweeping reforms, knowing full well that time was on their side.

The architects of the Pendleton Act also proposed the establishment of an independent civil service agency to ensure that appointments and promotions would be isolated from political influence. The agency itself was to be independent of Congress and, to the extent possible, from the executive. It was also to be a multimember agency with wide representation, certainly not from just one political party. The commissioners were to be presidential appointees, subject to Senate approval.

There are two points we need to highlight here. First, with all the concern about insulating the civil service from political patronage, the American reforms stopped short of completely reversing past practices. Indeed, the concept of a politically neutral civil service fell far short of what the British had done. Although the reformers were set on eliminating patronage, they were also worried about giving rise to an entrenched bureaucracy taking on a life of its own. They made provisions for the Civil Service Commission to provide a list of the three best qualified applicants, rather than naming a single winning applicant. Senior appointments were to remain "political" and within the prerogative of the president. The Americans, for example, have never appointed permanent and politically neutral under secretaries or deputy ministers to manage departments and agencies, as the British and the Canadians have.

It took some time for the Pendleton Act to deal with patronage in a substantial fashion. Initially, the act applied to only 10 percent of the service, and its application only increased through presidential order. "Inclusions" grew to about 50 percent under Theodore Roosevelt. The numbers gradually increased so that, by 1930, some 80 percent of employees were included under the act. There was some backsliding initially under Franklin Roosevelt, but he subsequently brought the numbers back up, until about 95 percent came under the jurisdiction of the Civil Service Commission. Some observers suggest that Roosevelt used the commission to push the bureaucracy in his ideological direction. That is, he gave patronage appointments to sympathetic supporters and later ensured their perpetuation in office by extending civil service protection to them. In any event, the inclusions number later dropped to 85 percent—about where the figure rests today. Thus, civil service reform in the United States was not adopted as fully in as short a period of time as it was in Great Britain or, as we shall see, in Canada.[21]

The second important legacy of the Pendleton Act is that personnel management became divorced from general management.[22] Executives would no longer be completely free to take decisions as they saw fit regarding staffing, promotions, and discipline. Indeed, key decision-making authority on personnel issues was diluted so that several voices, including some from central agencies and far removed from the day-to-day operations, would have a say on recruitment, promotions, compensation, and discipline.

CANADA

Although Canadian political institutions have their roots in British tradition, the administrative practices found in the Canadian public service reveal both British and American influences. In the case of the merit system, for instance, the influences have been predominantly American.[23] The Canadian battle to rid government of the political spoils system took place at about the same time as the British and American ones. In Canada, however, the early efforts were less successful than in the other two countries. Spurred on by a number of reformers, including a growing number of members of Parliament, the government established a parliamentary committee in 1877 and later, a royal commission, to look into the matter. Although the Civil Service Act was passed in 1882, it lacked teeth and little actually changed. R. MacGregor Dawson explains,

> The entrance examination was not competitive and the minister was therefore still free to appoint anyone he chose, subject to the trifling restriction that the candidate was required to pass a very elementary test. Subnormal and illiterate candidates were shut out; but almost anyone else could squeeze through and, if he had the necessary political influence, he could slip into the appointment as before.[24]

Although the pressure for effective reform toward the end of the nineteenth century in Canada was great, the government of the day looked for every opportunity to slip back to the old ways of doing things. It is important to realize that at the turn of the century "the distribution of patronage was the most important function of the government."[25]

But things began to change in the early 1900s. People with the necessary skills to carry out more complex tasks were increasingly required, and reformers pointed to developments in Great Britain and the United States. Moreover, the call for dealing with political patronage began to fall on attentive ears among the general public, which started to comprehend the great value of "efficient administration" and appreciate the wasteful results of patronage.[26]

Growing public demand for the government to do something, coupled with the need to call a general election, prompted the Laurier government in 1908 to pass a new civil service act. This established a civil service commission and effectively curtailed the autonomy of departments in the management of all personnel matters. Above all, the act sought to ensure that individual ministers could no longer appoint public servants after consulting cabinet colleagues, members of Parliament, defeated candidates, and the local patronage committee.[27]

Canada's Civil Service Commission was to be nonpartisan, and members of the commission given tenure during good behavior were to be subject to removal only by the Governor General on a motion passed by both the Senate and the House of Commons. The commission was charged with setting examinations for entrance to a large number of government jobs. The examinations would be held in open competition and the winning candidate would secure the appointment. As in the United States, however, the old ways of doing things proved difficult to abandon. Although the 1908 changes were far-reaching, the reformers were not at all satisfied. The policies of the Civil Service Commission applied to only parts of the service, the "In Service." The "Outside Service," which grew considerably after 1908, operated under the old political rules. The Outside Service was so large that, when the Laurier government went down to defeat in 1911, some eleven thousand public servants resigned or were fired, mostly for having been guilty of political partisanship.

The reformers finally won the day in 1918 when nearly the entire civil service and virtually all appointments were placed under the Civil Service Commission. The mandate of the commission was strengthened and a new system of classification and pay was introduced. On this front, Canada again looked to the American system for inspiration. It did not, for example, recognize a distinct administrative class to which young university graduates would be recruited. It sought to classify positions "minutely," according to specific duties and tasks.[28]

These developments strengthened considerably the hand of the commission, turning it into a powerful central agency.

Again, the reforms proved difficult to implement, and departments began to question the need for a highly centralized personnel-management system. Some line department officials even became nostalgic about the old days, when they appeared before parliamentary committees. Two senior deputy ministers went so far as to argue for "a restoration of the pre-1908 period, claiming that the maligned patronage system was in reality the only democratic way of managing the service."[29] Some senior officials felt that it was easier to cope with political patronage than with all the requirements of an independent central agency and with having to define and classify all positions. But this time there would be no turning back.

FRESH THINKING AND SOME REFORMS

By the end of World War II, government was playing a far more important role in society than it had previously. Prior to the change to a nonpartisan public service, the role of government had been highly restricted and any expansion was carefully monitored. It was William Gladstone who, at the time of the Northcote-Trevelyan report, had said that frugality in government spending was a matter of the most basic of principles and, in his opinion, the way to ensure this was "to estimate expenditures liberally, revenue carefully and make each year pay its own expense."[30]

Despite Gladstone's caution, government in all three countries began to expand on all cylinders in the late 1930s. This was on the heels of the Great Depression, and the "Keynesian revolution" had captured the Budget Office in the United States and the Treasury in Britain and Canada. The New Deal in the United States, Lord Beveridge's Full Employment Report in Britain, and the Rowell-Sirois Commission in Canada all pointed to a greatly expanded role for government, to attenuate the sting of economic misfortune, to promote employment opportunities, and to direct economic activities. The need to plan the war effort also saw governments move into areas that were traditionally the preserve of the private sector. By the end of World War II, it was no longer possible for any of the three governments to apply the Gladstone principle of frugality to budget making. Government was now too complex, multifaceted, and ever expanding for a handful of individuals poring over detailed expenditure plans around a table to counterbalance provision for new wants by new economies. Things were no longer that simple and, with the close of World War II, calls were increasingly heard to make the government more efficient.[31]

In the United States, President Roosevelt recognized even before the war that administrative reforms were necessary. He had established a number of New Deal agencies, and critics were increasingly complaining of the "crazy-quilt character of the federal government."[32]

Roosevelt responded to the charges in 1936 by establishing a president's committee on administrative management. The Brownlow Committee, as it became known because of its chairman Louis Brownlow, recommended a major overhaul of departments and agencies. It urged the establishment of twelve major departments, which would provide a home for the various agencies. It recommended a considerable strengthening of the president's own office, the creation of a single civil service administrator to replace the Civil Service Commission, an expansion of the merit system, and an ambitious overhaul of the government's accounting system.[33]

Roosevelt supported Brownlow's recommendations but Congress resisted, at least initially. Interest groups lined up to oppose the consolidation of their particular agencies into large government departments, and the president's reorganization bill went down to defeat in Congress in 1937. A few years later, however, Roosevelt submitted a new, watered-down reorganization bill, which Congress approved. The creation of large new departments and the modernization of the civil service system were dropped from the bill. The legislation, however, enabled the president to submit reorganization proposals to Congress, and Roosevelt turned to this legislation to establish a new Executive Office of the President (EOP) and to transfer the Budget Bureau to his office. Notwithstanding a poor start, the Brownlow Committee report had an important impact on government operations and continued to make itself felt for a long time.[34]

The Brownlow report, however, remained closely identified with the Roosevelt administration. Some ten years after the report was tabled, a Republican Congress felt the need to "straighten out" once again the executive branch.[35] In 1947, the American Congress passed, without opposition, legislation to establish a commission to explore ways to make the government more "efficient and economical." It established yet another commission in 1953 to look into the "Organization of the Executive Branch of the Government." Both became commonly known as the Hoover commissions, because of their chairman, former president Herbert Hoover. The first Hoover Commission tabled its report in 1949 and the second in 1955.

To be sure, the Hoover commissions were not the first review of the structure and functions of the executive branch of government. They were different, however, in that they were very ambitious in scope, they were inspired by Congress, and they enjoyed presidential support. In both, some members were appointed by the president, some by the Senate, and still others by the House of Representatives. Commissioners came from the private sector, the bureaucracy, and from both houses of Congress. The task at hand—and on this everyone seemed to agree, not least the legislation establishing the commissions—was to make the federal government "efficient and economical." Legislation that created the second commission, for example, records:

> [it is] the policy of Congress to promote economy, efficiency, and improved service in the transaction of the public business by 1) recommending methods and procedures for reducing expenditures to the lowest amount consistent with the efficient performance of essential services, activities, and functions; 2) eliminating duplication and overlapping of services, activities, and functions; 3) consolidating services, activities, and functions of a similar nature; 4) abolishing services, activities, and functions not necessary to the efficient conduct of government; 5) eliminating nonessential services, functions, and activities which are competitive with private enterprise; 6) defining responsibilities of officials.[36]

Hoover himself and the commissioners saw their task as one of tidying up (in the words of Ronald Moe) "the organizational residue left in the wake of the New Deal and the war." Hoover explained that "major functions of the government are determinable as needed by Congress. It is not our function to say whether it should exist or not, but it is our function to see if we cannot make it work better." Although the commissions, particularly the second, did in fact venture into the debate as to whether a function should exist, they mostly concentrated on how to make government more economical and efficient. In doing so, they looked to the private sector for solutions, since a majority of them "believed the government to be a morass of well-intentioned, but essentially incompetent bureaucrats who needed to be guided by the principles of private sector management."[37]

Both commissions put together ambitious work plans. In the case of the first Hoover Commission, some twenty-four task forces were established, with personnel drawn largely from leaders in the business community and professional associations. Most were set up to study a specific function (federal supply, for example), although there was not always an apparent link bringing all the task forces together. This no doubt explains why nineteen separate reports were sent to Congress.

The first commission concentrated on organizational structure, arguing that "we must reorganize the Executive Branch to give it simplicity of structure, the unity of purpose, and the clear line of executive authority that was originally intended."[38] Underpinning its recommendations was the view that the executive branch needed to be organized hierarchically and to have a strong president at the top acting as an executive manager. The commission was highly critical of the tendency to disperse functions to various independent agencies—hence the call for a strong hierarchical structure. It also recommended a more orderly grouping of the various functions into departments and agencies. The commission found the internal activities of the federal government to be lacking in overall direction and concluded that supply, records management, and the operation of public buildings required stronger central authority. The solution, in the view of the commission, was to set up an Office of General Services that would coordinate all such activities.[39]

Hoover himself believed that politics and administration could be separated. He felt that what was required to make government more efficient was to place responsibility for making policy and setting standards in the hands of the president and departmental secretaries, but to decentralize administrative-type decisions down the line. The commission also challenged the budget process, insisting that the executive branch budget was an inadequate document. The line budget approach, it reported, was outdated. Line budgeting concentrated exclusively on requested funding for objects of expenditure, and funds were allocated on that basis. This was fine for the Gladstonian era when a handful of politicians were able to sit around a table to review carefully and in considerable detail proposed spending plans. Hoover urged the government to drop its approach to budgeting in favor of one "based upon functions, activities and projects: this we designate as a performance budget."[40] The commission also came forward with numerous recommendations on personnel management. It declared its support for the Civil Service Commission as constituted. It urged agencies, however, to ensure greater mobility among senior managers to broaden their perspective and to gain wider experience.

The first Hoover Commission came forward with 273 recommendations. The Truman administration quickly declared its support, as did many key leaders of Congress. Eventually, 196 of its recommendations (72 percent) were adopted. Certainly, the commission's work in leading to the reorganization of departments and functions was significant and at the time widely applauded. Still, some observers suggest that the commission's main accomplishment was to provide a sense that government activities could be well managed, that they could be both economical and efficient. This, we are now told, served to undercut the conservative opposition to an expanding government. Peri Arnold, for example, concluded, "In the end, Hoover and his commission provided the bridge over which . . . the old political enemies of Franklin Roosevelt could embrace the managerial Presidency."[41] In short, the commission did not (as some had initially hoped it would) propose ways to cut back the size of government. Instead, it brought forward measures to strengthen the managerial hands of the president and departmental secretaries and pointed to ways to manage departments, agencies, and programs more effectively.

The second Hoover Commission was no less ambitious than the first. Once again, Congress unanimously approved the legislation setting it up. The commission also retained essentially the same membership, many of the same staff, and even the same name as the first commission. It also turned to nineteen task forces to carry out the research. This time, however, supporters of the commission, in Congress and elsewhere, made it very clear at the outset that Hoover should attack big government at its roots. This explains why the second Hoover Commission was asked not simply to consider the efficiency of internal administration, like its predecessor, but also to consider public policies. Indeed, some felt that the first commission had let them down by giving rise to more, rather than less, government. Senator Ferguson explained:

> The most important difference between this bill and the first Hoover Commission is found in the declaration-of-policy section. This is . . . intended to make certain that this commission has full power to look into the activities of the Federal Government from the standpoint of policy and to inquire. Should the Government be performing this activity or service, and if so, to what extent? This Commission must ask questions of this nature which the original Hoover Commission did not ask.[42]

The second commission submitted to Congress, along with its final report, twenty related reports. Again, the reports dealt with a number of issues, ranging from managing the expenditure budget and accounting to water resources and power. They proposed 314 recommendations and a citizens' committee reported in 1958 that the government had fully or partially accepted some two hundred of them. This latter figure has been challenged on numerous occasions, and observers now agree that the second commission was not nearly as successful as the first.

One important contribution of the second commission, however, was its focus on personnel management. It urged the government to recruit more noncareer civil servants to senior executive positions. It recommended more political appointees in key policy positions. It saw the need for a new, distinct senior group, with individual civil servants holding a rank and status not necessarily linked to the classification of the job they currently held. In short, the commission felt that staffing should be done to level rather than to position. Finally, it called for a new emphasis on the training and development of junior- and middle-rank managers.

The commission also tried its hand at attacking big government at its roots. It argued, for example, that there were three thousand units in government that were in competition with the private sector, and it urged their elimination. A recurring theme in the various reports was that the government's being inefficient and uneconomical was the fault of the system, not of individuals or even specific agencies.[43] The solution was, whenever possible, to turn the activities over to the private sector.

The commission, however, had very limited impact in cutting big government down to size. Ronald Moe explains that, by the time the commission tabled its report in 1955, the Democrats controlled both houses of Congress. The Democratic leadership claimed the commission had been captured by "big business," which was committed to "repealing the New Deal." This—combined with the fact that federally run programs, if not the civil service itself, were held in high esteem in the 1950s—meant that there was no political will to carry through on the second Hoover Commission. President Eisenhower and his moderate Republican wing sensed this and decided to put some distance between the White House and the commission.[44]

The work of the Hoover commissions, however, was not lost on the Canadian government. A Progressive Conservative government elected in 1957—the first time the Conservatives had been in office in nearly thirty years—quickly concluded that the public service had many shortcomings. Prime Minister John Diefenbaker, in particular, viewed the public service as possessed of its own policy agenda, as administratively inefficient and, above all, as not to be trusted.[45]

He looked south for inspiration and became highly interested in the work of the Hoover commissions. The second commission, in particular, contained the right message for Diefenbaker: it wanted to attack big government at its roots by turning to the private sector for at least some of the solutions. Diefenbaker clearly borrowed from the American experience when he announced in 1960 the establishment of a royal commission, commonly known as the Glassco Commission, on government organization. Glassco and his team were asked to "inquire into and report upon the organization and methods of operation of the departments and agencies of the government of Canada and to recommend changes therein which they consider would best promote efficiency, economy, and improved service in the dispatch of public business."[46]

Like Hoover, the private sector was well represented both on the Glassco Commission itself and at the staff level. Indeed, some critics observed later that the strong private sector presence was the reason some of the commission's recommendations were not practical to government. They argued, for example, that Glassco's "appraisals and recommendations . . . were unduly biased and tended to dismiss the essential differences between management operating in the private sector and in the public sector."[47]

The Glassco Commission was strongly critical of both personnel and financial management in the Canadian public service. Only two years after it was established, it documented its findings in four voluminous reports:

> There is a waste of human resources, because of the failure to give orderly consideration to the best methods of providing and utilizing people and the consequent frustration of many individual careers; the procedures are costly and time consuming; personnel management in departments is generally misdirected, mainly because accountability for the effective use of personnel is fragmented or virtually non-existent.[48]

Glassco also slammed the government's approach to budgeting, as being hopelessly out of date and certainly inefficient. The commission argued that the "ponderous system, virtually unchanged in the past thirty years, is regarded by many as the price that must be paid under democracy in order to hold public service accountable." It concluded that "the system in place no longer did the job." What was relatively simple government organization in 1939, it reported,

> had become today a complicated system of departments, boards and commissions engaged in a multitude of different tasks. Obviously, the methods found effective for the management of the relatively compact organization of the prewar days cannot control without extensive alteration, the vast complex which has come into being in the past twenty years.

The commission found the government's financial controls were too cumbersome and that there was a wide variety of "checks, counterchecks and duplication and blind adherence to regulations."[49]

Glassco came forward with a series of sweeping recommendations designed to overhaul management practices in the Canadian public service. Like Hoover had done before, the commission urged the government to replace its line budgeting approach by a program-and-performance-base budget system. The commission also concluded that a new central agency was required to coordinate human, financial, and material resources. It rejected out of hand any suggestion that the Civil

Service Commission become that agency. It argued that its role was to act as an arm of Parliament and its primary concern should be to ensure fairness, to see that the merit principle applies in the staffing process. The Civil Service Commission would have other responsibilities, but Glassco insisted that the Treasury Board and a much expanded Treasury Board secretariat take the lead role in both personnel and financial management. There is little doubt that Glassco's goal was to see the Treasury Board emerge as the government's general manager. Above all, Glassco wanted to clarify the roles and responsibilities of the various agencies, arguing that, as the matter stood, "central agencies, together with a given department, constitute a complex triangle of authority and responsibility in countless detailed problems and requests sometimes travel lengthy circuitous routes before decisions are made and action taken."[50]

It was hoped that the Treasury Board would set the broad parameters to guide managers in line departments to modernize their operations and their management practices, which, Glassco demonstrated, had seriously lagged behind those in the private sector. This is not to suggest that Glassco wanted to see a heavy management hand from the center imposed on line departments. It wanted quite the opposite. Glassco's rallying cry to the government was "to let the manager manage." A central agency should provide the leadership and the know-how and set the standards, but then the line manager should be left free to manage.

Central agencies, including the Public Service Commission, were also to be transformed into servicing agencies rather than controlling agencies. The commission's role would now emphasize auditing, reviewing, and appellate functions arising from "personnel decisions—on appointment, promotion and disciplinary matters."[51] Similarly, Glassco strongly urged the government to devolve to departments the authority to make spending decisions free of central controls. Managers, Glassco argued, were not free to make even the most minor of spending decisions without central controllers looking over their shoulders. The commission noted the precedent provided by Britain and the United States in this respect and urged the Canadian government to scrap many of the central financial controls.

In recommending the delegation of spending controls to departments, Glassco was careful to insist that managers be held properly accountable for their decisions. Glassco explained, "This re-location of financial powers is in no sense intended to place departmental managers beyond the complete control of the Executive."[52]

The Glassco Commission also wrote about the "make-or-buy" concept, arguing that government should contract out to the private sector many of the activities it was currently operating. In addition, much like Hoover, Glassco called for a greater degree of coherence in government procurement and supplies. It also called for the establishment of specialized bodies or agencies to handle common services or needs. Like Hoover, it recommended the centralization of several common service functions, including property management, procurement, and records management.

The Diefenbaker government endorsed the findings of the Glassco Commission and immediately appointed a minister responsible for the implementation of its recommendations. A new government bureau headed by a senior deputy minister was also established to act as a "ginger group" to ensure that the recommendations would not fall by the way side. J. E. Hodgetts explains,

> Uneasily housed, under somewhat indirect supervision, and with slender resources, the bureau nevertheless played the invaluable role of instigator, gadfly and facilitator. At least, it ensured that all the major recommendations of the commission were canvassed and, where agreements were secured, that action on them was initiated.[53]

A change in government in the spring of 1963 did not signal the end of Glassco. On the contrary, Lester B. Pearson's new Liberal government announced its support very early on in its mandate. The bureau overseeing Glassco's implementation was moved to the Department of Finance, and its director was appointed secretary to the Treasury Board. The Treasury Board staff, as Glassco recommended, was realigned around three broad functions: programs, personnel, and administrative practices and procedures. The Treasury Board was also organized as a separate ministry reporting to a new minister rather than through the Department of Finance. In addition, the government's financial management system was completely overhauled. The line budgeting approach was abandoned for a program-base budgetary system and many of the centrally imposed financial controls on line departments were discarded. Some five years after Glassco submitted its report, the president of the Treasury Board reported, "if I were to read the forty-eight recommendations in the first volume, I would be able to insert after thirty-six of them, the response: and we have implemented that."[54]

The civil service also came under attack in Great Britain in the early 1960s, and some of the criticism came from an unpredictable quarter— the political left. Thomas Balogh, an influential supporter of the Labour party and a close friend of Labour prime minister Harold Wilson, took the civil service to task in his widely read "The Apotheosis of the Dilettante: The Establishment of the Mandarins," in which he argued that the ways of the civil service had become outdated. He applauded the work of the Victorian reformers but insisted that fresh thinking and a new orientation were now needed. He blamed the "very success of the boldness of the effort of the Victorian reformers" for the service's difficulties, claiming that it had given rise to a recruitment process "favouring the smooth, extrovert conformist with good connections and no knowledge of modern problems." Put differently, the civil service was now directed by an "entrenched" administrative class of generalists that was giving short shrift to the specialist. Balogh also questioned the civil service's reputation as a smooth and efficient institution, arguing that civil servants had "effective power without responsibility, the complete freedom from all criticism."[55]

The Fabians also put together a special group to look at possible civil service reform. This collection of high-profile politicians, academics, and even civil servants produced a paper, *The Administrators*, which acknowledged the work of the Northcote-Trevelyan Commission as the world leader of its day but which went on to argue that the civil service was falling far short of modern-day expectations. The paper suggested that the civil service was particularly inept at planning and policy development. Although some new policy and planning units had been established, they "seemed to assume the colours of the rest of the machine, and no plan emerged." The problem was that the civil service's administrative class was staffed by the wrong people—too many generalists, Oxford and Cambridge arts graduates—and was all too often operating as a monastic order, isolated from industry, local groups, and society in general. There was, as well, a certain malaise within the service itself at the time. A senior Treasury official observed

a few years later that "there is a general feeling about the Civil Service—both inside and outside it—that something is wrong. Indeed, a
great deal is wrong."[56]

Criticism of the service did not fall on deaf ears. The Estimates
Committee of the House of Commons in 1965 issued a call for reform.
The committee pointed with deep concern to the preponderance of
Oxford and Cambridge graduates in the upper echelons and to what it
considered to be highly restricted access to the administrative class. It
then called for an ambitious inquiry into the recruitment, management, and structure of the civil service.[57]

Prime Minister Wilson responded by establishing a committee of
inquiry and asked Lord Fulton, a longtime friend and the vice chancellor of Sussex University, to chair the committee. Fulton was asked
to examine the structure, recruitment, and management of the service,
including training of the Home Civil Service, and to make recommendations. Although Fulton was given a sweeping mandate, he was specifically instructed not to address the "machinery of government."
Wilson explained that his government's decision to establish the inquiry did not

> imply any intention . . . to alter the basic relationship between
> ministers and civil servants because civil servants, however emi-
> nent, remain the confidential advisers of ministers, who alone are
> answerable to Parliament for policy; and we do not envisage any
> change in this fundamental feature of our parliamentary system of
> democracy.[58]

This was a crucial exclusion. Indeed, some observers argue that it
crippled the work of the Fulton committee. They maintain that nothing should have been declared out of bounds, for one thing. For another, this exclusion would provide senior civil servants determined to
fight a rearguard action a ready-made argument that Fulton's "work
was . . . unduly circumscribed and, as a consequence, that there were
considerable doubts about most, if not all, of its recommendations."[59]

Still, the Fulton Committee pushed ahead and inquired into a wide
range of issues. It began work in 1966. Twelve members were appointed to the committee, of which three were senior civil servants.
Aside from its inability to look at the relationship between ministers
and permanent officials, the committee roamed wherever it wanted

and studied whatever it wished. It commissioned numerous studies, including a detailed investigation of what civil servants did and how they did it. A special four-person management study group was established to do this, and it immediately set out to examine twenty-three blocks of civil service work from twelve departments. The group sought to identify the specific tasks civil servants were carrying out and to determine whether they had the necessary skills and experience required to do so.[60] The group also looked at the relationship between administrators, including those between the most senior-level positions and specialists.

The management group concluded that the concept of the generalist administrator needed to be completely overhauled. It considered a number of definitions of the generalist administrator, including one suggesting that:

> The essential function of the generalist administrators is to bring together the disparate issues involved in taking major decisions of policy, to advise on what these decisions should be and subsequently put them into effect. . . . Collectively they know about the whole range of governmental and parliamentary affairs; they know how to cope with the complexities of the government machine; finally, they are politically aware in the sense of regarding politics as the art of the possible.[61]

The Fulton Committee did not quarrel with this definition. It did, however, find numerous shortcomings with the concept, arguing that the process through which a civil servant became a generalist gave rise to instability in the service. The management consulting group reported that, on average, administrators only stayed 2.8 years in a position before moving on to another job. Only by changing jobs frequently, it discovered, could an administrator develop an understanding of the whole machinery of government, appreciate the wide range of activities in government departments, and develop the necessary background to become a well-rounded generalist. The consulting group told Fulton that far too many administrators had too brief a stay in their positions and, as a result, very few of them could assess whether the policies and programs they had been implementing were successful or not. The group also argued that the constant change at senior levels led to inefficiencies and much slower decision making.

The Fulton Committee agreed and concluded that administrators did not

> develop adequate knowledge in any aspect of the department's work. . . . This can lead to bad policy making; prevent a fundamental evaluation of the policies being administered; and lead to the adoption of inefficient methods for implementing policies and obstruct the establishment of fruitful contacts with sources of expert advice.[62]

Fulton was also critical of the educational background of the generalist. The preponderance of Oxford and Cambridge graduates was one thing. An even more serious concern, however, was that the great majority of graduates recruited to the administrative class (over 70 percent) had degrees in general arts and the humanities. Only 25 percent had degrees in the social sciences, and only a fraction in applied science. The generalist, the argument went, did not even have the necessary educational background to be familiar with many of the modern economic, social, and scientific problems the government was expected to deal with. Fulton also felt that an old boys' network had come to dominate the senior levels of bureaucracy and had a strong control over who gained access to it. The civil service, his committee argued, had a vested interest in maintaining "the cult of the generalist," which they achieved by insisting that senior positions required "above all the virtues of the generalist." This meant an Oxbridge education in the arts or humanities, and preferably in English, history, or classics. Fulton lamented the extremely limited access of entry to senior positions for those from other disciplines. The committee also singled out for criticism the class divisions found in the civil service. It noted the horizontal line that set clear divisions between mechanical and simple tasks at the lower end, the work of the intermediate level, and the executive class, which looked after policy formulation and the general direction of the departments. Fulton was particularly critical of the vertical line that divided the work of the administrators and the work of the scientists which effectively prohibited the latter from gaining access to senior positions.[63] The result was that the specialists—including the scientists, the economists, and the accountants— were invariably relegated to a second-class status. Their role was to give advice to the generalists who determined when, if, and how ministers should be advised. In addition, the Fulton Committee insisted that the generalist approach had left gaping holes in the general management—particularly in financial management—and in policy-making.

The Fulton Committee presented a number of recommendations designed to do away with the cult of the generalist, to strengthen the management capacity of senior civil servants, to increase the capacity of ministers to control their departments, and to abolish the class structure of the service. It attached considerable importance to management, suggesting that the service should continually review the tasks it is asked to carry out, in order to identify what new skills are required and how to find and train the right people.

More specifically, Fulton urged the government to establish a new civil service department that would take over the Civil Service Commission and the Treasury's pay and management group. The new department, Fulton concluded, should report directly to the prime minister to secure the necessary political clout to ensure its success. Fulton also recommended that "all classes . . . be abolished and replaced by a single, unified grading structure covering all civil servants from top to bottom in the non-industrial part of the Service."[64] The report went on to make the case for greater professionalism among specialists in administration and recommended the development of financial and economic administrators. Fulton also sought to strengthen the management capacity of senior officials by recommending the setting up of a civil service college. The college would not only provide major training courses in management but also have an important research function. The college would initially, at least, run courses for specialists who needed management training.

Some observers suggest that Fulton urged the establishment of the civil service college and department mainly to undermine the position of the generalist. New management courses for specialists, for instance, would enable them to assume more responsibilities and authority. The new department, the thinking was, would implement the Fulton report, and this explains why Fulton urged that it report to the prime minister, since "No other Minister could assert the needs of the government service as a whole over the sectional needs of powerful departmental ministers." Fulton also recommended that the principles of "accountable management" be applied to the activities of the departments. His report called for the "clear allocation of responsibility and authority to accountable units with defined objectives and a corresponding addition to the system of government accounting."[65]

The old mandarins' hold on the civil service would also be challenged by new planning units to be set up in each department. These units, to be directed by specialists, would provide for someone to plan for the long term and also ensure that day-to-day decisions square with long-term plans. Fulton sought to strengthen the ministers' position in their dealings with their departments by having in most departments "in addition to the Permanent Secretary, a Senior Policy Adviser to assist the Minister. The Senior Policy Adviser would normally be head of the Planning Unit."[66]

Fulton also recommended that the government overhaul its recruitment policies so that future civil servants not be solely "intelligent all-rounders," destined to become generalists. The committee recommended that "a number of appointments at senior levels within the new department should be made from outside the Service of people with appropriate knowledge and experience of managing large organizations both at home and abroad." Finally, Fulton pointed to other issues that required further research. These included "the desirability of hiving off activities to non-departmental organizations, ways of getting rid of unnecessary secrecy both in policy-making and in administration and methods of making recruitment procedures as speedy and objective as possible."[67]

Fulton knew that it was one thing to come up with recommendations, and quite another to see action taken on them. There was concern that there would be "massive civil service resistance since the Civil Service would have to be the engine of reform as well as the subject." Put differently, "the class Fulton was trying to transform was the very class which would have to advise ministers on the reforms—and then implement them."[68]

Fulton and some of his colleagues lobbied senior cabinet ministers to have the government commit itself early to supporting the report or, failing that, at least some of its key recommendations on the day of its release. As so happened, the prime minister announced the day the report was published that his government embraced, if not the entire report, at least all of the committee's key recommendations, including the establishment of a new civil service department and a civil service college and the abolition of civil service classes, to be replaced by a unified grading structure.

REFORMING GOVERNMENT BUDGETING

The first Hoover Commission, it will be recalled, called for a new approach to budgeting. The line-item budgetary process, it argued, was out of date, and the government needed to introduce a performance-based budgetary system. Performance budgeting became the holy grail of a more efficient government, and the search was on for a new system that would challenge the traditional, line-item, incremental style of budgeting.

The U.S. Department of Defense argued, in the late 1950s and 1960s, that it had designed such a system. It pioneered, during that period, a new approach to budgeting and labeled it Planning, Programming Budgeting System (commonly referred to as PPB or PPBS). President Johnson liked what he saw and in 1965 ordered all government agencies to adopt it. He explained later that PPBS was "a means of encouraging a careful and explicit analysis of federal programs." He added that it would "substantially improve our ability to decide among competing proposals for funds and to evaluate actual performance."[69]

The workings of PPBS have been described in great detail elsewhere, and there is no need to go over them here. Suffice to note that PPBS is different from traditional budgeting in that it concentrates on the objectives to be achieved rather than on the means of achieving them. PPBS was also seen as a means by which the cost benefits of alternative programs could be evaluated, as well as providing a capacity to ascertain the costs of future programs and spending proposals. This would leave politicians free to consider larger issues and broader questions. The thinking was that if politicians were given information on administrative details, they would make decisions on details, but if they were given information on policies and programs, they would make policy decisions. In short, under PPBS, the emphasis would shift to goals and performance and away from administration. This squared with the findings of both Hoover and Glassco commissions, both of which were highly critical of line-item budgeting, and both of which had encouraged the introduction of private sector management practices to government. PPBS signaled a sharp shift from control to planning and held the promise of letting the manager manage.[70] At the same time, it was felt that PPBS would strengthen accountability because, by presenting government spending in terms of objectives, performance could be measured. The system would also force legislators to look to the big issues and force them away from detailed information on such things as accounts spent for furniture and travel.

The Canadian government soon heard about the implementation of PPBS in the United States and liked what it heard. A few years after President Johnson announced that PPBS would be introduced throughout the American government, the Canadian finance minister followed suit. "PPBS," he declared, "is a major budget breakthrough." Most informed people in Canada believed that PPBS held great promise, and few dissident voices were heard. A leading practitioner explained that "PPBS seeks almost by definition to bring under review all that has been, as well as all that might be, to query the conventional wisdom, and to advance if necessary unconventional alternatives." The new approach was considered to be such a powerful instrument that many believed it would actually remove politics from the budgeting process—it would provide such clear and rational answers that ministers would be compelled to embrace them. This was so widely accepted that senior officials felt the need to reassure ministers that they would continue to make the key decisions and that politics would still weigh heavily in the decision-making process. The then-secretary to the Treasury Board wrote, for example, that "PPBS must not seek to substitute science for politics in the decision-making process."[71]

By the late 1960s, Britain also began the search for new ways to link policy and expenditure decisions. Certainly, by then, few inside government were happy about ministerial and bureaucratic decision making. For one thing, Fulton's report had exposed weaknesses in the civil service. For another, many politicians and a good number of officials came to accept that ministers in Britain "lacked sophisticated information and analysis such as that used in the United States programme budgeting to make important decisions." Britain did not embrace PPBS but came close when it introduced a "rigorous" system of Programme Analysis and Review (PAR).[72]

The Conservatives, while in opposition in the late 1960s, studied new approaches to budgeting and management. Edward Heath boldly declared in 1966 that a war on government waste, based on new Amer-

ican systems analysis techniques, "would result in dramatic savings."[73]
Advisors to Heath, both from his own party's research staff and from
the private sector, argued that the government's expenditure system
was too much oriented toward inputs and not enough toward performance or the quality of programs. Indeed, the Conservative party was
not alone in looking at what the Americans were doing. Treasury
officials also sent emissaries to United States to study PPBS techniques. However, when they arrived in the late 1960s, the bloom was
already off PPBS. They liked what they saw, but returned convinced
that the new approach would have a greater chance of success if it were
implemented piecemeal, or in carefully selected departments that had
bright young analysts eager to introduce the changes and make them
work.

The Conservatives won the 1970 election and pledged a new style of
government. The Heath government pushed ahead with the implementation of PAR. There was some jostling for position initially between the Civil Service Department, the Treasury, and others about
which would take the lead role in implementing PAR, but it soon
became clear that the powerful Treasury would take charge. As Hugh
Heclo and Aaron Wildavsky report, PAR became "the province" of the
Treasury, and not (as initially envisaged) of an "independent group of
long-term thinkers or of the Civil Service Department."[74]

The Treasury decided to launch PAR by commissioning a dozen or
so major studies of selected policy areas and to attempt later any necessary adjustments to improve the process. In addition, all departments
were asked to think about their objectives and to identify ways to
measure the performance of their programs. Heclo and Wildavsky
explain,

> Suggestions for PAR studies can come from almost anywhere—
> a minister, a department official, a treasury, or Central Policy
> Review Staff (CPRS). . . . They usually originate with depart-
> ments, are accepted or modified by the treasury and CPRS, rati-
> fied by a Cabinet committee, and wind their way down the de-
> partmental apparatus where they are modified again, worked
> upon, and hopefully emerge at the appointed time. The minister
> then presents his department's PAR report to a Cabinet commit-
> tee of his colleagues. The subjects of the studies, their timing,
> their sensitivity, the analysis that goes into them, the options that

are considered or ignored, the talent invested in them—all are subjects for negotiations.[75]

The hope was that, in time, departments would apply the same kind of rigorous thinking to all their programs and operations as that applied to the PAR process. Introducing modern PPBS-type management techniques to the civil service would lead departments to ask fundamental questions about their programs, their performance, their desirability, and their alternatives. Certainly, initially at least, politicians were enthusiastic about PAR. Edward Heath explained that, because of PAR,

> Ministers collectively can see what their department's up to. So this is . . . a major means of seeing the particular activities of individual departments. . . . What we are trying to do is to take each aspect of work in a department and say: Right, for this year we're going to analyze this, see what its origin, what its purpose and cost are.[76]

Permanent officials also saw merit in PAR, thinking that it would help ministers take the tough decisions. One permanent secretary explained, "PAR provides the minister with more prompting to undertake these major shifts in programme; it means he needn't be quite such a hero to carry important changes through the department."[77]

DISILLUSIONMENT

By the mid 1970s, it became clear that the various reforms and new budgeting systems introduced during the previous twenty years in all three countries were in serious difficulty. Disillusion was rampant. A new growth industry had sprouted, which consisted of consultants and academics explaining why things had gone wrong or coming up with suggestions to fix them.

To be sure, the Hoover commissions were important in the historical development of the American public service. Their lasting contribution was to provide key support to the "institutional presidency as manager of Government and to the notion of departmentalism."[78] Hoover successfully made the case that the Americans should give the president the authority and resources to manage the executive functions. This was no small achievement.

By the 1970s if not earlier, however, the Hoover commission reports held little value for those searching for a greater understanding of government organization and management.[79] If Hoover's objective had been to attack government at its roots, it had failed. The reports had called for some centralization of common services, including government procurement, as a cost-saving measure. Many critics would later come to argue that centralized purchasing made for a much more complex and slower decision-making process than formerly. They also questioned whether actual savings were ever realized. Hoover had also pointed to performance budgeting as the way ahead for more efficient government. The call was taken up but, as things transpired, PPBS hardly lived up to expectations.

In Canada, the Glassco Commission picked up on the themes found in Hoover, including a shift to a performance-base budgetary system. It centered on the call of "letting the manager manage" and demanded the abolishing of many centrally imposed financial, personnel, and administrative controls. The Canadian government implemented the great majority of the Glassco recommendations, and there is no doubt that the changes were quickly felt inside government. If nothing else, Glassco and PPBS had considerable impact on the attitudes of public servants, particularly managers, and on the types of administrative requirements found inside the government. One senior official explained, "Those who were not in the federal government before Glassco can't begin to imagine what it was like. We were constantly nickled and dimed to death. Ordering office supplies and planning a trip were no easy matter. All that changed after Glassco."[80]

While the government was implementing Glassco and PPBS, the auditor general shocked the nation when he wrote, "Parliament—and indeed the government—had lost or was close to losing effective control of the public purse." Some critics blamed Glassco for the crisis: one suggested that "Glassco failed to address itself to the operation of Cabinet and Parliament." Others argued that Glassco wrote about the need to delegate authority down the line and to make spending decisions closer to where programs were actually being implemented, but they failed to provide a clear direction for how managers would be held accountable for their decisions.[81]

The Canadian government responded to the criticism by establishing a royal commission on financial management and accountability, the Lambert Commission. The president of the Treasury Board explained that "the difficulties that have been encountered in attempting to develop, in the post-Glassco era, the concept of managerial accountability in the government environment are accordingly, one of the factors which have prompted the initiative." The commission came forward with numerous recommendations to "rediscover a sense of frugality" in government, including a substantial reorganization of central agencies. It also called for a strong emphasis on management rather than policy and presented a series of recommendations on how to hold officials more accountable for their decisions. Although some recommendations were accepted, the Lambert Report has had very little impact on government operations.[82]

The British government in 1978 looked back to the work of the Fulton Committee and declared that its acceptance "resulted in a number of radical changes in the organization and management of the Civil Service." The majority of students of British government, however, disagree. Although many of the Fulton recommendations were implemented, the key ones were not. In addition, some measures that were accepted never enjoyed the support of civil servants, so they broke down in the implementation stages. Prime Minister Wilson, himself, backed down on one of Fulton's key recommendations—the so-called preference for relevance—when recruiting young administrators of the future.[83]

We have seen that a civil service department was established a few months after Fulton tabled his report, along with a civil service college. However, the department had limited impact during its relatively short and rather tortuous life, at least in Margaret Thatcher's opinion, and the Thatcher government finally abolished it in 1981. A civil service college was set up less than two years after Fulton recommended its establishment. It was asked to establish an important research program and to provide major training courses in management. A quarter of a century later, the college has yet to make much headway on the research front and only recently has it been able to put together important management-development courses.[84]

One of Fulton's most important recommendations was that "the present multitude of classes and their separate structures should be replaced by a classless, uniformly graded structure." Prime Minister Wilson stated his complete support for this recommendation, on the day the report was made public, as did Opposition leader Edward Heath. Peter Kellner and Lord Crowther-Hunt report, however, that "ten years later the open road to the top remained unbuilt. Classes were replaced by groups and some of the lower hurdles to career progress were removed. But only for the 800 or so most senior civil servants was a unified grading system created." "More fundamentally," they add, "the philosophy of a classless Civil Service has been rejected." Civil servants charged with implementing Fulton, while admitting that the vertical barriers remained, did acknowledge that the horizontal barriers had been removed, with the administrative, executive, and clerical classes merged into a new administrative group. Although some efforts were made to recruit people from outside Oxford and Cambridge (and outside the humanities), these efforts did not amount to much. Indeed, the preponderance of Oxbridge graduates was as great by the late 1970s as it was when Fulton carried out his inquiry.[85] By the late 1970s, there was still only extremely limited access to senior positions for individuals occupying comparable positions in other sectors.

Fulton fell short of the mark in the implementation phase. There is little doubt that a good number of senior civil servants were less than enthusiastic over the work of the committee and its recommendations. One explained, "Fulton was a joke. The Civil Service is much too smart to worry about Fulton. They accepted everything he said, then did what they wanted to." Another reported, "Oh, there have been loads of changes. We have renamed everything." Peter Hennessy sums up the position of the civil service: "For a decade and more, the Fulton report continued to be the butt of private abuse from many, though not all, administrators. . . . The opposition was imbued by the kind of snobbery and arrogance that goes with an entrenched ruling group secure in the tradition of a century." In opposing Fulton, the senior civil service had, as always, an important advantage. Peter Kellner and Lord Crowther-Hunt explain, "The mandarins' greatest ally . . . was time. Politicians are, often, stimulated by brief enthusiasms, while civil servants are motivated by the need to survive the longer term."[86]

The biggest disappointment, however, was with the shift to a performance-base budgetary process. It is not too much of an exaggeration to say that the attempt collapsed everywhere and that, in the end, it constituted a step backward.

Within a few years, it became obvious that PPBS had serious short-comings, and by the mid 1970s, it was pronounced dead in the United States and Canada. The fact also became widely accepted that if "any-one did a cost-benefit analysis on the introduction of PPBS, he would be forced to conclude that it was not worth the effort."[87] Certainly, PPBS entailed considerable paperwork, countless meetings, and the hiring of a great number of systems analysts and operation research specialists. Yet, looking back, we now see that it led to very few pro-gram terminations or dramatic shifts in expenditure patterns. Aaron Wildavsky explains,

> I have not been able to find a single example of successful imple-mentation of PPBS. . . . Even where implementation was serious-ly carried out and a large investment made, the primary goal—changing budgetary procedures and decisions—was never achieved. Why? Did ugly politics beat up nice young PPBS? No doubt. But that is not half of it. Practitioners of program budget-ing were never able to define programs or attach costs to them, or make it worthwhile for organizations to figure out how to do so. What is worse . . . PPBS deserved to die because it is an irrational mode of analysis that leads to suppression rather than correction of error.[88]

If anything, PPBS led to increased spending in the administrative costs of government. Numerous new positions were established to implement PPBS, particularly in the areas of planning, evaluation, and policy and program coordination. Moreover, in moving away from line budgeting, the Budget Office and the Treasury loosened their control over costs such as travel, consultant contracts, and the like. Some senior officials now report that, as a result, departmental budgets for these items mushroomed in the late 1960s and 1970s. "It became too easy," said one, "for departments to get money for travel, for consult-ants, for staff, for new equipment and the like. We lost control over spending and we got little in the way of program reduction. PPBS itself became the problem."[89]

Bringing quantitative analysis into the expenditure process proved a particularly difficult task. As Wildavsky points out, in most instances, defining quantifiable objectives for programs and activities proved impossible. Officials soon discovered that there was often more than one objective for any given program, and virtually every program impinged directly or indirectly on the goals of others. Thus, in defining its program objectives, a department had to contend with those of another, which could be in conflict. Program objectives, if ever defined at all, were more often than not vague and of little value even as a checklist to evaluate the program's effectiveness. In turn, it became virtually impossible to develop a set of criteria to determine the success of a program. There was little in the way of experience to draw from. In any event, in the United States, the authors of PPBS reforms soon realized that their initiative, which had a centralizing tendency, would run up against the system of checks and balances and the separation of powers, with Congress constituting a significant budgetary force.

The PAR experiment enjoyed no more success in Britain than PPBS did in the United States or Canada. PAR eventually went the same way as PPBS and received its last rites in 1979. Observers now report that in the end it accomplished very little. One wrote that "the story of Heath's quiet revolution is of one revolutionary element after another being taken away and shot or allowed to expire because of neglect. The sickliest of them was what was supposed to be the vigorous system of policy and programme review." Another reported that

> in the heart of Whitehall's central departments, behind locked doors (and sometimes under the tea biscuits), lies a set of impressive but almost unused documents. Expensively produced, in a variety of stiff coloured covers and up to half an inch thick, the only sign of their ever having attracted attention is the odd short (and often dismissive) memorandum pinned to them. . . . They remain as fossilized memories of a dead species—the PARs, Whitehall's major and perhaps only effort at institutionalizing rational policy analysis.[90]

Why did PAR fail? PAR resembled PPBS in many ways, and so do the reasons that led to its failure. It also appears that civil servants often looked to PAR from a self-serving perspective. Heclo and Wildavsky wrote,

> When PAR is not a growth area, it is an odds-on bet that this is because political administrators of the department have already

decided that they want to switch resources away from this area to another. "It's conceivable," said a permanent secretary, "that we might do a PAR in a weak area if we want to get rid of something."[91]

The quality of the studies carried out under PAR varied considerably. Overall, however, the departmental management of PAR frequently "fell to generalist administrators best known for their consummate skills as essayists. Thus, the final product was often just that—an essay with little evidence of rigorous appraisal or of prescriptions for action." One government official explained his dilemma succinctly when he observed, "Socrates was the first person to do a PAR. He did it on Athens, going around asking fundamental questions. Athens put him to death. That's why I don't want to do any more PARs." Traces of provocative thinking were accordingly hard to find, and when it did surface, too many senior civil servants "could get at its findings before they reached ministers and erase any traces of radicalism."[92]

The failures of the various reforms to have any lasting impact on the operations of the civil service were not lost on many. Failures were apparent in different settings. Many—even those who had been in the past supportive of the civil service—began to question the ability of bureaucracy to reform itself. By the late 1970s, there was a growing consensus among politicians (irrespective of ideological bent) that the bureaucracy would invariably resist change and keep on doing things the way it wanted to, despite the numerous public inquiries, accusations of government inefficiency, and recommendations for sweeping change.

Politicians began to talk openly of the failures of their public service. Conservative politicians in Britain, particularly after the defeat of the Heath government, blamed both the trade unions and the civil service for the decline of Britain's economy. Now Labour politicians began to express publicly their deep displeasure with the civil service. Richard Crossman detailed in his widely read diaries his difficulties in dealing with public servants. He argued,

Whenever one relaxes one's guard the Civil Service in one's Department quietly asserts itself. . . . Just as the Cabinet Secretariat constantly transforms the actual proceedings of Cabinet into the form of the Cabinet minutes (i.e. it substitutes what we should have said if we had done as they wished for what we actually did say), so here in my Department the civil servants are always putting in what they think I should have said and not what I actually decided.[93]

The Crossman diaries opened a veritable floodgate of criticism from the political left. Tony Benn, for one, insisted that the problem with the civil service was that it "sees itself as being above the party battle, with a political position of its own to defend all comers, including incoming governments armed with their philosophy and program." Even more moderate politicians who had been highly supportive of the senior civil service in the past began to hurl criticism at the mandarins. Shirley Williams, for example, took to the lecture halls less than a year after holding office to document the weaknesses of the British civil service. At that point, argued Peter Hennessy, "the spectrum of criticism directed at the Civil Service was complete." Once again, in 1979, the Fabian Society put together a study group to look at government operations in the aftermath of Labour's electoral defeat. Again, its membership included former ministers, political advisors, former civil servants, and academics. The group reached several conclusions, notably that the civil service has "distinct ideologies of its own," that the "nature of departments limits a minister's capacity to produce a long-term and radical approach," and that "civil service advice needs to be augmented by alternative sources of ideas and analysis."[94]

Criticism against the civil service was also increasing in the United States and Canada. The Republicans under Richard Nixon had long believed that the bureaucracy was subverting their policy objectives. James Q. Wilson reports that Jimmy Carter and Gerald Ford could agree on very little during the 1976 presidential campaign other than that "the bureaucracy was a mess." President Carter's presidential campaign was based in large measure on his perceived ability to reform "bureaucracy" and "Washington." His track record on this front in Georgia was promising. He launched in 1978 an ambitious reform of the Civil Service Act, established a new Senior Executive Service (SES), and sought to introduce new ways to measure the performance of civil servants. The Carter reforms, however, proved disappointing. Evaluating the performance of civil service managers proved as difficult as evaluating programs under PPBS. The Carter reforms also failed to strike a new balance between expertise and political loyalty to the president and, in the end, "they had an immediate effect that was exactly opposite to the desired one: Instead of encouraging the best senior executives to stay with the public service, it encouraged the most senior and most capable ones to leave."[95]

Canadian politicians from both the right and the left also became critical of bureaucracy by the late 1970s. The right-of-center Progressive Conservative party had long been suspicious of the public service, and their suspicions turned to public criticism after the Joe Clark government lost a confidence motion in Parliament in 1979 after only a few months in power. They lost the subsequent election, and Flora MacDonald, minister of External Affairs in the short-lived government, went on the lecture circuit to denounce senior public servants, claiming that they employed clever ruses to push their own agenda and to circumvent cabinet and ministerial direction. She itemized what she termed the officials' entrapment devices for ministers, which included bogus options and delayed recommendations. Joe Clark, himself, became critical of the public service and spoke of misguided programs "concocted by a small group of theorists" within the public service.[96]

That members of the Progressive Conservative party would be critical of the public service surprised few people. It was, however, a different story to find leading members of the center-left Liberal party also doing so. The Liberal party, which held office for some forty-six of the fifty years between 1930 and 1980, had struck a particularly close working relationship with the public service. They had built Canada's welfare state together, and by the 1970s some were even arguing that an incestuous relationship had developed between the ruling Liberals and the senior civil servants. It surprised more than a few people when a senior and longtime leading member of the Liberal party and deputy prime minister, Allan MacEachen, reported that if Liberals had learned anything during their brief stay in opposition it was that his party would no longer rely as much as they had on the advice of senior public servants. Other senior Liberals joined in and publicly criticized the policy advisory and management capacities of public servants.[97]

Peter Drucker diagnosed government in the late 1960s as "sick."[98] The emerging political leadership, together with some leading members of the outgoing governments were convinced that the various reforms of the 1960s and 1970s had failed to bring the patient back to health. By the late 1970s, bureaucracy stood accused of many things, and there were few supportive voices heard anywhere. Indeed, those who had sung the praises of the public service in the 1950s, 1960s, and early 1970s were now silent or, worse, had become openly critical. Everywhere, as never before, the public service was on the defensive. The late 1970s and early 1980s would see new right-of-center governments coming to office in Great Britain, the United States, and Canada. They were all determined to roll the state back, and an important feature of their agenda was to modernize and cut bureaucracy down to size. In short, they were determined to attack big government at its roots—and this meant the bureaucracy.

PART 2
AS YE SOW

4

Rhetoric and Reality

THE ROLE GOVERNMENTS played in society fell out of favor in many Western countries during the late 1970s, and a slowdown in economic growth coupled with rising inflation gave birth to a new and dreaded word, *stagflation*. The confidence of many of those reared on the merits of Keynesian economics began to sag as they discovered that the scope and cost of government kept growing in both good economic times as well as bad. By the late 1970s, a good number of countries were witnessing double-digit inflation and a growth in the costs of government that outstripped growth in the economy. The standard Keynesian response of increasing government spending to deal with rising unemployment appeared ever more inappropriate in the face of inflationary pressure and growing government deficits. Observers began to write about a crisis of "governability" or "governmental overload." Political parties favoring a greater role for government in society and increased public spending were losing public support. For instance, in California, a grass-roots movement in 1978 successfully championed Proposition 13, a measure designed to limit taxation and, by extension, government spending.[1]

One concern was related to the apparent inability of governments to deal simultaneously with the issues of unemployment, inflation, balance of payments, and debt. Another concern extended to the apparatus of government itself and specifically bureaucracy, which was regarded as a barrier against, rather than a vehicle for, progressive change. Those few who still argued against tampering with the existing machinery of government and its "armies" of entrenched officials were dismissed by both political left and right. Even people who had supported the ideas and social welfare programs of leaders such as Franklin Roosevelt, Clement Attlee, Harold Gaitskell, T. C. Douglas, and Adlai Stevenson were now calling for changes to the apparatus of government.[2] We have already noted, for example, that barely a few months after the Labour party was out of office, the Fabian Society produced a report highly critical of the British civil service and calling for important changes. Academics by and large also became increasingly critical of bureaucracy. One scholar wrote that "Bureaucracy is a word with a bad reputation." Another argued, "Government functionaries work hard and accomplish little. Many people would question the first part of that statement." Herbert Kaufman concluded in the early 1980s that "antibureaucratic sentiment has taken hold like an epidemic."[3]

It was much more difficult for the political left than it was for the right to take the lead in redefining bureaucracy. Bureaucracy was largely a creation of the political left, which had held power for much of the Depression years, the immediate postwar period, and in key periods during the 1960s and 1970s. It was the political left that had been prepared to attempt daringly radical policies to combat the Depression, to plan the postwar reconstruction, and in the 1960s and early 1970s to introduce a Just, Equal, or Great Society. In short, the political left had articulated the visions, defined the new policies, and established the new agencies that led to big government. At least in the cases of the United States, Great Britain, and Canada, it was the political right that now took the lead in defining a new political agenda and that attempted to redefine bureaucracy.

THE RHETORIC

Margaret Thatcher came to office in 1979, Ronald Reagan in 1980, and Brian Mulroney in 1984. All three led their parties to resounding victories at the polls after being highly critical of big government. Thatcher won a majority of seventy seats over Labour. Reagan's victory was equally, if not more convincing in that he defeated an incumbent president. He won 50.7 percent of the vote, and 489 electoral votes to Carter's 44. In addition, on Reagan's coattails, the Republicans gained control of the Senate for the first time since 1954 and reduced the large Democratic majority in the House by 33 votes.[4] Brian Mulroney's victory was no less impressive. He captured 211 seats out of a total of 282, thus winning the largest number of seats ever recorded in Canadian history.

Some observers argue that Thatcher, Reagan, and Mulroney did not so much win a mandate to introduce a conservative agenda as step into the breach created when the incumbent governments self-destructed. To be sure, the incumbent governments were confronting difficult international economic circumstances that no regime could have handled well. Still, much has been written in Britain about the country's 1979 "winter of discontent." The rash of strikes, the perceived militancy of the trade unions (political allies of the governing Labour party), the slowdown in economic growth, the inability of the government to manage spending, and the actual decline in the average citizen's standard of living in the late 1970s led the British to "repudiate" the Labour party in 1979.[5] In the United States, the 1980 election was described as "a referendum on Carter" who had lost public confidence in his second year in office and failed to regain it, so that "in July 1980 Carter's approval rating . . . was 21 percent, a record low for any President."[6] Carter had come under heavy criticism because of the country's high inflation rate and the frustrating and highly publicized captivity of the American hostages in Iran. In Canada, the Liberal party (often referred to, for much of the 1960s and 1970s, as the natural government party) had been in office virtually uninterrupted for over twenty years and for forty-three of the previous fifty years. The party could not thus deflect responsibility for growing public disenchantment and criticism over the economy to someone else. To make matters worse, in his last weeks of office, Prime Minister Trudeau announced a veritable orgy of patronage appointments, naming hundreds of close political associates and friends to government positions. The new Liberal leader, John Turner, called a general election within days of becoming prime minister, but he proved particularly inept throughout the campaign.[7]

Although there is no doubt that the electorate in all three countries repudiated the parties in power, there is also little doubt they knew that, in voting for Thatcher, Reagan, and Mulroney, they were voting for a political agenda that would turn their countries to a more conservative tack. In Britain, Thatcher made clear her position on government intervention in the economy.[8] In Canada before the 1984 election, Mulroney published a collection of his speeches and policy positions that left little doubt he favored less government intervention in the economy.[9] In the United States, William Schneider reports, Reagan clearly offered a conservative perspective, but Americans were willing to go along with that not because they were convinced of the essential merits of the conservative program but they were willing to give conservatism a chance. It is as if, having got nowhere for the past four years with Jimmy Carter at the wheel, the voters turned to Ronald Reagan and said, O.K.—you drive.[10]

The new political agenda had various labels, including Thatcherism, Reaganomics, the New Right, and Neo Conservatism. The agenda spoke to a number of issues, but particularly to the role of government in society. Keynes was out and "supply-side economics" was in. The new agenda also rediscovered the works of Joseph A. Schumpeter. His 1942 book *Capitalism, Socialism and Democracy* argued that capitalism would eventually destroy itself—mostly through its own success. Capitalism, Schumpeter argued, would give rise to a new class of bureaucrats, intellectuals, and lawyers who would reap the benefits of capitalism to the point of becoming "parasitical," and ignore the need for wealth production. Schumpeter also warned that the "range" of political decisions should not be allowed to be pushed too far.[11] These views were music to the ears of the emerging political leadership. The new agenda had many targets, including trade unionism, welfarism, and government as an economic manager. The public service was singled out for criticism.

The rhetoric of politicians, particularly at election time, is often adversarial, but it also speaks to some of their fundamental values and basic beliefs. Thatcher, Reagan, and Mulroney often took full flight when speaking about the public service. They all regarded it as part of the problem and no one tried to attenuate their obvious dislike for the institution, even in public speeches.

Indeed, Thatcher's reservations about the civil service, in particular the senior civil service, were already well known. She, like many of her close advisors, wanted to tame what they described as "a greedy and parasitic public sector." When asked by a friend if she hated all institutions, she replied, "Not at all, I have great respect for the Monarchy and Parliament."[12] She saw senior civil servants as "protagonists of the failed Keynesian-Beveridgite consensus who had brought Britain low. She appeared to treat them, almost as a Marxist might, as a class with their own values." Peter Hennessy went on to sum up Thatcher's views succinctly: she "detested senior civil servants as a breed."[13]

Reagan shared Thatcher's views. Like Carter in 1976, he built his election campaign around the theme of running against the Washington establishment. Unlike Carter, however, Reagan did not suggest that the civil service needed to be updated and reorganized. Carter felt that the system was broken and that it needed fixing. Reagan felt that the system needed to be cut back to size. Few doubted that, if elected, Reagan would set out to "pare back extensively" the size of the federal government. He argued time and again, in the months leading up to his election, that the "unconstrained" growth of government and bureaucracy was one of the main causes of the poor performance of the American economy.[14] During the election campaign, he often referred in his speeches to the "government goliath" and "tons of bureaucracy."[15]

Mulroney could hardly hide his disdain for the public service. In his convention speech when he won the leadership of his party, he said that his government would be "prudent and frugal with taxpayers' money and eliminate the deficit by 1990."[16] I noted earlier that he promised to give "pink slips and running shoes to bureaucrats," once he was elected to office. In a major campaign speech shortly before coming to power, Mulroney pledged that his government would "spend smarter" and would employ the most advanced techniques to eliminate program duplication and overlap. He declared that since "coming to Ottawa (as opposition leader) from the private sector, I have been appalled by the waste of time and talent in government."[17]

The leaders' rhetoric did not die down once they were elected. Thatcher made it clear that she had won a mandate to smash the "established order." In her early days in office, she repeated what she had often said in opposition—government had limited capacity to do lasting good but a great capacity to do harm. She also brought along with her the "guilty men" theory, suggesting that it was the senior civil servants, once again the protagonists of the failed Keynes-Beveridge consensus, who had undermined Britain's economy. She felt that the civil service by instinct sought a consensus on virtually every issue, and for her *consensus* was a dirty word. She explained, "To me, consensus seems to be the process of abandoning all beliefs, principles and policies. It is the process of avoiding the very issues that have got to be solved merely to get people to come to an agreement." She was determined not to let herself be "educated" by the senior mandarins.

Indeed, the phrase "Deprivilege the Civil Service" became a key objective of the newly elected government.[18]

When the Thatcher government came to office, the size of the British civil service stood at 732,000. Within days, Thatcher announced a ban on recruitment, the scrapping of the previous government's plan to add another 16,000 to the government payroll, and a 3 percent cut in the civil service. A few months later, a further cut of some 39,000 positions, to be fully implemented by 1983, was also announced. Within a year, Margaret Thatcher rose in the House of Commons to report,

> In the past, Governments have progressively increased the number of tasks that the Civil Service is asked to do without paying sufficient attention to the need for economy and efficiency. Consequently, staff numbers have grown over the years. The present Government is committed both to a reduction in tasks and to better management. We believe that we should now concentrate on simplifying the work and doing it more efficiently. . . . All Ministers in charge of Departments will now work out detailed plans for concentrating on essential functions and making operations simpler and more efficient in their Departments. . . . When the Government took office, the size of the Civil Service was 732,000. As a result of the steps that we have already taken, it is now 705,000. We intend now to bring the number down to about 630,000 over the next four years.[19]

During his 1980 presidential campaign, Reagan described the federal bureaucracy as "overgrown and overweight" and pledged to bring "corruption fighters" into government.[20] It will also be recalled that he declared, on his inaugural day as president, that he had come to Washington "to drain the swamp." He explained, "Government does not solve problems, it is the problem." He also pledged to "limit government to its proper role and make it the servant, not the master of the people."[21] Two students of American government wrote,

> Throughout the campaign and into the first years of his administration, Reagan made the federal civil service the whipping boy of his rhetoric. The overall image that emerged was that of a bloated and misdirected behemoth staffed by incompetent zealots, hardly an image likely to encourage bureaucratic self-esteem.[22]

Key Reagan advisors were quick to elaborate on the meaning of Reagan's mandate. One wrote,

> the election of Ronald Reagan to the U.S. Presidency in 1980 was a statement by the American people that their government has become too large, too expensive and too intrusive. It is now time to translate that mandate into pragmatic, sensible actions to bring about responsible change in the boundaries that separate the sovereignty of the individual and private institutions from the sovereignty of government.

He explained that the Reagan election constituted a reaction against the current role of government and strong support to cut back the size and scope of the federal government. He added,

> the huge job of government—begun a century ago—of building the nation and integrating its parts, of allocating the costs and benefits of change and progress, of correcting the major abuses of business, and of alleviating human problems and improving the lot of the populace, has largely been completed and the reforms of a generation ago are themselves sorely in need of reform, as mistakes, excesses, waste, and scandals appear, and as the inevitable institutional arteriosclerosis sets in.[23]

Reagan, immediately after the election, put together an ambitious and costly transition machinery to assume power. The total cost of his transition-planning process was estimated at some $4 million financed equally by public and private services. At one point, Reagan had 132 staff on his transition team.[24] The scope of Reagan's transition planning was so great it led one observer of American politics to charge that "It is marvellous how the people who most bewail bureaucracy . . . are now conducting the transition in Washington by staging a bureaucratic orgy that those around who recall the transition from Eisenhower to Kennedy in 1960 can only watch with stupefaction and incredulity." The Reagan entourage explained that "it required a large bureaucracy to try to take control of a runaway one."[25] The Reagan transition saw nearly a hundred citizen task forces of "Reagan loyalists" sent to various federal agencies. The task forces were largely made up of Reagan ideologues, many of whom were seeking jobs, and they were organized to link agencies into a government-wide network to ensure the implementation of the Reagan agenda.[26]

Mulroney, a close advisor reported, "walked into the Prime Minister's Office with deeply held prejudices about bureaucrats. He disliked them, thinking that they were self serving, incompetent and certainly unable to earn a living in the real world. He also hardly needed much effort to convince many of his ministers that his views were correct."[27] The day after coming to office, he announced the establishment of a task force to review government programs with a view to eliminating those that no longer served a purpose, to consolidate others, and to point the way to better government. He also announced that an advisory committee and a number of working committees would be established to carry out the work. Membership to these committees would be drawn about evenly from both the private sector and the public service. The reason for the large private sector representation, according to a senior Mulroney minister, was simply that "we did not trust the bureaucrats to do anything right on their own."[28]

In the government's first major statement on the economy, tabled a few weeks after coming to office, the minister of Finance reported to the House of Commons that

> Government has become too big. It intrudes too much into the marketplace and inhibits or distorts the entrepreneurial process. . . . Some programs designed to facilitate investment have the perverse effect of distorting investment decisions. Other programs carry on long after the need for them has passed, and are only a fiscal drain. In many cases, the federal government has not done the job it should have, in support of private sector initiatives. . . . This is a discouraging litany.[29]

A few days later, the government announced a series of spending cuts and revenue increases totaling $4.2 billion. In addition, the government declared its firm intention "to improve the management of existing programs."[30]

REALITY

Political rhetoric is one thing. Working with the machinery of government is quite another. Both the newly elected politicians and the career civil servants knew full well that the new political agenda would not square with the views and the interests of the latter. Senior public servants had seen governments, presidents, and prime ministers come and go and had grown accustomed to election-time rhetoric. They know that, when in opposition, politicians invariably promise a new beginning, with new men and new women, if elected to office. Opposition election manifestos and promises often point to nothing short of the need to change the course of history.

The election campaign promises of Thatcher, Reagan, and Mulroney were not different on this front. What was different was the open hostility to the civil service and large parts of the public sector. There was a strong commitment on the part of the three leaders to tackle head-on the ever-expanding role of the state. In the foreword to her party's 1979 election manifesto, for example, Margaret Thatcher wrote that the election might be the "last chance voters had to reverse the extension of state power at the expense of the individual."[31]

The transition to power is a particularly tender moment in the affairs of government. It has been described as a "peaceful coup."[32] There is little doubt that it is also a time of intense activity. The newly elected government will want to take charge quickly, and to be seen to be doing so. It will usually have already given some thought to how it wants to carry out the first weeks in office, what new policies to promote first, what existing policies and programs to scrap or modify. If it has not done so, it will invariably put together transition teams consisting of party faithfuls or, at least, known sympathizers to the party's broad policy orientation. There are also party faithfuls hovering about looking for rewards for services and always willing to provide advice or assistance during the transition period.

The public service, meanwhile, will not have stayed idly by simply waiting for new direction. It will have laid out elaborate transition plans and prepared briefing books designed to welcome the new government and its advisors to power. There are often hundreds of decisions that a newly elected government should take early on in its mandate. The public service will identify where the decisions should be taken and also brief their political masters on all policy fronts.

To be sure, the first few weeks of a government's life are crucial for everyone. Wittingly or not, the new government will set the tone for how it will govern. The public service will be watching carefully to discern a style of governing. Meanwhile, the media will be watching for clues on priorities and for signs of how well the government is working with the public service and interest groups. A president or a political party with little experience in government is likely to know a great deal about politics but very little about governing. The two are, of course, quite different and require far different sets of skills. With no experience in governing, the new government indeed faces a steep learning curve.

In short, a transition signals the arrival of a new government that, in many ways, has maximum energy but minimum knowledge. It is replacing an outgoing government that often has maximum knowledge and minimum energy. The public service, the architects of continuing public administration, will often want to steer the incoming government away from courses it thinks unadvisable. It will seek to strike what it considers to be a proper balance between educating a new government on the ways of governing and ensuring that the new government is able to introduce its policies and programs. One thing the public service has, perhaps above all else, is knowledge. It knows how government works and it knows about government policies. It will use this knowledge to assist the new government in making a smooth transition to governing and to avoid making mistakes. The dangers of running into difficulty are many and varied. For instance, a new government quickly discovers that it is facing an overloaded agenda and is expected to deal with far more demands than it can possibly accommodate. Still, expectations are high, and the new leadership is invariably eager to move on a number of fronts. In his study of the American presidency, Stephen Hess listed a number of factors that could contribute to a difficult transition process. There is often animosity between outgoing and incoming governments. There is also the risk of depression on the part of the loser and exhaustion on the part of the winner. Then there is a whole series of decisions that have to be made by a government with no or very little experience at governing.[33] He added that no matter what level of experience the president may have or how much he may have read about the presidency, "a new president is deeply ignorant about the job to which he has just been elected. Thus each new president will face a period of orientation and learning."[34]

From a public service perspective, transitions are both a period of uncertainty and a key part of their responsibility. To start with, no two political leaders are alike. Every president or prime minister will bring his or her own style, values, and skills to office. Public servants know that if they are to serve successfully, they must quickly gain an appreciation of the working habits of the new political leadership and adjust their own working style to it.

The transitions under Thatcher, Reagan, and Mulroney, however, were different. Throughout the 1960s and 1970s, the transition of power from one party to another had not entailed a significant break from the past. To be sure, there had been some differences between Harold Wilson, Edward Heath, and James Callaghan and between John Kennedy, Lyndon Johnson, Richard Nixon, Gerald Ford, and Jimmy Carter. The differences, however, were not nearly as pronounced as were those between Callaghan and Thatcher, Carter and Reagan, and Trudeau and Mulroney. Thatcher went to lengths to point out that her political ideology was not only different from that of the Labour party, but also from some of her conservative colleagues, including Edward Heath whom she labeled a "wet." Reagan's antigovernment rhetoric was certainly considerably stronger than Nixon's. Mulroney's election broke down Canada's one-party rule, which had lasted for much of the 1960s and 1970s, and very few leaders of a major Canadian political party had ever been as critical of the country's public service as Mulroney was.

All of this is to suggest that the transition to power of Thatcher, Reagan, and Mulroney constituted uncharted territory for public servants. Never before had they been asked to welcome a political leadership that was so eager to question what they did and how they did it. Time and again, the new leaders made it clear that they were determined to make the shift from incremental to decremental government. Yet, what role civil servants were expected to play in this shift was never spelled out. And the civil service was fingered as part of the problem.

Thatcher, unlike her American and Canadian counterparts, came to office with some experience in the government she was being asked to lead. By her own account, her experience in the Heath government where she served as minister (secretary of state for Education and Science, a post she held from 1970 to 1974), was hardly a positive one. Although some claim that she was selective in her memory of the Heath government, she became highly critical of its policies. She felt that the government had lacked political will, clung to out-dated Keynesian thinking, and continually attempted to make the old system work. Her experience with civil servants "did nothing to lighten her dim view of permanent officials."[35] She found many of them patronizing, less than straightforward in presenting advice to ministers, and not very competent to boot. Hugo Young wrote of Thatcher's experience in the Heath government:

> In the plenitude of their self-confidence, which had not yet been broken by economic decline or any perception that the consensus which they embodied might be in error, top civil servants looked upon junior ministers as a very low form of life—and here was one junior minister less prepared than some to overlook the slights.[36]

Intuitively, she grew to mistrust senior civil servants, convinced that they had successfully captured every Labour and Conservative cabinet to their own way of thinking from the immediate postwar period up until her own election to power.

Thatcher became leader of the Conservative party in 1975 and immediately began planning for the day she would come to office. She was able to push her party to the right, as she turned more and more to her trusted lieutenant, Sir Keith Joseph. Joseph was both tough-minded and convinced that the growth of government was the cause of inflation, high taxes, and poor economic performance. By the late 1970s, there were two camps in the Conservative party: the Wets on one side, associated with Heath and Keynesian economics, and the Drys on the other, associated with monetarist economic policies, cutting government spending and taxes, and a greater reliance on free market forces. Thatcher left no doubt in anyone's mind which side she was on.

Thatcher and Joseph established in 1974 a free-market think tank, the Centre for Policy Studies. The center set out to challenge established views and to outline a series of free-market options for when the Conservatives would come back to power. She looked to the center, to the party's research staff, and to selected individuals from outside (mainly from the private sector) to prepare plans to ensure that her government would hit the ground running the day she assumed power. Her prime target was the machine of government itself. Hugo Young argued,

Never was this clash of purposes more explicit than in the summer of 1979. No government has been elected whose leader was as deeply seized as this one of the need to overturn the power and presumption of the continuing government of the civil service: to challenge its orthodoxies, cut down its size, reject its assumptions . . . and teach it a lesson in political control.[37]

Once elected, Thatcher wasted little time in demonstrating a hands-on approach to the management of government operations. For one thing, she immediately asked Sir Derek Rayner of Marks and Spencer to come in to lead a crusade against waste and inefficiency in government. For another, she made it clear to Whitehall that she would take a strong interest in the promotion of senior civil servants. Whitehall and the Civil Service Commission had long looked on senior appointments as pretty well their preserve, with their political masters merely rubber-stamping their decisions. Thatcher soon put a stop to this. She took a direct hand in who was being promoted as permanent secretaries, often looking to less obvious or less senior candidates, favoring those who appeared impatient with the status quo and who demonstrated a capacity "to manage."[38]

It soon became obvious that the Thatcher government and the senior civil service would form an uneasy coexistence. Thatcher unleashed Rayner on the civil service and took advantage of every opportunity to show her full support and commitment to his task. She repeatedly told her ministers and senior officials that Rayner's was an "action" exercise, not a "study" exercise. Rayner himself was also quick off the mark in identifying his two chief enemies as "paper" and the "tyranny of the past."[39] All in all, Thatcher's arrival to power is best summed up by Peter Hennessy: "she struck Whitehall with the force of a tornado." Hugo Young wrote,

> From the first hour, she established her desire to see everything and do everything. At the end of the first week, one of her officials told me: she reads every paper she gets and never fails to write a comment on it. "Nonsense," "Needs more briefing," "Do this again," are what she's constantly writing.[40]

Within days, there developed "a clammy air of mutual distrust, as unsatisfactory to the mandarins as it was to politicians." One senior official sought to improve the situation by organizing a dinner meeting between the prime minister and all permanent secretaries. The occasion was at least in part to teach the prime minister a "polite lesson or two and restore at least a portion of pride to the scions of the public service." In the event, it had the opposite effect, for Thatcher asked the assembled officials to help her "beat the system." One responded, "but we are the system." Another got into an open and acrimonious argument with her. Thatcher later told a member of her staff that the dinner meeting "would be etched on my soul." Still, the "lady was not for turning"; she did not let her guard down at any moment during her first six months in office. Indeed, she could look back on those six months and take heart in the fact "she had refused to be diverted, either by senior ministers or by the conventional wisdom available in endless quantity throughout the civil service."[41]

Reagan came to office with experience in government but all of it at the state level. Washington was foreign to him. Like Thatcher, Reagan claimed he had a strong mandate for change and, like her, he had a distinctive political philosophy to guide his initiatives. He also at once set out to exploit the momentum generated during the election campaign to implement his "new" agenda, to cut government down to size.[42] He promised, for example, to abolish the departments of Education and Energy.

Reagan's conservatism looked a great deal like Thatcher's, but his management style did not. It is important to stress again that, unlike Thatcher with Whitehall, he had no firsthand experience with Washington. He understood the workings of the machinery of government less than Thatcher did, and he did not carry with him into office the memory of past slights. Reagan also preferred the role of chairman of the board, defining the big picture. He liked to delegate and was constantly on his guard against getting too immersed in detail. He did decide, however, not to surround himself with "California cronies" or with a "California mafia" because both he and they lacked Washington experience. Instead, he turned to people with firsthand experience with the federal government. He also gave a green light in the months leading up to the election to a "pre-election transition planning" scheme that was "modest in scope and clandestine in style."[43]

As we have already seen, Reagan put in place, immediately after the election, the most elaborate and costly transition machinery in history. He also brought on board many veterans of the Nixon and Ford administrations to fill key positions. In planning their transition to power, Reagan and his key aides turned to conservative think tanks like the Heritage Foundation for advice. These proved helpful by bringing forward detailed policy prescriptions.

Reagan's appointments to his cabinet and to senior positions in his administration fell into two categories: pragmatists and ideologues. Carl Brauer points out, they "tended to be the right of center—right and far right. . . . Liberal Republicans were a scarce commodity in the Reagan administration." To offset the influence of career officials, Reagan also brought in Washington outsiders from the private sector. Reagan himself explained that he wanted business people in his administration who did not need or want a job and who would be prepared to tell him when the positions they occupied were no longer necessary. He explained, "I want people who are already so successful that they would regard a government job as a step down, not a step up." Borrowing a page from Thatcher, he added "there's an awful lot of brains and talent in people (in the private sector) who haven't learned all the things you can't do." Certainly, Reagan's appointees—particularly those from the private sector or from outside Washington—had a low opinion of permanent public servants, convinced that they were "indolent, liberal and self-serving."[44]

The Reaganites took other steps to ensure that they would not be "captured" by the permanent bureaucracy. They asked Harvard's Kennedy School of Government to organize a series of seminars in public management to introduce some of them to ways of governing. Some appointees took more dramatic steps on their own. One secretary was advised to hire his own staff quickly and to avoid looking in his in-basket for fear that it would always be filled with the agenda of his bureaucrats. He was advised to pick a few priority areas, to concentrate on them, and to ignore what the bureaucrats wanted.[45]

Reagan essentially looked to three areas of government—defense, the economy, and the federal budget—to implement his mandate. He had stressed during the election campaign that it was time to reestablish America's strong position in world affairs and to stand up to Communism on behalf of the free world. Thus, increased military spending was an important component of the new agenda. But so was the need to get a handle on the expenditure budget.

Reagan appointed David Stockman—described as ambitious, self-assured, and articulate—as head of the Office of Management and Budget (OMB). Stockman knew Washington well. However, he reported shortly after his appointment that, "in digging into details of its vast expanse of programs, regulations and bureaucracy, I discovered that it was riddled with waste, excess and injustice. I came to believe that Ronald Reagan had been right all along."[46]

Stockman wasted no time. The day he was appointed, he and his staff began planning strategy, and they soon prepared a series of policy papers outlining numerous cuts in spending, both in programs and in the overhead cost of government. However, he quickly ran up against difficulties: Reagan's management style—the president was not going to take an interest in detail—and a serious lack of that rarest of commodities, time with the president. After a nonproductive first meeting, where he felt the discussions never got beyond generalities, he reported,

> Back at my office, I took a hard look at the timetable to see how much time Meese had allotted in the President-elect's schedule for the budget sessions we would need to have. Suddenly, the utter scarcity of presidential time hit home: only four more sessions, totalling six hours, between now and the inauguration. We'd just used up a quarter of this allotted time discussing the administration's highest priority, and we hadn't even scratched the surface.[47]

Stockman pressed on and put together a series of cuts amounting to $40 billion from a budget that ran over $700 billion. The proposed cuts were in a number of domestic programs, notably agriculture, housing, education, transportation, energy, and health services. In addition, Stockman convinced the president to approve, just before the inauguration, a series of "first day" directives to demonstrate that the Reagan administration would be hitting the ground running. These directives included an across-the-board hiring freeze, a 15 percent cutback in agency travel budgets, a 5 percent reduction in consulting fees, and a freeze on the purchase of new furniture and office equipment. What in the event transpired fell short of Reagan's announcement. Some of the program cuts met with a cool reception in Congress, and some projected cuts were restored. On the administrative side, Stockman explained,

Within hours of the first full day I was swamped with urgent demands as to the meaning of the directives. Did the travel cut apply to FBI agents on their way to apprehending a felon? Did the equipment freeze cover the blood circulating machines essential to coronary by-pass surgery? How did the hiring freeze impact on the guy promised a federal job in Washington on 1 February who had already moved there from Utah? My staff and I held a desultory debate on it all and ended up exempting as much as we included.[48]

Unlike Thatcher and Reagan, Brian Mulroney had no government experience at all when he became leader of his party in 1983, a year before he led it to a sweeping victory at the polls. Unlike Reagan, Mulroney decided to recruit mainly outsiders to his staff. These came mostly from the private sector, academia, and the media, and they tended to reinforce Mulroney's view that Ottawa was "fat city" and bureaucracy was a "bad word." In addition, as with Mulroney himself, most of the people who were to assume key cabinet posts also had limited or no experience in governing. Still, Mulroney insisted on an early start in planning the transition to power. Within weeks of winning his party's leadership, he assembled a transition-planning group. Its task was not only to lay down plans for the transition, but also to come up with specific proposals to revise government policy in several areas, notably energy, the machinery of government, appointments, and staffing. The group consisted of senior members of Parliament and outside experts. By March 1984, the group had put together a comprehensive set of proposals on a wide range of issues on specific policy matters, on the structure of ministries and government departments, and on the staffing of ministerial offices. Word quickly leaked that Mulroney was planning a major reform of the machinery of government and that, in particular, he favored the kind of large political bureaucracy found in the United States.[49]

A few months before the election, Mulroney declared in a major address that he and his party were "prepared to take over the responsibilities of government." He also outlined the principles that would guide his transition to power. He spoke about bureaucracy having a life of its own and that it was "impervious—or at any rate able to resist the political will to change direction or priority." He added, however, that "We do not intend to be obstructed in any way in our plan to initiate beneficial change for Canada." He explained that he would not hesitate to let senior public servants go and that there would be changes "in the relationship between deputy ministers and the Prime Minister who appoints them, and to whom they owe a prior loyalty." He reported that there would "have" to be fundamental changes, the most important being "frugality in government," and he made it clear to public servants that the "way to preferment and promotion is to save money rather than spend it." He also spoke about the need for "government to fundamentally change its attitude in its relationships with the governed" so that people would have a greater say in policy and decision making.[50]

Mulroney also announced that policy changes in his government's first mandate would be made with "a minimum of structured and bureaucratic reorganization." On the basis of what he had seen since his arrival in Ottawa, he concluded that "reorganizations in government . . . had become a way of life . . . an end in itself for many people in the Capital." He wanted, he argued, to get the bureaucrats away from "the organizational charts and back to work on the problems of the country." He added, however, that some branches in government and administrative units were superfluous and could be "collapsed quickly."[51]

The important point to note here is that Mulroney planned changes in personnel rather than a massive government reorganization to implement his agenda for change. And, indeed, he did make some changes in deputy ministers. But he also reorganized ministerial offices. Borrowing a page from the Americans—although some claim only halfheartedly—he announced a new senior staff position in each ministerial office. The appointment, chief of staff, was to be political and would be at the level of assistant deputy minister, that is, immediately below the deputy minister, the most senior position in the public service. The position was designed to provide ministers with political and policy advice, to balance the advice they would be receiving from their public servants. The transition planners provided a detailed job description for the chiefs of staff and put together a list of potential candidates for the new positions. Although the move sent a clear signal that Mulroney wanted politicians to take charge of the bureaucracy, it was also seen by many in the public service as an attempt to politicize the bureaucracy, something considered anathema to the Westminster model of a neutral and career-based public service.

It was also viewed by others as a vote of no confidence in the public service and a blatant challenge to the authority of deputy ministers.[52]

The public service viewed the new government's agenda with deep concern and a sense that its very credibility was at stake. They recalled Mulroney's threat to distribute "pink slips and running shoes" to bureaucrats and his intention to root out Liberal appointees. In his speech on transition, Mulroney had promised that the heads of some deputy ministers would roll. In addition, the mood of the country was hardly sympathetic to bureaucrats. To make matters worse, some of Trudeau's cabinet ministers took parting shots at the bureaucrats on leaving office.

It was in this climate of apprehension that senior public servants made elaborate plans to welcome the new government. The head of the public service laid down two objectives: civil servants were to provide all possible assistance to the new government, and they were to ensure that "the public service was not damaged." He asked that all senior public servants be forthcoming in their first contacts with the new government, to ensure that the transition process contained "no surprises." He personally met with members of Mulroney's own transition team to explain how the public service was readying itself. He commissioned several briefing packages dealing with issues of immediate and long-term policy issues, machinery of government, appointments, and major departmental matters. The material was divided between background information and recommendations. The objective was to generate trust and to avoid any suspicion that the public service might have a hidden agenda.[53]

They were hoping that if they could survive the initial transition period then relations with ministers would improve and serious damage to the public service would be avoided. In fact, they did survive the initial transition period, but not without some casualties. Within a few months a number of senior public servants left government.[54] In addition, the new government pressed ahead with the chief-of-staff concept, and after only a few weeks virtually every minister had one appointed to his or her office.[55]

DEFINING THE PROBLEM

The rhetoric of the new right and the directions that Thatcher, Reagan, and Mulroney brought to power spoke to a deep disenchantment not just about the role of government in society but also about bureaucracy. Not one of the three leaders had many positive things to say about the public service.

But what specifically were they saying about bureaucracy? And what problems were they trying to fix? What was the substance of their criticism? We know that Thatcher recommended reading on public choice theory to people around her, including senior public servants. Other than this, there is little evidence from their speeches or their writings that would suggest they were even aware of the basic concepts underpinning public administration.

Still, all three leaders spoke about cutting government down to size. They all spoke also about the need to strike a new balance between the political and bureaucratic levels and for a greater accountability in government. All three leaders felt that career officials exerted too much influence over policy and that they were inherently biased in favor of the status quo. None, at least in their first months in office, favored large-scale organizational reforms to implement their policies and, once elected, they were certainly anxious to get on with the job of putting things right. Yet, despite the fact that they all had highly sophisticated transition-planning teams, not one was immune to the "maximum energy and minimum knowledge" that afflicts new governments.

The problems Thatcher, Reagan, and Mulroney identified were not new nor had they not been studied in the past. Indeed, the leaders' views on bureaucracy bring to mind the Northcote-Trevelyan Report, which was written some 140 years ago:

> Admission into the Civil Service is eagerly sought after, but it is
> for the unambitious, and the indolent or incapable that it is highly
> desired. Those whose abilities do not warrant an expectation that
> they will succeed in the open professions, where they must en-
> counter the competition of their contemporaries . . . where they
> may obtain an honourable livelihood with little labour, and with
> no risk.[56]

The one difference was that, now, civil servants were also being accused of having too much influence over policy, which often meant favoring the status quo.

There is, in fact, a growing body of literature on the very problems the new right spoke to in its criticisms of bureaucracy, including a spate of books and articles arguing that bureaucracy intuitively favors the status quo. Francis Rourke and Paul Schulman wrote, bluntly, "bureaucratic organizations are commonly seen as lacking in imagination, unwilling to depart from past policies and precedents, and devoutly attached to one and only one objective—the protection and enhancement of their own status and survival as part of the government process." They are just two who have reached this conclusion.[57] The public choice school is built around a similar theme, with the exception that it argues that bureaucrats are continually on the lookout to maximize their budgets and the scope of their activities. Even those who write in defense of bureaucracy acknowledge that the civil service tends to favor the status quo—although they usually add that this is not unlike what is often seen in other large institutions or organizations.[58] This is little comfort, however, to politicians who have fought their way to office on the promise of change.

Opposition parties that had previously held power shared the new right's views on the bureaucracy. One former senior British cabinet minister warned, "the deal that the civil service offers a minister is this: if you do what we want you to do we will help you publicly to pretend that you're implementing the manifesto on which you were elected. And I've seen many ministers, of both parties actually, fall for that one."[59]

Thatcher, Reagan, and Mulroney spoke not only about the tendency of bureaucracy to be wedded to the status quo, but also about its power and ability to thwart the wishes of its political masters. Again, a substantial body of literature exists that confirms this perception. Norton Long began his seminal essay in public administration with the sentence "The lifeblood of administration is power." Max Weber wrote that bureaucracy

> has been and is a power instrument of the first order—for the one who controls the bureaucratic apparatus . . . under normal conditions, the power position of a fully developed bureaucracy is always overtowering. The political master finds himself in the position of the dilettante who stands opposite the expert, facing the trained official who stands within the management of administration.[60]

There are various reasons, scholars point out, that lead bureaucracy to secure power. For one thing, bureaucracy will invariably move in to fill the void when the political leadership has no concrete plans to implement. James Q. Wilson also wrote that bureaucracy will become powerful when the growth of the administration apparatus becomes so large that it can no longer be subject to regular control; discretionary authority is then delegated to a government agency to the point where the exercise of power can no longer be made responsive to the public good. Others suggest that professionalism in the civil service has given rise to the view that the institution is better informed than politicians, who can never possess the technical knowledge to make the right policy choice or decisions. This in turn has led the civil service to develop a rigid resistance to the views of the outside world, including politicians.[61] In addition, particularly in Great Britain and Canada, politicians claim that officials are scarcely held accountable for what they do—that they fall back on the principle of ministerial responsibility to unload the blame on ministers.

Thatcher, Reagan, and Mulroney only had to look to what their predecessors in office had to say to see their concern with the public service shared. Edward Heath declared in 1980,

> The Civil Service . . . today is an admirable administrative instrument, but it is not primarily designed for the formulation of policies to meet the problems of the modern world. . . . [It has] an inherent quality of inertia which leads to a refusal to accept innovation. . . . I have never yet been able to put forward to the civil service an idea to which I would get the latter coming back saying, "That is a good idea. We think we might want it."[62]

Roy Hattersley, a veteran of Labour governments, argued that civil servants

> sometimes fight for what they believe is the right policy and sometimes they're blinded by their own convictions and thinking that they're not interfering with policy, that they're not involved in politics, they're just taking that sort of common sense which they have been brought to believe transcends party differences.[63]

Richard Crossman's *Diaries of a Cabinet Minister* spoke of exasperation with a bureaucratic machine that took on a life of its own, like an uncontrollable monster. The Crossman diaries gave rise to the popular BBC television series "Yes, Minister," which attracted some nine million viewers in Britain alone and became the favorite television program of the permanent secretaries. Mrs. Thatcher had each episode videotaped and reported that she subscribed to the caricature view of the senior civil service. The series also gained a worldwide audience and became highly popular with some politicians and civil servants in both Canada and the United States. The not-so-subtle message of "Yes, Minister" was that public servants were running the country, their deference to politicians was pure pretense, and the Sir Humphreys of the bureaucratic world wielded considerable power. The series actually served to give credence to bureaucrat-bashing. There is now a veritable who's who from all sides of the Canadian political spectrum who have publicly questioned the work of their own public service. Meanwhile, in the United States, "Congressional and presidential candidates get elected by promising to go to Washington to control the bureaucracy or to cut it down to size."[64]

The new political leadership in the three countries thus had little difficulty in identifying the problems with bureaucracy. This was the easy part. On closer inspection, however, the actual problem is difficult to pin down.[65] No one said much about what needed to be done other than "cut government down to size." In addition, all three leaders had to work with the bureaucracy—the very institution they were assaulting—to implement their policies, including those designed to cut bureaucracy down to size. Also, cuts to the bureaucracy was only one issue. To make it more responsive to the political leadership, more creative, accountable, and frugal required new policy prescriptions.

The public administration literature is replete with studies explaining why things are the way they are, with how bureaucracy has not performed well, and with how things work or do not work in specific circumstances. Most studies are highly critical of bureaucracy, although a few do take the opposite view. The debate, however, is often a contradictory one, with some arguing in the same breath that bureaucracy is by nature expansionist and timid, lazy and power hungry, arrogant and fear-ridden, incompetent and imperialistic, unaccountable and overly concerned with red tape, process, procedures, and forms. We have very few studies, however, that offer specific prescriptions for what to do to make bureaucracy more responsive, creative, efficient, and accountable. One ambitious study, for example, reports that bureaucratic habits die hard. Simple remedies will not do. Contemporary administrative problems require new approaches, new organizational designs, new laws, new commitments, new relationships, new attitudes, new techniques, new inventions. We are in no position to discard so tried and tested a strategy as the reform model. We need to understand better when its strengths warrant its exclusive use and when circumstances warrant its combination with other strategies, such as experimentation. Much more needs to be done to improve our administrative capabilities. We ought to keep raising our sights and persist with our normative concerns.[66]

The study ends on this note, offering little advice as to what kind of new laws, new commitments, new relationships, and new organizational designs are required.

The point here is that the new leaders could turn to the public choice literature and to numerous politicians to support their views that something was wrong with the bureaucracy. They had, however, few places to turn for ideas. Their own rhetoric spoke more to the problems than to the solutions. John Greenwood and David Wilson explain about Thatcher, "Despite the political and ideological underpinning it is unlikely that the Thatcher government entered office with any grand strategy for the civil service."[67] The new right appeared to know what not to do rather than what to do. Mulroney made it clear shortly before assuming office that he would not launch ambitious organizational reforms, at least not in his first few years in government. And Thatcher and Reagan did not attempt to, either, beyond saying that substantial cuts were required in the size of government departments and agencies. Although the three would in time unveil public service reforms, they had plenty of reasons to doubt the effectiveness of reorganization or sweeping reform. Much of the public administrative literature—and on this there even appears to be agreement among practitioners and scholars—argues that reorganizations of government take up a great deal of time and energy but that they invariably fall short of expectations. Guy Peters wrote, "Reading evaluations of major government reform efforts from a number of national settings appears to indicate that a finding of no significant results is often the indicator of a reform success, while a failure often is characterized by serious negative side effects."[68] Thatcher, Reagan, and Mulroney only had to take a cursory look at past attempts at reform to see that they had all fallen short of expectations.

They could, of course, have asked career public servants to assist them in defining the problems and in suggesting solutions. But this too was fraught with potential problems. Public servants have seen electoral commitments come and go. With their well-honed sense of déjà vu, they tended to assume things would not be different under Thatcher, Reagan, and Mulroney and that things would settle down within a few months of the new governments taking office.[69]

It would have been nothing short of a breathtaking jump in logic to assume that civil servants could be convinced that their institution—the public service—had indeed serious shortcomings and that they would come forward with suggestions to make things right. A good number of them would argue that those politicians who complain that civil servants are too powerful are themselves weak or incompetent. Power, they say, initially lies with politicians and only devolves to the civil servants when politicians fail to use it. Many civil servants will readily admit that they are cautious, but they will also insist caution comes with the territory. They are cautious because criticism for failure is enormous while credit for success is rare. A good number of civil servants also argue that society places unfair expectations on bureaucracy, that we ask public servants to come up with new solutions when a community's economic viability breaks down, and to deal with pollution, poverty, alcoholism, drug abuse, and so on. No doubt many civil servants identify with Charles Goodsell's comment "Bureaucracy is expected not only to be perfect, but to perfect society."[70]

Some civil servants are prepared to admit that bureaucracy has serious shortcomings. Indeed, many will speak openly about its inertia and the proliferation of paperwork. They will also report that to get anything done in government is often a trial and that there is a great deal of activity with little result. Others readily acknowledge that the urgent inevitably crowds out the important in their work. The result is that senior civil servants, in particular, get so caught up in the rush of day-to-day activities they do not take the time to sit back and ask if they, and their staff, are operating as efficiently as possible. A former British civil servant wrote that he is a "little embarrassed," looking back on his own time as a civil servant, to recall how unreflective I was about my own responsibilities as a manager in the full sense. I had little idea of the cost of the resources I deployed, and no responsibility for some of them. I was also fairly confident of my ability to disguise from my superiors, if necessary, precisely what I was doing and how far their view of reality matched what was happening on my small patch of the ground.[71]

Some civil servants also believe that bureaucracy can be insular, lacking in creativity, skeptical about new ideas, and insensitive to other institutions and the general public.

Although many civil servants will readily admit to their institution's shortcomings, they are not always willing to accept that the problem lies with the civil servants themselves. Politicians, they claim, are at the root of many of the problems associated with bureaucracy. It is the politicians who will insist on new administrative rules when confronted with a public crisis or scandal. They also say that it is the politicians who will insist that a local government office remains open even though it no longer serves a useful purpose. It is politicians who raise expectations at election time about what can actually be accomplished, when, in fact, they have no concrete ideas about how to proceed. Politicians, the argument goes, are rarely willing to look in the mirror to see why they, or their governments, have failed. They much prefer to blame the bureaucrats, the one group in society that cannot fight back (at least not publicly). It is also worth stressing, as Max Weber observed, that politicians and bureaucrats often have vastly different values and tend to view the world from markedly different perspectives. One former senior civil servant summed up the difference: "Self-advertising, irresponsible nincompoops. . . . They embody everything that my training has taught me to eschew—ambition, prejudice, dishonesty, self-seeking, light-hearted irresponsibility, black-hearted mendacity."[72]

To be sure, permanent civil servants will want to welcome all new governments and attempt to establish close working relationships with them. This is true even in the case of a new leader intent on hitting the civil service with "her handbag."[73] There is evidence that all three services made special efforts to ensure a smooth transition to power for Thatcher, Reagan, and Mulroney. And, even though all three were "profoundly suspicious" of the civil service, within a few months of their coming to power, one heard how well they were being served by individual civil servants.[74] Very quickly the problem was no longer a matter of individual civil servants but of the civil service as an institution.

This should come as no surprise. It will be recalled that the two overarching objectives of the head of the Canadian public service in planning the Mulroney transition to governing were to effect a smooth and orderly transition and to cause no damage to the civil service. Most civil servants will want to protect their institutions, many of them intuitively. They have over the years developed a strong sense of public service and a profound respect for their institution. "Public service," as one former civil servant wrote, "is its own reward." For long-serving career civil servants, as the more senior ones invariably are, the public service is not so much a job as a vocation: "chosen for life, to be seen through to the end whatever the fluctuations in job satisfaction or the temptation of higher salaries elsewhere."[75] Since few of them have worked in other settings or institutions, they do not readily see the flaws in their own institution. The same is probably true for most people who have made a career in only one institution, be it a university or a large corporation.

Even civil servants who can see shortcomings in their institution will not automatically want to see them corrected. Overstaffing is a case in point. In return for accepting fluctuations in job satisfaction or for overlooking the temptation of higher salaries elsewhere, many will argue that governments and ultimately the public should accept that the public service will be overstaffed. Civil servants looking to public service as a vocation rather than as a job expect in return a career-long tenure with the institution.

In addition, senior civil servants who recognize the flaws in their institution, including overstaffing, must contend with a sort of "prisoners' dilemma" in deciding whether something should be done about it. They see firsthand how decisions are made to spend public funds and they see many decisions made solely on the basis of political considerations. Such decisions may include the establishment of a military base; the favoring, which makes little administrative sense, of a military supplier from a particular region; a government subsidy to locate an economic activity where it will have limited chance of long-term success; costly public relations campaigns designed to sing the praises of a government program closely identified with the party in power; and so on. They will thus be reluctant to see cuts made in their institution while politicians spend public funds on misguided initiatives. In short, civil servants are likely to argue that,

> If it is waste and mismanagement politicians are looking for they should look to the "political boondoggles" and not to the bureaucracy. If the finger is pointed at their own department, they are likely to point their fingers to the politicians where, they will claim, waste is even more spectacular.

One public servant explained the dilemma well when he observed,

> To be frank, I am being kept busy at turning cranks not connected to anything. But what do you expect me to do? Walk up to the Treasury and say cut my position because it is really not necessary? Ministers blow more money on strictly political things in one day than my salary will ever cost taxpayers in twenty years.[76]

Civil servants will also resist, in an almost knee-jerk fashion, politicians' meddling in the running of the public service. The role of politicians, after all, is to set policy, not to manage the civil servants. Indeed, civil servants are likely to consider politicians particularly ill-equipped to understand the working of the public service. They will continually want to steer politicians away from administrative matters to broad policy issues. This is particularly true in the case of newly elected governments with little or no experience in governing. The politics-administration dichotomy still survives for many public servants, especially the part that says, "administration lies outside the proper sphere of politics . . . administrative questions are not political questions."[77] Public servants are in an excellent position to protect their institution and to make the case that cuts in personnel are not advisable. They know their operations better than anyone else and can easily defy outsiders to demonstrate how their units are overstaffed. In the British television satire "Yes, Minister," the permanent secretary scolded one of his subordinates for putting forward the wrong question on internal departmental management. The subordinate had asked how they would justify before the parliamentary committee the department's person-year levels and overhead costs. The permanent secretary explained that he was asking the wrong question—the point, he insisted, was for the parliamentary committee to demonstrate that the department did not require these resources, not the other way around. "Let it try," he boasted. It is not too much of an exaggeration to suggest that this resembles the real world of government.

Thatcher, Reagan, and Mulroney soon came up against this type of institutional resistance to their plans to cut down the size of bureaucracy, to make the public service more responsive to political direction, and to make the institution the "servant," not the "master." The new political leaders would not, however, give up easily. To be sure, they would all look to individual civil servants for help as they pressed ahead with their plans to modernize their public services. They would, however, also turn to the private sector as no other government had ever done before.

5

Looking to the Private Sector

THE NEW POLITICAL LEADERSHIP lost little time in looking to the private sector for ideas, advice, and a helping hand in implementing new approaches to management in government. For example, President Reagan, in his administration time and again as soon as he came to office, highlighted the role the private sector would be asked to play. Indeed, he featured private-sector-led initiatives in eighty-four speeches, public appearances, or similar events during his first twenty-two months in office, an average of about once a week.[1]

The conservative ideology, of course, has close ties to the business community, which believes that when a firm becomes "fat" it tends to make poor decisions, waste resources, and drift toward uncompetitiveness until, in time, bankruptcy results. To stop the drift, competent managers must be brought in to cut costs, eliminate waste, cut out unprofitable product lines, and return the firm to a competitive footing. This process is labeled "turnaround management." Thatcher, Reagan, and Mulroney were all convinced that the bureaucracies they inherited had become "fat," and all three leaders turned, albeit to varying degrees, to senior business executives to introduce turnaround management to government operations.[2]

Co-opting the private sector as an ally had the added benefit of lessening the chance of being captured by the bureaucracy. This was particularly important for the new political agenda called for deprivileging the public service and for more decisions to be taken by the market. The goals of the new political leadership were obviously threatening to public servants. Dead aim had been taken at their jobs, their benefits, and the programs they presumably believed in. To be sure, undoing the Keynesian consensus meant there were fewer opportunities for advancement and less interesting work for public servants to fine tune the economy and the bureaucracy.

Public servants also soon learned that the new political leadership

116

had little interest in traditional issues of public administration, in Fulton-type reforms, in tinkering with the bureaucracy, in shuffling around public servants. These had been tried and, in the new leaders' opinion, had failed. If anything, traditional concepts of public administration were being called into question.[3] Management practices found in business became the new fad in government, and books like *The Pursuit of Excellence* became required reading. Indeed, several articles were published in the United States suggesting how management prescriptions found in this book could also be applied to the federal bureaucracy.[4]

A PRIVATE SECTOR PERSPECTIVE

Thatcher, Reagan, and Mulroney (and their advisors), it will be recalled, had decided to bring the private sector on board even before they were elected, and they wasted little time in doing so once in office.

As a keen student of government explained, the three leaders believed that "the means of management and intervention used in the private sector are superior to those of the public sector, and that whenever possible the public sector should either emulate the private sector or simply privatize the function."[5] And the leaders were not reluctant to tell public servants they had a thing or two to learn from the private sector. Indeed, some senior civil servants complained a year after Thatcher came to office that it was "a bit much . . . to be told by politicians that they have several friends in the private sector who could do their job in a morning with one hand tied behind their back."[6] The issue then for the three leaders was never "if" the private sector could help shake up the public service but rather "how" and to what extent.

Business people were invited to serve full time in all three governments. One of Thatcher's advisors went so far as to suggest that the entire senior civil service be cleared out and replaced by outsiders, preferably from the private sector.[7] This was too radical a proposal even for Thatcher—and certainly for her ministers—but she still wanted private sector executives in the civil service, either indefinitely or for a set period of time. Ronald Reagan's transition team similarly sought out business executives, as did Brian Mulroney, within days of assuming power.

All three, and Reagan in particular, were successful in this venture—

although many of those invited to serve full time declined, particularly in Britain. If nothing else, the salary scale of government positions made the idea unattractive.[8]

But getting business executives in government was only one part of the plan to involve the private sector.[9] A new government, as we saw in the previous chapter, is ideally positioned to take stock and to call for a fresh review of existing government operations. This is why most new political leaders call for such a review before they implement their own agenda and before they fully take charge of government operations. Once they have set on a policy course and asserted control of operations, it becomes, of course, risky to call for a review.[10]

Thatcher, Reagan, and Mulroney all called for a review of government operations shortly after coming to office. There were some differences in how they initiated the reviews: for example, Thatcher's was publicly financed, Reagan's was not, while Mulroney's was a joint public and private sector effort. They had, however, far more in common than not. All three reviews were extremely ambitious, all involved people who had little or no stake in protecting government programs and operations, and all specifically looked to the private sector for help.

RAYNERISM

We saw in the last chapter that, in coming to power, Thatcher asked Derek Rayner, chief executive officer at Marks and Spencer, to lead an efficiency exercise in government. There is no need here to review in detail the workings of what has since been labeled Raynerism. We now have some excellent studies on the topic. Still, it is important for the purpose of our study to highlight some points.

Rayner, much like Thatcher herself, had strongly held views about bureaucracy, and like Thatcher, he had worked in the Edward Heath government. That experience had convinced him that government operations were by and large poorly managed and that financial management, in particular, was seriously lacking. The people in charge were generalists, with little knowledge of the area they were asked to manage, inclined to follow the rule book rather than modern management practices. Further, he maintained that at a different level—at the macro level—senior officials managed the system by "private, and indeed, by unspoken rules."[11]

Thatcher gave Rayner carte blanche to achieve greater "managerial efficiency in Whitehall and the spending departments."[12] Thatcher made her support clear to her ministers and to the senior officials, that she was four square behind Rayner, and this considerably strengthened Rayner's hand. Peter Hennessy, for example, reports that "The Rayner experience has one thing in common with the Fulton experience— both demonstrate how absolutely and utterly crucial is the patronage of the occupant in No. 10: Wilson lost interest; Thatcher did not."[13]

Rayner declared very early that his work would be guided by a number of principles: the two greatest enemies of government operations, he reported, were paper and the tyranny of the past. Never, he insisted, try to defeat bureaucracy by creating another bureaucracy, and never attempt to put everything right at once. Rather, select targets, stay away from committees, look to those who have the authority and continually ask them, What value does this work add? True to his word, he established a small, seven-people office within the Prime Minister's Office. He then had each minister in charge of a department select projects for study by teams of officials. These were labeled "scrutinies," and their purpose, he stressed time and again, was to be action, not study. They were designed, Rayner explained, "a) to examine a specific policy, activity or function with a view to savings . . . b) to propose solutions . . . c) to implement agreed solutions, or begin their implementation, within 12 months of the start of the scrutiny." Rayner made it clear that his ultimate goal was to change the "civil service culture . . . and the attitudes held by civil servants."[14]

The scrutiny exercise in each department was in turn led by a handful of civil servants and occasionally outside consultants. A sense of urgency accompanied the scrutinies, which were expected to be completed within ninety days. The selection of a scrutiny was vetted by Lord Rayner himself. He then briefed the scrutiny teams and established the ground rules. He or his staff were always available to the teams if there were problems.[15] But full responsibility for scrutinies rested with the ministers and the departments, and Rayner made certain that neither he nor his staff would interfere in their preparation. In time, it was hoped that scrutinies would become top management tools in all departments. In short, Rayner and his staff would prompt scrutinies, ensure follow-up, and seek to disseminate the important lessons learned throughout government. The scrutiny exercise was to be an

insider's job. When completed, the scrutinies were presented to the
minister and Lord Rayner (and, in some instances, to the prime minister and cabinet). Thatcher took a keen interest in the scrutinies,
insisting that she be regularly briefed on their progress. In addition,
she selected from the list of scrutinies those that were of particular
interest to her, for which she would request in-depth briefings. When
she took such an interest, the department and its minister had to secure
approval from the Rayner's Efficiency Unit before any action could be
taken.[16]

The scrutinies approach pointed quite clearly to a "minister-as-
manager" concept. Indeed, the key players in selecting and approving
scrutinies were ministers and not permanent secretaries. Ministers,
thus, were not just being asked to set broad policy directions, they were
being asked to take a direct hand in reviewing government operations
and management practices. There was, to be sure, some skepticism—if
not outright opposition—to the concept, notably from retired permanent secretaries who could speak out publicly, and even from some
ministers themselves. Said one former permanent secretary,

> Ministers are amateurs of management; it is not their skill or, fre-
> quently, inclination. Extremely few have had experience in genu-
> inely managing a large organization over a prolonged period. And
> in the isolated cases where they have, they have not been notably
> successful as politicians—which is what they essentially need to be.

Said another,

> In many ways it would be better if the Civil Service was left to get
> on with the management job. What ministers need to do is to
> take more time and have better advice on the political direction in
> which they want to go and have a coherent strategy which hangs
> together and will stick. And, on the whole, if the Civil Service
> knows what the policy is and the strategy is, it will make quite a
> good fist at carrying it out.[17]

Not all ministers welcomed the management role. Some made it clear
that they preferred to concentrate on partisan politics and making
policy choices.[18]

Thatcher dismissed such reservations out of hand, convinced that it
was little more than the old order trying to cling to the status quo. She
strongly encouraged her ministers to take a direct interest in the ad-

ministration of their departments and supported them when they came forward with ideas to strengthen the minister-as-manager concept. Michael Heseltine wasted little time in meeting the challenge. He reports that when he was appointed minister of Environment, he discovered that his department had no adequate system to keep him and even senior officials informed of new financial commitments. Heseltine set out to revamp financial management in his department, and his initiative soon became "the rallying cry for the proponents of management innovation in government."[19]

Much as early reform measures like PPBS and PAR had done, Heseltine's initiative sought to clearly define program objectives, to set a strategy to meet these objectives, and to put in place a method for monitoring progress. Subunits were asked to provide new analysis and up-to-date financial information, to establish links with other subunits and programs, to determine how successful the subunits were in meeting their objectives, and to outline the methods employed to measure success.

Both Thatcher and Rayner were delighted with Heseltine's system, and it was transformed into a government-wide Financial Management Information (FMI). All ministers and all departments were directed to sign on and to develop within several months a system equivalent to Heseltine's. Formally launched in May 1982, FMI sought to redefine financial management in government. It was designed to promote the minister-as-manager concept; decentralize decision making to line departments; reduce, if not eliminate, the case-by-case review of the work in line departments by central agencies; stress monitoring of the effectiveness of government programs; and highlight cost or responsibility centers to clarify tasks and accountability. It took a shot at the Whitehall culture by shifting the focus to line management and away from centrally designed and imposed rules and constraints. Indeed, it sought to delegate budgets as far down the line as possible to enable public servants at middle- and even junior-management levels to have greater control over their resources. The goal was to give managers, for the first time, responsibility for managing their own budgets.[20] In turn, FMI would provide ministers and senior departmental officials information on the scope of operations, the use of resources, and on how well activities were being managed and delivered.

Les Metcalfe and Sue Richards report that FMI involved "the management of change on a grand scale."[21] It is ambitious and comprehensive in that it involves all departments. It places departments on a specific timetable to get things done. It looks to establish centers of responsibility and seeks to break the business-as-usual syndrome by establishing expectations of year-on-year improvements in performance. It seeks to restructure government operations in the sense that it is designed to transfer decision-making responsibilities for finance, personnel, and program management away from specialized units to the line managers. The objective is to create centers of responsibilities and then cluster all management functions in them so that departments can have relatively self-contained organization units.

This concept—as well as many others found in FMI, including delegated budgets as a management tool for improving performance—are borrowed from the private sector. Indeed, FMI has been described as "the bureaucracy's surrogate for private-sector stimuli."[22] For Thatcher, Rayner, Heseltine, and others of like mind, the way to ensure that government operations were more efficient and more businesslike, was simply to see them operated more like a business.[23]

To be sure, introducing FMI throughout the government was a far more ambitious undertaking than Heseltine's own departmental initiative. There were many roadblocks, and there were many people inside government who were convinced that FMI would meet the same fate as other, earlier reforms such as PPBS and PAR. But Thatcher was not for turning. Her government invested large amounts of money (when compared with past investments) for computer systems to run FMI, and the Treasury was directed to ensure that FMI be completely integrated in the expenditure budget process. To ensure follow-up, a small, new, financial-management unit consisting of about a dozen civil servants and outside consultants was established as a joint venture between the Treasury and the Management and Personnel Office. This, once again, reflected Rayner's view that you do not take on a large bureaucracy by establishing another large bureaucracy. As Rayner's own group, this new unit sought to assist departments to implement FMI and central agencies to coordinate their efforts. The onus was on departments themselves to get on with the job.

By early 1983, all departments had submitted their FMI plans according to specifications. All were then published in a government white paper. The initiative was reviewed in 1986, a sort of scrutiny of the system itself. The review was positive, and the government decided to extend it by devolving still further budgetary expenditure responsibilities to line managers. In addition, the government continued to press departments to define ways to measure the success of their operations, and by 1987, in its annual white paper on expenditure budget, the government was able to report on some eighteen hundred performance indicators of the work of government departments.[24]

GRACE

After two years in office, President Reagan asked a flamboyant business executive, J. Peter Grace, to direct what he labeled a Private Sector Survey on Cost Control (PPSSCC). The president left no doubt that he wanted to bring a business perspective to bear on the operations of government. He insisted that the survey provide "an objective outsider's view on improving management and reducing federal costs."[25] He asked Grace and his people to work like "tireless bloodhounds" in uncovering waste, inefficiency, and poor management practices in government.[26] Reagan made certain that the initiative was planned and carried out by the business community by turning over the whole exercise, including its funding. The president was looking for sweeping changes to the established order, rather than changes merely at the margin. He thought he would do this by "putting the fox in the chicken coop," or by turning business executives "loose in government administration."[27] Reagan asked Grace to look at government agencies as if he and his colleagues were considering a merger or a takeover. When he submitted his findings, however, Grace bluntly told Reagan, "The President's private sector survey would not acquire the government."[28]

The Grace survey was a highly ambitious undertaking. Charles Goodsell reports that when it was compared with previous reviews of government operations, including the Hoover Commission, not one has approached Grace in terms of size and format.[29] Its executive committee alone had 161 members, 80 percent of which were key executives in some of the nation's largest corporations. As well, another two thousand volunteers from the private sector worked on thirty-six task forces, of which twenty-two looked at specific departments or agencies and fourteen studied such government-wide functions as personnel management, procurement, and data processing. The private sector also paid all the expenses of the Grace Commission (estimated at $75 million), including the services of all participants.

In the end, Grace produced 47 reports and an astounding number of recommendations (2,478) dealing with 784 different issues. The commission presented the president with a two-volume 650-page "summary" report on 16 January 1984.

Little wonder (Grace told the president), the Grace survey concluded that the business community would not buy, take over, or merge with the government. It had found poor management practices virtually everywhere in government, as well as waste and duplication. The commission argued that if the recommendations were fully implemented, some $424.4 billion would be saved over three years without eliminating a single essential service or raising taxes.[30] To ensure that his report would not be put on the shelf, Grace, together with columnist Jack Anderson, organized a grass-roots movement called Citizens Against Government Waste, to promote the implementation of the commission's recommendations. The group put together a nationwide network of members, purchased nationally televised advertisements promoting ways to cut waste in government, and promoted the establishment of a "congressional Grace caucus committee," involving 169 senators and congressmen to ensure the continued implementation of the recommendations.

The Reagan administration applauded the findings of the Grace Commission and pledged to work on its implementation. Certainly the findings suggested that Reagan's rhetoric on the failings of the federal bureaucracy had been right all along. The commission looked at a multitude of targets. Grace told the president 37.9 percent of the potential savings would result from eliminating "program waste," 35.7 percent from system failures, 21.4 percent from personnel mismanagement, and 5 percent from structural deficiencies and "other" opportunities.[31] The commission told the president that it would not recommend buying or taking over government at least in part because the government reporting and accounting systems were found so lacking that it was not possible to decide whether it should make the acquisitions. The Grace Commission also became convinced that the federal bureaucracy was much too large and poorly managed. It argued that overgrading of positions was rampant, and that the government's retirement benefits for public servants were far too generous when compared with those in the private sector.

The solutions? They were as varied as they were numerous. Privatization, the contracting out of work, increased imposition of user charges, substantial cuts in retirement and fringe benefits for public servants, wage reductions for some employees, a fundamental rethink of some government regulations, consolidation of certain services, the implementation of new personnel and financial management practices, incentives to seek greater efficiency and economy for managers, eliminating needless red tape, and so on. A good number of observers have concluded that the central purpose behind many of the Grace recommendations was nothing short of transforming "public management into business management."[32] E. Goldenberg wrote, for example, "The Grace Commission's enchantment with private sector is . . . intense. . . . The Grace Commission report emphasizes neither distinctions between public and private sectors nor diversity within either one. Instead, it glosses over differences between and within sectors."[33]

Grace not only sought to introduce business-management practices to government, he also carried out in his own right a scrutiny exercise of the kind Rayner was undertaking in Britain. In the case of Grace, however, it was one massive scrutiny of everything and all at once. In addition, his exercise, unlike that in Britain, unleashed over two thousand outsiders to roam wherever they wished throughout government, to sniff out waste and mismanagement. There is little doubt that, whether an ongoing process as in the case of Rayner or a one-shot deal like Grace, the search-and-destroy tactic provides solid ammunition for those who want to cut government down to size.

The thirty-six Grace task forces were staffed mostly by private sector executives, with many of them working in their areas of expertise. In most instances, they went about their work in a systematic fashion. At the risk of oversimplifying what was a complex, intense, and at times chaotic work environment, I would say the Grace task forces undertook their work in an orderly, step-by-step sequence. First, they gathered detailed information on the issues under review. Typically, they would look to a variety of sources for their information, including the bureaucracy itself, independent agencies and think tanks, the General Accounting Office, and the Congressional Budget Office. Second, they would often compare the operation of the departments or the crosscutting functions (such as procurement) with experiences in the private sector. Third, they would formulate recommendations and objectives.

Not long after making its findings public, the Grace Commission came under heavy criticism. Charles Goodsell argued that it had ignored the terms of reference of its mandate, which was to look at improving efficiency not to propose new policy initiatives. He then went on to insist that Grace's analyses and proposals contained "serious instances of misrepresentation." Robert M. Hayes went even further, calling the findings "specious, pernicious, deceitful and dishonest . . . Grace is a political document. To hide what are essentially political debates under the guise of 'good management' is to work a con game of the greatest magnitude. That is what that document is—a massive con game."[34]

Goodsell and Hayes were not alone in leveling strongly worded criticism at the Grace Commission. The congressional committees on the budget directed both the U.S. General Accounting Office (GAO) and the Congressional Budget Office to analyze the commission's recommendations and related budgetary savings estimates. What both reported served to undermine the commission's credibility. The offices reviewed close to 400 of the 2,478 recommendations, which accounted for nearly 90 percent of the net three-year cost savings estimated by the commission. They reported that 122 of the recommendations were too vague to permit a proper evaluation of the proposed savings. The other 274 pointed to savings of only $98 billion, rather than the $298 billion Grace suggested they would generate. The GAO even undertook a review of government pension benefits and concluded that they were not as generous as those for many private firms, including Grace's own company.[35]

The criticism, however, did not stop the Reagan administration from applauding the findings of the commission and from reporting that it would press ahead with their implementation. Donald Devine, director of the Office of Personnel Management, reported a few months after Grace tabled his final report that the Reagan administration was already reaping important savings. He pointed to his office's decisions to tighten up on disability retirements, to reduce the "bulge" of middle-management positions, and to consolidate supervisory training courses. Some three or four years after the Grace Commission tabled its findings, the White House claimed that the government had already achieved 80 percent of the savings identified by Grace.[36]

NIELSEN

It will be recalled that the day after coming to power, Prime Minister Mulroney announced the establishment of the Ministerial Task Force (MTF) to review existing programs, with a view to eliminating those that no longer served a purpose and consolidating others in the hope that not only savings, but better government, would result. The prime minister explained, in making the announcement, that he was asking the task force to review government programs to make them "simple, more understandable and more accessible to their clientele" and that decision making be "decentralized as far as possible to those in direct contact with client groups."[37] The new government also hoped that the exercise would pave the way for more businesslike practices in government.

Mulroney turned to Erik Nielsen, his deputy prime minister, to chair the task force and appointed three of his most senior ministers as members. Nielsen was thought to be particularly well suited to the task: it was widely believed that he profoundly disliked bureaucrats, he was regarded as one of the most tough-minded politicians in Ottawa, and he was a veteran of many parliamentary wars.[38]

Nielsen immediately established an eleven-member private sector advisory committee, chaired by a senior partner of one of Canada's largest accounting firms. One of the first initiatives the task force undertook was to prepare an inventory of existing programs. This uncovered over a thousand government spending programs and tax expenditures. The task force subsequently divided these programs into nineteen program families. Only a few of these families were limited to single departments. The bulk of them crossed departmental lines. The inventory, if nothing else, revealed the enormity of the challenge that confronted the task force. Nielsen described the problem:

> The inventory has shown us the extraordinary complexity of our task. Each program in its own way is a monument to some problem of the past. Programs are often designed on an ad hoc basis,

and targeted to a single problem without much reference to other programs that may address similar problems. From the client's viewpoint, this can result in a confusing hodgepodge of sometimes conflicting programs. We must, therefore, ask ourselves to what extent the original problems still exist and to what extent the original solution is still valid. For instance, through Agriculture Canada, the federal government still manages pastures and livestock in western Canada. Is there still a need, I must ask, to have bulls or sacred cows in federal pastures?[39]

The ministerial task force established nineteen study teams to review the nineteen program families. The teams—with both public servants and private sector representatives—usually consisted of about fifteen members. Some were led by public servants and others by private sector people, but in all instances, their makeup was about equally divided. All in all, 102 business people served on the various teams, compared with 99 public servants. There were also twenty public servants from some of the provincial governments invited to participate. Erik Nielsen explained in his autobiography why he opted for a mixed private and public sector approach:

> Similar program reviews had been conducted in Great Britain, under Margaret Thatcher, and the United States under Ronald Reagan by J. Peter Grace. The difference between them was that the Grace review was conducted entirely by means of contributions from the private sector, with no public financing whatsoever, while the Thatcher review, although it was chaired by a private businessman, was paid for by public funds. The Grace review produced twenty-nine volumes of detail and a wide-ranging set of recommendations, which, if implemented, would have caused certain chaos. Although much of the research was excellent and informative, it did not have much impact. The publicly financed report in Britain did rather better. It was my theory that our approach in Canada should be halfway between that of Britain and the United States; that is, it would be a joint public- and private-sector effort. My colleagues on the task force agreed.[40]

The study teams were given a mandate, a list of programs, and three months to complete their reviews. While the teams sought out new information, in many instances the programs under review had already been evaluated earlier, either internally, by the auditor general, or by outside consultants. The study teams could easily tap in these sources of information. Early on, the task force decided to complete the study in one year. The teams were asked to report sequentially, but each was given about three months to complete its work. All were able to meet the deadline. Once this phase was over, the study teams would discuss their reports with their private sector advisory committee and subsequently submit them to the MTF.

All the reports have been made public and there is no need to discuss them here. Suffice to note that all of them sought to reduce the scope of some programs and to eliminate others. None recommended that programs be expanded or that new ones be introduced. All teams asked questions such as Why is the federal government in this field? and What should be its role? All teams were well aware of the new government's desire to "downsize" bureaucracy and to reduce its spending. They sought to respond by finding programs that could be cut back or by looking at possibilities for devolution to the provinces, privatization, and contracting out.

The nineteen study-group reports were tabled on 11 March 1986.[41] The review recommended one-shot expenditure and tax reductions of between $7 to $8 billion. It also recommended substantial reductions in subsidies to agriculture, fisheries, transportation, business, and the arts. One report recommended sweeping changes to the government procurement policy and urged that the government adopt a comprehensive make-or-buy (that is, contracting out) policy. Some members of the private sector advisory committee stated that in their view the make-or-buy proposal was the single most important recommendation of the review. There were numerous other recommendations covering all policy fields and the great majority of programs surveyed.

Nielsen's task was to carry out a program, not a management review. Still, some of the cuts Nielsen proposed were because the programs were poorly managed. They were sometimes in conflict with other programs or, more often, involved overlap, duplication, and redundancies. The study team on procurement made numerous suggestions to improve management practices; in particular, it urged the government to reorganize the management of its procurement system, by privatizing or contracting out to the private sector a number of functions.[42]

The first Nielsen report, *Management Initiatives*, was tabled as part of the Mulroney government's first budget on 23 May 1985. It not only provided a detailed account of what the study teams were uncovering, it also reported that the government was supportive of the Nielsen findings and would take steps to "inject new ideas into the management of the Government of Canada."[43] The nineteen study reports, however, were tabled nearly a year later, on 11 March 1986.

Notwithstanding its early support, the Mulroney government did not follow through on the great majority of the Nielsen recommendations. The government claims that $280 million in direct ongoing spending reductions and $215 million in tax expenditures can be attributed to the Nielsen task force. Even if we accept the government's figures at face value, they are far off the $7–8 billion cuts proposed by Nielsen. All in all, the Mulroney government did cut training expenditures, adjusted an investment-tax credit scheme, and issued guidelines on the "stacking" of business subsidies and tax credits. It also sold some surplus land, as Nielsen had recommended, and established a new unit in the Treasury Board secretariat to manage government property more effectively and, in September 1986, approved a make-or-buy policy. There are, however, still bulls and sacred cows in federal pastures several years after Nielsen reported its findings. Indeed, the great majority of programs reviewed are still in place and virtually intact.[44]

Three months after tabling the reports, Nielsen was dropped from the cabinet after charges that he had mishandled the resignation of a cabinet colleague. After this, the Nielsen task force became an exercise in a search of support in government. Some decisions were taken immediately after the reports were tabled, but most were minor ones with very limited impact. It was estimated that at least seven hundred decisions were required to deal with the task force recommendations. Major decisions were deferred or rejected. Over two hundred recommendations were immediately turned over to policy committees for further review and were labeled "callbacks." Another forty were not acted upon. Precious few of these callbacks have ever been acted upon.

The reports were tabled in Parliament, but there was little apparent interest in pursuing the findings. Although they were referred to the appropriate standing committee for study, they "were quickly forgotten." Vince Wilson reports that the first session of the Thirty-third

Parliament spent approximately twenty hours on the fifteen thousand pages and three million words of the Nielsen task force volumes.[45]

Senior public servants were less than enthusiastic about the Nielsen recommendations. One explains that a few months after the reports were tabled, his job was to put out a press release saying that some action was being taken—but then immediately to deep-six the whole exercise. He said that very few ministers and fewer officials wanted to hear anything about the Nielsen exercise.[46] This is not to suggest that officials had been reluctant partners in the Nielsen exercise. Indeed, many had been indispensable to the task force and, in some instances, had been instrumental in highlighting program weaknesses and activities. In such instances, however, they had been trying for some time to cut what they felt were "politically motivated" programs.[47] Private sector representatives were always willing to support proposed cuts identified by public servants. However, they wanted to push the exercise much further by identifying deeper cuts and exposing what they considered to be particularly weak management practices. In the end, a good number of officials felt that there had been a clear "we/they" mentality, with business executives holding a dim view of the bureaucrats' abilities. According to one official who participated in the Nielsen review, the business people believed that government "had to be put right in a hurry and that bureaucrats have neither the inclination or the ability to do the job."[48]

ON THE INSIDE, LOOKING AT THE INQUISITORS

Rayner, Grace, and Nielsen arrived in government at the invitation of Thatcher, Reagan, and Mulroney. Government reform measures do not often surface from inside the public service, although some do (the PS 2000 reform initiative in Canada is a case in point). A good number of high-profile reform exercises have originated outside the civil service (Hoover, Fulton, and Glassco reforms are examples). There are various reasons this is so. For one thing, senior officials are often too busy with day-to-day issues. Walter Bagehot's explanation in 1856 as to why administrators intuitively shy away from questions about what they do and how they do it, still applies: "the brain of the administrator is naturally occupied with the details of the day, the passing dust, the granules of that day's life; and the unforeseeing temperament turns away uninterested from reaching speculations, vague thoughts, and from extensive and far-off plans."[49] For another, there is inside bureaucracy a "disbelief culture," which suggests that no attempted reform will stick or work.[50] Thus, when reforms are announced, public servants simply go through the motions of implementation, convinced that this is just another passing fad that will soon die out. Things will shortly get back to normal. As well, senior officials at the pinnacle of their careers are hardly disposed to question the very system that judged them worthy to make it to the top.

The Rayner, Grace, and Nielsen exercises, however, were different from past attempts at government reform. They were all highly ambitious, and all three involved business executives to a greater extent than ever before. The idea of questioning what public servants do and how they do it was probably perceived by permanent officials as a rather quixotic idea some politician brought in from an election campaign, like a baby on a doorstep. Only in the case of the Nielsen task force is there a suggestion that the idea had been proposed by senior public servants. Even here, however, there is a view that the clerk of the Privy Council made the recommendation knowing full well that Mulroney had already decided to announce an "independent" review of government programs.[51]

The role the private sector played varied in all three cases and ranged from doing virtually everything (in the case of Grace) to playing a lead role (in the case of Rayner), but with permanent officials doing much of the work. Public servants, at the best of times, resent outsiders roaming about reviewing their work. They believe outsiders do not understand their problems and cannot possibly appreciate the intricacies of public administration. We saw in an earlier chapter that several authors have identified numerous important differences between managing in the public and private sectors. In addition, with bureaucracy under attack as it was in the early 1980s and with its image in decline, public servants undoubtedly would have preferred to be left to their own devices. Most are convinced that outsiders simply do not have the necessary skills and background to understand government operations. In the case of the Grace Commission (where business executives essentially ran the whole show), at least, a good number of public servants must have been reminded of the *Jungle Book*, in which the "elephants marched from here to there with a military air and it didn't much matter where." Certainly, the many shortcomings that Goodsell and others were so quick to report as soon as Grace made his findings public suggest that the two thousand business executives who worked on the commission lacked basic knowledge about government accounting, public policy, and managing in government.

There is no denying that support for the status quo is characteristic behavior for career officials in bureaucracies, whether public or private.[52] Still, public servants insist that their work and their organizations are vastly different from the private sector. Some will also accept that private sector management practices may apply to government. However, they are likely to insist that, to have any chance of success, senior public servants must be the ones doing the picking and choosing of what will and will not work.

The operations of the public and private sectors differ in many ways.[53] For instance, there is hardly any agreement on how to measure the performance of public servants, while performance measurement is often a relatively straightforward matter in the private sector. Although governments have produced numerous papers on the attributes of competent career officials, there is hardly any consensus on how to measure competence. One senior official in Ottawa spoke to this problem when he pointed out that, for every ten people who will approve the work of any deputy minister, one can easily find ten others who will claim that the same person ought never to have been promoted to that level.[54] Unlike in business, sports, law, entertainment, and academe, there are no hard criteria to judge the success of the work of senior public servants. There are so many variables that have an impact on the success of a policy, a policy proposal, or a government program, that it is difficult to single out one or even several officials for the success or lack of success of departmental operations.

Senior government officials usually operate in a competition-free environment, in that there is no one across the street producing the same products so that one can compare levels of competence. The chief executive officer of a private firm is judged on the basis of his firm's earnings—the bottom line. The head of a government department or agency, meanwhile, is often judged on the basis of appearance or perception of success. James Q. Wilson explains that success here "can mean reputation, influence, charm, the absence of criticism, personal ideology or victory in policy debates." He adds that many government employees "often produce nothing that can be measured after the fact." Michael Blumenthal is much more blunt. He argues that, in Washington, "you can be successful if you appear to be successful. . . . Appearance is as important as reality."[55]

We also know that governments invariably attach importance to ensuring equity among different groups or constituencies, while in business the emphasis is on efficiency and competitiveness. The work of government officials is also subjected to far greater public scrutiny than is the case for private sector managers, where much of their work is internal and far removed from public view. On the other hand, the public sector is fair game for anyone. One can hardly imagine two thousand government officials roaming through General Motors or IBM, intent on exposing management weaknesses and pointing the way to improvements.

In short, the main difference between the public and private sectors is that the private sector manages to the bottom line, while the public sector manages to the top line.[56] The difference has less to do with size than with the rules and constraints under which they operate. Government agencies—to a far greater degree than private bureaucracies—must serve goals or purposes that are not always the preferences of the agency's senior administrators. James Q. Wilson explains, "control over revenues, productive factors and agency goals is all vested to an important degree in entities external to the organization—legislative, courts, politicians, and interest groups."[57] The result is that government officials will often look to the demands of the "external entities" rather than down the organization. It is for this reason, Wilson argues, that government managers are driven by the constraints on the organization, not by its tasks, and that public sector managers will invariably manage to the top line.

One senior government official explained his work environment aptly, if crudely: "in this work, I have come to learn, we suck from above and we kick below. That is, we play to what our political masters or officials more senior than we are want and then we tell our subordinates what to do, how to do it, and what not to do."[58] To be sure, goals in government departments and agencies are vague, and often deliberately so. Indeed, their goals, when viewed from a government-wide perspective, frequently work at cross-purposes. The classical example here is the U.S. Department of Agriculture, which encourages tobacco farmers, while the Surgeon General is busy promoting antismoking campaigns. There are countless such examples in economic-development policy, environment protection, social policy, and government procurement policy. All in all, few government organizations can define their tasks on the basis of clearly stated goals in legislation or resulting from policy reviews. Government, by its very nature, speaks to different objectives and policies, not always wholly compatible with one another. This explains why senior government officials often tend to be cautious administrators rather than daring managers.

Many government officials also remain convinced that business executives have a stereotyped view of government departments and agencies, thinking they are basically all alike. Government officials now often point to the work of Henry Mintzberg and James Q. Wilson to explain differences in government organizations. Mintzberg identifies seven organizational configurations, four of which—entrepreneurial, machine, professional, and innovative—can be quite useful in classifying public sector organizations. They vary in terms of the primary means used to coordinate work, which part of the organization dominates its work processes, and the extent and nature of decentralization. Meanwhile, James Q. Wilson employs a four-way classification system based on the extent to which outputs can be measured and work observed. He refers to these as production organizations (controllable on the basis of outputs and processes readily observable), procedural organizations (not controllable on the basis of outputs and processes readily observable), craft organizations (controllable on the basis of outputs and processes not readily observable), and coping organizations (not controllable on the basis of outputs and processes not readily observable). In the case of production organizations, he reports, the tasks are simple, stable, and specialized. Consequently, they are often centralized and formal, including examples such as the processing of tax returns and government printing bureaus. Examples of procedural organizations include peacetime armed forces; examples of craft organizations include audit services and inspection and enforcement services; and examples of professional organizations include central government consulting services and some policy and advisory units.[59]

Government officials increasingly call upon this literature to make the point that their work is complex, rarely straightforward, and not easily understood by outsiders.[60] The government environment is one where, because goals are vague, circumstances and organizational culture become important. Officials claim that even this tells only part of the story. For instance, work incentives in government are far different from those found in business. Government managers are not able to capture surplus revenues for themselves or often even for their own organizations. This begs the question alluded to earlier in discussing the prisoners' dilemma: Why would they want to scrimp? Added to this are the myriad rules and procedures they continually face. All government bureaucracies have one thing in common—decisions about hiring, promotions, and firing staff, as well as financial, procurement, and contracting decisions are all guided by prescribed processes, rules, and regulations. A business executive who wants to hire staff, relocate, downgrade or even let someone go, or who wishes to purchase a computer, can usually do so with a minimum of administrative constraints or red tape. Not so for the government official. Indeed, the steps one must go through to get rid of an employee whose work is not satisfactory, are such that it is rare, indeed, that a government manager attempts it. A long-drawn-out process is required, and most managers have learned that it is far better and easier to invest their time and energy on initiatives that have greater payoffs. It is a rough road for any managers who wish to pursue a dismissal. Government employees have a right to appeal any decision to fire them, demote them, or suspend them without pay. The appeal process can be lengthy—over six months in many instances—and can sap the energy of the most determined manager.[61] Rules and regulations prescribing decision making in government are rarely the product of what government officials want. Much more often than not, such rules are there for political reasons. The application of the merit principle, the push toward equity in employment practices, centrally prescribed rules guiding financial decisions, procurement policies favoring certain regions or firms displaying certain employment policies, and so on are largely driven by politicians, not by public servants.

All of this is to make the point once again that management and decision making in government are tied to conditions and circumstances that differ substantially from those found in the private sector. These conditions often stress "procedural values" over "substance." Such values do not encourage efficiency. Indeed, they often run counter. Public servants must continually take their cue from politicians, whose work is always tied to a political function. While a chief executive officer of a large private firm may meet with the board of directors several times a year and nearly always get what he or she wants, the senior public official must navigate in a complex, conflict-ridden, and highly charged political environment. Since this entails keeping an eye on interest groups and the media, there is little time left to look down the organization to shape its activities. There is seldom an easy road to success in government. Simply getting things done "remains a wearisome and frustrating business."[62]

To many senior government officials, "coping" becomes important. For the ambitious, networking, visibility, and appearance of success also are important. The system is such, however, that there are few rewards for competence, as defined from a private sector perspective.[63] Given that government goals are nearly always vague, that there are numerous constraints inhibiting efficiency, and that good management is rarely rewarded, one may well wonder why there is any management at all in government.

Government officials know all of this intuitively. Indeed, they understand the administrative culture in government and know what is on, what can work, and what will not. What they may lack in management skills and in the ability to shape the activities of their organizations, they make up for in their ability to cope with an unpredictable political environment and with external forces. To protect their organization becomes a key preoccupation. Wilson spells out with great insight how they often set out to ensure that their agencies will survive, if not expand. The dos and don'ts include fighting other government organizations that seek to perform similar tasks as your own, avoiding tasks that will produce divided or hostile constituencies, avoiding "learned vulnerabilities" or risks, and so on.[64]

Officials do not deny that fighting for one's corner is an important part of their work. But this, they insist, comes with the territory. Their purpose after all is not to fight for markets but rather to compete with others in government for a policy position, for jurisdiction, legitimacy, and resources in support of their political masters. Old habits die hard. Managerialism is one thing, but a good number of officials still strongly value their ability to observe the workings of power and influence and to identify their sources, applications, and constraints. In their opinion, this and their ability to keep their eyes on both the ideal (what is best) and on reality (what is possible in the political environment) still constitute one of the most important contributions they can make for their country.[65]

This, then, is the world of career government officials, whether in London, Washington, or Ottawa. Little wonder that a clash in culture and outlook is unavoidable when business executives are given a mandate to turn around government operations. By temperament, business executives will want to cut through the nonsense, jump to solutions, and make sweeping judgments about what is required. They are likely to give short shrift to the interdependence of functions in government, to the vague and conflicting goals, to the built-in administrative constraints, and the sundry requirements of the political world. Public servants—well versed in the ways of their village and capable of sniffing out the most subtle of messages emanating from any part of the government machinery—are likely to become exasperated with business executives, who briefly invade their turf and sell simple solutions to complex problems.[66] Indeed, many civil servants are disdainful of such exercises, aware that the functions to be performed in government differ in many respects from those involved "in the running of Marks and Spencer."[67] Some that I consulted accepted that private sector management practices can be introduced in certain instances to government operations, particularly in the case of machine- or production-type functions, that is, in routine and predictable tasks. But even in these cases, government officials are quick to argue that private sector practices must be adjusted to fit the "realities of government."[68]

Few government officials gave Rayner, Grace, or Nielsen much chance of success. Some were opposed to the exercises from the outset and, in the case of Nielsen at least, deep-sixed the whole initiative as soon as the first opportunity arose.[69] Although they could not speak out publicly, a good number were contemptuous of the findings of the various commissions. This was particularly true of the Grace Commission.[70] The disbelief culture that Les Metcalfe and Sue Richards wrote about was in play in the case of Rayner and Whitehall.[71] The culture, they argue, acts as a psychological defense mechanism against proposals or initiatives that threaten the stability of public servants' belief system and their work. Thus, many dismiss out of hand new management concepts, especially those imported from the private sector. They view them as self-serving promises for politicians seeking election. Their value is limited to political campaigns and to the short term. For many, Rayner, Grace, and Nielsen amounted to little more than yet another occasion to batten down the hatches and wait out the descent of the private sector and the passing storm. Past experience told them things would soon get back to normal. The new political leadership would shortly get comfortable with the levers of power, then turn to the bureaucrats as a kind of fire brigade to help them extinguish political fires and the inevitable government crisis.

LOOKING BACK

Thatcher, Reagan, and Mulroney all turned to the private sector to perform a "management turnaround" operation on the government bureaucracies they were inheriting. The business community happily took up the challenge. Although many of them declined to serve full-time in government, a good number, particularly in the United States and Canada, agreed to serve on a temporary basis.

Looking back, we can see that the operation was, from the perspective of the new political leadership, successful in certain areas but considerably less so in others. Rayner can claim some success from his efforts and indeed has done so. He was at the center of a whirlwind of activities that asked fundamental questions about the costs and results of government operations. He launched the scrutiny exercise that is still being carried out today.

There is now a veritable catalogue of scrutiny stories to tell. Many involve the realization of substantial savings. Others refer to the inability or unwillingness of government officials to ask fundamental questions about their operations. The now widely reported £30 rat is a case in point. A scrutiny of support services in research and development operations discovered that rats were being bred in-house for experimental purposes, to the cost of £30, while a nearby private sector laboratory sold similar rats for only £2.[72] Another scrutiny revealed that the Inland Revenue kept two different sets of registers on small businesses, both containing the same information; yet another scrutiny revealed that it cost £91 to give out £100 under a woodland scheme.[73] The point here—and one that Thatcherites often made—is that, left to their own devices, civil servants would not uncover such wasteful practices simply because they do not walk around asking questions about what they do, about the status quo, and about government operations.

By the time Rayner left his position in government in late 1982 to return to the private sector, 133 scrutinies had been completed, recommending onetime savings of £56 million, recurrent savings of £400 million, and the elimination of twelve thousand positions. The government had taken firm decisions to cut the twelve thousand positions and to realize a onetime savings of £29 million and recurrent annual savings of £180 million.[74] Scrutinies, as noted earlier, did not stop with Rayner's departure. A scrutiny was even carried out on the scrutiny process itself in 1985, and the report was positive. Thatcher made the report public and wrote a foreword reporting that it demonstrated "conclusively the effectiveness of the scrutiny as a method of identifying better ways of achieving value for money in government departments."[75]

The scrutinies constituted just one element of introducing good management in government. The FMI was also launched to introduce a more disciplined approach to financial management. Looking back on its implementation, most observers and senior public servants now report some progress and success on several fronts. All departments now have a financial management system in place that has enabled a further decentralization of decision-making authority down the line. The systems have also been institutionalized in the ongoing dealings between the Treasury and the departments. In some instances, performance indicators have been developed that have enabled the Treasury to loosen some administrative and financial controls on departments.

Thatcher asked Rayner's successor, Sir Robin Ibbs, to carry out an assessment of FMI and her other efforts to strengthen management practices in government. His review, made public in February 1988, reported that progress had been made. Civil servants were now more cost conscious, and the FMI constituted an important and successful start at changing the attitudes of senior civil servants toward management. The review stressed that budget cuts and the FMI were the two most important forces in this change of attitude. Still, the review revealed some important shortcomings and recommended new measures. It argued that there was insufficient focus on the delivery of government services as opposed to policy and ministerial support; that there was a shortage of solid management skills; that there was still too much emphasis on spending money and not enough on getting results; and that it was necessary to find new ways of organizing government activities. It urged the establishment of agencies to carry out the executive functions of government. Thatcher endorsed the findings of the report and, as we shall see, directed new efforts to be launched in these areas.[76]

None of this is to suggest that Thatcher's reform measures had no blemishes or that they were widely welcomed inside government. Indeed, the important shortcomings identified in the Ibbs report suggest that many senior officials were not taking FMI and the new emphasis on management as seriously as Thatcher had hoped. Rayner himself wrote about the resistance he met from the bureaucracy. Many senior officials had looked to just wait out the storm and sought to limit the damage of scrutinies, at least in their implementation phase. In one instance, for example, a head office manager wrote to a field manager that he had "cleared the action plan. I think it is the minimum we are likely to be able to get away with, and I hope you will feel it is something you can live with."[77] There were also numerous delays in arriving at firm decisions on scrutinies and, again, in their implementation.

FMI did have an impact. It appears, however, that its impact was not evenly felt. For one thing, the system concentrated on administrative costs and did not place sufficient emphasis on program spending. For another, the system has been much more successful in machine- or production-type functions than elsewhere. FMI has also had precious little impact on policy work, other than being able to monitor running costs more accurately. In addition, notwithstanding Thatcher's directive to ministers that they take a much stronger interest in the management of their departments, ministers remained "disinclined to use" FMI systems.[78] Some also questioned, initially at least, whether the scrutinies and FMI systems would have much of a lasting impact on the culture and values of the senior civil service. Rayner himself expressed doubts when he was asked if there were any real change at the top under the "whip of Thatcherism." He said: "Taken as a whole, I must be frank and say no."[79]

Yet Thatcher was far more successful in making her reform measures stick than were either Reagan or Mulroney. To be sure, the Grace Commission was highly visible, created a great deal of interest in certain quarters, and produced a series of voluminous reports. Peter Grace did place the need for better management practices in government high on the public agenda. As we saw, a citizens' organization was founded to promote the commission's proposals. In addition, the Deficit Reduction Act of 1984 required an annual review of the implementation of the Grace Commission.[80]

In other respects, however, Grace is far short of a success story. Grace and his two thousand business executives came, formulated recommendations, and left. Their findings were challenged on several fronts from various quarters and soon the credibility of the commission and its findings were under question.[81] The recommendations lacked a central and coherent purpose, they were all over the map, and in many ways agencies were left to pick and choose what they wanted from the menu. With Grace and his team no longer around and the president and his advisors unable to work through the details of the many recommendations, career officials waited for the storm to pass—and it did.

Reagan insisted, however, right up to his last days in office that Grace had been a successful exercise and that he had supported its recommendations. In his last report on the *Management of the United States Government*, he reported that he had accepted some 80 percent of Grace Commission recommendations.[82] The report, however, quickly added a number of caveats. It made the calculation on the basis of what it labeled "unduplicated" recommendations, which numbered 2,160 rather than the 2,478 Grace said his report contained. Reagan's report then revealed that Congress agreed with some 1,600 of the recommendations. However, the report also dismissed as misleading the savings identified by Grace, pointing out important differences between "Grace savings estimates" and actual "budget savings." In any event, Congress "support" for the recommendations is not the same thing as actual "implementation." When asked to comment on the implementation, a government official observed,

> Grace had an impact. A number of recommendations have been acted upon because they made sense and because many agencies had been promoting such measures for a long time. Grace picked up on them and it then became easier for agencies to do things that they had been wanting to do for some time. That said, it is easy to play the numbers game with savings and the White House

played the game. On the whole, it is quite difficult to make the case that Grace was successful and rather quite easy to make the case that it was not. I have to conclude that Grace was not a success story.[83]

Another official argued that,

> Grace was anything but a success story. No one has ever been able to figure out how the administration was able to claim that it had implemented many Grace recommendations. Grace was a friend of the president and there was a concerted effort to make Grace look good. There was certainly a lot of playing around with the numbers and some "partially" implemented recommendations became somehow fully implemented.[84]

Looking at the implementation of Grace, one is reminded of the comments of an official who reported after Fulton that British officials "accepted everything Fulton said but then did what they wanted to."[85]

The Nielsen task force in Canada suffered a similar fate. The hundred or so business executives involved in this initiative came and went. The exercise created considerable interest in the media, but it gradually lost its place on the public agenda. Public servants played a key role in placing he Nielsen findings on the back burner. There is now hardly a trace left of the Nielsen exercise. One official summed up its legacy by pointing out, "There are still bulls and sacred cows in federal pastures."[86] Another, perhaps sarcastically, suggested that one of the few lasting impacts of Nielsen was that "maybe we were able to educate a hundred or so yahoos that government administration is not as simple as it may at first appear to outsiders."[87]

Although there were important differences in how Rayner, Grace, and Nielsen approached their tasks and although the three exercises had varying degrees of success, one can easily pick up a common thread. All three looked to the private sector, not only for people to do the job but also to borrow ideas. This was even true of Rayner, who constantly looked to his business background for inspiration. The phrases he employed to describe his work were clearly the language of a business executive, not of public administration. He spoke about "rules being contrary to good management," about "robust systems of management," and about the need to look at "the operation of the State from a management perspective."[88] Some of the techniques he employed, however, were at times quite another matter. One can make the case, for example, that the Programme Analysis and Review (PAR) of the early 1970s sought to scrutinize programs in the hope of eliminating waste in government in the same manner that Rayner did. Still, the British civil service had never before witnessed such an intensive and determined attempt at modernization.

There are two important reasons why Rayner and the FMI were more successful and left a far more lasting legacy than either Grace or Nielsen. Thatcher made the initiatives her own, made them central to her government's agenda, and took a strong personal interest in their success. She-who-must-be-obeyed left no doubt that she was deeply committed, expected results, and was prepared to hold her ministers and permanent secretaries accountable. Mulroney's interest in government reform came in fits and starts.[89] He was deeply committed to the idea until another issue (whether national unity or negotiating a free-trade agreement with the United States) came along to claim his interest and priority. He would always come back to government reform and the need to eliminate waste, but never with the kind of intensity that Thatcher had. Reagan's views on government waste never wavered but, like Mulroney, his interest in pursuing the matter did. In addition, the task was much harder for Reagan, given the kind of relationship that exists between Congress and executive departments and agencies.[90]

Thatcher, with previous government experience, turned to Rayner, also with government experience, to lead the charge. Reagan, with no Washington experience, turned to Grace, also with no Washington experience. Mulroney, with no Ottawa experience, turned to Nielsen, also with no government experience.[91] In turn, Rayner turned mostly to public servants for help, Grace did the opposite, while Nielsen sought a middle course.

His government experience, if nothing else, enabled Rayner to keep his bias in check when working with government officials and gave him a sense of what could and could not work. He wisely decided to avoid "a grand scheme" and a "detailed blueprint."[92] He chose to proceed step-by-step with departments and to ensure that permanent officials would ultimately take charge of the work plan. He also sought to be "credible" with the civil service and often spoke out publicly about the wealth of talent and expertise to be found in government.[93] He took to heart Edward Bridges's warning that the "real economy of administration is something which is best done from inside, and cannot be applied externally like an ointment."[94] Still, with Thatcher's full backing, he "stayed determined" that there would be a radical change in the quality of management in government.[95] Above all, he stayed around, knowing full well that if he did not, he would in the end amount to little more than just another passing storm, providing still more fuel for Whitehall's disbelief system.

Government officials soon discovered that there was more to the Thatcher, Reagan, and Mulroney agendas than Rayner, FMI, Grace, and Nielsen. This was only the first volley, there was more to come. However, two things would remain constant. The emphasis on management was here to stay, and the private sector would continue to represent the role model for government operations. Indeed, Thatcher, Reagan, and Mulroney would not only look to the business community for inspiration, they would also turn to it to take on some of the functions previously assumed by governments.

6

Turning to the Private Sector

THE ENTHUSIASM of the new political leadership for the merits of private enterprise did not end with the introduction of private sector practices to government operations. There was also a readiness to experiment with market approaches and to turn over public sector activities to the business community.

Privatization became fashionable in the 1980s in London, Washington, and Ottawa and, indeed, subsequently in much of the world. The term *privatization* has become closely identified with Margaret Thatcher, as Britain was the trailblazer. Privatization began to spread "outward from Britain" in the early 1980s, affecting more than "100 countries throughout the world."[1]

In fact, the term *privatization* dates back at least forty years. The Hoover commissions pointed to privatization or contracting out in the United States in the late 1940s and again in the 1950s. The former U.S. Bureau of the Budget put out a directive in 1955 discouraging federal government agencies from producing for themselves "any product or service which can be procured from private enterprise through ordinary business channels."[2] The Glassco Commission in Canada also urged the federal government to look to the private sector to produce some of the services or products that departments were producing in-house.

Although the term *privatization* has been known since the 1950s, however, it never made much headway as government policy. One observer explained that even "during the 1970s those of us who appealed for reform via privatization were still generally regarded as nuts."[3] It is Thatcher who first introduced privatization to the public policy agenda and made it stick. She also gave the term a much broader meaning than it ever had before. Under previous conservative prime ministers, it meant handing industries or property back to their previous owners. Under Thatcher, *privatization* became "the process by

146

which the production of goods and services was transferred from the public to the private sector."[4] First with Thatcher, and later with Reagan and Mulroney, it meant contracting out; soliciting bids; deregulation; user fees, by which citizens are charged for the use of public facilities or services that could be supported through tax revenues; voucher systems, by which citizens are provided coupons redeemable for purchasing goods or services from private firms; and load shedding, by which the public sector withdraws from providing certain services in the expectation that those services can be provided by other levels of government or preferably through voluntary institutions or self-help.[5] Some now argue that Thatcher was far more successful than her predecessors at "denationalization" because she went well beyond merely selling government-owned ventures, as is, "to private buyers."[6]

Although Thatcher's example made privatization a dominant theme in the public policy agenda in much of the industrialized world throughout the 1980s, she hardly made reference to it during the 1979 election campaign or in her first days in office. By 1983, however, it had become a key part of her government's agenda and a central theme in her party's plan for the next election.[7] In the United States, the Grace Commission and the Heritage Foundation, a conservative think tank with strong connections to the Reagan White House, pointed to privatization as a means of introducing market forces to the activities of government and a way of cutting the government deficit. Like Thatcher, Reagan had not identified privatization as a key feature of his first election campaign and, as with her, it became an important focus of his administration only after a few years—so much so that "by the second Reagan term, officials took to joking that virtually any proposal could become administration policy if it carried the label of privatization."[8] By the time Mulroney fought his first election campaign, Thatcher had completed her first mandate while Reagan was nearing the end of his. Although privatization was by then well entrenched in the public policy agenda in both Britain and the United States, the concept formed no part of Mulroney's first election campaign. About all he would say on the matter was that he had established a task force to study the issue and to make recommendations.[9] Within a few weeks of being elected, however, the Mulroney government unveiled ambitious privatization plans. Although several announcements about privatization were made within days of his coming to office, the plans were slow in getting off the ground. By the end of Mulroney's first mandate, however, his government's privatization plans were also in full flight.

IDEOLOGY AND THE NEED FOR CASH

Privatization was attractive for two reasons: first, the concept is rooted in the conservative ideology of the three leaders, and (in the case of Thatcher and Mulroney at least) the sale of government assets would generate much-needed cash. The new political leadership was determined to turn more and more to market mechanisms. Charles Wolf wrote in the mid 1980s that a cardinal policy issue facing modern economic systems was to decide "the appropriate role of government and of the market in the functioning of the economic systems." The new political leaders left little doubt where they stood. Their philosophy embraced the Friedman view that "a freely functioning market economy results in economic and technological progress, efficient utilization of resources, [and] a rising standard of living that is distributed with reasonable equity."[10] In the Friedman view, the expansion of government beyond minimal functions related to the public good inhibits economic progress. For example, defense and public order properly belong within government, but postal services do not. Government intervention, according to Friedman, not only impedes achieving full employment but also gives rise to large government organizations that invariably "mismanage" their tasks.[11] The solution then was not simply to stop the state from growing, but also to roll back the state. Privatization represented an important policy instrument to put these plans into action.

The new political leadership could and did point to a number of studies making the case that private or market supply was much more efficient than public or nonmarket supply. One such study looked at fifty cases in five countries, comparing the efficiency of both sectors, and reported that in at least forty, the private sector was considerably more efficient. Nonmarket supply appeared less costly only in the case of electric utilities, veterans' hospitals, and garbage collection. In seven cases, the verdict was unclear, because either the results showed no difference or they were too ambiguous to draw any conclusions. In forty cases, however, private supply was more efficient. The study looked at a variety of areas ranging from insurance sales and servicing, airlines, bus services, cleaning services, banks, slaughterhouses, fire protection, to weather forecasting. In many instances, the differences were substantial, with the private sector being 50 percent more efficient in the case of cleaning services, 200 percent in debt collection, and from 12 to 100 percent in the case of the airline industry.[12]

Privatization was favored by the business community. Rayner made certain to ask in his scrutinies whether what was being done by the government could not be more efficiently carried out by the private sector. The Grace Commission singled out privatization as a key recommendation, while business executives on the Nielsen task force considered the make-or-buy recommendation to be one of their most important recommendations. Private sector pressure on government to privatize some functions has also been well documented.[13] Patrick Dunleavy wrote that in Britain "The Conservative party's move towards public service privatization has been under corporate pressure since 1979 and the congruent objectives of ministers and corporate groups has created a privatization bonanza."[14]

Privatization has been described as a "new right project" and as the "central prescriptive maxim of the new right." It certainly squares with the public choice literature Thatcher urged her advisors and senior government officials to read. Public choice theorists, it will be recalled, argue that government departments and agencies are weakly controlled by sponsors (politicians), with the result that bureaucracies inevitably oversupply outputs. Privatization takes the decision making from the hands of the bureaucrats and turns it over to market forces, which (the thinking goes) will, by their very nature, ensure more efficient decisions and allocation of resources. It also "attacks the integrity of public sector organizations" by exposing and removing the protective ideologies that government agencies build up "to insulate their over-supply behaviour from external scrutiny or criticism."[15] If public bureaucracies cannot, by definition, operate efficiently (as public choice theorists claim), then the solution for Thatcherites and people of like mind is to move the bureaucracies into the private sector.

Privatization also constituted a powerful tool for politicians wishing to ensure lasting change to government and to bureaucracy. One of the fears of the three leaders was that bureaucracy would, as in the past, simply wait out the political crowd in power and then see to it that things got back to normal. A sympathetic observer of the new political leadership maintained that politically driven efficiency drives or campaigns only bring at best limited success and this only during the actual period of pressure. He explained that, "When the novelty has died, the practices of public supply gradually reassert their effects. The history of the public sector in Britain is littered with the names of whiz kids who wrought beneficial but short-lived influence from the private sector."[16] The new political leadership also felt that imposing budget cuts or spending limits would simply result in bureaucracies' spending less—but not necessarily more efficiently. Indeed, some argued that when asked to cut spending, bureaucrats would cut programs and services rather than endanger their own jobs or reduce the overhead cost of government.

The broader definition of privatization, it was hoped, would not only see public sector management responsibilities exported to the business community but also see private sector management ideas and practices imported to government. Contracting out, for example, forces government managers to deal with the business community and to compare their operations with those in the private sector. Contracting out is widely employed in the private sector where large firms decide what they should produce in-house and what ought to be produced by other firms under contract. Contracting out has become even more popular in recent years, as firms look more and more at divesting to the core in order to ensure a more concentrated focus on the "business of the business."[17] The new political leadership strongly felt that government was producing too many of its services in-house (thus overlooking excellent opportunities to save public funds by contracting out services to the private sector) and that large government had become unmanageable and should return to its core responsibilities, as defined by Friedman and other neoconservative thinkers. The new leadership was convinced that savings could be realized, because contracting out would unleash competitive forces and expose the lack of efficiency and cost control found in government. Contracting out held an added bonus for governments who were committed to reducing the size of their bureaucracies, since it transferred jobs from the public to the private sector.[18] Lastly, the political leadership felt that contracting out would also strengthen the private sector and make it more competitive in the international market place.

LOAD SHEDDING

The new leadership, but particularly Reagan, also introduced load shedding to the public policy agenda. The argument was that government and the collectivization of public goods, such as health care, education, housing, and various social services, had failed to achieve even the most modest of expectations.[19] In addition, they had given rise to waste and inefficiencies by overloading government and rendering it unmanageable. The solution was for government gradually to withdraw from a number of policy fields. It was felt that the private sector, voluntary associations, and even state governments would pick up the slack.

Load shedding is also deeply rooted in conservative ideology. It looks to the family as the principal decision-making unit in society to arrange health care, education, and social services. The family should be free to choose where to secure such services. The poor, it was argued, need not fear that the ax would fall on them. Vouchers (or a negative income tax scheme) would also enable them to pick and choose services and goods, thus giving them new freedoms. An advisor to Reagan suggested that, as government gradually diminished the supply of collective goods, private firms would move in to fill the breach. It was possible, he argued, to imagine that one day McDonald's could start a franchised day-care business.[20]

Reagan established a special task force and internal study teams to identify ways for the private sector to take up the slack left by cuts in government spending. In October 1981, he announced the creation of a special presidential task force on private sector initiatives and asked it "to promote private sector leadership and responsibility for solving public needs, and to recommend ways of fostering public-private partnerships." In time, the task force became a highly visible blue-ribbon panel of forty-four business and civic leaders. The panel decided to enlarge the scope of its tasks; to review the rules and regulations of government agencies to see how they inhibited private sector involvement; to look at existing government programs to see if they could be more productively carried out by private firms; to come up with ideas to stimulate private sector investment in areas that had been the preserve of the public sector; and to identify ways to lessen dependence on government and encourage new public and private sector partnerships.

Reagan had high expectations that the panel would give rise to concrete results. He told the chairman that he did not "want a committee report. Give me action and results. Get the private sector in the driver's seat so we can start using market incentives and philanthropy to find lasting solutions to community problems."[21] The panel produced a report and a number of studies, including one on volunteering and another on community and economic development. It also came up with a number of recommendations, including specific measures to involve the private sector in employment creation, to promote charitable giving, and to encourage voluntarism. There were also, however, some proposals for concrete action, including the establishment of job-search clubs, business-education programs within chambers of commerce, and new forums to encourage employers to establish day-care facilities. The work of the panel also gave rise to new public and private sector partnerships in urban redevelopment and to a system of vouchers under which low-income families could rent from private landlords rather than from federally funded housing projects.[22]

Much has been written about Reagan's "new federalism" and his attempts at load shedding by turning over responsibilities to the state level and by cutting back grants to state governments. Reagan's new federalism called for a review of the roles and responsibilities of the federal government, later of state and local governments and, later still, of the public and private sectors. The thinking was that federal government responsibilities would initially devolve to the lower levels of government, and from there perhaps to the market or to organizations that were neither market nor government. In time, it was hoped, responsibilities for such areas as human resource development or even social services could be assumed by nonprofit foundations funded by the private sector and individuals.[23] Reagan successfully set out to cut back revenue-sharing programs with state governments, as well as some block funding, and to consolidate some intergovernmental grants.[24] *Consolidation*, however, simply became a code word for cutbacks to state governments. Indeed, viewed from the perspective of the state governments, Reagan's new federalism meant that some federal responsibilities were turned over to them without any accompanying funding. The Reagan administrators did not deny this. They pointed out, however, that it had become clear "there is a decision overload at the Federal level, and that Washington, D.C. was too intrusive in the lives of citizens and their State and local government."[25] They reported that the Reagan administration had consolidated fifty-eight programs into nine block grants, and they acknowledged that some cuts in funding had occurred. They argued, however, that in return decision making had become streamlined and that the states would be spending less time filling out federal application forms and attending intergovernmental meetings. The new federalism in short meant less bureaucracy.

The Reagan administration also pressed ahead with efforts to deregulate the American economy and to identify opportunities to contract out government activities to the private sector. Indeed, deregulation became the most important part of Reagan's privatization plans. The administration attacked what they labeled the paper burden of government on businesses and even on government agencies and the "heavy hand" of government regulations. They later argued that, in six years, they had been able to reduce by three hundred million hours the effort required to deal with the federal government's paperwork. The administration's Office of Information and Regulatory Affairs, located in its Office of Management and Budget, also reported that "superfluous" government regulations and statutory requirements had been successfully eliminated. The Information Office pointed out that it had eliminated some sixty requirements, including many restrictions imposed on businesses receiving federal grants or contracts, and that it had been able to cut thirty thousand pages from the Federal Acquisition Regulation.[26]

The Reagan administration also issued a policy directive encouraging the contracting out to private firms of all activities and services that could be provided at a lower cost than by in-house government workers. The directive not only made it easier for agencies to contract out services but also to carry out reviews to identify services that could be contracted out. The central purpose of the directive was to introduce a competitive process in government operations. It even provided for the restructuring of government operations to enable them to compete with private sector firms. The hope was that government operations would be "de-bureaucratized" to enable them to go into head-to-head competition with private firms to win government jobs. Whoever wins, the administration made it clear, would be "held accountable for meeting the performance standards, be it the Government or the private sector."[27]

The Reagan administration reported considerable success in its efforts to introduce the "benefits of marketplace competition into the operation of government programs and operations."[28] It declared that during its eight years in office, it saw to it that government operations competed with the private sector for ninety thousand jobs, and that it had contracted out thirty thousand jobs.[29] The move, it claimed, gave rise to over $800 million in annual savings, insisting that it saved on average some $9,300 for every position it identified for competition with private firms. It also reported that, through this policy, it was able to realize a 30 percent cost reduction in government operations without a loss in service. To prove the point, the administration outlined a number of examples of government operations where important savings had been realized without any loss in service. Examples were given in the fields of defense, computer programming, library management, and prisons.[30] The Reagan administration also reported that when government operations were restructured to become more efficient, they won about 45 percent of the time against private firms. The administration applauded these numbers but insisted that the most important benefit flowing from its contracting-out policy was the overall "change in management culture" in government.[31]

The Reagan administration reported toward the end of its second term in office that it had accomplished a great deal with its new policy but that still more was required. It proposed to amend its policy directive to increase "competitive" pressure in government operations and announced plans to allow private sector firms to review government operations or jobs directly and to nominate candidates for contracting out rather than relying on government to do so. It also urged government agencies that provide services to other agencies (such as data processing or financial-management services) to restructure their operations to become more competitive and, in turn, subject more of their activities to competition with the private sector. The administration also sought to make it easier for government employees to organize themselves as employee cooperatives to compete as outside firms for their jobs.[32]

Mulroney borrowed a page from the Grace Commission and Reagan's contracting-out policy to formulate his own make-or-buy policy.

Nielsen, it will be recalled, had looked to Grace and had stressed in his findings the importance of introducing the make-or-buy concept to government operations. The Mulroney government responded to developments in the United States and Britain and to the Nielsen findings by unveiling in July 1986 a "phased" implementation of a make-or-buy policy. The policy provided for competitive tendering between the public and private sectors, for employee takeovers, joint public and private sector ventures, and community enterprises. Underpinning the new policy was the desire to foster "an entrepreneurial, innovative, cost-conscious public service which is accountable for results."[33]

The policy was designed to encourage government departments and agencies to cost the most efficient way to deliver their services and then identify alternative sources of doing so, including contracting out. On the advice of secretariat officials, Treasury Board ministers decided to introduce the policy through pilot projects, with departments invited to participate voluntarily. To assist in implementing the policy, a small group was established in the Treasury Board secretariat. In addition, some funding was made available to retain the services of consultants to determine the most cost-effective organization to deliver current government services.

The make-or-buy group in the Treasury Board secretariat was quick to argue that most government services were amenable to the policy, or at least to some restructuring of the delivery of services. It also argued that important savings could be realized by challenging the in-house delivery of such services as training, claims processing, facility management, and even program delivery, including the growing of seed grains, research, laboratories, and the provision of health care for prison inmates. The make-or-buy process was intended to work in this fashion: the first task was to describe in detail the specifications for a job, or what was actually being done; second, a "most efficient organization" study then looked at alternative sources of supply and expected cost (this study was usually conducted by an outside consultant to ensure, among other things, that the study was impartial); the third task was to solicit bids from the private sector; and the fourth was to implement the most efficient option, either private or public.

By mid 1988, a dozen pilot projects had been launched, including one on a hydraulic laboratory, another on an airport, another on health care for inmates, and another on a vehicle test center. The results of all pilot projects pointed to potential savings of from 12 to over 20 percent. Still, very little beyond the study phase has actually been accomplished under Canada's make-or-buy policy. In one instance, word leaked out that the government was considering contracting out the government's mapping service to a large Canadian business.[34] Ministers now report that they were caught off guard with no time to plan a political strategy and that, under the circumstances, they had little choice but to deny they were about to privatize the service. These ministers maintain that the leak was deliberate, planted by public servants in the mapping unit who feared that they would be forced to relocate to another community. They also claim that the responsible minister was not aware of the developments, because the push to look at the mapping service had come from the group in the Treasury Board secretariat and not from the department.[35]

The public controversy resulting from this incident dampened the government's interest in its make-or-buy policy. From that moment on, the Treasury Board secretariat abided strictly by the rule that pilot projects would have to be identified by the departments themselves, on a voluntary basis, and this decision served to cripple its implementation. Since implementation of the policy has been voluntary, there has been no burden of proof on managers to justify retention of in-house delivery. In contrast, government managers in the United States and in Great Britain, when challenged, are required to demonstrate cost effectiveness for all commercial-type functions if they are to keep them in-house.

Government managers, of course, see no incentives and plenty of disincentives to transfer an activity to the private sector. A former official in the make-or-buy group now reports that the pilot projects identified by departments were invariably self-serving—only those projects were selected that would have absorbed a good part of the reductions in person-years already set for their departments.[36] The thinking was that if a service could be transferred to the private sector, it would show a net reduction in the department's total person-year complement. It would not, however, necessarily mean a savings in financial resources since the funds would be transferred to the private sector to carry out the service. Still, he argued, accommodating person-year cuts constituted about the only incentive for deputy ministers to implement the policy. The make-or-buy policy, however, held plenty of disincentives for managers. Some were administrative, such as penalties on pension transferability for affected government employees. Others were much more visible, including outright opposition from public service unions. Still others included the impact the transfer of a particular unit or service to the private sector was likely to have on all senior departmental managers. Such a transfer would have had, in time, some negative impact on their classification levels and hence on their salaries.

There were also some broader issues that line managers felt were never addressed. They argue that it is unfair to compare the cost of running their operations with costs in the private sector.[37] They point to various government policies and measures over which they have little control that serve to increase their costs and make them uncompetitive with private firms. These include employment equity policy, access to information legislation, the requirements of central agencies, the Public Service Employment Act, and so on. Senior government managers quite naturally also looked upon the government's make-or-buy policy as a vote of no confidence in the public service on the part of the politicians. And yet (they insist), if the public service has become inefficient and costly over the years, it is because of various measures the politicians themselves have put in place. A good number of managers also saw a link between the make-or-buy policy and morale problems in the federal public service.

The make-or-buy policy made little headway in the Mulroney government, and it was quietly dropped in 1990. The group promoting it in the Treasury Board secretariat was also disbanded. Departments are now being asked to identify, on their own, opportunities to contract out in-house activities and services. A senior government official who played a key role in developing the make-or-buy policy reported that very little is being done on this front, even now, and that prospects for the future are not much brighter. The only incentive now for managers to look at the make-or-buy option is when they are asked to absorb across-the-board spending cuts.[38] But even here, he insisted, it is not much of an incentive. Spending cuts are announced without warning, and it is invariably too late to look at applying the option in any serious fashion.

In Britain, Sir Keith Joseph promoted the contracting out option and measures to improve government purchasing in the early 1980s when he was secretary of state for industry.[39] The Thatcher government turned to the private sector for assistance and recruited a senior business executive to take charge of its contracting-out policy. The Thatcher policy was also designed to promote competition between government operations and the private sector. The approach, however, was far more proactive than the Canadian one, with Thatcher herself taking a personal interest in the application of the policy. While there was no burden of proof on government managers in Canada to justify the retention of in-house activities and services, in Britain, managers were required to demonstrate cost effectiveness to keep any commercial-type activities in-house. One can hardly overstate the importance of this decision. Indeed, contracting out was undertaken and savings realized, British officials report, only because the government "insisted" that competitive tendering be mandatory for certain government activities.[40]

The Thatcher government claimed that its contracting-out policy saved over £50 million over the first five years of its application, and that the cost of providing the same level of services went down by about 25 percent when the services were transferred to the private sector. After only a few years in office, Thatcher could point to important savings through the contracting out of services in the National Health Service and also in the "mandatory" tendering activities of catering, cleaning, laundry, security guarding, and maintenance.[41]

Both Thatcher and Mulroney, like Reagan, also made efforts to attenuate government regulations and the government-driven paper burden on the private sector. Special offices to promote deregulation and to reduce red tape were established in both governments, and they reported progress on both fronts. Thatcher and Mulroney, again like Reagan, argued that reporting requirements had been reduced, government forms made more simple, and regulations governing business activities substantially curtailed. By the late 1980s, they, like the Reagan administration, could give numerous examples where deregulation of certain sectors had been realized.[42] Mulroney could point to sweeping deregulations in the financial services industry and, among others, in the oil, gas, and transportation sectors. Certainly during her first term in office, Thatcher placed more emphasis on deregulation than on selling government assets. By the end of her first term, her government had brought in legislation designed to liberalize markets and remove entry barriers in telecommunications, transportation, oil, and gas sectors, and also measures designed to streamline statistical and licensing requirements. There were also some 120 specific items of work her government had undertaken to deregulate the economy and to simplify government-business relations. She also later introduced important regulatory reforms in the financial markets and in housing, and she published a series of reports and white papers on the matter with such telling titles as "Lifting the Burden," "Building Businesses, Not Barriers," and "Encouraging Enterprise."[43]

To be sure, all facets of privatization squared nicely with the ideology of the new political leadership since privatization held considerable promise as a way to check the growth of what the new leadership considered hyperactive governments. But privatization also held the promise of reducing the government deficit. One could debate the merits of selling government industries and argue whether or not they would become more efficient if sold. What was clear was that, once sold, the industries would look to private financial markets rather than to government for funding. In addition, selling assets meant, in many cases, an influx of cash for government coffers.

Concern over government deficits had long been a conservative theme, and the new political leadership felt quite at home speaking to that theme. And yet, by the mid 1980s, deficit fighting became a concern that would cut across the political spectrum. Left-of-center politicians began to view it as a serious problem, and some began to call for new measures to control its growth.[44]

The new conservative political leadership found it difficult to cut public expenditures, however. To cut programs means confronting interest groups, and government backbenchers representing areas directly affected by the proposed cuts (in the case of parliamentary governments) or an independently minded Congress (in the case of the United States). In addition, the early 1980s was a time of recession, rising unemployment, inflation, higher interest rates, and a steep decline in manufacturing output. All in all, it was hardly the best of economic times to introduce sweeping cuts to government programs. To contract out services and sell public assets became considerably easier politically than to cut government programs—so much so that some observers argue Britain's privatization program was politically as well as economically driven. If anything, it was more a matter of pol-

itics than economics. They also wrote about privatization as a fill-in for
the failure of Thatcher's monetarist policy and for her unwillingness to
cut as many programs as she had hoped. There is no denying that the
direct budgetary windfall flowing from British privatization efforts became substantial, bringing in about £400 million in the first year but
rising to about £5 billion a year by 1987.[45]

In the United States, Reagan began to lose budget votes in Congress, particularly after his first year in office, and some of his advisors
urged him to look to privatization as a way to reduce government
spending. Reagan went along with the advice and argued that privatization was necessary if the deficit-reduction targets set by Gramm-
Rudman laws were to be met.[46] In the end, however, privatization in
the United States brought in very little in the way of new revenues.

Brian Mulroney had insisted during the election campaign that, if
elected, his government would introduce important cuts in government programs. His Nielsen task force, it will be recalled, suggested a
number of possible program cuts but the government ignored most of
them. However, crown corporations represented an inviting target for
the Mulroney government in its trying to get at the annual deficit. Not
only would the sale of assets bring in new revenues, but the corporations also represented a drain on the government budget. The annual
cost to the Canadian government to subsidize the operations of crown
corporations amounted to over $4 billion when Mulroney came to
office.[47]

SELLING ASSETS

Thatcher may not have said much about selling public assets in her
1979 election manifesto and may have been slow off the mark in putting them up for sale when she first came to power, but she quickly
made up for lost time, and she took to selling government assets on "a
grand scale."[48] By the mid 1980s, her government had sold British
Gas, British Telecom, British Aerospace, British Petroleum, British
Steel, one million public housing units, and various public utilities. By
the time she left office, her government had sold half the industrial
assets owned by the government when she came to office. Total revenues from the sales of assets during her tenure amounted to about £20
billion. She also claimed time and again that the sale of public assets

was a key part of her strategy to transform the ailing British economy. She pointed to the success of her initiative and invited other governments to follow suit. Many did. We already saw that both Reagan and Mulroney looked to Thatcher's efforts for inspiration. Between 1979 and 1991, over a hundred countries were affected by privatization, and seventy of them introduced it as policy. During this period, we saw countries in Western Europe, Asia, and most dramatically, in Eastern Europe and Latin America accept Thatcher's clarion call.[49]

To be sure, Thatcher had plenty of scope to sell government assets on a grand scale. In contrast, the sales of public assets, particularly public industries, had to be a small part of Reagan's privatization plans because there were not that many to sell. Mulroney had more scope on this front than Reagan, although less than Thatcher.[50]

Labour governments in Britain, in particular the postwar Attlee government, had successfully nationalized the "commanding heights of the economy." The thinking, at least initially, was that it would be far too easy to make a profit in key industries like coal, rail, steel, shipbuilding, and public utilities. The solution then was to redraw the boundaries between the public and private sectors in favor of the public sector.

We already noted that Thatcher's plans to sell government assets was slow in getting off the ground. The reason in part was because she and her party while in opposition had not defined a plan to implement when in office. Indeed, the possible sale of public assets did not figure prominently at all in her speeches when she was in opposition or in her first election campaign. Thatcher, in her 1979 election campaign, referred only to the sales of the shipbuilding and aerospace industries and the National Freight Corporation. Total sales of assets from 1979 to 1980 had produced only about £400 million.[51] The lack of planning made some observers conclude that Thatcher "stumbled on privatization almost by accident."[52] The sale of assets gained momentum when its potential for reducing public sector borrowing and spending became clear. Government accounting procedures also favored the sale of assets since they counted as negative expenditures rather than revenue, thus showing a reduction in public spending. This is not to take away from the importance of political ideology or the fact that Thatcher wanted the chill winds of the market to shake up public industries that had become in her opinion "bureaucratic" and "uncontrollable." Indeed, many have stressed the importance of ideology in the development of Thatcher's privatization plans, including the sale of government assets.[53] It is simply to reiterate the point once again to say that Thatcher's plans had to do with both the government's budget and ideology. Two keen observers of Thatcher's efforts to reform government operations explain, "expectations that the privatization programme would soon run out of steam were confounded; a combination of ideological commitment and hard cash has kept it going." A strong supporter of the Thatcher reforms put it this way: "Privatization in Britain was not the end-result of an ideological victory in the world of ideas; it was something which was so successful in practice that the governments did more of it."[54]

That said, I must point out that not everyone approved of Thatcher's decision to sell government assets, and many were quick to say so. Opposition came from a number of quarters. As could be expected, the labor movement was highly critical, especially of contracting out and of the sale of assets. Thatcher's own views on the labor movement were hardly a secret: she was convinced that the unions were not only a major cause of Britain's economic woes, but that they had also brought down the Heath government. In its turn, the labor movement believed that Thatcher was turning to privatization as a means of curbing the unions' power and influence. Trade union leaders became highly critical of Thatcher's privatization efforts, while the labor movement published reports insisting that labor was being shortchanged in the plans. Companies that had been privatized, some of the reports argued, had all declared major redundancies while, at the same time, increasing management salaries substantially.[55] Criticism was even heard from friendly quarters, including from within her own party. Former Conservative prime ministers Harold Macmillan and Edward Heath became highly critical of Thatcher's plans, with Macmillan arguing that selling off government assets would no more secure a lasting economic solution than selling off the family silver. Even the right-of-center magazine *The Economist* reported on the "storm of criticism and abuse" that the privatized British Telecom-BT had created and acknowledged that "many people had concluded that privatizing a monopoly intact may be worse than leaving it in the public sector."[56]

Thatcher was anything but deterred by charges that she was selling the family silver or, for that matter, by any other charges. She weathered the storm of controversy in the wake of the first sales of government assets and pressed ahead with others. No sooner was one major sale completed than another was announced. One by one, prestigious British names like Jaguar, British Airways, and Rolls Royce went the privatization route. The Thatcher government was soon looking at privatizing assets and government activities that it would have been unthinkable to consider even in the early 1980s. By the end of her tenure as prime minister, Thatcher was looking to privatize parts of the health care system, prisons, the coal industry, and the railways.[57]

Thatcher pressed ahead, and not without assistance and encouragement from some of the country's leading business executives. She also secured the cooperation of key senior government officials to implement the process of selling off government assets. For any government, to sell assets can be as complex and difficult as it is to acquire them. The government officials were able to put in place and operate the necessary process to sell assets as varied as British Gas (valued at six billion pounds) and a single council house (valued at a few thousand pounds).[58] By most accounts, the process worked well. If there was any opposition from government officials, it was subdued. There has hardly been any criticism, from Thatcher or from her senior ministers, of the support permanent officials gave the government after it decided to sell public assets on a grand scale. In fact, some observers report that the sale of public assets met only "low-level resistance from the public service bureaucracies."[59]

To be sure, public opinion was more supportive of the sale of public assets in the 1980s than it had been for at least twenty years. Still, the push to sell came from the politicians and not from public opinion or from the bureaucracy.[60] Well aware of this, Thatcher sought to anchor the sales solidly so that future labor governments would be discouraged from renationalizing them. For this reason, her government decided to encourage ownership of the newly privatized industries by its workers and by small investors. The government also decided to sell public housing at discounts of up to 50 percent of market value.[61]

Selling industries, even a part of them, to the workers also served to attenuate somewhat the opposition of the labor movement—a group normally strongly opposed to privatization. Measures designed to encourage ownership by small investors would give rise, it was hoped, to grass-roots capitalism. For this reason, special preferences were instituted to favor applicants requesting small numbers of shares.[62] There is evidence to suggest that small investors did take up the challenge. By 1990, nine million people in Britain were shareholders, representing 20 percent of the population, compared with 7 percent in 1979 when Thatcher came to power. This and Thatcher's strong desire to see the sale of public industries successfully launched gave rise to substantial discounts on the market value of shares, discounts that varied between 14 and 100 percent. To be sure, people's capitalism did not come cheap, with financial losses resulting from underevaluations amounting to over £300 million in the case of British Airways.[63] Such losses, however, did not deter Thatcher. A former official in the British Cabinet Office explains why:

> Thatcher was profoundly convinced that the privatized firms would become so much more efficient in a short period of time that the resulting savings would more than make up for the losses in no time. It all comes back to her strong conviction that, by definition, the private sector is efficient and the public sector is not.[64]

Reagan also sought to make privatization a dominant theme in his approach to governance.[65] His administration contracted out some thirty thousand jobs to the private sector and introduced sweeping changes to government regulations. Reagan served notice that his administration would also be putting public industries and government assets up for sale. He embraced the findings of the Grace Commission, which had urged the government to privatize a number of activities through an aggressive contracting-out policy. The commission had concluded that up to 20 percent of what the federal government does could be turned over to the private sector.

Like Thatcher, however, Reagan did not come to office with a plan in hand to privatize government industries and public assets. He only "seriously" proposed to sell public assets after several months in his first term. In addition, he did so "less as part of a coordinated strategy for shrinking the public sector, than as a series of discrete and seemingly ad hoc manoeuvres designed to reduce the current year's budget deficit." Still, Reagan felt strongly that government should withdraw from most commercial-type activities. He explained: "Over the years, the Federal Government has acquired many commercial-type operations. In most cases, it would be better for the Government to get out of the business and stop competing with the private sector."[66] He also established a new office within the Office of Management and Budget to promote privatization. He later set up a presidential commission on privatization, which reported in March 1988. The report contained seventy-eight recommendations urging the administration to do much more on the privatization front.[67]

Reagan consistently put the sale of assets on his budgetary wish list to Congress. He proposed several important land sales, as well as plans to sell Conrail, marketing operations, government loans, the petroleum reserves, and the National Technical Information Service. There is little doubt that ideological criteria more than economics dictated the selection of targets to be privatized. This may, however, explain why Reagan's plans ran into difficulties. The administration sought early on to sell government land and to increase access by private developers to government-owned forests and offshore oil reserves. For Reagan and his advisors, this constituted a clear signal that government was prepared to get out of the way of the private sector so that it could get on with creating wealth and jobs. It will be recalled, however, that the move was seen as a serious threat to the environment. A public outcry resulted, and Reagan's secretary of the interior had to step down. This wounded Reagan "politically," resulting in the "administration pulling back, at least for a while, from an aggressive pursuit of the privatization goal. And its subsequent choice of privatization targets has been more modest and politically pragmatic."[68]

The sale of government industries and assets fell well short of expectations in the Reagan years. Although he tried, a good number of Reagan's proposals died on his annual budget wish list. But he was successful on some fronts. The administration successfully sold 85 percent of the government's ownership of Conrail, which brought in $1.65 billion. The Reagan administration also sold $5 billion in government loans, a coal gasification plant, an electricity-generating plant in Alaska, as well as some buildings and land.[69]

Although Mulroney was careful not to commit his party to privatizing any crown corporations, during the election campaign, there was a flurry of activities on this front within weeks of his coming to power. The minister of Industry declared after less than two months in office that the government would sell all assets of the Canada Development Investment Company within twelve months. The assets included large concerns, including de Havilland, Canadair, Teleglobe, and Eldorado Nuclear. Addressing the issue of privatizing crown corporations, the minister of Finance declared in his first budget that "Crown Corporations with a commercial value but no ongoing public policy purpose will be sold." The government also moved quickly to put other corporations up for sale and to dissolve a handful of others that were either nonactive or in direct competition with other levels of government.[70]

The government's privatization initiatives, however, were soon in difficulty as charges of favoritism were hurled by the opposition and the media over the handling of some sales. Word also leaked out that the bidding process was "in chaos." The sale of Teleglobe ran into problems when government-imposed guidelines included limits on foreign ownership. One observer labeled the sale "Act First, Think Later."[71]

Mulroney sought to put order in the government's privatization initiatives by establishing a new ministerial task force on privatization, chaired by the Treasury Board president assisted by a small secretariat inside the Treasury Board. In June 1986, the task force was turned into a cabinet committee and a minister was asked to establish a new privatization office.[72] The secretariat (and later the Office of Privatization and Regulatory Affairs) set out to "manage better" the various activities, including overseeing the preparation of necessary legislation of the sales already announced. The office also pressed ahead with the development of a comprehensive privatization plan. The plan called for a series of initiatives, some of which could be carried out quickly (that is, over six months), while others took a medium or longer term. The thinking was always to have plans for the privatization of crown corporations on the shelf so that initiatives could be pursued when the economic and market conditions were right. In preparing the plan, it was decided that all crown corporations would be considered for privatization and that the onus was on ministers to explain why they ought not to be involved. Candidates for privatization would be identified on the basis of two principles: if they were no longer serving public policy purposes, or if they had sufficient financial viability and prospects to attract investors. The office quickly identified two flagship candidates—Air Canada and Petro-Canada—and about fifteen others.

Notwithstanding the establishment of a privatization office, the development of a comprehensive plan, and the big push in Mulroney's first months in office to act quickly on the issue, the government's privatization plan ground almost to a halt by 1987.[73] For one thing, the policy demanding justification as to why a crown corporation ought not to be privatized proved difficult to apply in practice. Many ministers simply ignored it, in part because the Department of Finance insisted that all proceeds from the sale of crown corporations or subsidiaries should go to the Consolidated Revenue Fund. As ministers became more familiar with their departments and the crown corporations for which they were responsible, they increasingly resisted the department's position. This position proved particularly controversial when crown corporations sought to sell some of their subsidiaries. Ministers and departments argued that the proceeds from the sales should be plowed back into the parent crown corporation, while Finance still insisted that they go into the Consolidated Revenue Fund. Finance's position prevailed and ministers and crown corporations lost interest in pursuing plans to privatize their subsidiaries.[74]

Mulroney's own commitment to selling public assets also wavered from time to time. Initially, at least, he eschewed the full rhetorical language of privatization but later began to speak cautiously about it. He decided to employ the idea "selectively" in some regions of the country and to "show the right wing of the Conservative caucus and the business community" that he was moving in the right direction. Indeed, Mulroney spoke often about the need to privatize crown corporations, but when the time came to make a firm decision, he backed down. A case in point was Air Canada. His government had agreed, as part of its comprehensive privatization plan, to sell the government-owned airline. However, coming out of a private meeting with a Quebec labor leader and a long-standing acquaintance, Mulroney announced that he had assured his friend that Air Canada was not for sale. Mulroney also backed down on specific privatization initiatives when strong political pressure, "particularly the regional factor," came into play.[75]

In addition, in Canada, the sale of government assets did not help in getting the government's fiscal house in order as much as had been initially envisaged. In some instances, the government on its book carried a debt load for a crown corporation that exceeded market value. Selling the corporation would have meant that the government would have had to absorb the difference, thus showing an increase in the government's net debt. In other instances, however, fiscal pressure pushed Mulroney to flip-flop once again. By 1989, Air Canada urgently required an infusion of equity to upgrade its aging fleet of airplanes, and it asked the government to come up with $300 million cash or to turn to privatization. Facing an annual deficit of over $30 billion, Mulroney agreed with the minister of Finance that it would be unadvisable for the government to come up with the necessary funding. The government decided to make a share offering, which raised about $250 million, and agreed to let Air Canada keep the proceeds rather than have the funds go to the Consolidated Revenue Fund.[76]

LOOKING BACK

Thatcher gave privatization a new look and new political support. She broadened its definition considerably by viewing it as a synonym for any action that reduces the role of government and expands that of the private sector. The term *privatization* now means contracting out and deregulation, as well as selling public assets—in short, the term encompassed a return to "profitable private motivation" of things and activities that had become lethargic or in decline either through state ownership or government reputation.[77] Both Reagan and Mulroney also tried to steer their governments in that direction. Certainly, the new broader definition squared nicely with the conservative ideology. It spoke to the view that governments had become so big they were no longer manageable and that, in any event, government was by definition inefficient. One permanent official explained:

> There is a view particularly prevalent among the more conservative politicians that government bureaucracies can never get it right and that they keep repeating mistakes over and over again, no matter how inefficient. It suggests that if government bureaucracies had introduced the Edsel they would still be producing it. To them the solution is easy—privatize government activities.[78]

The enlarged definition of privatization also spoke to the general hostility the new political leadership felt toward the public sector and nationalized industries. In brief, government action was inhibiting the functioning of the private sector—hence the decision on deregulation;

it was interfering with spontaneous acts of charity and self-help—hence load shedding. The three political leaders also used the new definition to send a message to the civil service that it had no inherent right to provide public services if others could do it better or more efficiently.[79]

There was another powerful force fueling privatization efforts, and that was the need to control government spending. Thatcher, Reagan, and Mulroney all pledged to get their government budgets quickly back in a surplus position. In Britain, the government deficit "disappeared in 1987–88 in large part from the dramatic increase in privatization receipts."[80] Reagan claimed that he would have a balanced budget before the end of his first mandate. Things, however, proved considerably more difficult once he was in office. Indeed, the U.S. deficit grew from $900 billion in 1980 to $1.6 trillion by 1984. Reagan's advisors argued that privatization held more promise to control the deficit than did cuts in government spending. His administration was successful in introducing sweeping deregulation and in contracting out a substantial number of government jobs. The sale of government assets, however, made no appreciable difference in bringing down government borrowing requirements. This was true partly because, as noted earlier, Reagan's privatization plan got off to a poor start with accusations that it posed a serious threat to the environment and partly because Reagan had a lot less to sell than Thatcher. Mulroney had much more to sell, for example, state-owned enterprises employed nearly 8 percent of the labor force when he came to office, compared with 1.7 percent in the United States. The Mulroney government did successfully deregulate a number of sectors but fell far short of his party's expectations in selling public assets. In addition, the Mulroney government's attempts to contract out government jobs or activities fell far short of what Thatcher and Reagan accomplished.

Still, all three leaders received strong support in their efforts to turn government activities over to the private sector. The business and financial communities had long contributed handsomely to the political parties in power and had long extolled the virtues of the market. They pushed hard for privatization and contracting out, as did the more conservative elements of the three parties. They were not alone in asking for radical or new solutions. The public mood, as we have already seen, was hardly sympathetic to public bureaucracies, and there was a growing skepticism about the efficiency of large government agencies. New policy prescriptions were in demand, if only because there was a fairly widespread view that the old ones were thought to have failed.[81] The new enlarged definition of privatization became a key part of the new solutions.

There is solid evidence that permanent public servants supported the efforts to sell public assets and to deregulate the economy. In the case of Britain and Canada, senior permanent officials played a key advisory role in selling public assets and successfully put in place a process to implement the decisions from initial assessment through final sale. They developed sophisticated techniques to transfer public enterprises to the private sector.[82] They also played a pivotal role in all three countries in putting in place the mechanisms to deregulate the economies. If Reagan and Mulroney were not as successful in selling public enterprises and public assets as they had initially hoped, it had everything to do with a poor political strategy (the environment lobby in the United States, for example) or lack of political will (in Mulroney, for example). It had very little to do with civil service resistance.

One can argue that deregulation and the selling of public enterprises did not directly attack the interests of the bureaucracy. Indeed, one could argue that self-interested bureaucrats saw the selling of public enterprises as a much better way to control the growth in government spending than cuts in government departments, agencies, and programs. Some also noted that senior managers in public enterprises saw full privatization as a way to switch to less restrictive salaries and more generous perks.[83]

The contracting out of government jobs is quite another matter. It seeks to move "government" jobs to the private sector and offers limited potential for senior public servants to cross over to the private sector.[84] It is interesting that contracting out was more successful in Britain and in the United States where policies were put in place requiring government managers to demonstrate cost effectiveness if they were to keep in-house commercial-type activities. In Canada, although a comparable policy existed, it was not applied and Mulroney's make-or-buy policy had little impact.

In any event, no matter how broadly applied, privatization could hardly affect all government operations. To be sure, the size of government could be reduced, and Thatcher, Reagan and Mulroney were moving in this direction. However, they recognized that a wide range of activities would remain in the public sector and that large-scale government was here to stay. So Thatcher, Reagan, and Mulroney would put in place measures to ensure that these activities would be better managed in future. All three would stress the importance of management in government, and "public management" became the new fad. However, others before them—notably Hoover, Glassco, and Fulton—had also stressed this need. In the 1960s and the 1970s, it was widely assumed that if the heavy hand of bureaucracy were removed, government administrators would learn to manage their operations more effectively. The call then was to "let the managers manage." The consensus was that the call had not been heard and that, if anything, government had become less manageable—a theme Thatcher, Reagan, and Mulroney exploited fully in their election campaigns. Their message now changed from "let the managers manage" to "make the managers manage."

7

Looking to Management

IN LOOKING to the private sector for inspiration, Thatcher, Reagan, and Mulroney's ideology on governance differed radically from that which gave rise to traditional thinking on public administration. The private sector works from the bottom up, with the hidden hand of the market providing the key signals.[1] Business firms employ the most advanced management practices to interpret these signals and marshal their resources as efficiently as possible to provide a solid base for competing in the marketplace.[2] To be sure, a corporation's senior management will lay down the broad corporate strategy to which everyone down the line must rally, but once the strategy is defined, managers are often free to improvise and to make decisions on the spot, so long as their operations turn a profit. Objectives are easily understood, and senior executives see no reason why they should not delegate authority, as long as the objectives are being met. Since the objectives are straightforward, it is also easy to check on the results.

The public sector works from the top down. According to Wilson's politics-administration dichotomy, those at the top make the decisions, which the lower ranks implement, following carefully prescribed rules and regulations. The word *management* scarcely appeared in government operations until the 1950s and 1960s with the advent of the Hoover commissions, Glassco, Fulton, PPBS, and PAR. When it did appear, it was often to signal "management by direction," designed to tie "staff into a closely organized set of tasks." The term *administration* rather than *management* best described government operations; administrators rather than managers were in charge. The role of administrator involved the applying of formalized procedures and somehow reconciling the separate priorities of politics and administration. It is important to recognize that the concept of administration in government acquired its definition when much of the government's work was routine and predictable.[3] When the scope of government activities

172

expanded into various areas, including the provision of goods and services, some people began to question whether traditional administration, with its rule-bound organizations and behavior, was still appropriate to the requirements of the modern state. Such questions were raised by Hoover, Glassco, and Fulton, but in the end these commissions had limited impact on government operations or did not change them in the direction hoped.

The new political leadership raised once again the need for management discipline in government operations. This time, the solution was seen as relatively straightforward: government bureaucracy should be reduced by contracting out activities to the private sector and by introducing a new management culture for the bureaucrats who remain. Nevil Johnson explains that the notion of introducing a management culture to government is derived from commercial operations. It has ideological overtones, emphasizes the effective use of resources of all kinds, is seen as dynamic, and constitutes a remedy for the defects of administration. Christopher Pollitt is more blunt. He argues simply that "managerialism needs to be understood as an ideology."[4]

To introduce a new management culture to government operations, notwithstanding its strong ideological underpinning, is no small task. Taken at face value, the rhetoric of Thatcher, Reagan, and Mulroney on the issue meant setting the civil service at its own throat. It meant a new mind-set, a new vocabulary, and a proliferation of management techniques and procedures to force government operations to become more frugal and more efficient, and it required public servants willing to make tough management decisions. Senior government officials would no longer be called administrators, principal officers, senior finance or personnel officers, or assistant directors. Now they were to be called managers.[5]

Changing the vocabulary was the easy part. Changing a mind-set anchored in years of tradition and in a firmly entrenched bureaucratic culture was another matter. Quite apart from having to rethink the myriad rules and other mechanisms designed to check administrative errors, it is a fact that both permanent government officials and politicians have long been mesmerized by the glamour of policy at the expense of innovative management. The challenge was to refocus the role of the civil service so as to stress management rather than policy-making. In any event, the new political leadership felt that the policy advisory role of the civil service was "deeply illegitimate." Nonelected officials had become too powerful in shaping policy, and it was important to send them back to a more legitimate role. Their job was to implement policy decisions and to manage government resources more efficiently. The new political leadership felt that to subscribe firmly to a set of political beliefs, to have partisan policy advisors on the public payroll and pollsters interacting with party strategists would make this possible and render obsolete the "Sir Humphrey" style of policy-making.[6]

Adjusting to the new role would not be easy, however. The road to the top for career public servants has more often than not been through policy rather than administration. "Have policy, will travel" had long been the byword for the ambitious in government. This is true even in the United States where, although partisan professionals hold many of the senior policy positions, it remains that top permanent officials "often preside baronially over policy domains." For these career officials, occupying senior policy positions is "the reward of a lifetime of work" and learning how to be "very sensitive to both congressional and presidential pressures" is an important part of their work.[7] In any event, senior career civil servants are trained as professionals and have over the years developed considerable policy expertise in their areas of work. They are thus frequently better positioned than political appointees to identify new policy directions.[8]

Looking back on his experience in government, Derek Rayner wrote, "the costs of administrating the policies were regarded as the candle-ends of public expenditure." He went on to report that he found an obsession with policy matters and a general hostility to management in government. The British civil service, he maintained, represents "a huge slice of the Nation's best talents. It is ironic that, despite the talent, the quality of so much Whitehall management should be so low and that leadership has too often in the past fallen into the hands of those who know nothing of management and despise those who do."[9] In short, the glamour of government work over the years in the three countries surveyed has been in policy, not in administration. Indeed, senior officials have been happy to live with elaborate rules and regulations, so long as they were free to play a policy role. The thinking in some quarters is that the functional units were there to worry about rules dealing with personnel, administration, and financial matters. The senior official's job was to concentrate on politicians and policy issues. Some go so far as to argue that in government (particularly in Britain and Canada) the managing of major departmental programs traditionally has been a job for "junior personnel or *failed* administrative class people who are seen by the mandarins as not being able to make it to the top levels."[10]

Thatcher, Reagan, and Mulroney all served notice through subtle, and at times less than subtle messages that management abilities and (particularly in the case of Reagan, but by no means exclusively so) loyalty to ideology rather than policy skills constituted the new road to the top. Having carved out the broad policy direction they intended to pursue, the three leaders now wanted competent managers on their team, "doers" rather than "tinkerers," and certainly not "can't do" types. The message was heard. Senior government officials in all three countries spoke as never before about the need to strengthen management practices. Sir Robin Butler, the British secretary of the cabinet and head of the Home Office, made management the central theme of his Redcliffe-Maud Memorial Lecture. He spoke about the road to "better management in government," the need for greater "freedom for local managers," and he compared the management of certain government units to a "subsidiary of ICI."[11] No secretary to the cabinet in Britain before the 1980s would have made better management and the need to empower local managers the underlying themes of his lecture. Paul Tellier, Canada's secretary to the cabinet, also made management the central theme of his John Carson Lecture and hardly touched on the traditional issues of public administration.[12] In the United States, the call for stronger management was made time and again by Reagan appointees, by members of the Senior Executive Service, and by the National Academy of Public Administration (NAPA). The academy published a report in 1983 entitled *Revitalizing Federal Management: Managers and Their Overburdened Systems.* The report carried the central message of its title throughout, insisting that the current government system and the decision-making process "reduce rather than enhance management effectiveness."[13]

This also represented a relatively new interest in management on the part of the academy. The public administration literature in the three countries had been accused of being dominated by political scientists, of being "information rich" but "skills poor," of being overly preoccupied with ethical and normative issues, and of offering little guidance for managers of public organizations. The public policy literature, meanwhile, was considered to be concerned too much with policy decisions and the policy-making process and not enough with the role of public managers in this process. In short, until Thatcher, Reagan, and Mulroney came to power, it was generally agreed that public management had been underemphasized in both practice and research.[14]

As far as practice is concerned, however, this underemphasis was not for want of trying. Zero Base Budgeting, PPBS, PAR, and other reform measures had all been designed to improve management in government—and all were consistently disappointing. When the scrutinies and the FMI were introduced, some senior public servants even wondered aloud whether they constituted new "challenges or familiar prescriptions?"[15] There is no denying that there is a common thread consisting of performance indicators, evaluation techniques, and review systems linking all reform measures introduced from the mid 1960s onward.

The risk for the new political leadership was that, again, little might actually change; the old failings might live on within the new vocabulary. However, the fact that previous efforts had bogged down only served to stiffen the resolve of the three leaders, who all arrived in office announcing important cuts in their civil service. Reagan's attempt, very early in his first term, to break the air controllers' strike by firing the controllers and hiring replacements left no doubt that he was prepared to engage in confrontational politics. Mulroney established the new chief-of-staff position in all ministerial offices to check the influence of civil servants over policy. And all three invited business executives to carry out a turnaround-management exercise on government operations.

The failures of institutional reforms in the 1960s and 1970s convinced Thatcher, Reagan, and Mulroney that they should keep government reorganization to a minimum, at least in their first months in office, and instead concentrate their efforts at the micro level, that is, the manager's level. The intent of previous efforts such as PPBS had been to increase efficiency, performance, and accountability government-wide. These efforts had been centralized and hierarchical and involved specific goals and measurements to determine if they were being met.

The new approach would concentrate as much on specific organizational units as it would on government-wide systems. It sought to transform public administrators into managers who could think, act, and perform like private sector managers and run their government operations like private concerns. For example, the contracting-out policy and the scrutinies looked at the efficiency of individual units, while the FMI was designed not just to provide higher management with aggregate numbers on financial commitments but also to provide "managers at successive levels down the line with the information they need to do their job properly."[16] The goal was to achieve greater efficiency, results, performance, and value for money in individual government operations. Traditional approaches to public administration (the argument went) had overlooked these aspects, concentrating as they did on the policy advisory function, on the values of probity, and on the maintenance of the process. In short, public administration had not kept pace with the increasing scale, scope, and costs of modern government. The new managerialism would seek to break this pattern and to bring home the point that management in government involved a great deal more than controlling and supervising routine functions so that senior officials could be free to concentrate on policy issues.

The new managerialism had three underlying themes: empowerment, improving service to clients, and strengthening efficiency in government operations. At least the last two would cut across jurisdictional boundaries. The first, empowerment, was a key concern of both Thatcher and Mulroney, while Reagan sent out mixed signals. Still, it was envisaged that, when combined, the three themes would point the way to a new management culture in the civil service and to lasting reforms.[17]

EMPOWERMENT

The term *management* became the buzz word of the new political leadership, and the search was on to find "doers rather than thinkers."[18] Doers, to be effective, require scope to take decisions, and "empowerment" became one of the new fashions of the 1980s. Indeed, the term *empowerment* goes to the very heart of the new leadership's ideology on governance. It emphasizes the importance of managers' taking the lead, getting things done, and dealing with clients and their needs. This is not to suggest for a moment that the new leadership rushed headlong into doing away with all centrally prescribed rules or in delegating full decision-making authority to permanent officials. In some instances this was done, in others it was not. In all cases, mixed signals were sent out. To be sure, there was a contradiction between the desire to empower managers, as large private sector firms were doing, and the strongly held reservations that the three leaders shared about the capacity of bureaucracy and bureaucrats to be efficient.

The literature on private sector management is replete with assertions that centrally regulated financial and personnel rules must be kept to a minimum. Henry Mintzberg argues that the central techno-structure must be kept lean so that line managers are left unencumbered. In their widely read book *In Search of Excellence*, Thomas Peters and Robert Waterman stress such issues as the need for simplified forms, for autonomy, and for entrepreneurship, the importance of being close to the customer and of instilling a bias for action among managers. Peter Block wrote about "empowering managers" as the single most important building block to success in business, insisting that the deepest wish of all employees is to contribute something meaningful. Employees—and in particular managers—can only do this if the organization is prepared to trust them to make decisions.[19]

Although their actions sometimes pointed in an opposite direction, Thatcher, Reagan, and Mulroney spoke the language of Peters and Waterman. Thatcher often referred to "decentralizing management responsibilities," Reagan spoke of "simplifying government," Mulroney referred to the need to turn the bureaucratic culture upside down and "place as much authority as possible in the hands of front line employees and managers."[20]

Empowerment became fashionable first in the private sector. When the concept arrived in government, however, its interpretation was not adapted to fit the different needs of the public sector. One government task force explained: "Empowerment cannot be accommodated within the traditional command and control culture: indeed, it offers a fundamental challenge to that culture." Borrowing from what was being taught in the schools of business, government agencies and units were asked to prepare "mission statements" and to restructure their management practices.[21] Specifically, they were asked to empower their managers to encourage them and their employees

> to try new ways of achieving goals, motivating them to be creative and innovative in improving the service they deliver. Empowerment asks employees to assume responsibility for change and to be accountable for their actions within an environment which accepts a degree of risk-taking and acknowledges intent as well as results. Empowerment puts a premium on energy.[22]

Thus, as in the private sector, hierarchy came under attack in government, at least in published reports and speeches given by politicians and senior public servants.[23]

Thatcher's FMI claimed to "empower budget-holders to make operational management decisions." Its underlying goal was to encourage middle-rank public servants to think of themselves as managers first, free to take action whenever circumstances required. Thatcher's target was the mandarins—the cautious careerists who constantly did battle in favor of the status quo. She also sought to rid the system of its rigid rules, to place responsibility for decision making squarely on the shoulders of line managers, and to instill in them a "bias for action." With an eye to deregulation, her "coherent and integrated culture of good management" also took dead aim at centrally prescribed rules on financial and human resources, and she launched a thorough review of such rules.[24]

Reagan's favorite solution to empower decision makers was to privatize or contract out government activities. Well aware that he could not contract out everything, he pledged in his 1981 inaugural speech not "to do away with Government but rather to make it work." After only a few years in office, he launched his *President's Management Improvement Program: Reform 88*. Because, he claimed, solid management practices had not over the years been a priority in Washington, a "costly, incompatible hodgepodge of management systems with ill-defined lines of responsibility had been spawned." There were many facets to his *Reform 88* initiative, ranging from new measures to curb waste and fraud in government operations to the development of new "management systems."[25]

Reagan's *Reform 88* also sought to empower line managers.[26] The initiative directed "all" executive departments and agencies to take a hard look at their management systems, to put in place performance measurements, and to give top-level managers the information and flexibility they needed "to manage." Like Thatcher, Reagan asked that decision making in government be "deregulated" and that officials borrow the best management practices from the business community. He asked that "overhead cost, and paper burden," be reduced to a minimum and that incentives to improve government operations be introduced. He also sought to remove constraints to good management, to free managers to make sound decisions. He criticized restrictions on closing "unneeded offices," redundant but legislated report requirements, and outdated human resources management directives. Reagan summed up his reform measures: "The strategy is to place the decision-making responsibility with agency heads and to establish a productivity measurement system to record the results."[27]

Mulroney also announced a plan to overhaul government management practices in Canada, a little over a year after coming to power. He labeled the initiative Increased Ministerial Authority and Accountability (IMAA). His minister of Finance explained that IMAA would give "individual ministers and their departmental managers . . . more latitude and more direct responsibility to manage the resources entrusted to them so that they can react quickly and effectively to the changing environment." The Treasury Board president added, "We will be more concerned with what departments do both in program results and in meeting service-wide policy objectives and less concerned with how well procedural rules are followed." The IMAA initiative is being implemented through two complementary actions: a gradual reduction in centrally prescribed rules and controls; and the introduction of agreements between the Treasury Board and individual operating departments, under which departments are given greater freedom of action and flexibility in the use of the funds voted to them by Parliament. In return, departments are asked to define concrete performance commitments, "indicators and targets related to program delivery."[28]

The Treasury Board did make some progress in reducing reporting requirements and in limiting its role in the day-to-day operations of line departments. Departments can now sponsor conferences without having to secure Treasury Board approval; the ceiling on competitive contracts for construction and consulting without reference to the board has been doubled; departments can classify positions on their own, except in the management category, and also undertake some organizational changes without approval. The information required in preparing annual expenditure budgets has also been reduced and simplified, and the Treasury Board's approval process in several areas has been streamlined.[29]

The second IMAA initiative involves the Treasury Board Memoranda of Understanding (MOU) with departments to provide them with much greater management flexibility on a number of fronts. The MOUs not only provide for greater flexibility, they also lay out how departments will be held accountable for the efficient use of resources. This involves accountability sessions with the Treasury Board secretariat, the preparation of an annual management report, performance indicators, and a "major accountability review" in the final year of the three-year agreement.[30]

All three leaders also sought to anchor an empowerment culture in their bureaucracies by borrowing personnel from the private sector. It was felt that business executives, including middle-level ones, know intuitively the management style that leads to the development of an empowerment culture. Thatcher, Reagan, and Mulroney either introduced or considerably strengthened existing government-business "exchange" programs, which promote the exchange of public and private sector managers. To be sure, people from outside government have always come in for a period of time to serve in the public sector. The new political leadership, however, took this a step further by setting up blue-ribbon committees to promote an exchange of personnel between the public and private sectors and by encouraging a constant flow of business executives into government to "energize and revitalize inert bureaucracies, insisting on higher performance standards and being free to manage."[31] Conversely, it was assumed that government managers going to work in business for a while would come back imbued with sound management practices and with a "bias for action."

The three leaders also took a strong interest in public service appointments, convinced that if their management revolution was to succeed they needed senior managers sympathetic to their goals. "A radical government," one of Thatcher's key advisors argued, needs "a radically minded civil service."[32] Thatcher did not, as her predecessors often did, simply rubber-stamp appointments to the permanent secretary level from a list of candidates put forward by a handful of the most senior permanent secretaries (much more often than not the list only had one candidate). She insisted on a choice of candidates, and at times she turned all of them down and asked for a new list. She also freely made her views known on candidates for promotions to levels below that of permanent secretary, traditionally the prerogative of the Civil Service Commission. Thatcher appointed several permanent secretaries who were younger than usual, who showed an interest in management matters rather than policy, and who had a style more to her liking. At the risk of oversimplification, I would say they embraced a "can do" approach rather than a "stuffy" and "detached" style "preoccupied with the finer points of policy."[33] Officials report that her choice did not rest on the political party affiliation or political ideology of the candidates, which in any event were rarely, if ever, known to her or the Cabinet Office. She wanted "to feel satisfied," however, "that newly appointed permanent secretaries were effective managers and not simply good at policy."[34]

Reagan was free to staff the upper echelons of the American civil service with political appointees, and he did. His appointees had to pass a litmus test of loyalty to the Reagan agenda. They were advised to avoid catching "Potomac fever," that is, adopting the traditional characteristics of bureaucrats. They were instructed to employ their powers energetically to overcome the tendency of career bureaucrats to pursue their own agenda and to continue with established ways. Indeed, Reagan and his advisors carried their litmus test beyond political appointees. They also looked to upper-level career officials to sort out who supported Reagan's agenda and put those who did not "on the shelf."[35]

Mulroney also sought to appoint doers rather than bureaucrats to senior positions. Although in the end he was not nearly as successful as he had hoped, he turned to business executives to fill senior government positions on a permanent basis. He and his advisors also looked around the civil service to identify career officials who had a neoconservative bent and whose image was not that of the traditional bureaucrat. Two students of Canadian public administration who studied senior public service appointments concluded that many of the career bureaucrats promoted to the most senior levels demonstrated either a partisan attachment to the governing political elite or were sympathetic to their policies.[36]

SERVICE TO CLIENTS

The emphasis placed on reform at the micro level, or program level, also led governments to review the quality of the services they were delivering to the public. This became another fashion of the 1980s, a fashion that caught on in many countries. Organization for Economic Cooperation and Development members urged the organization to launch a number of initiatives in this area. This it did, and a major report was tabled in 1987. The report opens with a provocative message: "Each OECD member country has a public service. Everybody can agree that it is public. But the public often wonder whom it serves. If the public service already exists to serve the public, then why are so many OECD governments embarking on campaigns to make it happen?" The report goes on to argue that not enough emphasis has been placed on improving service to clients and to report on the reasons. These include "old" bureaucratic values, bureaucratic hierarchy, and weak internal and external communication systems. The report concludes by urging governments to undertake "real" reforms and not simply to deal with "cosmetics." It calls for stronger political leadership, to adjust the workings of the public service, and to introduce to government operations the notion of accountability to clients.[37]

Political leaders—including Thatcher, Reagan, and Mulroney—became convinced that to empower employees working at the "point of delivery" constituted a key element in any attempt to reform bureaucracy and improve the quality of service to the public. It is not too much of an exaggeration to write that from the days of Franklin D. Roosevelt to the late 1970s, it was widely accepted that the professional bureaucrat knew better than anyone else how to run government programs. The political leadership of the 1980s set out to challenge this view. Privatization, contracting out, and the issuance of vouchers for public goods all flowed out of this challenge. One not only heard of empowering middle-level managers in government, but increasingly of empowering the "clients" and "consumers" of government services.[38] Civil servants again understood the message. Some British officials reported that "increasingly, consumers expect to determine publicly standards of service and quality. They are no longer prepared to accept the standards laid down by producers often with an eye more to their own convenience than to that of their customers."[39] In Canada, a government white paper declared that "The Government wants to create a client-oriented Public Service, a major change since the Public Service has not been used to regarding Canadians as clients."[40]

These statements and, indeed, the whole emphasis on service to the public are rooted in the public choice literature, which argues that bureaucracies are inefficient at least in part because sponsors and ultimately clients have so little influence in shaping the programs and services and in deciding whether they should continue or be terminated. The emphasis on service to the public is also borrowed from the private sector. The thinking is that successful businesses stay close to the customer, and so should government.

Whatever its inspiration, the emphasis on service to the public speaks once again to the goal of changing the "culture of Whitehall," eradicating "Potomac fever," and altering the attitude of the "Ottawa mandarins." Staying close to the customer, it was felt, would lead to a new bureaucratic culture that would be more open and responsive and that would place a stronger emphasis on management. A technique that came in fashion in the business community in the 1980s to ensure that greater attention was paid to the customer was the corporate "mission statement." These brief statements are designed to instill a central purpose in all employees as they go about their work. Government departments and agencies soon jumped on the bandwagon, holding staff meeting after staff meeting to define a central mission to which all employees could relate. Once again, the client was invariably put front and center. In Canada, for example, each government department and agency was directed

> to assess its management practices and to develop a mission statement. This statement should be developed in close consultation with employees at all levels, and provide members of the department with a charter to guide their activities. It should reflect the mission of the Public Service generally, support the importance of an adaptable and consultative management, and incorporate specific service-oriented objectives.[41]

The goal here, once again, was to break down formal systems of control that lead to inaction and cautious behavior. To emphasize the customer would, it was hoped, release managers and employees all the way down the line to be innovative and to act.

It is hardly possible to overstate the point that the purpose of empowering public servants at the point of delivery was not only to improve the delivery of government programs but also to open up the government bureaucracy. This would serve a number of objectives. It would force bureaucrats to deal directly with the complaints of the consumers, since they would no longer be able to hide behind centrally prescribed rules and controls. This would empower the public or the customer of government programs and force bureaucrats to deal with the public view about what ought to be done. Invariably, this would serve to attenuate the influence of career officials on government programs.

A new emphasis on service to the public would also bring home the point that the public service needed to refocus its role, away from policy and toward management. It would drive home the message that the new political leadership wanted people who "had handled a product" and who had "actually talked to clients" to rise to the top, rather than the policy specialist.[42] In short, the focus on clients as the most important function in government would encourage the ambitious to look to the operational side of government in carving out a career path.

Looking to clients would also ensure a leaner, more frugal government. For one thing, it meant a move toward more simple organization, with government departments and agencies concentrating on their "core business" or on their programs. Again, the private sector provided the inspiration. Large multinational firms began to shed jobs in their "corpocracies" during the deep recession of the early 1980s. These corpocracies, it was concluded, were taking more from the business units than they were giving to them. The likes of GE, EXXON, AT&T, and BP had reduced their overhead, all the while seeing their businesses "grow in number, size and complexity" (a development that was not lost on Thatcher, Reagan, Mulroney, and their advisors). The businesses did this by contracting out, by "delayering," and by dramatically cutting back head office staff. This served to place in the hands of those closest to the problem the capacity to deal with the problems and create the solution. One chief executive officer of a leading private firm summed up the view when he observed, "If you want to know how to do a job right, ask the people who are doing it. Don't have some corporate bureaucracy tell them how to do it."[43]

Large businesses began to "delayer" their management structures in the early 1980s. In the United States alone, private firms were able to shed some five hundred thousand middle-management positions between 1980 and 1985. By the mid 1980s, the public sector jumped on the bandwagon, and "delayering" became the fashion in London, Washington, and Ottawa. There would be fewer managers, and those who remained would be asked to play a different role in future. Their new role would be geared to "leading" and "coaching" employees whose own responsibilities would now be "radically upgraded" to deal with clients.[44]

The new role called for doing away with many of the controls that had been built up over the years to bring a degree of stability in what is invariably a politically charged environment.[45] Service to the public entailed a higher degree of decentralization, deregulation, and delegation of decision-making authority. It also meant that senior government officials would move into uncharted territory. They could no longer rely on a hierarchical process of institutionalized regulation designed to secure conformity to prescribed rules and to avoid error. They would have to embrace new concepts, such as the importance of defining a vision or mission, of communicating this vision down through the organization, of "empowering" operational staff, and of building up a framework of shared values. They would also have to streamline their departments in order to ensure "simplicity" and clarity of purpose in their organization. More important, politicians would have to trust the newly empowered bureaucrats to make the right decisions in their dealings with their clients. This was no small task. As we have seen, politicians had shown time and again a general disdain for public bureaucracies and had accused bureaucrats, among other things, of being uncreative, lethargic, and insensitive. To make the new managerialism work required a new mind-set, not just on the part of career government officials but also on the part of politicians.

THE SEARCH FOR EFFICIENCY AND CONTROL

Those who espoused the new approach argued that traditional government bureaucracy is more concerned with the administration of rules and the maintenance of formal controls than with action and the efficient management of resources; that it focuses too much on policy advice and not enough on sound management practices. From the

1930s to the late 1970s, policy skills were what counted in the civil service. For much of this period, the perfect civil servant in a nonpolicy role was one who demonstrated "due respect for rules and regulations and red tape." No one was ever rewarded for taking risks, no matter how well the risks paid off in the long run. And no one was rewarded for sidestepping rules, regulations, and red tape.[46]

Managerialism, it is argued, is designed to deal with these lacunae head-on. It emphasizes management and directs officials in their day-to-day work to look to clients or to the public rather than to the requirements of the system. Managerialism bears the clear imprint of Thatcher, Reagan, and Mulroney, and one of its main objectives was to get at "mismanagement and waste" in government.

The managerialist school wants to debureaucratize the system, trim bloated bureaucracies, improve productivity, encourage creativity, reward efficiency, and again, place clients first. To accomplish this, management practices found in the private sector should be imported to government operations. The proponents of managerialism also argue that government managers must be taught how to manage. Some even insist that the politicians should become the managers of both policy and administration.[47]

Although managerialism has spread to numerous governments (including many beyond the three we are studying), it would be wrong to assume that the school flows out of an articulate, conceptually sound and coherent strategy. It has a number of inherent inconsistencies and contradictions. Nowhere is this more apparent than in its attempt to improve efficiency in government operations and to eliminate waste and mismanagement. This objective comes up squarely against another—the desire to reduce bureaucratic power over government decision making and to return control over their bureaucracies to the politicians. The pursuit of the two objectives invariably gives rise to tensions, if not outright contradictions, in the implementation of both sets of ideas.[48]

To regain control over their bureaucracies requires some degree of centralization for prime ministers and presidents and their ministers and advisors if they are to adopt a hands-on approach in directing government operations. Indeed, some would also insist on the necessity not only of centralization but also of new financial and administrative controls if waste, fraud, and mismanagement are to be eliminated. Yet, managerialism points the other way—to clients, to empowerment, to making the manager manage, to mission statements, and to the need for "trusting employees." This may well explain why Thatcher's FMI initiatives had two objectives: to provide managers with the necessary information to manage their operations better, and to provide the center, the Treasury, with information on how well those managers were doing. Thatcher also urged her ministers to take a strong interest in the implementation of the FMI and to become managers of their departments. Mulroney's IMAA initiative clearly identified ministers as the target for increased authority. Mulroney also borrowed a page from the Americans and appointed a chief of staff in all ministerial offices. The appointments were both political and senior, and they were made expressly to check the influence of career public servants.

Not long after coming to office, the Reagan transition team was handed a copy of the study prepared by NAPA, which called for sweeping deregulation of the governmental decision-making process. It argued that "the role of the government manager was being undervalued and that management systems had become burdensome and constraining" and concluded that the systems serve to "choke off the kind of individual innovation and initiatives which are crucial to real management effectiveness."[49] The report made a number of recommendations all around the theme of providing more authority and discretion to individual managers—in short, empowerment.

Reagan did embrace a number of features of the managerialist school. His administration certainly spoke about empowerment, placing new emphasis on clients, defining a mission, and encouraging management leadership in government agencies.[50] His *Reform 88* sought to simplify government management systems, establish clear lines of responsibility, and strengthen agency delivery systems to ensure better services for clients.

The Reagan administration, however, also took a number of steps in the opposite direction. Reagan believed in the politics-administration dichotomy. He wanted nothing from career officials except management and the implementation of decisions. His first head of the Office of Personnel Management argued emphatically in favor of a "firm demarcation separating policy and administration." Reagan and his most senior advisors carefully screened all political appointees to ensure loyalty to their conservative agenda and followed up with measures to promote a strong "cohesion" among them.[51] The administration also sought to control the appointments of senior career officials.

Reform 88 also claimed to be concerned with "reducing waste, fraud, abuse and improving productivity." Reagan announced in March 1981 the establishment of a president's council on integrity and efficiency to make recommendations on how to manage financial resources more efficiently. The council consisted of the inspector generals of the departments and agencies, the deputy director of the Office of Management and Budget, and six other appointees. One of the main aims of the council was to broaden the impact and coverage of the inspector general's role. On arriving in office, Reagan fired all inspectors general appointed by Carter. He wanted his own appointees occupying these positions, and he left little doubt what type of individual he was looking for. His White House spokesman, James Brady, said the president would pick people "meaner than junkyard dogs" to fill the positions.[52] Reagan also made sure that the budget of departmental inspectors general and their staff would see greater increases than other nondefense areas.[53]

The Council on Integrity and Efficiency moved on a number of fronts but centered its efforts on "preventing mismanagement."[54] It questioned many practices, identified billions in savings as a result of audits, launched civil and criminal actions, and introduced many sanctions against government agencies or employees.[55] The council also strengthened auditing practices and conducted numerous studies to detect waste in government operations. In addition, it promoted stronger internal control programs and measures to reduce overhead costs, including travel, office, and printing costs.

The work of the council speaks more to Reagan's desire to get at the bureaucrats, at wasteful government agencies, and at "draining the swamp" in Washington than at implementing managerialism. Reagan's annual report on *Management of the United States Government* always dealt at length with his accomplishments in "Controlling the Cost of Administering Federal Programs." The emphasis was always on administrative and financial controls; the report rarely touched on new management techniques that would free managers to manage.

Yet, this did not stop Reagan from occasionally introducing new management thinking to government operations. Total Quality Management (TQM) is a concept that came into vogue in the 1980s among the largest American firms. It was first conceived in the United States, but after World War II it was exported to Japan where it flourished. Americans rediscovered TQM when studying Japanese management techniques and immediately set out to implement it in their own businesses. Edwards Deming, one of several gurus of the TQM movement, explains, "It's so simple. Improve quality and you automatically improve productivity. You capture the market with lower price and better quality. You stay in business and you provide jobs." Elements underpinning the movement are equally simple—they include listening to customers, focusing on the prevention of poor quality, doing the right thing right the first time, ensuring continuing improvement, and fostering leadership.[56] Many of America's leading business people embraced the new movement, and they became convinced it would apply equally well to government operations.

Reagan heard their message and, in his second mandate, decided to introduce the concept to government, insisting that it had met with considerable "success in well-managed, private sector companies." The approach, he explained, called for setting "productivity and quality goals" and demanding accountability of managers in meeting them, developing measures to track progress, rewarding employees for their achievements, and seeking the participation of employees in improving operations. Reagan reported that his initiative constituted a new and "systematic management approach," and a year or so after its introduction he claimed specific improvements in many areas. The success stories, however, were essentially a collection of specific cases. For example, the passport service in the Department of State was able to reduce its error rate to 2 percent, and the geological survey in the Department of the Interior reduced the number of working days to process customer orders for maps from twenty to ten working days between 1986 and 1987. The Reagan administration acknowledged that successfully implementing Total Quality and Productivity Management required, as the private sector had discovered, "a fundamental cultural shift within the organization." It also acknowledged that "many of the agencies have yet to catch the spirit of total quality and productivity management and have not yet implemented the changes that are essential to creating such an environment."[57]

Reagan also introduced other management practices commonly seen in business. A "just-in-time" inventory system is one example; another was what he labeled "standard private sector cash management practices," which include electronic banking, a thirty-day payment schedule to reduce early payments, a more businesslike payment schedule of grants to state governments, and more demanding collection policies of funds owed to the government.[58]

Mulroney also introduced many of these practices to government operations in Canada. He introduced electronic banking, reduced the number of departmental bank accounts from a hundred to twenty-two, intensified efforts to reduce the level of outstanding amounts owed the government, and introduced a thirty-day payment schedule.[59] In Canada, as in the United States, these new practices were introduced to government by central agencies that issued formal instructions on how they should be implemented and followed up to ensure they were being adopted and implemented properly. Similarly, when Thatcher introduced just-in-time inventory control systems and other "keep-it-lean" measures, they were introduced by the Treasury and implemented under its watchful eye.[60] The point to note here is that the center led the way. The new practices did not bubble up from the newly empowered agencies and employees.

TEACHING MANAGEMENT

At the same time that Thatcher, Reagan, and Mulroney began to import private sector management practices to government, they concluded that government officials were ill prepared to make the transition. It was impossible to "make managers manage" unless they knew how. The political leadership certainly felt that the civil servants they had inherited were not up to the task and subscribed to the view that they were "badly trained, lacking in expertise and devoid of managerial skills."[61] In any event, private sector experience also suggested that training programs were required if a new management culture was to take root. Thus, the three political leaders again took their cue from business and introduced development programs (and this at a time when budgets were being squeezed in most areas). In all three cases, private sector experiences played an important role in shaping the new programs.[62]

In Britain, Fulton recommended the establishment of a civil service college to provide training courses in administration for senior administrators and specialists in mid career, to offer a wide range of shorter training courses to a variety of staff, and to conduct research in the problems of administration. The college was established in 1970 and by the end of the decade was able to offer courses in quantitative analysis, economics and social administration, statistics and operational research, and law.

The emphasis on management studies, however, only began in the early 1980s. Margaret Thatcher gave her formal approval in April 1984 to a new program at the college, the Top Management Programme (TMP). It is important to note that participants came in about equal numbers from the public and private sectors. Still, the program is designed for public servants, in particular for those expected to reach the rank of deputy secretary, the level immediately under the permanent secretary.[63] The thinking here is that the superior management knowledge of private sector participants would encourage government managers to focus on management issues rather than on policy. TMP was also developed by specialists from both inside and outside the government. It is operated by the Office of the Minister for the Civil Service, and it is an intensive residential program. The participants are high fliers with strong potential for advancement in both sectors, and all are expected to possess a strong record of success. The course is mandatory for anyone wishing to break into top management positions. While participants are not required to take the course in order to be promoted, they are expected to take it shortly after being promoted.[64]

Underpinning the TMP is the Senior Management Development Programme (SMDP), which was established in 1985.[65] This program is designed for managers, from assistant secretary to what is labeled the principal level. The purpose of the course is to prepare future top managers and also to develop further the effectiveness of all managers at the designated levels, whether or not they reach more senior levels. Unlike the TMP, the SMDP is not an intensive course. Indeed, the SMDP is not a formal course at all. Rather, it is an ongoing process involving short four-day courses, secondments, and the development of a personal development plan. The SMDP is built around a series of core competencies: the management of resources, the management of staff, a thorough knowledge of one's work, information technology, required specialized knowledge, and the management of one's work. Participants are asked to assess their current performance against this set of competencies and then to identify short courses or learning opportunities to improve their performance. They prepare a performance assessment by completing a personal development plan.

The British government has also developed a series of other management-development programs: a "best practice programme" where information is shared on what works; a senior professional administrative training scheme (a three-week course to equip specialists with management skills, followed by a management posting); and a "management charter initiative."[66] The latter is a private sector initiative launched in 1988, designed to encourage collaboration between the public and private sectors and to assist management education. It was set up with the full support of the Department of Trade and Industry, and an important element of the charter initiative is networking, or "the opportunity for employers who have joined the initiative to meet and share information about personnel management and management development issues."[67] The TMP group also organizes winter and summer "Nodes," which are joint public and private sector seminars for high fliers.

Government departments are also being encouraged to launch new management-training programs for their employees. They are being asked to concentrate on "hard" management themes, including leadership, change management, information technology, commercial management, finance, marketing, quality management, managing for results, and service to the customer. In short, as an official of the Cabinet Office explains, departments and agencies are being told to "strengthen their training provision in areas which have traditionally been regarded as being predominantly of interest to business managers."[68]

The American counterpart to Britain's Civil Service College is the Federal Executive Institute in Virginia, which celebrated its twentieth anniversary in 1988. Few would dispute that both the institute itself and the concept of public management development fell on difficult times for much of the 1970s and early 1980s in the United States. At one point, senior officials considered moving the institute to a new location and completely overhauling its curriculum, and the Reagan administration considered abolishing the center in the early 1980s. It was felt that the institute provided "too much soft management and not enough hard—i.e. too much psychology and not enough business administration."[69]

The appointment of a new director to the institute in the mid 1980s inspired new efforts to strengthen the management-development programs. The institute now offers a four-week Executive Excellence Program, as well as a number of one-week seminars on special topics. The four-week program is developed around core themes ranging from the fundamental values of constitutional government to the role of the career executive in implementing policy. Although members of the Service Executive Service (SES) are given priority, private sector representatives are also invited to attend.[70]

Reagan also encouraged new management-development programs to complement his Total Quality and Productivity Management Program, maintaining that the training of employees was essential if a change in culture inside the bureaucracy was to take place. Departments and agencies were strongly encouraged to set up new management-training initiatives. Some did. The Department of Commerce, for example, introduced a training program called More With Less. The program offers training sessions on motivation and improving performance and makes it clear that it expects "employees to return to their offices and implement productivity improvements strategies."[71]

In 1987 Reagan also invited private sector firms noted for a commitment to quality and a customer orientation (Westinghouse, IBM, Marriott, John Hancock Insurance, among others) to meet with government officials to look at ways to introduce a new quality culture to government operations. The group recommended the establishment of an educational institute to strengthen management practices in government. Reagan strongly endorsed the recommendation and a new Federal Quality Institute was opened in the late 1980s. It has since grown from a three-person to a thirty-person operation essentially promoting a TQM approach in government operations. In 1988, the Reagan administration initiated an annual productivity conference to encourage the introduction of innovative management techniques throughout the government. The conference features "private sector successes in instituting total quality management" and provides a forum for presenting the Presidential Productivity Award for outstanding productivity achievements by government agencies and employees.[72]

Like Britain, Canada established a training facility for its senior officials in the 1970s. The facility offered only orientation courses to newly appointed managers, however, and until the mid 1980s, these consisted essentially of lectures by other government officials. The courses lasted from one to three weeks and were designed to acquaint participants with the kind of knowledge required to perform at the senior level, including an appreciation of how the policy process actually works and the impact of central agency requirements on their duties and responsibilities.

Prime Minister Mulroney unveiled the new Centre for Management Development in April 1988. In making the announcement, he reported that the center would bring together "leading practitioners and scholars to help further develop the art of management."[73] He also said that the work of the center would be guided by an advisory body, consisting of representatives from the federal government, the private sector, and the universities. That same day, the deputy prime minister outlined the role of the new center. He explained that the center was necessary to provide government officials with the required management skills to operate in a new environment. He argued that "we have to deregulate the Public Service for the same reasons we deregulated many areas of the private sector—efficiency." He added that the government would be looking to the business community for advice and knowledge to make the center work.[74]

As soon as it was established, the center set up streamlined orientation courses. It also put forward objectives: "to help ensure that managers in the Public Service have the managerial skills and knowledge necessary to develop policy, to respond to change, and to manage government programs and services efficiently and effectively." The center then set out to develop several major new programs.[75] It was given a generous new budget (three times the amount allocated to the old training facility) in the order of $10 million annually, and one of Ottawa's most respected senior officials, John L. Manion, was appointed its first principal.

The center brought together a group of advisors from inside government, from the private sector, and from the universities to develop management courses. It settled on two kinds of courses. The first is a series of short courses, designed to develop problem-solving and managerial skills. Each has a specific focus, which may include "managing a small government agency, managing at the regional level, managing the working relationship with the business community," and so on. The center's flagship course, however, is a seven-week advanced-management program.[76] This is restricted to private sector managers and to senior government managers who have the potential to rise to the top of their organizations. The number of course participants is limited to about twenty-five a year. The curriculum is designed to encompass several themes, including managing complex organizations in changing environments, developing personal skills, managing public sector changes, and managing organizational responses to change. Although there are obvious differences between the two, it is clear that the British Advanced Management Programme influenced the development of the Canadian course.

A CIVIL SERVICE PERSPECTIVE

To be sure, civil servants went along with the new emphasis on managerialism. Managerialism was what their political masters wanted and civil servants do not as a rule openly challenge political authority. We also know, however, that civil servants are traditionally adept "at playing and adapting to games."[77] In the end, civil servants in London, Washington, and Ottawa designed and implemented a number of the reforms, and many spoke out publicly in support of these measures. Certainly, countless meetings were held to develop mission statements, to design ways to improve internal communication, to plan management delayering, to see how front-line employees could be empowered and how exchange schemes with the private sector could be implemented, and to prepare new measures to teach management to government managers.

This is not to suggest that civil servants—in particular senior civil servants—saw only merit in the shift toward managerialism or that they accepted fully that it would transform what they do and how they do it. Certainly, the disbelief system kicked in.[78] The system, as we have already seen, is a psychological defense mechanism against proposals and events that serve to threaten the civil servants' beliefs and the stability of their institutions. In any event, there is in government everywhere considerable skepticism as to whether announced changes will, in the end, amount to much. Senior government officials who have lived through Hoover, Glassco, Fulton, PPBS, and PAR have reason to assume that reforms are essentially short-lived affairs that end in failure and amount only to a waste of time and energy.

Certainly, there were reasons to be skeptical. Government officials are acutely aware of the pitfalls inherent in applying private sector management techniques to government operations. TQM and mission statements, they argue, are better suited to private sector organizations, where goals can be easily stated and the tasks to be accomplished easily understood. Obviously, IBM, for example, is in business to realize profits, to secure a greater market share, and to produce goods and services as efficiently as possible. There are no conflicting goals here, nor are there politicians pulling and pushing the organization in different directions.

Many government officials report shortcomings in exchange programs with the business community. Business executives coming to government invariably arrive with simple solutions to complex problems and without the necessary expertise and background to make a positive impact, at least over the short term. They often return to their firms, after a few years, frustrated with having accomplished so little. In their study, Les Metcalfe and Sue Richards arrive at the same conclusion, "The results of exchange schemes rarely seem to live up to expectations."[79]

Career officials are also convinced that Thatcher, Reagan, Mulroney, and their advisors did not fully understand the role of senior public servants as policy advisors. Rediscovering the politics-administration dichotomy, they insist, is hardly realistic. Politicians have all the power to make policy decisions, but to attempt to do so without considering what officials have to offer is shortsighted. In any event, they insist, it is not possible. One senior official observed,

> in the 1970s, I spent over 50 percent of my time on policy issues. Notwithstanding all this management stuff, I did the same in the 1980s and I am still spending over 50 percent of my time on policy issues in the 1990s. I do so not because I insist on it but because the system, in particular politicians themselves, demand it.

After a year or two in office, they come to accept that they and
their advisors simply do not have the expertise to deal with all
policy issues and they have—reluctantly or not—to look to us for
advice.[80]

Policy work in the 1980s, however, took on a different meaning. Senior
officials insist that their most important policy functions in the 1980s
was to act as a "dis-embarrasser" of politicians, to be a "fixer," and to
work out the "impracticalities of proposals that came down from the
politicians."[81]

Officials will also point out that, although empowerment may hold
considerable promise in the private sector, it cannot be as straightforward in government. Civil servants, they explain, are indeed cautious
people, no doubt because politicians do not easily tolerate errors. For
empowerment to have any chance of success, it must be accompanied
by a number of elements or values. Empowerment requires openness,
trust, a tolerance for errors, and a significant deregulation of controls
and processes governing personnel, administrative and financial decision making. Some even go as far as arguing that "in a hierarchy,
empowerment is a hoax."[82] These are not the values one commonly
encounters in government. Career officials report that it is the politicians, not them, who insist on error-free work. Politicians in office do
not like to have to explain to their colleagues, to the media, and to
interest groups that an administrative blunder has been committed by
newly empowered bureaucrats.

Although politicians sang the praise of empowerment and the
business-management model, they were not as forthcoming when it
came to demonstrating trust and tolerating errors. For instance, Reagan showed little hesitation in issuing an executive order on drug
testing for government employees in 1986 or in unleashing his inspectors general at every turn in search of bureaucratic blunders. Similarly,
Mulroney did not hesitate to issue a directive publicly instructing officials not to provide off-the-record background briefings to the media
or to the public without prior ministerial approval. He added that
ministerial approval for such briefings would only be made in exceptional circumstances.[83] There have also been numerous examples
throughout their stay in office when Thatcher, Reagan, and Mulroney
showed little or no tolerance for errors on the part of career officials.[84]
Some officials also report that the Thatcher, Reagan, and Mulroney
management revolution in government operations was more mean

spirited than it was genuine.[85] It involved privatization, contracting out, and importing the business-management model to government without making the necessary tough decisions to free government managers from excessive controls and formal rules.

Certainly, it did not take long for the political leadership to see that their efforts at changing the administrative culture in government operations were stalling. Some wrote that the disbelief system was still very much at work even after the introduction of reforms such as FMI. IMAA was hardly a success, with numerous departments declining to sign an MOU with the Treasury Board.[86] In the end, the Treasury Board could offer little incentive to departments to sign. In addition, some that did reported that the process created more paperwork than it reduced.[87]

The point was increasingly being made that it was not possible to graft a new management culture on to an old structure. To make matters worse, the political leadership was torn between wishing to impose controls that would bring the bureaucrats to heel, on one hand, and empowering them as the business model suggested, on the other. Thatcher, Reagan, and Mulroney had decided before coming to office that they would keep government reorganization to a minimum. All three had been highly critical about past reorganizations that had accomplished little other than keeping some bureaucrats busy. In time, however, they would themselves not only reorganize some agencies and departments but also (particularly in the case of Thatcher) undertake ambitious efforts to restructure government operations substantially.

8

Restructuring the Machinery

Most politicians initially, at least, have little interest in government reorganization. To start with, outside the capital (and indeed government itself), there is no constituency for such measures. More telling, there are no votes to be gained. Once in power, however, politicians much more often than not become unhappy with the organization of government. They often add new committees, reorganize an agency, abolish another agency, create yet another agency, in the hope of finally getting things right and of achieving more efficient government administration. Most politicians also long to leave their own imprint on government, and few areas offer as many possibilities to do so as does reorganization, which allows them to point to tangible evidence that they were able to clean up the mess their predecessors left behind. Carter, Trudeau, Heath, and Wilson all established new cabinet committees, departments, and agencies, reorganized others, created new policy advisory groups and program evaluation units, and introduced important changes to senior personnel management.[1]

Nor did it take long for Thatcher, Reagan, and Mulroney to follow suit. Some of their reforms were highly ambitious, by any standards. We saw that they privatized and contracted out many activities. Thatcher and Mulroney also sought to hive off parts of their civil service into separate agencies, to operate under new rules. They also set up new committees, abolished some agencies and departments, and created new ones.[2] Reagan would turn to one of Carter's most important innovations, the 1978 Civil Service Reform Act, to implement his agenda.

A common thread linked the various efforts. The new political leaders were less concerned about policy matters and the policy advisory function than their predecessors had been, and in the 1980s, management in government—defined to encompass considerably more than expenditure control—became an end in itself.

THATCHER

Thatcher, at least in her early years in office, perceived "the civil service, especially the higher civil service, as an adversary and relics of indulgent reformism like the Civil Service Department (CSD) were always unlikely to survive the attack." Within two years of coming to office, she concluded that the CSD was little more than "a pack of poachers turned gamekeepers," and she abolished the department.[3] The CSD, which flowed out of a recommendation of the Fulton report, was designed to play a leading role in implementing Fulton's findings. Fulton had argued in 1968 that a modern civil service required its own central-management focus and that the answer was a "stand alone" department, with a permanent secretary carrying the title of Head of the Home Civil Service. The department grouped together everything that was considered relevant to civil service management, from pay, human resources, and planning and development, to various support services, including telephones, computers, medical services, and even cafeterias.

There were a number of reasons why Thatcher decided to abolish the department, including her unhappiness with what she felt were high wage settlements negotiated with the unions. But she also became exasperated with the officials of the CSD who were constantly defending the department's practices, insisting that government administration was entirely different from business management. Some of Thatcher's key advisors had also been taking aim at the CSD from the start. Rayner, for one, believed that the department was just another cog that had to be taken account of in decision making. He felt that "the people in the Department, placed elsewhere in the Treasury, in the Cabinet Office would be able to deliver that task more efficiently."[4] In short, the CSD did not fit the business-management model. It took away from efforts to simplify decision making and inhibited attempts to introduce a bias for action in government operations.

In abolishing the department, Thatcher transferred its pay and manpower planning functions to the Treasury. Meanwhile, its efficiency, recruitment, and selection functions went to a new Management and Personnel Office (MPO) in the Cabinet Office. The head and deputy head of the disbanded department were both dispatched by the prime minister into early retirement.[5]

From her very first days in office, it also became clear that Thatcher had little time for the Central Policy Review Staff (CPRS), or "the think tank" that had been created by Edward Heath following a recommendation in the white paper *The Reorganization of Central Government*. Heath wanted CPRS to look to the long term and to help define a broad strategy for the government. He saw it as serving all cabinet, not just his own office. According to his most senior advisor, Heath wanted above all to "rub ministers' noses in the future." The group was off to a fast start. Lord Rothschild was at its head and a handful of brilliant economists and policy analysts were on board. They were left to define their work pretty well on their own, with Heath offering little more than a very broad vision of what he wanted CPRS to do. They soldiered on and produced some provocative "think" pieces on a wide variety of issues, ranging from airstrips to empty office blocks.[6]

Rumor had it that Harold Wilson had planned to disband CPRS when he came to office. But he did not. Indeed, Wilson later claimed that the Labour government itself had been working on establishing such a think tank just before losing office in 1970 and that Heath had simply picked up their ball and run with it. A new head, Sir Kenneth Berrill, had been appointed to replace Lord Rothschild just months before Wilson came to power. He continued to attract solid talent and to prepare, albeit with varying degrees of success, a number of policy papers, ranging from the state of the economy to a review of overseas representation. Wilson also established a small unit in his own office to provide him directly with policy advice. This concentrated mainly on economic policy, if only to avoid duplicating the planning efforts of CPRS staff.[7]

Few informed people held much hope that CPRS would survive for long after Thatcher came to office. It was felt that her impatience with generalists and her politics of conviction would not square with the work of CPRS or with the people working there. Although she did not move to abolish the group immediately, her early months in office hardly proved reassuring. "There was a period early on," a keen observer wrote, "when I think she felt it had no real purpose." Still, her key advisors and some senior civil servants set out to save CPRS, and Thatcher agreed, but only after she had substantially redefined its work so as to diminish its importance. The group saw the writing on the wall and quickly immersed itself in Thatcherism and, to the prime minister's delight, however brief, became "more Thatcherite than the Cabinet."[8]

Still, by the spring of 1983, Thatcher had made up her mind to kill CPRS. After more than three years, she felt it was simply not delivering the goods. She wanted a larger and stronger policy unit working out of her own office and to do this she needed to cut spending elsewhere. More important, however, her view was that CPRS could never completely shake itself free of the "generalist" civil service view of the world. One of her advisors explained, "CPRS seemed to become more donnish and detached from hard day-to-day decisions." For Thatcher, hard day-to-day decisions were in many ways the essence of government. Professor Ashworth explained, "Of its very existence the CPRS sort of encapsulated a view about government for which she had no great sympathy. She was what she called a conviction politician. There is a difference between being a conviction politician and being a rationally guided politician."[9]

In the aftermath of CPRS's demise, Thatcher went on to strengthen considerably her own policy unit, later claiming that its cost was a fraction of the cost of running CPRS. More important, she argued, it was more responsive to her policy preferences and to her requirements, right down to its "paper clips." One of her advisors who worked in the unit later said that it gave Thatcher a "non-Whitehall" perspective on departmental advice and that it had the capacity to be a "creative" think tank, which presumably a Whitehall-based CPRS did not have. Above all, he explained, a policy unit attached to the Prime Minister's Office provided Thatcher with the necessary support "in implementing the strategic goals of her government." The emphasis of the Cabinet Office, he noted, is to ensure that the machinery of government runs smoothly. This invariably inhibits candid and unorthodox policy advice. A policy unit reporting directly to the prime minister, on the other hand, had her political agenda at the top of its priority. The staff in the unit, like the prime minister herself, were convinced that "there is no such thing as policy advice resting solely on objective facts."[10]

What this amounted to was little patience for what Whitehall was good at: providing nonpartisan, professional policy advice that was above the fray. This was the same thinking that led to the creation of Thatcher's efficiency unit, which was established to carry out scrutinies and to improve management practices in government. What Thatcher wanted was straightforward advice. She was convinced she would not always receive such advice from long-serving career civil servants who tended to look at all facets of an issue, seek a middle course, and package the findings in a cleverly crafted paper that would not offend relevant ministers and departments. Thatcher decided to set up her own machinery, staffed by people willing to call a spade a spade. She also sought to undermine Whitehall's traditional administrative culture, which placed a premium on intellectuality and gamesmanship, by demonstrating what could be accomplished by two units with a bias for action.

In the fall of 1987, Thatcher decided to revisit her reorganization decision of 1981 that had led to the abolition of the CSD. She had become impatient with the tension between the Treasury and the Cabinet Office, through the MPO. She saw it as a classic case of "bureaucrats fighting over turf" and, rather than sorting out this tension by redrawing mandates, she decided to put an end to it by abolishing the MPO.[11] This time, she transferred most of its functions back to the Treasury. The remainder of the office was reorganized under an Office of the Minister for the Civil Service attached to the Cabinet Office, with the secretary to the cabinet assuming the title of Head of the Home Civil Service.

The Thatcher government also introduced a number of modifications to personnel-management policies. Borrowing a page from the private sector, the annual staff-appraisal system was modified substantially. Personal objectives were now set for most civil servants, together with performance indicators, showing how well they were meeting their objectives. The government also began experimenting with performance bonuses for managers. The Treasury developed (albeit with little success) proposals to implement a discretionary pay scheme at all management levels so that those who performed well would receive higher pay than those who did not.[12] True to her goal of importing the business-management model to government operations, Thatcher decided that the salaries of senior government officials should move closer to comparable rates for senior business executives. She agreed in 1985 to salary increases as high as 50 percent for permanent secretaries—the salary of her secretary to the cabinet, Sir Robert Armstrong, went from £50,000 to £75,000 in one year. Thatcher's decision appeared contradictory to some of her most ardent supporters in the Commons and it very nearly caused a back-bench revolt.[13]

Thatcher's most ambitious reform to do with the machinery of government stemmed from the report *Improving Management in Government: The Next Steps*, published by her efficiency unit. The report had argued, predictably, that the measures introduced since 1979 were having a positive impact. It argued, however, that much more was required. Indeed, it clearly gave the impression that, after her eight years in office, Thatcher's call to add emphasis to managing government operations and to reduce emphasis on policy was not being heard. The report stated,

> Most civil servants are very conscious that senior management is dominated by people whose skills are in policy formulation and who have relatively little experience of managing or working where services are actually being delivered. In any large organization, senior appointments are watched with close attention.[14]

This was true, even though the report admitted only 5 percent of the civil service was directly concerned with policy. The remaining 95 percent was directly concerned with the delivery of government services.

The report made the point that the work of civil servants is dominated by the demands of ministers and Parliament. It also made a number of general observations, including that the machinery of government itself—together with continuing demands from Parliament, from the media, and from the public—had contributed to the problem of "ministerial overload." Too little attention was paid to results and too much was paid to expenditures and activities, in departments, and there were relatively few external pressures demanding improvement in performance. The report's most important finding, however, was that the civil service was "too big and too diverse to manage as a single entity." This had led to the development of a machinery of government that "fits no operation effectively." A unified civil service had given rise to all kinds of uniform controls and rules so that managers were not free to manage effectively. Controls, it reported, existed on recruitment, dismissal, and choice of staff, promotion, pay, hours of work, accommodation, organization of work, and even on the use of communication equipment. The authors summed up their findings by identifying five critical issues confronting management in the civil service:

> *First*, a lack of clear and accountable management responsibility, and the self confidence that goes with it, particularly among the higher ranks in departments. *Second*, the need for greater precision about the results expected of people and of organisations. *Third*, a need to focus attention on outputs as well as inputs. *Fourth*, the handicap of imposing a uniform system in an organisation of the size and diversity of the present Civil Service. *Fifth*, a need for a sustained pressure for improvement.[15]

The solution was to reorganize the work of individual departments so that the job to be done received priority rather than the centrally conceived rules and controls. The focus in future should be results, not process. The report revisited the politics-administration dichotomy and put forward a radical proposal: agencies should be established to carry out the executive functions of government within a policy-and-resources framework set by ministers and the relevant department. The managers of the agencies would be given substantial freedom to manage their operations as they saw fit, but they would be held "rigorously to account for the results achieved." The report essentially argued that if government operations were allowed to operate at arm's length from ministers and from the Whitehall culture, then one would soon see a "release of managerial energy." In brief, the goal was nothing short of redefining the way the "business of government" was conducted.[16] It was envisaged that, some day, the civil service would consist of a small core at the center engaged in policy work, supporting ministers and managing departments, with the bulk of civil servants working in relatively independent executive agencies, delivering services.

The report, however, issued a number of warnings in implementing the new approach. It insisted that ministers and civil servants must learn to stand back from operational details and show confidence in the competence of managers by leaving them free to manage. Flexibility and management-development training, as well as the development of new skills in the delivery of services to the public, were critical to the success of the approach. So, too, was the full support of ministers, in that the changes being proposed were so fundamental that their only chance of success was through the firm leadership of ministers.

The report sought to deal head-on with the principle of ministerial responsibility, or the relationship between ministers and civil servants. Prime Minister Harold Wilson, it will be recalled, had directed Fulton not to deal with this issue in his review. Thatcher issued no such instruction. The report again turned to the politics-administration dichotomy and argued that ministers should be fully accountable for policy, but not for day-to-day management decisions. It insisted that there was nothing new in this suggestion, since there were already a number of government functions carried out at arm's length from ministers. These included the review of tax cases and regulatory functions. The solution lay in an accountability framework that was tailored for each agency. The underlying principle, however, would see heads of executive agencies delegated authority from ministers for managing the agencies "within the framework of policy directives and resource allocations prescribed by ministers."[17]

Finally, the report stressed time and again the magnitude of the changes being proposed. It laid down a fairly detailed timetable to implement the Next Steps. It insisted that the changes would only be successfully implemented if an "extremely" senior official was appointed "project manager" and given "unequivocal personal responsibility for achieving the change." The report added that the project manager should provide briefing papers on a regular basis to the prime minister on the progress being made by departments in "setting frameworks for their agencies and on the timetable for relaxing constraints on management."[18] This would ensure continuing political-level commitment to make the changes work.

Thatcher accepted the report's recommendations as "a major step in the reform of the civil service," which would serve to improve in a substantial fashion the "management of Government business." New agencies would be created, she explained, and "each will have its own Chief Executive, responsible for managing day to day operations." She provided a list of twelve candidates for immediate agency status, ranging from the Passport Department to Historic Royal Palaces.[19] She directed that the function of the agencies be carried out within a policy-and-resources framework set by ministers, that staff be properly trained for management and for the delivery of services, and that a project manager oversee the creation of the agencies. She appointed Peter Kemp, a senior and highly respected official, as project manager.

Kemp took up the challenge with enthusiasm. He described the magnitude of his task to be as great as the reforms carried out in the aftermath of the Northcote-Trevelyan report and predicted that "history will show" this to be so. He reported that there was scope for about 75 percent of the civil service to operate as agencies. Above all, he wanted to see "genuine change." What was required was a new mind-set that would give the agencies' chief executives the freedom to develop new management tools "geared to the type of business they are running." Kemp acknowledged that there would be some important problems to overcome if the changes were to take hold firmly. Chief among these, he wrote, was "the need to reconcile Parliament's ultimate control with the need to give managers freedom to manage." Still, he was able to report that a parliamentary committee took a strong interest in Next Steps and saw little difficulty in securing the necessary accountability to make the concept work. The Commons' Treasury and Civil Service Committee simply urged that an agency's chief executive be also designated its accounting officer. This would permit the executive to appear before the Public Accounts Committee to account for the agency's expenditures. The accounting officer is responsible for the accounts of the organization, which are presented annually to Parliament. The accounts present a detailed record of the expenditure of public funds and are subject to audit by the comptroller and the auditor general. In addition, once audited, the accounts may also be reviewed by the Public Accounts Committee of the House of Commons, and the accounting officer may be asked to appear before the committee to answer for the audited account. The government agreed with the committee proposal but not without some strong opposition from senior civil servants in the Cabinet Office and the Treasury.[20]

The government's final decision was to make the agency heads "additional" accounting officers, so that permanent secretaries retain the status of accounting officers for the whole of their areas of responsibilities, including the agencies. However, Treasury officials are quick to point out that, for all practical purposes, the agency heads will act as accounting officers for the work of their agencies and will answer for it before the Public Accounts Committee. "Only under extraordinary circumstances or when things have gone completely out of control," they explain, "will a permanent secretary want to involve himself directly between the Public Accounts Committee and an agency."[21]

Thatcher told the Commons the day the report was released that, "there will be no change in the arrangements for accountability."[22] Officials interpreted her statement to mean that there would be little difference between agencies and departments—indeed, Sir Robin Butler, head of the Home Civil Service, did not even think "it would be necessary to revise the rules on civil servants giving evidence to select committees" of Parliament.[23] He wrote,

> No doubt this is because ministers, notably the minister for the civil service, Richard Lace, made it clear that any constitutional changes to redefine ministerial responsibility were out of the question as were any suggestions to end Treasury controls over budgets, manpower and national pay bargaining.[24]

The House Committee took a strong and lasting interest in Next Steps. It held a hearing and issued its own report within months of Thatcher's making the report public. In fact, it proved more forthcoming on the issue of accountability than did the government. The Treasury's permanent secretary, Sir Peter Middleton, expressed some concern not just over the accountability issue but also over the removal of Treasury controls to permit agencies to operate at arm's length from government. He made clear that he wanted to keep "those central controls which remain essential" and would only be prepared to consider greater decentralization if there were "better information with which to carry out responsibilities for management control."[25]

There were other problems. When pressed, Kemp could not explain why certain government operations would be more appropriate than others for the agency model. He explained that areas where one could not make a sharp distinction between policy and executive positions would not be appropriate, although he admitted that it was "not very easy" to come up with examples.[26] Some, notably the labor movement, expressed concern that Next Steps was really the first step toward privatization. Thatcher was asked in the Commons if the agencies would be exempt from the government's privatization program. She replied,

> The Government's privatization policies will continue. Before an Agency is established, alternative options, including contracting

out the work and privatization will be examined. *Next Steps* is primarily about those operations which are to remain within Government. I cannot rule out, however, that after a period of years Agencies, like other Government activities, may be suitable for privatization. Where there is a firm intention of privatization when an Agency is being set up, this should be made clear.[27]

Some of her ministers, however, were less reassuring. Michael Heseltine worried that "the forces of reaction gathering" within the civil service would stifle the reforms and argued that the agencies be removed as far as possible from the public sector: "in other words, privatize them."[28]

The biggest problem, however, was the confusion that existed over the structure of agencies. This, no doubt, resulted from the differing values and motives behind the concept.[29] Thatcher, her efficiency unit, her key cabinet ministers, and her advisors saw Next Steps as another nail in the coffin of the old Whitehall, the traditional civil service with the generalists' emphasis on policy rather than management. The executive agencies were to be decentralist, consumer oriented, and compatible with the business-management model. Although they accepted the new emphasis on management, the traditionalists had strong reservations about Next Steps. Senior officials began to speak and write about management and to draw parallels between large business concerns and government operations. Some approved of the Next Steps initiative, although it was not at all clear that their thinking on the matter squared with that of the Thatcherites.[30] Indeed, a good many permanent officials felt that there was no need for the agencies, that the changes could be accommodated within the existing structure. Treasury officials remained convinced that the structural changes would in the end be much more modest than the advocates of reforms were hoping for. The relationship between the Treasury and Customs and Excise and Inland Revenue were already of an agency-type nature or could easily be adjusted to be so. In any event, both the Cabinet Office and the Treasury insisted that delegation of authority be devolved gradually over time.[31]

To be sure, senior officials were concerned about the implications Next Steps held for the long-term health of their institution. Some were worried that the baby would be thrown out with the bath water. They also questioned how agency staff would relate to public service ethics and how loyal they would be to the civil service as an institution. Many felt that the principle of ministerial responsibility and accountability in government operations was, in fact, far more complex than described in Next Steps. Some also feared that a government agency, all of a sudden freed of controls and "energized," could run off in all kinds of directions without anyone having effective control.[32]

There was, however, no shortage of advice on how to make the Next Steps initiative work. The report made a number of specific recommendations, but so did the Treasury and civil service committee report. The Commons committee urged the government to remove any uncertainty there might be over whether an agency would be privatized. It also rejected the suggestion that managers earn freedom gradually, arguing that the government should show greater confidence in its senior employees. It insisted that the "right people" be hired to run the agencies and urged that, as much as possible, "outsiders" be recruited. It argued that in future every effort be made to ensure that the "golden route" to the top be through management, not policy. The committee also recommended that every effort be made to encourage the momentum for reform by setting up performance indicators and fostering intra-agency competition.[33]

Notwithstanding concerns and confusion over structure, the initiative "caught alight in 1988-89." Peter Kemp oversaw the creation of eight agencies within the first year. He sold the initiative, both inside government and out, as the most promising vehicle to improve the quality of service to the public and to increase the satisfaction civil servants can find in their work. He and his Next Steps team also quickly put together a process to guide the implementation. First, departments were directed to review their activities and to look at five possibilities: abolition, privatization, contracting out, relocation in an agency, or no change. Once activities were identified as candidates for agency status, they were submitted to a Project Liaison Group and then to the project executive teams, made up of representatives from Kemp's group, the Treasury, Thatcher's efficiency unit, and the sponsoring department.[34]

By early 1991, 50 executive agencies had been established, employing 183,000 people, and another 20 with 23,000 employees were under review for agency status. Kemp predicted that about half of the civil service would be operating under Next Steps by mid 1992 (an objective that has been realized). He deliberately picked small, relatively self-contained operations, ranging from 50 to about 3,000 employees, as candidates to launch the initiative. This was to minimize the difficulties and political controversy and to allow for important lessons to be learned before attacking the larger and possibly more politically controversial operations.[35]

The strategy worked. The flurry of activity in support of Next Steps in the first twenty-four months took most observers by surprise. Government operations as varied as the civil service college, the Statistical Office, the Stationery Office, defense non-nuclear research establishments, and the Driver Testing and Training Office were given agency status. Prime Minister Thatcher was delighted with the progress and wrote,

> One of the great tasks we face for the 1990s is to improve our
> public services and make them more responsive to the people's
> needs. *Next Steps*, which I launched two years ago, put this to the
> top of the agenda. *Next Steps* sets the direction for the Civil Ser-
> vice of the future. I am sure this is what we will see.

Even the opposition Labour party was supportive of Next Steps and made it clear that it would not turn back the clock if elected to office. The Shadow Chancellor of the Exchequer declared in a speech to the Royal Institute of Public Administration in 1991 that there would be no

> merit in a new government seeking to uproot all the plants in the
> garden, rearrange their roots, and then, having planted them
> again, expect them to grow well. It is worth noticing that the
> framework agreement controlling the agency can be altered by
> government and one option for a government which has different
> aims and values, is to change the agreement in line with its pur-
> poses.[36]

The key elements in implementing Next Steps are relatively straightforward. Once a candidate for agency status has been identified, a great deal of work is done to prepare a framework document. The document outlines the objectives of the agency, covers the financial regime (including arrangements for auditing and annual reports), presents a business or corporate plan, reports on what decision-making authority is being decentralized (including personnel, pay, and training delegations), and contains a clause stipulating that the document will be reviewed after three years. The document also makes reference to the direct accountability to Parliament of the agency's chief executive and reports on the administrative arrangements linking agencies with the core department. Once the framework agreement has been defined, a chief executive is appointed, normally by open competition, and the agency is launched. The relationship between the chief executive and the responsible minister is established in each framework document. It is the minister who appoints the chief executive and approves the framework document. Executive agencies can also establish a board of management or a steering group—and most do. These boards enable agencies to bring in people from their core departments, as well as outside experts with "business experience to provide advice."[37]

REAGAN

British prime ministers have far more scope to reform the machinery of government, and an easier time of it, than do U.S. presidents. British constitutional arrangements are such that Thatcher did not have to introduce any legislation before Parliament to create her executive agencies. In fact, there was no debate in the House of Commons on Next Steps or on the new executive agencies before May 1991.[38] The Thatcher government did introduce legislation in the early 1990s, but its purpose was to allow agencies to benefit from trading funds. Such funds enable agencies to establish a financial framework to cover operating costs, to borrow to meet capital expenditure and working capital requirements, and to establish reserves out of surpluses. Accordingly, trading funds operate outside the parliamentary supply system. Still, by the time this legislation was introduced, the Next Steps initiative was well launched, with some fifty agencies already operating.

Things are very different in the United States. Congress has the power to accept or reject major reorganizations, including the establishment or dissolution of departments. Standing committees of Congress are very powerful and jealously guard their influence. Indeed, they are continually on the lookout for any proposed changes, not just from the president but even from Congress itself. There have been

instances when committees of Congress have simply ignored enact-
ments of Congress, if they were perceived as threats. In 1990, for
example, Congress passed the Chief Financial Offices Act designed to
reform certain aspects of financial management. Convinced that this
constituted a threat to its power, the House Appropriations Committee decided in 1991 to incorporate a clause in all agency budgets that
read, "none of the funds available shall be used to carry out the Chief
Financial Offices Act."[39]

Reagan did at first attempt some major surgery on the machinery of
government but was rebuffed by Congress. For example, he did not
pursue his announced proposals to eliminate the departments of Education and Energy because he knew that Congress would balk him at
every turn. He had also advocated a consolidation of all trade functions
in a single Department of Trade, and a merger of the Bureau of
Reclamation and the Army Corps of Engineers, but then he abandoned
the ideas, again because of anticipated problems with Congress. In
short, "administrative reorganization was not a hallmark of the Reagan
administration." Reagan decided rather that his legacy would be management reform. The Reagan administration did not try to duplicate
Thatcher's Next Steps initiative and potential problems with Congress
was not the only reason. Next Steps was introduced in Britain during
Reagan's final months in office. By then he had little appetite for
reforms beyond those he had already introduced, preoccupied as he
was with the Iran-Contra scandal. In any event, the machinery of
government in Britain and the United States is so different that Next
Steps would make little sense in Washington. Indeed, government
officials claim that a version of the executive-agency concept has been
in place in the United States for some time.[40]

Although administrative reorganization was not a hallmark of the
Reagan administration, it was not for want of being at the top of the
public policy agenda. Charles H. Levine wrote that perhaps one of
the most lasting legacies of the Reagan presidency

> has been to legitimize debate over the tools and techniques of
> policy implementation. The Reagan administration has brought
> into the open the full implications of the subtle shift in federal
> management over the past fifty years from direct service provision
> and production to greater dependence on third party service pro-
> viders.[41]

Although not nearly as successful as he would have liked, Reagan promoted privatization, contracting out, and user fees at every opportunity. We saw earlier that Reagan was particularly concerned with redefining the proper scope and even the organization of government by rebalancing the respective roles of public, private, and voluntary organizations in the delivery of public goods and services.

Although Congress has the power to stop a major reorganization, it has delegated much of its power over internal agency organization to the Secretaries, thus creating an opening for Reagan and his advisors. They took it.[42] Certainly they tinkered time and again with the machinery of government so as to introduce "management to the United States Government" and "took full advantage of changes introduced by President Carter . . . in particular, to redefine the role of civil servants in policy making."[43]

Initially at least, the Reagan administration turned to the Office of Management and Budgeting (OMB) to implement a major part of its agenda. Indeed, interviews with Reagan's White House staff in the early 1980s reveal that OMB was regarded as the single most important organization, even more important than the high-profile National Security Council. In any event, the president can reorganize or tinker with OMB more easily than the rest of the government. Initially, at least, the administration concentrated on the budget and the budget process. In appointing David Stockman to head OMB, Reagan made it clear that it would not be business as usual. For one thing, the expenditure budget would be a top-down rather than a bottom-up operation. For another, OMB would become highly politicized and mainly concerned with selling the agenda to Congress, rather than weighing policy options and analyzing long-term fiscal trends.[44] The Reagan administration knew precisely what it wanted (and that was less government) and denied any need for sophisticated policy reviews. The only issue to resolve was how to package the agenda and how to sell it to Congress.

The Reagan administration also tinkered with OMB's organization and later with the Office of Personnel Management (OPM). Colin Campbell wrote, "What happened to Britain's Civil Service Department in 1981, two years into the Thatcher Government, would, in fact, serve as a harbinger of the fate of OMB's management side and the Office of Personnel Management." The administration was unhappy with President Carter's reorganization of OMB and abolished the intergovernmental affairs and personnel policy divisions, as well as collapsing two others into one to create the Office of Information and Regulatory Affairs. This office, with a substantial number of new staff and a high-profile task force, set out to overhaul how government agencies implement policies. Regulatory reviews permitted appointed officials in OMB to travel into territory long considered to be the domain of the permanent bureaucracy and to question or shape decisions that would have otherwise remained the prerogative of permanent officials. Stockman, meanwhile, held the limelight and effected a hiring freeze and spending cuts. Resources were shifted to the budget and the deregulation sides of OMB to the point that during the first eighteen months, the management side of the office "withered to a tiny fragment."[45]

Things started to change, however, halfway through Reagan's first term. By 1982, OMB increasingly talked about developing solutions to "government wide management and systems deficiencies."[46] During that summer, two major initiatives were announced. One was an ambitious study to deregulate government management, and the other was *Reform 88*, which OMB described as a "major, far reaching project to restructure the management systems of the federal government." As Chester A. Newland argues, although Reform 88 lacked precision, it did suggest two things.[47] First, although the Reagan administration had not given a high priority to management reform until 1982, it was now prepared to do so. Second, the reform would require a long time to implement and would continue throughout a second term. Reform 88, as we have seen, became a catch-all for all kinds of management reform, ranging from electronic information systems to financial management and accountability.

Thus, in 1982, the administration's emphasis on management went into high gear. The Grace Commission on cost control was established that year, as was the cabinet Council on Management and Administration. This was chaired by Edwin Meese, a powerful member of Reagan's inner group of advisors. Meese was one of a few members of Reagan's close advisors who had the reputation of having some interest in and respect for career civil servants. He later appointed Ralph Bledsoe, a respected professional public administrator, as the council's executive director. The new cabinet council was announced on the same day as Reform 88, and its mandate was to oversee the implementation of Reform 88. It reviewed the findings of the Grace Commission and more generally sought to "bridge policy and implementation in all managerial initiatives."[48] The council became very active, meeting twenty-one times between 1982 and 1983 to consider a host of issues. In addition, the council's secretariat was able to involve a number of senior-level officials from OMB and OPM in a review of management practices.

The establishment of the Grace Commission and the Council on Management and Administration shifted OMB's attention from an almost exclusive concentration on budgeting and deregulation to issues of management. If nothing else, the Grace Commission and the new president of the council challenged OMB to prove it was up to the task.[49] Certainly, the Grace recommendation that a new Office of Federal Management (OFM) be established to replace OMB raised more than a few eyebrows. It did not take long for the office to pick up the cue and hurry to put the "M" back in OMB. This is not to suggest for a moment that the "M" became more important than the "B," or even more important than it had been under previous administrations. Still, OMB played the key role in packaging Reform 88. In addition, in 1983, it required federal government organizations to prepare management plans, with a special emphasis on improvement efforts. These plans were to be submitted along with their annual budget requests.

In May 1984, the president also established the new Council on Management Improvement in which OMB would play a pivotal role. This brought together assistant-secretary-level officials responsible for management from all major government agencies to work with OMB and other central agencies to develop and oversee the implementation of Reform 88. The group was also asked to develop long-range management-improvement plans, identify best management practices from the agencies, promote these practices to other departments and agencies, and resolve interagency management issues.[50]

In 1986, Reagan launched a program designed to improve productivity in government agencies by 20 percent by the year 1992 and also to strengthen the delivery of government services. This was part of his TQM initiative discussed earlier, which gave rise to a number of changes, including the creation of a federal quality institute and the formation of a small council to assist small government agencies, or those employing fewer than five hundred employees, in implementing measures to improve productivity.

Reform 88 also led to the appointment of OMB's head of management as chief financial officer of the United States in July 1987. Subsequently, government agencies each appointed a chief financial officer to participate in a newly created Chief Financial Officers' Council, which was designed to improve financial management in government. The Reagan administration directed the council to "reduce obsolete systems, eliminate redundant systems, and make systems compatible so that financial information can readily be exchanged, aggregated, and reported to all management levels in a timely manner to support managerial decision making."[51] OMB also established the new Office of Privatization to work with agencies to identify potential candidates for privatization and to manage privatization initiatives. This office was one of seventy-eight recommendations the Reagan-appointed commission on privatization made when it reported in March 1978.

Reagan also restructured his cabinet to create seven cabinet councils. These councils were designed to provide general direction in specific policy areas: Economic Affairs (CCEA), Commerce and Trade (CCCT), Human Resources (CCHR), Natural Resources and Environment (CCNRE), Food and Agriculture (CCFA), and Legal Policy and Management and Administration (CCMA). Reagan, initially at least, was convinced of the importance of institutionalized cabinet consultation, and he made full use of those councils, particularly in his first twenty-four months in office. He was an active participant in some of the meetings, especially those dealing with economic affairs. Over time, however, the councils lost their importance and some became dormant. Three remained active, in part because of the president's interest in their work but also because of the quality of the staff work. These were the councils on Economic Affairs, Commerce and Trade, and Management and Administration. They were supported by executive secretariats and working groups, involving mostly appointed officials.[52]

Within the administration, two key policy groups underpinned much of the policy decisions of cabinet, cabinet councils, and the president: the president's Office of Policy Development (OPD) and OMB were both very close to the work of the councils. The OPD is noninstitutional in that it is "personal and partisanly political." Notwithstanding its noninstitutional nature, there is agreement that it did some solid staff work in support of the president and some cabinet councils.[53] OMB, meanwhile, has had little difficulty in securing its place in the Washington sun, given its role in the budget process.

Reagan's OPD—essentially the equivalent of the domestic policy staffs all presidents have had since Kennedy—did much of its work through the cabinet councils. It played an important role in this arena and for a while, at least, became adroit at integrating potentially conflicting actors and agencies. Terry Moe reports that the office

> gave cabinet members and bureaucratic officials a sense of meaningful participation and a means of direct, continuing input, while it also gave the administration a regularized means of reemphasizing the president's agenda and the coordinated actions required throughout government for its pursuit.[54]

The Reagan administration also proved adventurous in reorganizing the internal structure of government departments and agencies. With Congress having delegated much of its authority in this area to the Secretaries, the administration eliminated some units, consolidated agency operations, reduced the number of regional offices, centralized to Washington some services performed in the field, and downgraded some regional offices to area offices. Reagan's annual reports on *Management of the United States Government* consistently gave details of such fine-tuning measures. Occasionally, they proved more ambitious and crossed departmental or agency lines. For example, the administration launched a review of the standard regional structure of government agencies. The argument was that Reagan's new federalism, which reduced the number of assistance grant programs and improved means of communications, had reduced the need for what was considered to be an elaborate field structure. These measures invariably recorded cost savings, with offices and positions being closed down or downgraded.[55]

The Reagan administration also looked to personnel policy to control, if not reshape the bureaucracy. It sought to politicize the upper echelons of the federal bureaucracy through both formal and informal means. It applied a political litmus test to appointed and even to career officials wishing to move ahead. The administration recognized even before assuming office how important appointments, notably at the assistant-secretary level, were to implement its agenda. Contrary to previous presidents (Carter, in particular), Reagan was willing to wait to secure the "right" appointment. The Reagan team did not hesitate to spend months interviewing a great number of people for positions throughout the government. We also know that they placed (in Terry Moe's words) "almost exclusive emphasis on loyalty and ideology. Their concern was not simply with filling the obviously important positions: they wanted partisans located deep within the established bureaucracy, even if expertise was lacking." When it comes to appointments, U.S. presidents hold formidable powers far more sweeping than British and Canadian prime ministers do, and Reagan showed no hesitation in making full use of these powers. Nor did he hesitate to apply the ideological litmus test as no other president had for half a century. One key Reagan advisor explained, "The three criteria we followed were, one, was he a Reagan man? two, a Republican? and three, a conservative? Probably our most crucial concern was to ensure that conservative ideology was properly represented." William Gormley sums it up best: "More than his predecessors, Reagan took an active personal interest in subcabinet appointments. More than his predecessors, Reagan used ideology as a litmus test in the appointments process. More than his predecessors, Reagan delayed appointments until he found the right people for the job."[56]

Reagan's plans to politicize the bureaucracy did not stop with appointed officials. They extended to the Service Executive Service (SES) group and to the Office of Personnel Management (OPM), both of which came into being following Carter's Civil Service Reform Act of 1978. The SES is an elite corps of about eight thousand senior managers. Employment in this group is secure, except for political appointees who constitute no more than 10 percent.[57] Employment is secure but the job is not, in that incumbents can be demoted or transferred within the agency or to another agency. The 1978 reforms sought to create a performance-management system to make it easier to remove or to demote managers whose performance is unsatisfactory, by simplifying procedures and by lowering the burden of proof required of agency management. It also created a performance or merit pay system for managers. Performance awards may be awarded annually as a lump sum payment of up to 20 percent of basic pay. Total performance awards, however, are limited to the greater of 3 percent of the aggregate SES career payroll for the previous fiscal year, or 15 percent of the average annual rates of basic pay. The senior managers are evaluated annually, according to both individual and organizational performance, and cash bonuses are given to the top performers. Carter's reforms also divided the old Civil Service Commission into two agencies—OPM and the Merit Systems Protection Board (MSPB)—and established the Federal Labor Relations Authority (FLRA).

Guy Peters describes the 1978 reforms as "Carter's gift to Reagan," and well he could. It is widely accepted that these reforms enabled the Reagan administration to dominate the federal government's personnel management as no other had before him. Indeed, by mid 1983, over 10 percent of SES appointees were noncareer officials. Although legislation requires that only 10 percent of noncareer officials be in the group, Reagan interpreted this to mean allocated rather than filled positions. Since there are invariably more positions allocated than filled, Reagan was able to secure over a hundred noncareer appointments to the group. This, among other things, led Bernard Rosen to conclude that the reforms have been a "disaster for merit." Chester A. Newland added that "under Reagan, responsibility of the personnel system to the political system is largely defined as responsiveness to ideological executive control."[58]

The Reagan administration came under repeated criticism, not just for using the SES to ensure that people loyal to the president's agenda occupied key positions throughout the government but also for the political aspect of performance bonuses. A good number of career civil servants began to question the fairness of their performance evaluations and the management of merit and bonus schemes. In any event, the number of SES members eligible for bonuses dropped from 50 percent to 25 percent in 1980, and again by another 20 percent a few months later. The result was that only one out of five SES members became eligible for a bonus, a drop from one out of every two as was initially envisaged.[59] It is important to stress, however, that the Reagan administration was not solely responsible for the drop in SES members eligible for a bonus. Indeed, Congress made the first cut and President Carter's OPM the second.

The Office of Personnel Management had an uncertain existence, particularly during Reagan's first mandate. Reagan initially toyed with the idea of abolishing OPM, much like Thatcher toyed with the idea of dropping the Civil Service Department (CSD). Although OPM has little interest-group support, it is unlikely that Congress would have agreed to its abolition. It is easy for Congress to cry foul when anyone tampers with the machinery of government that is responsible for the management of the civil service personnel policy or the merit principle. Still, the Reagan administration successfully introduced a series of budgets cuts. From a base of about $170 million, Reagan cut 4 percent in July 1981 and another 12 percent the following December.

If career officials ever viewed OPM as an ally in promoting their interests, they quickly discovered that things would be different under Reagan. Indeed, the Reagan administration showed no hesitation in politicizing OPM. Donald J. Devine, an outspoken archconservative, was appointed to head the office. He immediately declared war on the bureaucracy, pledging to "bring the tanks up to the border." He made a habit of publicly demeaning bureaucrats, insisting that they were overpaid underperformers with an overly generous pension scheme. Devine argued, time and again, that Wilson's politics-administration dichotomy was an apt description of how government works (or at least should work), saying that career bureaucrats were there to implement decisions, period. He slashed the number of career officials at OPM while substantially increasing the number of political appointees. During Devine's tenure at OPM, the number of career officials fell by 18 percent while that of political appointees shot up by 169 percent. He openly advertised his close association with the Republican party and campaigned for thirteen candidates for Congress during 1984. Some of his political appointees at OPM also campaigned for Republican candidates, with one taking a leave of absence to manage a congressional campaign, only to return to his position after the candidate was defeated.[60]

Career officials were shocked and demoralized by Devine's hostility to them. If there is any position in the United States equivalent to the head of the civil service in Britain and Canada, it is the head of OPM. Although it was hardly welcome, civil servants could tolerate the criticism of politicians. They could not accept that the head of the civil service would declare open war on the bureaucracy and use appointments to reward friends and punish enemies. William Gormley summed it up well when he wrote that career officials can accept bureaucrat-bashing from a number of quarters, but "to be bashed by the head of the civil service was the last straw."[61]

Devine also reorganized OPM three times between November 1981 and November 1982 in order to centralize policy-making and to put it firmly in the hands of appointed rather than career officials. He created a new policy unit, which operated very close to his own office. He sought to recentralize control of the operations and at the same time to reduce the number of units reporting to him.[62]

Carter's gift to Reagan also included the establishment of an independent Merit Systems Protection Board (MSPB) to adjudicate employee appeals. To be sure, under Reagan, the board adjudicated specific appeal cases but it did not challenge the work of OPM. Indeed, observers and career officials became convinced that the Reagan administration had taken charge of the board and that it could hardly be called independent, unlike the old Civil Service Commission. The MSPB did produce a report in late 1984 that was critical of Devine's OPM, but board members deferred its submission to Congress until the following year—too late for it to have any impact on Devine's reconfirmation hearing. Indeed, one Reagan-appointed board member argued before a congressional committee that Mr. Devine had "scrupulously respected the independence of MSPB" and that "using any criteria that the Senate has applied to nominees in the past, I believe that Mr. Devine deserves to be reconfirmed."[63]

Devine's management of OPM did not go unnoticed by Congress. The chair of the House Committee on the Civil Service put up four principles that should guide the work of the director of OPM: faithfully execute the law, motivate civil servants, work effectively within the political process, and safeguard the merit principle. Knowing full well that Congress would not reconfirm him to another term at OPM, Devine withdrew his request for reconfirmation in 1985.[64]

MULRONEY

Mulroney had been more outspoken during his first election campaign against administrative reorganization than either Thatcher or Reagan, claiming it to be only an exercise to keep bureaucrats busy doing nothing. He pledged to get the bureaucrats away from "the organizational charts and back to work on the problems of the country." Once in power, he said, he wanted to get on with the work of managing government operations efficiently, put in place the right policy mix, and stay away from any temptation to tinker with the machinery of government. He insisted that his party would simply introduce "productive management" to government, adding, "Our goal is simply to govern—and to let managers manage." Clearly, he did not think that this required any reorganization or changes to the machinery of government.[65]

No sooner was he elected, however, than Mulroney lost his resolve. He created a new and politically partisan senior policy position in all ministerial offices. This was a departure from the British and Canadian traditions of public administration and drew its inspiration from the American model. He restructured the cabinet committee system, completely overhauled several economic-development departments, and established new departments.[66] In time, he went on to establish still more new departments and to abolish or reorganize over forty departments and agencies. He decided to scrap the government's budget-making process, introduce a version of Thatcher's Next Steps, and launch a high-profile initiative to redefine personnel management and, some would argue, government decision making itself.

Mulroney's decision to establish a chief of staff in each ministerial office had one purpose—to check the permanent officials' influence on policy. The position was established at the assistant-deputy-minister level, a senior-level position in the Canadian public service. Government press releases describe the position as an "official in the American style." Although senior government officials and outside observers argued that the move was incompatible with Canada's machinery of government, Mulroney pressed ahead with his decision.[67]

Mulroney was concerned that the machinery of government he had inherited would be resistant to "conservative" policy proposals, which were certain to be contrary to the preferences of the permanent civil service and to the bureaucratic interest in big government with its advantages of higher ranks and perks for individual mandarins. Most of his closest advisors subscribed fully to the politics-administration dichotomy, claiming that the influence of permanent officials had over time "crept up" to such an extent that politicians had lost control. Officials, one senior Mulroney advisor explained, "should get back to their real job—implement decisions and see to it that government operations run smoothly and leave policy to us."[68] There is no doubt that many of Mulroney's key ministers and advisors were pushing him to go even further on this front. One senior minister explained:

> Something is basically wrong with our system of government. We are the only ones elected to make decisions. But we do like the British. We move into government offices with no support. Everything in these offices belongs to the permanent government. We are only visitors, barely trusted enough not to break the furniture. I prefer the American way. Politicians there move in with their own furniture (i.e., their own partisan advisors) and run the show for however long they are elected to office. Then they move out with their furniture to let the next crowd in. I have discussed this with the Prime Minister and so have many of my colleagues. But, you know, this kind of thinking so upsets the bureaucrats that he feels he cannot go much further than he has. Appointing chiefs of staff was seen in many quarters in the bureaucracy as a revolutionary act—no, an act of high treason.[69]

All ministers had a chief of staff within days of Mulroney's coming to power. His transition team had put together a list of potential candidates for ministers to pick from as they were appointed. The chiefs of staff, however, had a mixed reception, often dependent on the quality of the incumbent. This introduced a new level between ministers and permanent officials, which has given rise to a number of misunderstandings and complications. In some instances, the chief of staff acts as a mediator between the minister and permanent officials, screening advice going up to the minister and issuing policy directives going down to officials, much to the dismay and objections of deputy ministers. Many chiefs of staff take a dim view of the competence of permanent officials, while senior officials take an equally dim view of chiefs of staff. The arrangement, one senior permanent official said, "has on the whole hardly been a happy or a successful one."[70]

Within weeks of being returned to power in November 1988, Mulroney unveiled far-reaching changes to the expenditure-budget process and to the structure of cabinet committees, in the latter case signaling the end of the Policy and Expenditure Management System (PEMS), which had been introduced by Mulroney's fellow conservative Joe Clark during his brief period as prime minister in 1979.

PEMS had been introduced with the widespread belief that Ottawa had finally found the budget process that would force politicians and officials to come to terms with their profligate spending. It was envisaged that PEMS would integrate policy and expenditure decision making more fully than PPBS ever did. Under PPBS, cabinet committees had approved policy proposals and left the spending issue to Finance or the Treasury Board, with the result that new commitments were easily made by the committees. They simply did not have to reconcile their policy decisions with the government's spending plans. A Treasury Board official explained the difference between PPBS and PEMS:

> You can compare policy and expenditure decisions to a pair of scissors. The two blades must meet for the process to be effective. Under PPBS they would never meet. Cabinet committees would make policy decisions and leave it to someone else to make resources available. PEMS has changed this. Now cabinet committees have to make both policy and spending decisions or see to it that both blades meet at the same time. They have expenditure limits or envelopes consistent with the government's fiscal plan.[71]

In short, the envelope accounting system would face the cabinet committees with the fiscal consequence of their decisions. In the past, a cabinet committee, if it wanted to approve new spending proposals beyond what was available in the budget, simply reviewed existing policies and programs and their resource levels and then brought about the necessary changes in funding levels to reflect their changing priorities. In theory, under PEMS, ministers would be forced to make tough decisions if they wanted to approve new spending proposals. In short, the intent was to place responsibility for saving squarely on the shoulders of those who spent. PEMS would also put first things first by establishing priorities, fiscal limits, and policy envelopes before developing expenditure plans. It was also designed to strengthen the hand of ministers in their relations with officials since all spending decisions would bubble up to them.

How did PEMS work?[72] First, it attempted to forge a link between operational planning and the broader government-wide strategic planning process. Second, it was conceived as a collective top-down decision-making process. Under PEMS, cabinet and cabinet committees set expenditure ceilings and established priorities. Programs were then developed within these constraints. Third, so the familiar story line goes, PEMS concentrated more on planned results in allocating resources than on program objectives, as did PPBS.

Mulroney, and for that matter nearly everyone in Ottawa, soon became disenchanted with PEMS. Indeed, Mulroney and his minister of Finance themselves hardly respected the requirements of PEMS in preparing spending plans. They turned to other mechanisms, such as the Nielson Task Force, to review spending plans. It thus came as no surprise when Mulroney announced in 1989 that the PEMS system would be disbanded.

There are several reasons why PEMS failed.[73] The main reason was its failure to instill the "financial and qualitative" discipline that was initially envisaged. Policy committees were always quick to approve new spending proposals and to spend their policy reserves. Once spent, ministers and departments did not always sit back and wait for reserves to be replenished in the next fiscal year. Many spending ministers went straight to the minister of Finance and the prime minister in search of new funds. Many were successful. Knowing that pressure for new spending would spill over from the policy committees, the minister of Finance put aside every year a central reserve to accommodate the inevitable pressure from the spenders. Once the minister of Finance agreed to fund one such proposal, however, he was in fact inviting other spending ministers to try the same route. A pattern developed whereby the Department of Finance supported the big-ticket items, while policy committees handled the less expensive proposals. Ministers with clout also bypassed PEMS when quick decisions were required.

Mulroney's changes did away with the policy envelopes and shifted effective decision making away from policy committees to a new Expenditure Review Committee (ERC), and to the existing cabinet committees for operations, priorities, and planning. Mulroney also created a number of new cabinet committees "down below"—fifteen in all, including several new ones: Economic Policy, Environment, Human Resources, Income Support and Health, Cultural Affairs, and National Identity. These committees did not have spending power in their own right as similar committees had under PEMS, and in time they became ineffective. Fewer meetings now take place, and a number of ministers skip the meetings that are called.[74]

One of the new committees established in 1989 was especially designed to keep spending in check. ERC, chaired by the prime minister, was set up to "ensure that the Government's expenditures continue to be directed to its highest priorities, and that expenditure control continues to contribute to deficit reduction." Much was made by the prime minister, cabinet ministers, permanent officials, and the media over the role of this new committee and its prospects for success. It was widely reported that Mulroney borrowed from Margaret Thatcher in "centralizing absolute power for spending cuts into a new committee."[75]

Mulroney attended the first ERC meeting where he explained to his ministers that to make the new committee work they would have to arrive at some tough decisions on spending. In the early days of the committee's work, it was widely assumed that it was, indeed, making some tough decisions. When asked whether committee members were "biting the bullet," a senior official responded that "they are not only biting the bullet, they are chewing it." The effectiveness of ERC, however, was soon questioned. Mulroney scarcely attended another meeting after the first and delegated the chairmanship to the deputy prime minister who was also later appointed minister of Finance. Spending decisions, in the words of one senior central agency official, "are now taken all over the place, depending on the individuals and the circumstances involved. In fact, there are now very few meaningful meetings of the Expenditure Review Committee ever held. The key player is the Minister of Finance."[76]

Mulroney unveiled on 12 December 1989 a high-profile and ambitious public service reform exercise, Public Service (PS) 2000. Inspired by similar reforms in the private sector, the purpose of PS 2000 is to cut red tape, empower employees, and improve service to the public. PS 2000 set up ten task forces to study specific areas, including service to the public, resource management, administrative policy, and various aspects of human resource management and organizational structure.[77] The task forces consisted almost entirely of senior public servants, and all were chaired by deputy ministers. Although PS 2000 was guided by an advisory group from the business community, academe, and government, it was on the whole an attempt by the civil service to reform itself.

PS 2000's main conclusion was that the Canadian public service needed to undergo a fundamental cultural change. The old culture and the new culture were defined as in table 2.

TABLE 2
Changing Civil Service Culture

Old Culture	New Culture
Controlling	Empowering
Rigid	Flexible
Suspicious	Trusting
Administrative	Managerial
Secret	Open
Power based	Task based
Input/process oriented	Results oriented
Preprogrammed and repetitive	Capable of purposeful action
Risk averse	Willing to take intelligent risks
Mandatory	Optional
Communicating poorly	Communicating well
Centralized	Decentralized
Uniform	Diverse
Stifling creativity	Encouraging innovation
Reactive	Proactive

Source: Public Service 2000 Secretariat, Ottawa

The PS 2000 secretariat said that the transition from the old culture to the new "requires a shift centred on prudence and probity, to one which recognizes the primacy of service to clients while accepting the need for reasonable prudence and probity."[78] It put together more than three hundred recommendations for "delayering," reducing central controls, reducing the number of job classifications from seventy-two to twenty-three, and making it easier to staff positions. The PS 2000 secretariat also put together a number of "broad strategies" to support the change: decentralization of decision making, empowerment, the notion of trust and confidence in a nonpartisan, objective, and professional public service, a reduction on controls on managers, more flexible organizational structures, upgrading the skills of government managers, and a stronger sense of service to the public.

To implement these strategies required changes, especially to ensure that centrally prescribed controls were attenuated, if not eliminated. A key target was the Public Service Commission, with its elaborate rules and regulations governing staffing, training, promotion, and dismissal. The secretary to the cabinet, in his J. J. Carson Lecture delivered on 8 March 1990, argued that, "For the Public Service Commission, the changes will mean getting out of the management business and focusing on its role as Parliament's agent in protecting the integrity of the personnel system."[79]

Changes such as these require not only alterations to the machinery of government but new legislation. On 18 June 1991, the president of the Treasury Board, Gilles Loiselle, tabled legislation "to support 2000 and to overhaul the federal public service." The background briefing material in support of the legislation reported that the government would be delegating more authority down the line, reducing levels of management, simplifying government budgets and the classification of positions. The new legislation provided for a number of changes, including measures to make it easier for departments to hire casual workers, to "release" poor performers, and to contract out activities to the private sector. The legislation also restated the merit principle as the fundamental rule for public service hiring and promotion. Collective bargaining also remained largely unchanged. The changes that were made were designed to give departments a greater role in collective bargaining and in handling grievance adjudications for cases that do not have a service-wide impact. The proposed changes made clear that employees could be "released" on grounds of "incompetence, incapacity and unsatisfactory performance." This was necessary not only to let the manager manage but also, the government explained, because poor performance on the part of some employees can "demoralize" others who perform and who often assume unfair work loads. Managers will be free to manage, but PS 2000 suggests that their performance will be evaluated. It reports that a "manager's performance evaluation will reflect how she or he has recruited and developed women and minority groups—members of visible minorities, aboriginal peoples and persons with disabilities."[80]

In the early months of PS 2000, it was thus widely assumed that important changes to central agencies would be introduced. The thinking was that they would be cut back substantially, with the secretary of the cabinet pointing out, for example, that the mandate of the Public Service Commission would be reformulated to perform essentially an audit role. Line-department managers were arguing that, if there were to be any real meaning this time to the "let-the-manager-manage" cry, then it was important to cut back central agencies. However, the legislation did not attempt to restructure central agencies, including the Public Service Commission. Employees at the commission put up, within government, a concerted defense of its organizational interest, and it was left intact.[81] In addition, no administrative reform has been introduced to cut back the size of the other central agencies.

As noted earlier, PS 2000 was unveiled on the heels of a new mandate for the Mulroney government. The government was looking for ways to breathe new life into its efforts to reform the bureaucracy. Mulroney's management innovations were floundering, with success only visible in such relatively modest schemes as cash-management policies. There were only minor cuts in the size of the civil service, minimal contracting out, and a modest degree of privatization of crown corporations to show for all the rhetoric, and the search was on for new initiatives. PS 2000 was not enough.

The Mulroney government was soon looking to Thatcher's Next Steps for inspiration. The secretary to the Treasury Board explained, "Canadian interest in special operating agencies [SOAs] was spurred by the Executive Agency, or *Next Steps* initiative in the United Kingdom."[82] Members of the Treasury Board secretariat staff were sent to London to study the agency concept and returned with ideas on how to adapt it to Canada.

The secretariat began to put forward option papers in the spring of 1989 under such headings as *Restructuring Government Service Delivery* and *A Blueprint for Redefining the Role of Government in Service Delivery*.[83] The papers suggested that there could be important savings if government service delivery was restructured. It recommended a Next Steps initiative for Canada, although the agencies would be called Special Operating Agencies (SOAs) rather than executive agencies. Other than the name change, the concept closely resembles the British initiative. However, its application to Canada has been vastly different from the British experience. The scope of the Canadian initiative is considerably less ambitious and it commands much less visibility than Britain's Next Step. Mulroney did not personally embrace the initiative, as Thatcher did, nor did he appoint a senior government official to oversee its implementation. There were no major reports commissioned, SOA has never been debated fully in a parliamentary committee, and no one has claimed—as Peter Kemp did in Britain—that 75 percent of the civil service could be reconstituted in special operating agencies. A small group—fully integrated in the program branch (that is, budget branch) in the Treasury Board secretariat—is responsible for the project.

The Treasury Board president announced the creation of five new SOAs in December 1989, and nine more in February 1991. He explained that these agencies would ensure better management in government operations and strengthen the quality of services to "customers." There is a wide mix of units granted agency status, ranging from the Passport Office to the Canadian Heritage Information Network. The government's Throne Speech on 31 May 1991 reported that more SOAs would be created to "provide better service to Canadians through more autonomy and a sharper focus on objectives."[84]

The Treasury Board secretariat has laid down criteria for the selection of SOAs. First, they must be discrete units, large enough to justify a change of status. They should be concerned with the delivery of services to the public, the private sector, or the government and should be independently accountable within their parent department. They must be subject to market discipline or otherwise to the development of performance standards; they should offer potential for performance improvement; they should currently operate under a stable policy framework, with a clear, ongoing mandate, thereby being able to establish firm performance goals; and they should be amenable to having their achievements measured. Finally, senior management must be committed to the concept and have an expressed interest in becoming an SOA.[85]

Government officials report that one of the main reasons for establishing SOAs was to provide "the first clear break with the traditional control and command model and to offer concrete evidence of the beginnings of a culture for government services that emphasizes the practices of management in place of the systems and processes of program administration." The Treasury Board secretariat made it clear that SOAs should be "business units oriented to good management" and should, over time, promote more "business-like services, improve service to the customer and demonstrate concern for efficient management." It also added that for SOAs to function properly, it was necessary to "separate policy from day-to-day operations."[86]

The SOA initiative did not attempt to deal with the principle of ministerial responsibility. Unlike in Britain, where there is a direct relationship between the agency head and the minister, in Canada the deputy minister remains the key point of contact. The Treasury Board simply reported that

> No change is contemplated in the current accountability relationship. If anything, accountability will be strengthened and made more transparent under the Agency approach. Similarly, the establishment of an Agency will not change the status of an employee as a public servant, nor will it change union representation. It will allow for the greater flexibility required to achieve agreed performance levels and clearer accountability.[87]

To become a fully operating agency, the unit has to negotiate a policy, resources, and accountability "framework agreement" with its parent department and then, through the department, with the Treasury Board. Negotiating such agreements takes anywhere from four to ten months.

Although they allow for flexibility, framework and accountability agreements are usually broken down into three parts. The first part outlines the policy and resources framework required and the flexibility and the delegation of authority needed to manage the operation. Another part presents a three-year business plan, which indicates the accountability relationship between the deputy minister and the agency, the planning assumptions, the key financial and other performance targets, and how the authorities granted under the framework document would be exercised. Yet another part is a formal Treasury Board submission, which requests approval for the agency and related authorities. The agreement also outlines in some detail the organization of the agency. All five original agencies became operational in early 1990.[88]

The purpose of framework agreements is to lay out the areas where the agency can secure more decision-making authority. It is possible to decentralize to an agency the power to introduce organizational change without going to central agencies for approval, establish a pay-for-performance plan, increase staffing authority, provide more flexibility in assigning tasks and duties to employees, and give the head of the agency freedom to move funds around to different tasks within an agreed total. The Treasury Board secretariat argued that this kind of decentralization would make government operations much more efficient and circulated a document to departments stating that the agency model would allow government operations to "apply and adopt the best private and public sector management techniques" and to "monitor performance of its main business lines to ensure progressive improvement."[89]

Inspired by the principles of PS 2000, the Treasury Board secretariat, in the summer of 1991, introduced yet another new management concept, labeled the Shared Management Agenda. The concept has four objectives: to improve communication between the Treasury Board and line departments; to improve service to the public; to encourage better "people management"; and to promote empowerment. The Shared Management Agenda works as follows: the secretary of the Treasury Board and deputy ministers agree—either in the form of a letter or a memorandum of understanding—on the management issues and objectives the departments want to address over a one- to three-year period. They then agree on the steps required to meet these objectives. Such steps can include, for example, decentralizing more authority to the department and improvements in the operations and policies of the Treasury Board.[90] The Shared Management Agenda, according to Treasury Board officials, is essentially another attempt at transforming the "command-and-control" model of government decision making into an empowered business-management model.

The Mulroney government has more recently borrowed a page from the Reagan administration and introduced the TQM concept to many government operations. It has not established a TQM institute in Canada, like Reagan did in the United States, but it has promoted a government-wide "TQM network." The purpose of the network is to promote TQM techniques and to exchange best practices in applying these techniques.

LOOKING BACK

Thatcher, Reagan, and Mulroney all looked to the reform of the machinery of government as a means of pursuing their management agenda. In each case, the underlying theme was to refocus the role of the civil service on management rather than on policy-making. Their approaches, however, differed somewhat. Thatcher and Mulroney concentrated on structural reform. Reagan, knowing that Congress would oppose such measures, used the reforms brought in by Carter to reorganize agencies internally, as well as to introduce management reform.

Thatcher showed little patience with turf wars, at least with the ones that came to her attention. She did not hesitate to put the ax to departments and administrative or policy units. The Civil Service Department, the Central Policy Review Staff, and the Management and Personnel Office were abolished. The reasons were to put an end to bureaucrats' fighting over turf, to secure a stronger handle on policy issues, and to ensure a better management of government operations.

Thatcher's most ambitious reform, however, stemmed from Next Steps, which in fact spoke volumes about the failure of her previous attempts to achieve a management revolution. Indeed, much of the report that led to the establishment of executive agencies is essentially an account of how futile previous efforts had been to get ministers and senior officials to devote more time to management and less to policy. The report claims that Next Steps was a logical outgrowth of the Financial Management Initiative (FMI). Yet, FMI was designed to improve the management of a unified civil service, government-wide. Next Steps, meanwhile, is designed to bring about a "decisive break" in the unified civil service by separating executive functions from their parent Whitehall departments.[91]

There is no doubt that Next Steps has generated a great deal of activity and strong interest on the part of many government departments. It is not at all clear, however, that the initiative will be as successful as Thatcherites would have us believe. To be sure, by May 1992, more than half of the British civil service was operating along Next Steps lines, and the program is expected to be complete by the end of 1993. In addition, there have been a number of large units—most notably the Social Security Benefits Agency, with its staff of seventy thousand—that have been given agency status.

As Robin Butler warned, however, there is a danger that agencies are being set up at a rapid rate for the sake of a scorecard to show that the Next Steps policy is successful. Others, including officials directly responsible for Next Steps, have made the same point. Some argue that, in the rush to create new agencies, a production-line look-alike model has developed, which makes the numbers look impressive, but in fact one monolith may have been substituted for another, because the agency has not been tailored to its own particular task.[92]

There are other concerns. Some insist that breaking down or attenuating Treasury controls is only half the challenge. Parent departments must in turn delegate control to the agencies, and there are indications that in a number of instances this is not taking place. Recent studies suggest that this has become a problem, that one of the main concerns among executive agencies is the amount of time spent dealing with parent departments. One agency official insists that the "biggest obstacle to providing a better service to its customers is the time spent on and the cost of activities required by the parent department, supposedly in the interests of departmental accountability." Another study, a survey of four agencies, reports that the parent department "had in all four cases interfered more not less, since they became agencies."[93]

The prime minister's own efficiency unit commissioned a review, three years into Next Steps, and its findings also point to some problems. Although the Fraser report, titled *Making the Most of Next Steps: The Management of Ministers' Departments and the Executive Agencies* predictably argued that Next Steps was going well, still it zeroed in on two problems: it stated that departments' dealings with agencies should involve strategy, not day-to-day operations, and that more authority should be delegated to agencies and their chief executives as they strengthen their track records. The report also revealed that agencies were experiencing difficulties using performance measures and information as a management tool. It also found that it was difficult to make a clean split between the policy role of the host departments and the service delivery role of the agencies. The report called for devolving still more decision-making authority to the agency heads. It called on central agencies, notably the Treasury, and the host departments to cut back up to 25 percent of the head office staff in finance and personnel areas. Finally, it called for the continued hiring of agency heads through open competition in order to bring in the best private sector people.[94]

Officials in host departments also claim that the emergence of "multiple accounting officers" has given rise to confusion with more than one voice answering for the accounts of departments before parliamentary committees. They report that this led to "management" problems in sorting out the roles of permanent secretaries and agency heads and their responsibilities to each other and to ministers.[95]

Certainly, the bureaucracy's disbelief system again kicked in with Next Steps. To make matters worse, senior officials at the Cabinet Office and the Treasury argued that the operations of the civil service could be adjusted to accomplish what Next Steps was trying to do, without having to hive off operations to agencies. The government did look to non–civil servants to fill chief executive positions and over half of the incumbents in the first thirty-four agencies established were through open competition. Still, about two-thirds of the chief executives selected were career civil servants. That tells only half the story, however. The fact remains that 99 percent of the staff in the agencies are career civil servants occupying the same jobs and doing the same sorts of things they did before. Notwithstanding the transition to agency status, agencies are not any smaller than they were as units of their departments.[96]

Although not always apparent, there were some similarities in the way Thatcher and Reagan tried to reform the machinery of government. Both, for example, used appointments to take charge of the bureaucracy and to stress the management function in government operations. Thatcher involved herself in the appointment of senior civil servants to a much greater extent than had been the case previously, and she stamped at least some appointments with a more managerial, if not more ideological seal than before.[97]

Without Thatcher's freedom to restructure at will the machinery of government, Reagan concentrated on appointments to drive home his agenda. Through the application of Carter's 1978 Civil Service Reform Act and the management of the Senior Executive Service (SES) group, Reagan sympathizers were infiltrated into the permanent bureaucracy. It is this infiltration, maintains Terry Moe, that permitted politically responsive bureaucratic decision-making criteria tied to the operation of Reagan's Office of Policy Development (OPD). The Reagan administration also went to some lengths to encourage a "networking" ethos between Reagan aides and conservative task forces and appointed officials. The purpose was to see to it that their appointees would not catch "Potomac fever" (or go native) and so to minimize the corrupting influences of career officials.[98] The Reagan administration also made use of internal agency reorganizations or reductions in force (RIFs), measures taken in the early months in office to eliminate offices staffed by career officials.

Reagan's administration already had a policy agenda, and what it was looking for was the right machinery to orchestrate its implementation: OMB and OPM were to disseminate the agenda throughout government. Stockman at OMB, with his top-down approach to budgeting, charted the course and left the details of administration to career officials. Devine at OPM did not hesitate to battle career officials head-on, to reduce their compensation and benefits, arguing all the while both inside government and in public speeches that they were overpaid for what they did. His tenure at OPM led one leading American scholar to write about the "Crises in the U.S. Civil Service." Reagan's success at infiltrating the bureaucracy and his attempts to limit the role of career officials to implementation came at a price. Members of the SES began to leave government at an alarming rate, and studies have indicated a morale problem among careerists since the early 1980s. Hugh Heclo, for example, reports that, as early as 1983, some 50 percent of those who entered the SES in 1979 had left government and another 22 percent were planning to leave.[99]

The Mulroney government was also very active, unveiling one reform measure after another, virtually from the day it assumed office. The government, as we saw, added a new senior level (a partisan policy position in each ministerial office), reorganized the economic-development departments, scrapped the government's budget-making process, established a series of new cabinet committees and SOAs, unveiled PS 2000, and introduced the shared-management agenda approach that appears to be designed to improve relations between line departments and central agencies. Despite the appearance of activity, however, Mulroney's reforms have not been successful, nor have they lived up to expectations.

The chief-of-staff position has at best played to mixed reviews. Quite apart from the fact that relations between chiefs of staff and the senior bureaucracy has on the whole hardly been productive, the government has not been able to attract to the position the kind of talent and expertise to make the concept work. It is important to bear in mind that partisan policy positions in government are an American invention and are anathema to the parliamentary form of government. They do not fit nicely with the constitutional theory of cabinet-parliamentary government, which recognizes only two types of actors: elected and accountable ministers, on one hand, and appointed and anonymous permanent civil servants, on the other. Permanent officials who have the requisite policy skills and expertise were not courted by the Mulroney government, and even if they had been, it is unlikely that they would have given up their permanent status and risked carrying forever the stigma of political partisanship. In part because of public administration traditions in Canada but also because of job security, policy analysts prefer permanent government employment to the uncertainty of a chief-of-staff position, let alone the stigma that comes with partisan politics. Mulroney has discovered that a capable and partisan policy expertise cannot be built up overnight, and appointments as chief of staff have largely been rewards to political operators rather than to policy specialists.[100]

Few observers believe that Mulroney's reorganization of economic-development departments and the budget process have been successful; many insist that they have not. The government's budget process amounts to little more than the minister of Finance's getting together with the prime minister, a few key ministers, and senior officials and deciding what can be spent and then striking a series of deals about who gets what and who loses what. One central agency official explained,

> We no longer pretend that there is any kind of planning going on in government. The expenditure budget process is purely an exercise in ad hocery. We are right back where we started from thirty years ago—a top-down budget process. We just keep our heads down and do what is expected.

Nor is the cabinet committee structure working as envisaged: only a few of the senior committees make "real" decisions.[101]

A good number of ministers are enthusiastic about the SOAs. Senior government officials, however, have openly expressed concerns and reservations about the concept, while middle- and lower-level officials have become skeptical and, in many instances, cynical. In addition, there appears to be a great deal of confusion about what an SOA is. One deputy minister wondered publicly "whether we really are going to be serious with this move this time, or is this just another of the long line of fads we have come up with over time—something that five years from now will have been forgotten." Another senior official wrote that while "a few" in the bureaucracy welcomed SOAs as a wonderful opportunity to improve government operations, a minority are cynical, saying that they have seen it all before while the majority have adopted a wait-and-see attitude.[102]

It is obvious that the Canadian government is still struggling with the proper definition of an SOA. One deputy minister described it as "a bureaucratic version of a halfway house. It is neither a jail, nor is it total freedom. It is part of a department, yet separate from it." He added that SOAs "are still very much part of the federal family. Staff in agencies are still public servants. SOAs still report to the department, to the Minister and to the Treasury Board." The secretary to the Treasury Board wrote that "SOAs are not quasi-Crown corporations. They remain a distinct part of the home department, albeit with enhanced operational authority."[103]

The uncertainty over what precisely an SOA is has given rise to problems. Senior officials readily admit that "Some Deputy Ministers are concerned about accountability and what might be called the *balkanization* of a department." This, in turn, has led to tension between the agency head and the parent department, with agencies pushing for more authority while departments are resisting.[104] Senior SOA officials complain about a lack of "authority," "empowerment," or overall support from the system to make the concept work. Unlike in Britain, where the head of the agency is the chief executive officer, in Canada the chief executive officer is the department's deputy minister, while the head of the agency is the chief operating officer. This, they insist, places the deputy minister in a conflict between the set of rules stemming from the department and those established internally by the agency. There are all kinds of incentives for a deputy minister to favor the department over an agency that is continually striving to secure arm's-length status. In any event, they argue, deputy ministers are far too busy with their own jobs to give much time to SOAs. Agency personnel also report that the lines of accountability for SOAs have never been properly defined.[105]

The biggest complaint one hears, however, is that SOAs have changed precious little, if anything. Central agencies still exercise control as much as before, and formal rules and guidelines still apply. The home department has, in turn, added a new set of rules and controls in the name of accountability. One agency head wrote that "The British are a year ahead of Canada, having launched the Next Steps initiative in 1988. However, in terms of scrutiny and will to succeed, they may lead by a light-year or more."[106] Middle-level officials in the SOAs insist that nothing has changed. One reports that

> The rules are the same and the senior executives are the same. We have seen no new blood coming from outside. If anything, the home department has made things more difficult, perhaps because they do not like part of their empire hived off. For me and my colleagues, SOA no longer stands for Special Operating Agency; it stands for Screwed Once Again. If anything, we have less freedom than before.[107]

Even its most ardent supporter readily admits that PS 2000 is not living up to expectations. To be sure, bureaucracy's disbelief culture may, in part, explain its lukewarm reception. Some officials argue, however, that PS 2000 has produced all kinds of voluminous reports and made numerous recommendations but that, in the end, it has failed to decentralize decision making and truly empower managers. Initially, it was hoped that PS 2000 would cut central agencies (in particular, the Public Service Commission) down to size. It did not, and this may well have crippled the initiative. One deputy minister explained:

> Unless you are prepared to deal with the structure and role of central agencies, then PS 2000 will be little more than an exercise of finely crafted words. You have a couple of thousand officials in the Public Service Commission, another eight hundred or so in the Treasury Board Secretariat, another couple of hundred in the Office of the Comptroller General, another two hundred or so in the Privy Council Office, and so on. These people want to be relevant. How do they keep themselves busy and relevant? Simple, they fight over turf and they get in the way of what we do. Remember, these central agency types do not have programs to deliver. So if you are not prepared to deal with this problem—and obviously PS 2000 is not—you are not prepared to deal with the real problems of government operations.

Another deputy minister reported that "I continue to modernize my operations but I do not call it PS 2000. It now lacks credibility."[108]

PS 2000 also has the stigma of being a top-down planning exercise, with ten deputy ministers chairing the task forces and then sitting down to review their own findings. A public service union leader, Daryl Bean was critical of the top-down approach, arguing that "Senior bureaucrats have no hands-on experience of either labour relations or service to the public. No wonder we got a bunch of reports designed to make life easier for managers." A representative of a private sector group with a mandate to improve the public policy process, David Zussman observed that the senior mandarins put together the package they wanted, and "all they wanted us to do was sell it after they had developed their blueprint." A student of public administration observed that he was "exasperated" by the top-down approach to middle-level managers where morale was low. The storm of protest served to erode Mulroney's support for PS 2000, and there are very few people left in Ottawa singing its praise.[109]

Although it is still early to report on its progress, the Shared Management Agenda is also being received with a degree of skepticism. Officials in line departments call it a "paper exercise," and a "make-work" project, designed to keep central agency officials busy. One deputy minister maintained that there is little to be gained in the exercise for line departments with all the "information going one way, and that is to central agencies. We still have not been able to figure out what advantages it holds for departments. Still, we go through the motions, not so much because it will accomplish anything. What it does, however, is avoid creating problems with the Treasury Board." Treasury Board officials disagree. Although they readily admit that there is a great deal of cynicism toward Shared Management throughout the "system," they remain confident that in time it will make an important contribution to better management practices. It is designed, they point out, to alert everyone to the key management and policy issues confronting departments, so that the "whole system" will be in a position to assist. It is also designed to provide some basis to evaluate the performance of senior line-department officials, to which every year Treasury Board officials are asked to provide input. At present, they have no substantive basis from which to do so, and they admit that their comments are often based on perception or hearsay. They hope that the Shared Management Agenda will in future provide a more solid footing to assess the work and performance of senior departmental officials.[110]

PART 3
SO SHALL YE REAP

9

Being There

THATCHER, REAGAN, AND MULRONEY arrived in office highly critical and suspicious of the bureaucracy. Bureaucracy-bashing had been a feature of all their election campaigns, and power did not alter their low opinion of bureaucrats as a breed. One of Canada's leading journalists wrote, eight years after Mulroney came to office, that the government still had "a visceral distrust of many public servants."[1] Nevertheless, they all claimed by the end of their terms in office that they had been able to improve their civil service considerably and to exert greater political control on policy.

Their rhetoric, at face value, implies that there existed a great deal of room for improvement. All three leaders were openly critical of the civil service. They spoke about giving bureaucrats "pink slips and running shoes," about the need to "deprivilege the Civil Service," and about aiming to "drain the swamp." The outgoing politicians did not jump to the defense of the civil servants, either. A good number of them took parting shots at the bureaucrats, convinced that the civil service had let them down. Prominent journalists and highly respected academics also—notably those from the public choice school—were less than enthusiastic about the civil service and its work. Meanwhile, public opinion surveys were reporting that public confidence in the civil service was low, ranking it barely above politicians and the tobacco industry. A former left-of-center politician in Canada reports that, in the 1960s, he signed a letter to all members of his departmental staff to thank them for serving him and the public in a competent manner during his stay in office.[2] One could hardly imagine a politician making a similar gesture in the early 1980s. All in all, it seemed that no one was speaking out in support of the civil service as an institution. Those who could and no doubt would have welcomed the opportunity, the civil servants themselves, were in no position to do so. And all of this was at a time when the public had begun to have "a pervasive sense that government agencies were not working well."[3]

Thatcher, Reagan, and Mulroney caught the mood of their electorates in calling for less government and more efficient management of the government operations that would remain. Voters who doubted the effectiveness of Keynesian economics and who had become disenchanted with the welfare state and its bureaucracy turned to those who were critical of the whole apparatus.[4] The rhetoric of the new political leadership, if nothing else, served to raise expectations that something would finally be done. Thus, the new political leadership had a window of opportunity to reform the bureaucracy. But although the window may well have been there, a carefully crafted game plan was not, as this study makes clear. The three leaders shared some strongly felt beliefs: government needed to be cut back to size; the business-management model was clearly the course to follow; it ought to be imported to government or, in the case of privatization and contracting out, government operations should be exported to it.

Lacking a grand design for reform, however, Thatcher improvised from her very first days in office and continued to do so until her last. Mulroney and Reagan (to a lesser extent) followed suit. Indeed, measures to reform the civil service in Canada were continually imported from Britain, always with a time lag and not always successfully. The 1980s featured Rayner, Grace, Nielson, privatization, contracting out, IMAA, Next Steps, SOAs, TQM, managerialism (and all that it implies, including empowerment, management-development training, and an emphasis on service to the public), PS 2000, Shared Management Agenda, cuts in personnel, and measures to strengthen the political control of the bureaucracy. New management magazines produced by central agencies—with titles such as *Management Matters* and the *Manager's Magazine*—sprung up in government departments and agencies. The level of activity directed at reforming bureaucracy was intense and far-reaching. One is tempted to turn Peter Hennessy's observation around and argue that the 1980s saw orgies of reform hardly punctuated by even brief periods of routine.[5]

Thatcher led the way. She was the first elected to power and, with the strong presence of the state in many sectors of the British economy, she had more scope to act than did either Reagan or Mulroney. She hit Whitehall like a storm and never relented. It did not take long for the Thatcher revolution to attract attention worldwide "because of its boldness, radicalism and apparent success against an entrenched system that had previously defied all attempts to change the pervasive administrative culture." Reagan, Mulroney, and their entourage kept a close watch on developments in the British civil service and they drew inspiration from them. One American official observed that

> there were lots of trans-Atlantic flights over to Britain to study developments there to see how they would apply back home. The difficulty for us was that our system is so different that a number of the measures could not be introduced. There is no denying, however, that Thatcher had an impact on Washington, perhaps not so much in the application of specific measures, but in setting the tone.

Her influence in Canada is obvious, even to the most casual observer. One senior Canadian official remarked, "Without doubt the politician who had the most significant impact in shaping PS 2000 was Margaret Thatcher."[6]

THE DETERMINED

When she arrived in office, Thatcher had three goals in mind with regard to the civil service. She was intent on cutting down the size of government, on making government operations more efficient, and on reclaiming political control over the bureaucracy. Short of a grand design, she needed outside help, people with no vested interest in the status quo, and she needed a dogged determination to pursue her agenda. She had both. She insisted on having someone from the private sector, starting with Rayner, close by her, not only to provide advice but also to play a lead role in reforming the bureaucracy. She understood that political authority was crucial to success, and she never hesitated to provide it.[7] She took a strong personal interest in all the reform measures and added a small but powerful central unit to her own office to direct developments.

Thatcher came face to face with officials and, like Wilson, Heath, and Callaghan before her, was given many reasons why she should not do what she was intent on doing. But she pushed on. In Walter Williams's words, "Mrs. Thatcher is a brute force who can override the political and bureaucratic blockages that would defeat an ordinary prime minister." And S. E. Finer claims that Thatcher "falls short of greatness, but she radiates dominance." Thatcher's deeply held conviction that her political ideology was the right one, her no-nonsense style of leadership, and her hostility to the premium attached to reaching agreement by consensus shook Whitehall. She would not be easily captured even by the most persuasive of the Whitehall mandarins. Indeed, she-who-must-be-obeyed was able to stare down most of the objections raised by senior officials. She did not hesitate to express, often openly, her disdain for professional advice that claimed to be above party politics. This is one of the reasons she abolished the Central Policy Review Staff (CPRS), preferring to strengthen her own policy unit, in addition to working with her own efficiency unit.[8]

No one disputes that Thatcher made good her promise to cut back the size of the public sector and the civil service. She privatized a number of high-profile industries, employing some eight hundred thousand people. She carried the logic of privatization to the civil service itself and earmarked a number of government activities for contracting out to the private sector.

The civil service felt Thatcher's clout in many other ways. She declared a freeze on hiring the day she came to office and scrapped plans to add new positions. She stared down the civil service unions, whose lengthy strike in 1981 ended in defeat. Sir Ian Bancroft, the head of the Home Civil Service and a widely respected figure in Whitehall, also became one of Thatcher's casualties.[9]

When she came to office, Thatcher ignored the claim in the civil service briefing books that the 733,000–strong civil service was already stretched to the limit. The books argued that there was no fat in the system and that "even modest" cuts in staff would inhibit departments from functioning effectively.[10] She announced a series of cuts early in her first mandate, and she directed that the civil service be reduced in size by nearly 15 percent. By the time she left office, it had been cut by over 22 percent, down to 569,000. She imposed the cuts by simply outlining targets. Convinced that more could be made without reduction in services, she said that cuts could be absorbed through the increased efficiency resulting from Rayner's scrutinies, and through contracting out. The Ministry of Defence, for example, reported that it would save 7,500 person-years by contracting out services such as cleaning and catering, while the diplomatic service reported projected cuts of 425 person-years by closing some overseas posts and by reducing the size of its largest missions.[11] It is important to note that in most instances contracting out constitutes false savings since the same people are employed doing the same things. They no longer appear as government employees, but governments still pay their salaries, albeit on a contractual basis. Still, departments were free to decide how to reach the targets. Many of them imposed across-the-board cuts, without regard to priorities or functions. One would be hard-pressed to make the case that the "planning" and "executing" of the cuts followed a comprehensive and rational process.[12] Some departments, like Environment, sought to identify functions that could be eliminated or substantially reduced rather than imposing across-the-board reductions. But this was the exception and, in the case of Environment, at least, it was the minister, Michael Heseltine, who insisted on this approach. Some departments did better than others, achieving their 1988 targets as early as 1984.

Fears that cuts could be made in the regions rather than in the head office did not materialize. The same is true for the industrial and nonindustrial categories of the civil service. The continuous decline in the ratio of industrials to nonindustrials simply continued. The industrials lost some 25 percent of their complement, against nearly 10 percent for nonindustrials, but this, the government pointed out, was in line with the long-term trend. The government also reported that the senior-level categories suffered the heaviest cuts, proportionally, while those who suffered least were in the lowest grades—clerical offices and below. It also revealed, however, that the heaviest losers by occupational group were blue-collar workers and the specialists—that is, the scientists, and the professional and technical groups. The administration group suffered the least.[13]

The government tried to determine the source of the cuts, to see if they were being realized through efficiency, contracting out, elimination of tasks, decrease in workload, general streamlining, decreased number of services, or a lower standard of service. It was quick to point out that a precise assessment was not possible, although it estimated that between 1979 and 1990, increased efficiency, general streamlining measures, and dropping functions accounted for 95,200 out of the 169,900 positions eliminated (see table 3). The remaining cuts came

TABLE 3
Manpower Reductions by Source Category 1979–1990
Numbers of Staff (in thousands)

	1979–80	1980–81	1981–82	1982–83	1983–84	1984–85	1985–86	1986–87	1987–88	1988–89	1989–90	TOTAL
Changes in work load (including new activities and functions dropped)	−4.9	+3.0	−3.0	−0.6	−7.8	+5.1	+5.8	+17.0	+11.7	−8.2	−2.6	−95.2
Efficiency and general streamlining	−20.1	−16.2	−13.2	−12.2	−11.3	−8.6	−8.0	−11.1	−10.0			
Transfers out												
a) Contracting out	−2.4	−1.5	−5.8	−3.7	−2.7	−2.4	−1.9	−2.4	−19.8	−2.2	−0.9	−45.7
b) Privatization and hiving off		−0.6	−1.2	−0.9	−3.2	−19.1	−0.5	−0.1	−0.1	—	−3.3	−29.0
TOTAL	−27.4	−15.3	−23.2	−17.4	−25.0	−25.0	−4.6	+3.4	−18.2	−10.4	−6.8	−169.9

Source: Based on information provided by Treasury officials, London, May 1992.
Note: Minimum estimates: full details of privatization and hivings off not collected since 1 April 1982. Figures in last column are from 1 April 1979 to 1 April 1990.

from contracting out (45,700) and privatization or hiving off (29,000).[14]

By and large, the cuts were absorbed through attrition and by the redeployment of staff so that, overall, in many areas they were not much in excess of natural attrition. Although Thatcher had no time for the "job-for-life" characteristic of the civil service, her actions did not serve to kill it completely. In 1985, there were only "five hundred non-industrial redundancies and nearly two thousand amongst industrial staff" who were actually let go, suggesting that nonindustrial employment at least remained fairly secure.[15]

Cuts in staff were only one part of Thatcher's changes in personnel management. Measures were introduced to modernize the employee-appraisal system so that performance would be evaluated against personal objectives; performance-related pay schemes were developed; and delegation to recruit employees was increased, particularly at the clerical level. A performance bonus scheme was tried in 1985, but it proved difficult to apply and was dropped. Subsequently, a new framework was introduced to link pay more closely to performance than in the past. The majority of civil servants are now covered by these flexible pay agreements. Hand in hand with the new emphasis on performance pay, the employee-appraisal system shifted from one based on intellectual qualities or some "hidden agenda in the manager's bottom drawer," to one based on performance.[16] Managers are asked to meet with their employees and set objectives against which performance can be reviewed.

Thatcher also sought to control the appointment process more closely than previous prime ministers had done, and to tap private sector expertise. She had ample opportunities to shape the senior levels of the British civil service since eleven of the twenty-three most important positions at the permanent-secretary level became vacant through "natural" retirement between 1981 and 1983 alone. She also sought to add a bit more "grit" to the civil service by appointing "doers rather than thinkers."[17] Thatcher carefully studied the list of potential candidates that the Cabinet Office put forward, and she rejected some. Whether the people she approved for appointment were markedly different from previous officeholders or from those who would be chosen by a different prime minister is, however, questionable.

To be sure, the people Thatcher appointed were younger and

showed an interest and a capacity in management. Many officials claim that a good number of Thatcher's appointments would have made any short list, whoever the prime minister, although perhaps a few years later in some instances. As Walter Williams argues, despite Thatcher's thinker-doer orientation, all the permanent secretaries appointed during the period from 1981 to 1983 were a product of the mandarin system. None came from outside. He added, "Each had travelled the normal, mighty route leading to the top of the British civil service."[18]

Thatcher met with some success in her attempts to bring business executives into government. Derek Rayner was one high-profile example and there were more. The British civil service made about seventy appointments or secondments from outside the service at the under-secretary level or above, between 1979 and 1985 alone. This may appear modest, particularly to the American reader. But to the British student of public administration, the number was high by past standards, with some observers suggesting that the "career concept" of the civil service had been undermined. To Thatcher and her advisors, however, the number was far short of expectations.[19] The program of secondments between the civil service and industry, commerce, and other outside bodies was expanded, with anywhere between eight hundred and a thousand secondments in and out of the service throughout the Thatcher years. This was not only high by past standards, it was impressive in light of the cutbacks in the civil service. One official observed that there are now always four of five senior managers from the ICI group alone serving in some capacity in government. This, he reports, was not the case in the 1970s.[20]

Thatcher's reforms extended far beyond changes in personnel management. We saw that when he was at the Department of the Environment, Michael Heseltine introduced a new financial-management information system for his department, which in turn gave rise to FMI, a government-wide system. FMI had two important objectives: to underline the importance of management in relation to policy, and to push for greater decentralization and delegation down the line. FMI was going down a well-traveled road. Fulton, the Plowden Report, and PAR had all tried to steer the civil service into this mind-set, and none had met with much success. The secretary to the cabinet, Robert Armstrong, admitted as much in 1982 when he observed that officials find policy work far more glamorous and interesting than management work.[21]

FMI resembles earlier efforts to promote a managerial culture in the civil service.[22] It has, for example, a striking resemblance to PPBS in that it is a comprehensive top-down system. Like earlier efforts, FMI seeks to establish clearly defined objectives and ways to make them operational, as well as to establish clear responsibility for achieving the objectives and a means of providing for feedback, to determine if the objectives are being met. FMI was largely designed at the center, to be implemented by departments under the guidance of a financial-management unit in the Treasury. This is essentially the same format, tried with PPBS in the United States and Canada and with PAR in Britain. The two differences with FMI are that the government gave the departments more time to implement the system and that the system received strong backing from Thatcher and from some of her key cabinet ministers.

It is debatable, however, whether FMI has been much more suc-cessful than were PAR or PPBS. Some British officials insist that it has been, while others are equally convinced that its impact has been lim-ited, notwithstanding all the activities, reports, and literature it has generated.[23] No one doubts that some Treasury controls have been loosened as a result of FMI and that the quality of information on financial and general management matters is now superior. Beyond this, however, improvements are less obvious.

Indeed, it is largely a concern that her management revolution was running out of steam that pushed Thatcher to launch her Next Steps initiative. The jury is still out on its success. To be sure, Next Steps has generated a great deal of activity in the civil service and a great deal of interest abroad. One can easily appreciate the underlying logic behind the initiative: the size, complexity, and diversity of tasks performed by the British government are now such that its civil service can no longer be treated as a single entity with formal rules and processes applying uniformly and at all times. However, making it work in the real world of partisan politics and government—as Thatcher and her officials were aware—was quite another matter, although they proved more willing to tamper with delicate questions regarding the machinery of government than Fulton was, for example, or than Canadians have been in introducing a similar initiative. In the face of strong concern (if not opposition) from senior officials, the Thatcher government accepted that the head of an executive agency should be directly accountable to a minister. Her government also recognized that, to make the concept work as envisaged, a cultural change was needed. Operations must be more businesslike and employees more entrepreneurial. For this reason, Thatcher directed the Civil Service College to prepare new programs to equip the staff of executive agencies to deal with their new responsibilities, and she insisted that business people be invited to participate in the programs.

The question that remains, however, is whether or not the decentralization of decision making has, in fact, been shifted to the agencies. While they clearly have more flexibility in hiring and redeploying staff, it is not at all clear that much else has changed.

Old ways die hard. The agencies, by and large, employ the same people who do the same jobs in the same places; they still deal with the same people in their host departments and with the same people in the same Treasury. There is no reason to assume that the disbelief culture—the inertia and resistance found in any civil service or, as D. Schon calls it, the "dynamic conservatism of institutions"—will be easily overcome. We now know that agency employees are complaining they spend too much time dealing with their "parent" departments, that they "yearn" for more independence from the system. We also know that many agencies are still concentrating on establishing themselves and that most do not yet "fully think and operate as businesses."[24] In the meantime, as we shall see in the next chapter, the executive-agencies concept will have raised—but left unresolved—fundamental issues of accountability and the continued application of the principle of ministerial responsibility.

This brings us to ask, What has Thatcher's overall impact been on the British civil service? Was she able to deliver on her rhetoric? Was she able to tame what she felt was a "greedy and parasitic" institution?[25] To what extent has she been able to make her management revolution stick?

There is no denying that Thatcher was a dominant figure in British politics and that her impact on the civil service has been strongly felt, perhaps more so than that of any other prime minister in this century. She took a keen interest in the work of the civil service and sought to reform it. To be sure, previous prime ministers had taken a similar interest. The difference with Thatcher, however, is that her interest never waned, nor did her determination to see the reforms through. She did not hesitate to confront her officials "face to face and stare them down with her own set views on the Civil Service." She was much more successful in forcing the pace of change than her predecessors were, in large part because of her "imperative style of leadership."[26]

There is strong evidence that productivity in the civil service increased under Thatcher. Indeed, the permanent secretary of the Treasury claimed in 1985 that public sector productivity was now equal to that of the private sector. A respected former senior government official, L. Pliatsky, said that between 1979 and 1985, growth in productivity in the civil service had been between 2 and 3 percent, again comparable to the private sector. There is no convincing argument, however, that this was the result of new management practices like FMI. Indeed, the government itself reported that the two most important measures in "altering the climate and the way the Civil Service works" were budget and personnel cuts.[27]

Thatcher also made it fashionable throughout government to consider "management" and "service to the public." This is not to suggest that management suddenly became more glamorous than policy, or that a profound cultural change had actually taken place. What it does suggest, however, is that management issues no longer seemed trivial to senior officials. From the cabinet secretary right down to lower-management levels, speeches were given in which management became a central theme. The Civil Service College launched new high-profile courses with management issues front and center. The completion of these courses became a new ticket to promotion, possibly to the top. And the ambitious understood the message. With not much of a market left at the top of the bureaucracy for policy analysts, many senior officials in Britain, the United States, and Canada embraced the merits of public management. Reading the speeches they gave in the 1980s, I was struck by two things: first, management had clearly become the fad; second, public management was never properly defined.[28] Inevitably, the speeches stressed the importance of effective management of human and financial resources in times of fiscal restraint. A number of recurrent themes were the same in the three countries: "empowerment," the removal of "constraints," effective management, improving the quality of service to the public. The speakers were much less forthcoming, however, on how to achieve all this and on how to reconcile empowerment with politics and political institutions.

This is not to suggest that the public sector management revolution was somehow not real. It was. In Britain, Thatcher's forcefulness and the length of her stay in office have made her message difficult to ignore or even circumvent. The public also gained an unaccustomed prominence with the new emphasis on service to the public. Courses, seminars on the topic, and market research became routine in government, something virtually unheard of ten or fifteen years earlier. Indeed, service to the public became so pervasive a theme that every government department and agency began incorporating them in mission or vision statements. *The Economist* observed, "Everybody—even absurdly, the Inland Revenue—talks about the customers."[29]

Has Thatcher's management revolution changed the face of the British civil service permanently? This is much less clear. To be sure, numbers are fewer, but a future government could quickly turn that around. The crucial issue is how the executive agencies will work over time. If they gain a degree of independence from the Treasury, their home departments, and their ministers, then clearly the operations of the civil service will have been changed markedly and permanently. Time will tell. But problems can easily be predicted (we shall return to this point in the next chapter), and the real test will come when the agencies make mistakes. How tolerant ministers, core departments, and Parliament—in particular the opposition—will be will determine how far agencies will be allowed to operate at arm's length, and for how long. The day the head of an agency goes public to say that the reason the agency is not functioning as efficiently as possible is perhaps owing to government policy will constitute another important test.

Apart from the fact that the British civil service is now much smaller, that some new and no doubt improved management-information systems have been introduced and the executive agencies set up, the institution looks very much as it did before Thatcher. Her strong interest and direct involvement in the appointment of permanent secretaries may, in the end, be only something peculiar to Thatcher's personal style. There are strong indications that John Major, for example, has limited interest in such appointments. When he arrived in office, the

Cabinet Office offered "to take such onerous duties [that is, senior appointments] off his hands—except for 35 sensitive posts." He agreed.[30]

The Victorian civil service is still recognizable, even after Thatcher. Clive Priestley wrote in 1984 that "the Civil Service is a great rock on the tide-line. The political wave, Labour or Conservative, rolls in, washes over it and ebbs. The rock is exposed again to the air, usually virtually unchanged. But Mrs. Thatcher has been applying sticks of dynamite to that rock."[31] The dynamite has left some marks, and if the executive agencies work as Thatcher hoped they would, then some chunks of the rock may well be blown away. But for the moment the basic structure remains. Even in the case of executive agencies, the contracts between ministers and agency heads are not legally binding. Nor has the civil service employment structure in London been broken up. Despite all the talk about ministers as managers, they do not have the authority even to decide on key appointments in their own departments. Career civil servants still occupy all senior posts, and they are the ones who still decide who makes it to the high-flier list—not an inconsequential matter in determining where power truly lies in government. Yet, civil servants have not been given full responsibility for managing departments. Ministers and departments still compete for funding, and central agencies still make the key decisions. The assumed demise of the generalist also appears to be premature.

Still, scratches are becoming more visible upon the rock. The overall structure of the civil service is becoming "looser" and more "dispersed."[32] The role of career officials in policy-making is being increasingly questioned on several fronts (including by politicians of all parties), and some changes appear to be emerging. Policy units within the Prime Minister's Office, consultants, and policy-making by public opinion surveys and party strategists continue to relegate career officials to a much less important role than in the past. Thatcher certainly played an important part in this shift.

THE EUNUCH

Reagan was fond of saying in his early days as president that it was "morning in America." It was not, however, morning for everyone— Reagan had, after all, come to Washington to drain the swamps. For civil servants, his arrival signaled "bedtime for Bonzo" more than it did a new morning.

Many people have drawn parallels between Reagan's approach to managing the civil service and Thatcher's. Both launched all-out attacks on bureaucracy, and both used outsiders to bring the civil service to heel. Both subscribed to the politics-administration dichotomy. Thatcher frequently talked about the government as if she were not a member of it, and only Reagan "could equal or better her in the rhetoric of dissociation."[33] Both had a dislike for "professional non-partisan" policy advice, and both abolished or downgraded policy units in the government structure. Both, the moment they came to office, immediately announced cuts in the size of the civil service.

The Reagan administration was successful, at least initially, in making the announced cuts stick. From January 1981 to September 1983, the civilian work force—which excludes the Post Office and Defense—dropped by 92,000 (from 1,240,000 to 1,148,000), a drop of 7.4 percent. Some of the cuts were made through attrition or redeployment, but the downsizing had more casualties than in the Thatcher exercise. Between 1981 and 1982, twelve thousand civil servants lost their jobs. The administration did issue new directives in October 1983 to give more weight to performance, to minimize agency disruptions, and more generally to limit the policy's negative impact on employees.[34] By then, however, the bulk of the cuts had been made, so the directives had limited impact. In addition, much as Thatcher had taken on the civil service union after the lengthy 1981 strikes, Reagan took on the air-traffic controllers. Both claimed victory.

Still, there were important differences in style. Thatcher's was hands-on. She made a point of carefully reading briefing materials and returning them with specific instructions written in the margin. She never deviated from her strong personal commitment to all reform measures. Reagan was more at ease playing the role of chairman of the board, leaving the details to his trusted advisors. His continuous display of nonchalance to the details of governing in fact led many to question the extent to which he truly applied himself to his job.[35] To some observers, the Iran-Contra scandal revealed that Reagan was guided throughout his presidency by his "handlers," that he was protected (and some even suggest cocooned) to a degree not seen elsewhere in modern political and executive leadership.

Still, Reagan's agenda met with considerable success during his first two years in office. Not only was he able to make cuts in the civil service, he successfully pushed through Congress major parts of his bold conservative agenda. His advisors and political appointees immediately set out to divide Washington into two camps: Them and Us. "Them" was anyone who had served in the bureaucracy for any length of time. David Stockman was initially of this view but later acknowledged that "the six hundred OMB career staffs were dedicated anti-bureaucrats."[36] Reagan's approach to civil service reforms in the first years of his administration largely consisted of top-down budgetary measures. Stockman and OMB staff went through agency budgets cutting programs, entitlements, and staff. They went after big- as well as small-ticket items. In the early weeks, they keyed in on management positions, eliminating some and, on occasion, pushing to eliminate whole levels in certain agencies.

This squared with what has been described as Reagan's supply-side-management approach. The key element in the approach is to limit or preferably decrease the number of managers in government. The thinking here is that fewer managers means less tendency for government to expand, and that those who remain manage programs directly. Supply-side management is also rooted in the politics-administration dichotomy. It implies that government is able to get along with few managers because it leaves "to career administration the details of administration while appointed officials chart broad policy directions."[37] Supply-side management explains why in many instances the top-down budgeting procedures of the Reagan administration left career officials out in the cold. In some agencies, they were not only excluded from packaging the cuts, they were scarcely informed until everything had been decided.

The administration moved quickly to push its cutback program through Congress, knowing it could ride the wave of popular support for the president for several months after the election. It sought to take full advantage of the honeymoon period every administration enjoys after an election victory and before the opposition can organize. In the early days, popular support for the cutback program was perceived to be so strong that members of Congress reportedly feared to express opposition to it.[38] David Stockman described the first days of the Reagan administration as "One blitzkrieg followed another as the revolution moved up to Capitol Hill." The goal was to get the program through, and he and other Reagan advisors had little time for constitutional niceties. Stockman explained that "enacting the Reagan administration's economic program meant rubber stamp approval, nothing less. The world's so-called greatest deliberative body would have to be reduced to the status of a ministerial arm of the White House."[39] The administration employed every means to ensure legislative victories. It knew that it was facing a democratic majority in the House and feared splits in the ranks of Senate Republicans. The administration employed several strategies to drive its agenda through Congress, including

> drawing on the president's personal powers of persuasion, making administrative changes overseen by carefully selected political appointees, centralizing the policy management process in the White House, implementing top-down budgeting at the Office of Management and Budget and using the reconciliation provisions of the congressional budget process in an unorthodox way.[40]

During his first year, Reagan secured Congress approval to enact a cut in income taxes, notably to businesses and upper-income individuals. He also won approval for important cuts in spending, amounting to $40 billion in constant dollars, implemented between 1981 and 1983.[41]

Although less ambitious over time, the administration continued until its last months in office to identify programs and specific activities it wanted eliminated or reduced, as well as cuts in the civil service. But, as early as the fall of 1981, the spirit of resignation evident among the House Democratic leaders in the aftermath of Reagan's first victory was giving way to a spirit of defiance. Congress also became concerned over press reports that the president was riding roughshod over its role and wanted to demonstrate once again its independence. The administration's new fall budget offensive met with a cool reception in Congress, and by 1982 and 1983 outright opposition became the order of the day. Not only were Democrats hostile to most of the Reagan proposals to cut into domestic programs, but even Republicans began to oppose them as well. In fact, the Republican-dominated Budget Committee flatly turned down the budget by 21–0 in April 1982. Reagan refused to back down, and the committee essentially rewrote the budget, denying most of the cuts and incorporating new tax increases. Reaching a consensus on where to cut began to prove difficult within the administration itself. Stockman explains that he started to sense a problem even in the early months of the administration, when he discovered

> that the glory days of the Cutting Room were over. Resistance began to crop up everywhere both within the Cabinet and on the Hill. In its totality, it amounted to a counter-revolution—a broad range of political signals that the free market and cut-welfare state premises of the Reagan Revolution were not going to take root.[42]

Stockman himself did not help matters. He was reported in Bill Greider's article in the *Atlantic Monthly* in late 1981 as having reservations about some of the Reagan measures. He observed that the president's tax legislation was "a Trojan horse, filled full of all kinds of budget busting measures and secondary agendas." The president, it will be recalled, took Stockman to the woodshed but did not remove him from OMB. Although it was later revealed that the "woodshed story" was a publicity stunt, Stockman's credibility and that of OMB itself were damaged, and so was the top-down budget process. There were very few people anywhere still willing to accept OMB's projections at face value as it valiantly continued to project a budgetary surplus in future fiscal years, beginning in 1984.[43]

Few in Congress—or for that matter in the administration—believed that Reagan could achieve a balanced budget by the end of his first mandate, let alone by 1983, as he had suggested before he came to power. It became clear that an important mid-course correction was necessary after the 1982 congressional elections. Congress would never again be as compliant as it had been during Reagan's early months in office. It would play havoc time and again with the administration's plans, particularly on the budget. In short, the democratic gains in the mid-term election and a split in the ranks of the Senate Republicans saw "stalemate set in" and the administration had little additional success in advancing its agenda.[44]

There is no doubt that if the Reagan administration could have had its way, we would have seen more cuts in domestic programs and a much greater shift of responsibility to other public and private bodies. One can also easily speculate that Reagan's majority in a parliamentary form of government would have led to major cuts in government operations, to more privatization, and to a much smaller civil service. Lacking the clout to do these things, Reagan's administration turned to improving the management of government operations as the new priority. It is as if the administration concluded that, since it was unable to cut domestic programs, it would see to it that they would be better managed. It is perhaps no simple coincidence that the Grace Commission was established in February 1982, at about the same time it became obvious that major surgery on most government programs and the size of the civil service was not going to happen.[45]

Members of the Reagan administration and observers have pointed to several reasons why Reagan's cuts were not as deep as he had hoped. Congress stands at the top of most people's list. The "iron triangles" where interest groups lobby both Congress and agencies also figure prominently. Some claim that Reagan failed because the presidency itself has become an impossible job, suffering from a serious "overload problem." Still others—including a number of senior Reagan advisors—blame a stubborn civil service of bureaucrats who resisted change and played to interest groups and Congress to protect their programs and their jobs.[46] For his part, David Stockman—the key architect of the plan to cut government spending and the size of the civil service—offers this explanation:

> The true Reagan Revolution never had a chance. It defied all of the overwhelming forces, interests and impulses of American democracy. Our Madisonian government of checks and balances, three branches, two legislative houses and infinitely splintered power is conservative, not radical. It hugs powerfully to the history behind it. It shuffles into the future one step at a time. It cannot leap into a revolution without falling flat on its face.[47]

Although strengthening management practices did not hold great promise as a way of rolling back the state, they were much easier to accomplish. Better management was less threatening to Congress and interest groups and, in any event, many important management reforms could be implemented without congressional approval. In short, the administration had a much more direct control of what it could do in management reform. The other side of the coin, however, is that the blame for any failures could not be shifted elsewhere.

Reagan began to introduce one management reform after another, starting in 1982. Taken together, they suggest a highly ambitious agenda, bringing forward an array of specific measures, ranging from the Grace Commission to the introduction of TQM to government operations. This is not to suggest that the Reagan administration had a coherent approach to improving management practices. It did not. His approach was much more schizophrenic, contradictory, and even more disjointed and ad hoc than Thatcher's reforms.

Reagan's Grace Commission, his desire to import the business-management model to government, his Cabinet Council on Management Improvement, his Council on Integrity and Efficiency, his Reform 88, his emphasis on providing better-quality service to the public, his Productivity program, and his endorsement of TQM all constitute an impressive list of initiatives. Taken as a whole, however, they do not add up to an overall strategy or even to a guide for managers.

The business-management model, the Productivity program, and TQM are concerned with the "empowerment" and the "trusting" of managers and employees to make the right decisions most of the time. They, like many of Thatcher's initiatives, hark back to the politics-administration-dichotomy model, by which policy is decided at the top, with the rest of the government being treated like a business organization, left to decide only how to implement the policy most efficiently. This requires decentralizing decision making and letting managers decide what can be cut from their budgets. But it also requires a tolerance of errors. To be sure, the U.S. government has long had many agencies that enjoy a greater degree of autonomy than is the case under a parliamentary form of government, and the argument can easily be made that, unlike Thatcher and Mulroney, there was no need for Reagan to embrace FMI or Next Steps–type measures, or to stress decentralization of decision making.[48] Still, the Reagan administration moved in the opposite direction. It sought to tighten White House control over the agencies, through OMB's budget process and OPM's policies on personnel management. Political appointees in agencies did not restrict themselves to setting policy or to deciding on the ends. Although the matter varied from agency to agency, they did get into the question of means—what should be cut and how, when, and where.

Reagan and his administration sought to do two things with the civil service. They wanted to break the political will of the traditional bureaucrats to make them more responsive to top-down political and policy decisions. At the same time, they wanted to turn public administration into public management, convinced that the business-management model based on identifying market need was far superior to the traditional public administration, with its emphasis on rules and procedures.[49] This gave rise to confusion, with career officials feeling that they were being asked to run in two different directions at once. The administration was never able to reconcile its desire to bring the bureaucrats to heel with its desire to make the private sector bottom-up model work in government.

Reagan's Integrity and Efficiency measures, the Grace Commission, and his decision to strengthen the role of inspectors general certainly spoke to other priorities than "empowerment" or the business-management model. These measures denoted a lack of trust in career civil servants. Certainly, public statements explaining their necessity hardly constituted a vote of confidence. The purpose of Grace, Reagan said, was to put the fox among the chickens, and he asked the commission's staff to work like untiring bloodhounds to sniff out waste and mismanagement. His inspectors general were to be "meaner than junkyard dogs." It is difficult to imagine any other message for career officials than that they must manage by the rule book.

Will Reagan's reforms have any lasting impact on the American civil service? Some will, but certainly not to the extent that Thatcher's have had on the British civil service. He did try to cut the size of the service, and he met with some success early on. By the end of his second mandate, however, the civil service was larger than when he first came to office. Reagan's shifts in policy and programs did entail a new distribution of civil servants across agencies. Federal employment in nonpostal domestic-policy agencies dropped by over 130,000, while increases in defense agencies, the departments of State, Treasury, Justice, and Veterans Administration totaled over 150,000. In addition, the size of the postal service grew by about 125,000.[50]

The Reagan presidency, in part thanks to Carter's civil service reforms, gave political appointees greater leverage than ever before in their dealings with career officials. As we saw, Carter's 1978 Civil Service Reform Act made it easier for the Reagan administration to appoint people to senior executive positions and to move them around, thus securing a high degree of political presence and control over the career civil service. The policy role played by top-level career officials has been greatly reduced. Indeed, in some agencies, they were purposely excluded from policy discussions and simply told to await specific orders from the political appointees. Charles H. Levine argues that this constituted an "assault on the concept of neutral competence which previously guided civil service doctrine." Reagan set the stage to replace "neutral competence" by "responsive competence" through his considerable power of appointment.[51] The pattern has been established for future administrations to do the same.

The administration has also successfully modernized the nuts and bolts of government operations. It has introduced a number of measures to correct deficiencies in cash management, debt collection, and real property management. It has also improved considerably computer planning and operations in government agencies. Although some claim that these reforms amount to little more than penny-pinching, taken as a whole they amount to important administrative improvements and cost-saving measures.[52] Still, with the TQM rhetoric set aside for a moment, the administration's management revolution essentially consisted of cost-cutting, the centralization of management policy-making, and stronger controls through auditing and more stringent accounting practices.

The Reagan administration also legitimized, as none had done before, a debate over the means of implementing public policy. The administration threw open a full public debate on privatization and contracting out, even though it was not nearly as successful as it would have liked to have been in shifting more government responsibilities to the private sector, state governments, and volunteer associations.

Still, the Reagan administration was not able to leave a lasting imprint or create a new institutional environment. Unlike Carter, for example, who left behind a new Civil Service Act that transformed personnel management in government operations, Reagan's legacy has been more in areas under the discretion of the president. He did not institutionalize his conservative revolution with landmark legislation or by bringing permanent change to the way the U.S. government works. With some important exceptions apart, most of the legislation and programs Reagan inherited from Carter in January 1981 are still in place and their funding levels are essentially the same as they were under Carter.[53]

THE NOT ALWAYS COMMITTED

Mulroney arrived in office full of bravado about putting the bureaucrats in their place. Even toward the end of his second mandate, bureaucrats were still the butt of many of his jokes, both in caucus and in private meetings.[54] Mulroney's goals in reforming the civil service were precisely the same as Thatcher's—to cut down the size of government, to make its operations more efficient, and to reclaim political control over the bureaucracy. He imported to the Canadian civil service many of the reforms Thatcher introduced in Britain. The Mulroney government also looked to the Reagan administration for new ideas, particularly with regard to the nuts and bolts of government operations, and even formulated a few ideas on its own. If one looked at the number of measures introduced as the sole yardstick of success, Mulroney would win hands down. By any other criteria, however, the picture is quite different. Mulroney lacked Thatcher's determination to push things through and Reagan's excuse that Congress had blocked his efforts.

Like Thatcher and Reagan, Mulroney decided to cut the size of the civil service shortly after he came to office although, as in Britain, there was pressure to increase it. The Mulroney government ignored the pressure, however, and announced that the service would be reduced by fifteen thousand within six years. It did not say how or where the cuts would be achieved. The minister of Finance simply reported that the government was confident that the public service would "adjust to achieve greater productivity and efficiency with a minimum amount of disruption in service to the public."[55] The Mulroney government did not—as Thatcher did and as Reagan attempted to do—try to cut the civil service beyond this initial fifteen thousand.

The Treasury Board secretariat picked up the ball and put together a five-year work-force-adjustment program designed to effect the cuts by the end of 1991. By 1990, it could report that cuts totaling over eleven thousand had been made, and more, with a minimum of dislocation to civil servants. In fact, throughout the life of the program, only a thousand people were actually laid off. The great majority of those affected were reassigned within the civil service after their original positions were eliminated. Treasury Board officials also report that a large number of employees welcomed being laid off because of the attractive pay package accompanying the work-force-adjustment program.[56]

It is necessary, however, to qualify the success of the program. For one thing, most of the positions shown as cut were in fact merely transferred or devolved to provincial governments, territorial governments, Indian bands, and the private sector. Treasury Board officials report this was the case for over 50 percent of the positions.[57] In thus devolving the positions, the federal government also transferred the required funds to pay their salaries. For example, between 1988 and 1989, the Department of Indian Affairs and Northern Development (DIAND) transferred 175 person-years to Indian control, and between 1987 and 1988, Correctional Services reported a decrease of 236 person-years, largely because it devolved some of its responsibilities to provincial governments. In both cases, the federal government signed an agreement to transfer the necessary funds to pay the salaries. The cost of the function obviously is still paid by the federal government, although it no longer carries the person-years on its books.[58]

The largest cuts—5,500 person-years—occurred in the first year and were relatively painless. The numbers were 3,100 from 1987 to 1988, 2,000 from 1988 to 1989, and just 1,000 from 1989 to 1990.[59] Departments do not always "burn" all their person-years. For example, a department may have twenty thousand person-years, but not all positions are likely to be filled for twelve months because it is not possible to plan for all promotions, retirements, and transfers to make full use of the allotment. In the first and second year of a person-year cutback, departments can manage the cuts by not staffing all vacant positions and by redeploying personnel.

The program ended on schedule, although not on target. The Mulroney government was not able to cut 15,000 person-years; the number stalled at about 12,000. The government, nevertheless, claimed a victory, of sorts, insisting that it had bravely made some cuts in the face of tremendous demands for increased staff to implement new policies and programs, such as the labor-intensive Goods and Services Tax introduced on 1 January 1990. Whatever the merits of the argument, the size of the Canadian civil service stood at about 232,000 at the end of Mulroney's second mandate, down 4,000 from the day he came to office. However, big government may yet make a comeback. The Canadian civil service grew again by nearly 4,000 between 1989 and 1991.[60]

To cut the size of the civil service was only one part of Mulroney's agenda to reform government operations. Like Reagan, Mulroney had pledged to have a balanced budget by the end of his first mandate. The annual deficit, however, has been stuck at $30 billion—about the same level as during Trudeau's last full year in office. This is so despite new taxes, numerous tax increases, and a much wider use of user fees.[61]

A number of reasons have been put forward to explain this inability to cut spending, either to the extent Mulroney himself had predicted while in opposition or to the extent his minister of Finance insisted on during his first major economic statement and his first budget. High among most explanations is Canada's regional factor, which fuels demands for new spending and inhibits cabinet from cutting existing programs. But Mulroney himself has frequently intervened: to secure new initiatives, on occasion to stop cuts from being made, or even to restore funding levels after the cuts were made.[62] A senior Mulroney cabinet minister explained,

> Contrary to what is commonly believed, Mulroney is not an ideologue. He likes to cut a deal. That is what he did for a living before he came to politics. He does talk about cutting spending, but it really depends on the day of the week. He will not very often let fiscal problems get in the way of a good deal or good politics.[63]

Unable or unwilling to cut spending, Mulroney did what Reagan had done earlier. He shifted his emphasis to the strengthening of management practices. Mulroney's initiatives have been even more varied than those of Thatcher or Reagan. They did not entail the contradictions of Reagan's initiatives; but neither have they borne the mark of a personal commitment and a firm hand that characterized Thatcher's. His government's attempts to improve management did have fairly consistent goals, however. The politics-administration dichotomy is central. A consistent emphasis is placed on management over policy, on the empowerment of line managers and employees, on quality of service to the public, and on the business-management model for inspiration.

The question that jumps to mind when one looks at the Mulroney initiatives is, Why the constant flow of new measures? The first was the Increased Ministerial Authority and Accountability (IMAA) initiative, introduced in 1986. IMAA was designed to remove constraints to good management, to decentralize decision making, to improve service to the public, and more generally to let the manager manage. A few years later, a mainly private sector group devoted to promoting a strong civil service urged the prime minister to launch a program of reform that would strengthen the management of people in government, eliminate unnecessary bureaucracy, and modernize the information and computer capacity of government operations. This was how PS 2000 was born. Like IMAA, PS 2000 is designed to remove constraints to good management (particularly in the area of personnel management), to remove many centrally imposed controls, and to emphasize service to the public. Later, a page was borrowed from Thatcher, and the SOAs came into being. Although this involved hiving off certain activities to be recast in an agency framework, again the underlying purpose was to empower managers, to free them to make decisions. More recently, the Canadian government, as the Reagan administration before it, has sought to introduce TQM to government operations.[64] TQM seeks to improve productivity and to encourage employees to focus on the quality of service to the public. It too speaks of empowerment and of removing constraints to good management. This came on top of the Shared Management Agenda, which was introduced by the Treasury Board secretariat in the early 1990s with identical goals.

Why this never ending parade of new measures? There are two possible answers. Either the government sought to reinforce managerialism by introducing one complementary measure after another or it felt that it needed to breathe new life into the system to prevent the reforms going flat. The latter is the most plausible explanation.

Some six years after IMAA was introduced, only about one-third of government departments had signed the MOU with the Treasury Board that was required to implement the concept fully. Those that have signed are not singing the praise of IMAA, insisting that the paperwork involved and the reporting requirements are not compensated for by the limited freedom they get from central-agency controls. The Treasury Board's pledge, made at the time IMAA was introduced, to review all centrally prescribed rules and regulations so as to remove constraints to good management does not appear to have come to pass. Four years later, the Privy Council Office declared in introducing PS 2000 that "the personnel and administrative management regimes are encrusted with barnacles of rules and procedures that are wasteful and hamper efficiency." A widely respected former secretary to the Treasury Board, now retired, explained that the reason for IMAA's failure to remove constraints to good management is because the "work was largely the responsibility of central agencies which had little motivation for change."[65]

The disbelief culture is certainly a major factor in the Canadian civil service. The head of the PS 2000 secretariat explains that what is required to instill a stronger managerial culture in government operations is "70 percent attitudinal change, 20 percent machinery change and 10 percent legislation."[66] One can easily appreciate that senior civil servants, especially long-serving ones, would have difficulty getting excited about IMAA, PS 2000, and Shared Management Agenda. One after another, for the past twenty-five years or so, measures to reform the civil service have been marched in front of them. It requires a particularly optimistic frame of mind to believe that this new parade after Glassco's call to "let the manager manage" will have a lasting impact.

The actions of central agencies also have not helped matters. When PS 2000 was launched, there was hope that the size and mandate of some central agencies, notably the Public Service Commission (PSC), would be substantially cut back. And it was not. This has served to reinforce the disbelief culture among civil servants who remain convinced that the machinery change must come first, if there is any chance of an attitudinal change. Both the PSC and the Treasury Board secretariat have retained virtually intact all their bureaucracies responsible for administrative and personnel policy. The same is true in the administrative, personnel, and financial policy bureaucracies in the head offices of departments, notwithstanding several measures to decentralize decision making and to remove centrally prescribed rules and constraints to management. The head of the PS 2000 secretariat reports the staff in these units are busy redefining a role for themselves and their organizations but without much success. He reports that recent surveys in the head offices of several large departments reveal a "deeply serious" morale problem, which he attributes to a lack of meaningful role for the staff.[67]

Some powerful central agencies have paid lip service to the new management reforms when it came to their own operations. All departments were asked to delayer their management levels so that there are only four levels of managers between the working level and the deputy minister. The Department of Finance, the most powerful economic ministry and the "guardian" of the public purse, has long had several levels, ranging from the deputy minister to associate deputy minister, senior assistant deputy minister, assistant deputy minister, general director, director, and managers. To delayer, the department simply declared that, henceforth, three of the levels would be considered staff positions and would no longer constitute management levels.[68] Everybody stayed in their positions doing precisely the same things as before. This only served to reinforce the skepticism of those in line departments and to fuel the disbelief culture.

Line department officials also claim that central agencies very seldom participate in activities designed to strengthen management practices in government. They report, for example, that senior central-agency officials are few on the ground in the courses and activities of the Canadian Centre for Management Development (CCMD), which was established to promote better management practices in government. According to one senior line-department official, "[the central agencies are saying] do as we say, not as we do. This is not the way to make the management message stick."[69]

One of the main reasons for the plethora of measures to strengthen management practices in government operations has been the lack of firm leadership at the top. Although Mulroney spoke Thatcher's language, he lacked her conviction. He adopted her agenda, convinced it would get his party back in power after being frozen out for so long. But once in office, he was much more at home cutting a deal than pressing for an ideology or a set agenda. This was as true in government as out. One of his senior ministers explained,

> Remember Mulroney was one of the most skilled labor lawyers in Canada before he came to office. He looks at problems one at a time and also looks to one solution at a time. He got briefed on IMAA all right and gave his blessings. The same is likely true for

the other measures. He agreed to each package, one package at a time. He is not the type to add them all together to make sense out of the whole thing. As far as I know, he never requested regular briefings on how things were progressing with the civil service. . . . Whatever you may hear, making the bureaucracy work better has never been a burning matter for Mulroney. As far as he is concerned, announcing that we would cut 15,000 bureaucrats and PS 2000 were good enough.[70]

A senior central-agency official who has worked closely with Mulroney agreed:

Mulroney is not the most focused politician. Nor would he very often request briefings on how the various management reform measures were progressing. Once in a while, he would declare that one issue—say, the deficit—was the priority issue for the government. That would hold for a while, or until another issue that caught his attention came around. I have seen him become consumed by the Canada/U.S. Free Trade Agreement, by national unity, by a looming general election, but never by public service reforms.[71]

How different will the Canadian civil service be after Mulroney? Not much. It is largely the same size today as it was when Mulroney first came to office. He never confronted the civil service, as Thatcher did during its prolonged strike or as Reagan did with the air-traffic controllers. When the Mulroney government announced a policy of wage restraint in 1991, calling for a 0 percent increase in wages in the fiscal year from 1991 to 1992 and for a 3 percent increase the following year, the union called a strike. The government legislated the employees back to work. In the aftermath of the strike, however, the government agreed to a job security provision for the unionized civil servants. It later decided to extend the provision to the management category. The president of the Treasury Board explained that in exchange for accepting the 0 and 3 percent increases in wages, the government was making a "commitment that every current employee of the Public Service will be offered a position on comparable terms, for the period for which the wage restraint applies, if he or she is willing to be trained and relocated."[72] In addition, despite all the talk of delayering, there are more managers today than in 1984.

Mulroney pledged to open up the civil service by bringing in people from the private sector. For a while, he got personally involved in an exchange program between government and the private sector. But here too his interest waned over time, and his government was no more successful than was Trudeau's in attracting business executives to serve in senior positions. The same holds for staffing the management category. In 1990, for example, only 69 appointments out of 829 came from outside the civil service. This is about the same level as before Mulroney came to office.[73]

To be sure, there were a number of changes at the senior levels. For instance, after two years in office in 1986, Mulroney had changed all deputy ministers. Some were simply reassigned to other departments. About 20 percent of all managers took early retirement, after being offered strong incentives to do so. But the government turned to the civil service itself for their replacements or, as one cabinet minister explained, "We replaced one bunch of bureaucrats by another." All the rhetoric about management rather than policy being the new road to the top has not in practice had much impact in Ottawa. There are fewer deputy ministers today in Ottawa with field and program experience than there were in 1977. In addition, the background of the bulk of deputy ministers appointed by Mulroney was in central agencies. This was true, for example, for eight of the ten deputy ministers he appointed between 1987 and 1990.[74] If there is any difference from the past it is that the new mandarins appear to have made their mark working on civil service and management reform rather than on preparing policy papers and on "fixing" high-profile political problems. In any event, Mulroney never insisted on a hands-on approach to the appointment process to the same extent Thatcher did.

It is highly unlikely that Mulroney's SOAs will have any lasting impact on government operations unless far-reaching reforms are introduced. As we noted earlier, the concept was borrowed from Thatcher's Next Steps. However, a number of key features of Thatcher's executive agencies were not incorporated in the SOAs. Perhaps more important, however, the SOAs lack a firm political hand to promote them. The head of one SOA recently wrote, "The most glaring differences (between Executive Agencies and SOAs) are that Canadian SOAs are not politically driven in the same magnitude."[75]

Certainly, the political forces that gave rise to the executive agencies in Britain were not the same in Canada. In Britain, the concept originated from Thatcher's efficiency unit, and she took a strong personal interest in their creation. In Canada, although ministers have welcomed SOAs, the impetus to make them work has come from officials who, however, report that in some instances they pushed for agency status because ministers were set on privatizing the unit. For them, it is preferable to be an SOA because the unit remains "part of the family."[76]

One also has to search far and wide in line departments to find more than a handful of managers who see a future in IMAA, PS 2000, Shared Management Agenda, or TQM. There is no doubt that the sense of déjà vu is overpowering. In the end, it may well be that the most lasting impact of the latest round of reform initiatives will have been to reinforce the disbelief culture in the Canadian civil service.

ON THE INSIDE

The 1980s constituted a hostile environment for civil servants. Guy Peters writes about Thatcher and Reagan "burning the village" and speculates that the job of the civil servant had to be difficult since the profession was "the object of so much vituperation." I asked most of the career officials I consulted to reflect on their work in the 1980s. Almost to a person, the response was negative. One American official summed up the general feeling when he observed,

> You are asking me how well the swamp dwellers fared in the 1980s. Frankly, not very well. It was not just one thing; it was many, many things. Sure, the rhetoric was one factor. But you can add such things as lack of trust, a desire to put us in our place and a general lack of appreciation of what the civil service has accomplished over the years and can still accomplish. The 1980s were not a time to be brave and to speak truth to power.[77]

Many civil servants have now come to accept that antigovernment feelings and bureaucrat-bashing come on schedule during election campaigns. Thatcher, Reagan, and Mulroney were different in that their rhetoric did not stop with their election victories. It continued, with all three at times sounding as if they were not part of the government. The underlying message that emerged from the rhetoric was that of a "bloated and misdirected behemoth staffed by incompetent zealots, hardly an image likely to encourage bureaucratic self-esteem."[78]

Officials in the three countries insist that political ideology was not the only force at play throughout the 1980s. Fiscal restraint, in their opinion, has also served as a major catalyst to managerial reforms in the three countries. The three leaders were not as successful in cutting government programs and spending to the extent they had hoped. When it became clear that Grace, Nielsen, and (albeit to a lesser extent) Rayner were not leading to substantial spending cuts, Thatcher, Reagan, and Mulroney turned to the only options available—privatization and better-managed programs and operations. A senior Canadian cabinet minister and a member of the Nielsen task force explained,

> With Nielsen failing to make much of an impact on the expenditure budget, we were sending out one heck of a message. If a newly elected government, committed to cutting back programs, handed out all kinds of ideas through task force reports to cut spending, but in the end could not cut spending, then one can easily appreciate why some people in government assumed that nothing else would work. I admit that it became easier for us to talk about better management practices than cutting spending.[79]

Officials in the three countries report that, by and large, the civil services are trying to make managerialism work. They also insist that, on the whole, career officials were far more receptive to Thatcher, Reagan, and Mulroney than is generally assumed. They add that, although there were a few "rejectors," there were a good number of "skeptics."[80] To be sure, many civil servants felt that Thatcher, Reagan, and Mulroney had an "impoverished" concept of management. They agreed with Christopher Pollitt's view that management requires something more "than a strong executive with a consistent set of prejudices."[81] Indeed, many say that the political leadership was highly selective in importing the business-management model to government operations, that they conveniently discarded things that did not square with their prejudices.

Thatcher, Reagan, and Mulroney approached managerialism in ways that had a number of things in common. At no time were any of their strategies coherent or comprehensive. All involved a series of piecemeal and ad hoc measures that emphasized routine and embraced the politics-administration dichotomy, with career officials being told that their job was to manage government operations. But even here the message was not always coherent. The three leaders at times spoke of "empowerment" and stressed "quality of service" to the public. At other times, they—particularly Reagan—wanted their senior officials to manage government operations like good accountants. One can but conclude that at times the politics-administration dichotomy was being interpreted by the politicians to mean that they themselves should manage both policy and administration.[82] Civil servants were never certain if managerialism was moving them toward or away from the Weberian type of bureaucracy—the new political leadership was never explicit on such a crucial point.

The call to let managers manage rang empty for a number of civil servants. For one thing, they had heard it many times down through the years and they were skeptical as to how it could be repackaged in the 1980s and sold as a bold new reform measure. For another, the three political leaders intervened in the appointments and promotions processes to a far greater extent than before. To be sure, new management-development courses were now in place. But to many, these courses—with their mixture of business and government managers brought together under one roof—only served to underscore the lack of trust in bureaucrats and in traditional public administration. In short, civil servants were made to feel that they had a great deal to learn from their private sector counterparts.

The politics-administration dichotomy also pressed home the belief that career civil servants should not be involved with policy. All three leaders took concrete steps to weaken the policy role traditionally played by career officials. Thatcher sought to centralize policy advice in her own office; Reagan went further than any president in fifty years in making sure that appointees and even senior career officials shared his political views; and Mulroney appointed political and policy "commissars" to all ministerial offices. Officials in the three countries report that, particularly in their first years in office, Thatcher, Reagan, and Mulroney made clear that the officials' policy roles and advice were not welcomed.

Officials, therefore, got on the management bandwagon. In all three countries, government departments and agencies prepared vision and mission statements, launched reviews to strengthen the quality of service to the public, and organized countless courses and seminars on strengthening management practices. There was hardly a fashion or fad in management that went by in the 1980s that at least two of the three leaders did not fully embrace. Government officials in all three countries for a while spoke the language of *In Search of Excellence*. They discussed visions, missions, and values. These were followed by empowerment, Shared Management Agenda, and TQM. By the mid 1980s, all three governments, like many leading business firms, stressed the employees as their most valuable asset. A variety of panaceas to solve bureaucracy's ills were presented to government departments, blushing debutantes all, beautifully gowned, soon to be embraced in marriage and not long afterward divorced. By the late 1980s, for example, few people were still singing the praises of *In Search of Excellence*. TQM was the new fad and *In Search of Excellence* was as old as yesterday's miniskirt.

As this study makes clear, Thatcher, Reagan, and Mulroney were smitten with the merits of the business-management model and tried to apply it to government operations. All their approaches to reform were rooted in private sector practices. The career officials, however, were able to pick and choose what they liked from the model, and they blatantly ignored the things they did not like.

Boards of directors and top management of large businesses do not as a rule engage in "bashing" their employees. If they did, they would lose consumer confidence and would soon be out of business. Civil servants insist, and rightly so, that they were under attack during much of the 1980s. This is hardly the way to motivate employees under any management practice, public or private.[83] In the United States, officials point out that the Reagan administration meandered all over the management map. Lip service was given to empowerment, service to the public, and TQM, but the next day government operations felt the heavy hand of more formal rules and processes. In the business-management model, empowerment entails a tolerance for errors. A leading member of Harvard's Business School explained that empowerment and risk taking is important for innovation and successful change. He added, however, "risk-taking involves the chance of error. A strong organization learns to profit from errors: a weak one tries at all cost to avoid them."[84] The Reagan administration did not adopt the

National Academy of Public Administration report *Revitalizing Federal Management: Managers and Their Overburdened Systems*, which sought to deregulate management in government and to empower managers. Instead, it moved in the opposite direction and placed new emphasis on administrative and financial controls. Indeed, the administration even encouraged whistle-blowing, by providing hot lines to inspectors general for tips on undetected wrongdoing.

Officials in Britain report that executive agencies were created mostly as a means to control costs and, some insist, to cut the civil service down to size, rather than as a positive management-development initiative. They point out that two of the main criticisms from people employed in agencies is that they are underfunded and that their core departments still retain too much control.[85]

A good number of officials in all three countries also note that the management revolution was a top-down affair. The "obsession with management" in the Thatcher era was a direct result of her views and tenacity. Business-management literature now reports that, to have any lasting impact, change must come from the bottom. Michael Beer, Russell A. Eisenstat, and Bert Spector, for example, wrote,

> in some companies, wave after wave of programs rolled across the landscape with little positive impact; in others, more successful transformations did take place. They usually started at the periphery of the corporation in a few plants and divisions far from corporate headquarters. And they were led by the general managers of those units, not by the CEO or corporate staff people.[86]

The management revolution in Britain, Canada, and the United States consisted of wave after wave of programs, coming neither from the bottom nor from the periphery.

The question then is, From the perspective of career officials, what lasting legacy will Thatcher, Reagan, and Mulroney have on the civil service? Civil servants in Britain believe that Thatcher's legacy will be lasting on two fronts: the size of the civil service has been cut back, and the executive agencies could in time have a far-reaching impact. Officials in the United States report that Reagan legitimated greater political control over the civil service and that the tension between appointed and career officials rose to "unhealthy levels." They argue that Reagan established a precedent: squadrons of political ideologues can now move into government to take control deep in the bowels of the civil service. By doing this, he undermined the morale of the civil service and discouraged competent professionals from serving in government. Officials in Canada report that the Mulroney government will be remembered for having raised management to a new prominence but that, at the same time, messages about management in government have been uncertain. One long-serving line manager put it succinctly,

> "Have policy, will travel" was replaced by "have management, will travel." But it isn't really management at all. It is fluff. All the group that were kept busy cranking out new policy stuff in the 1970s simply started to turn out new management stuff in the 1980s. It occasionally makes for fine reading, but there is very little substance here. You know it is quite an art—giving the appearance of progress when you are really not going anywhere.[87]

There is little doubt that a price was paid for the management revolution whether judged successful or not. There is plenty of evidence that a mood of frustration gripped many civil servants, that it gave rise to a crisis in morale, and that the confidence civil servants had in their institution was badly shaken.[88] To career officials, the message from the political leadership was clear and hardly positive: a good part of the civil service had no intrinsic value since much of its work could be turned over to the private sector or to agency employees who were expected to behave as though they were in the private sector.

In Britain, the 1980s posed a strong challenge to the fundamental values of the civil service. Many officials want to perform well. They are proud to be in the civil service and in an institution that is not always on the lookout to make a profit. Thatcherism, they insist, put a damper on this. Many observers of the civil service under Thatcher also wrote about the morale problem that developed among civil servants. Committees of Parliament and even the government itself recognized the need to restore morale in the civil service.[89]

In Canada, senior civil servants began to talk openly about a civil service "in trouble, demoralized, losing confidence in its leaders and themselves, unsure of their roles and their futures, overburdened with work, and chafing under perceived unfair criticism."[90] A survey of senior public servants in 1986 confirmed this view. A second survey, commissioned in 1988, sought to determine if the various reforms—especially IMAA—had brought about an improvement in morale and confidence. It found none. Indeed, if anything, the situation had deteriorated. The survey also compared morale between public and private managers and concluded that "almost without exception, the private sector managers had a more positive view of the management practices in their organization than did their public sector counterparts, working at similar levels in their organization." It also found that "as one moves down the bureaucratic hierarchy, managers are less satisfied and less positive about managerial practices in their organization."[91] Surveys at the departmental level were even more worrisome. A 1990 study on the Department of External Affairs reported that "External Affairs' advice is ignored and its staff made subject to public scorn, rebuke and ridicule. Motivation has plunged and morale is abysmal. The department is under siege from the outside and consumed by ferment from within."[92] It seemed that by the early 1990s, every large department could produce similar studies revealing serious morale problems. The deteriorating morale problem perhaps more than anything else gave rise to the PS 2000 exercise.

The situation was no better in the United States. Several studies in the mid 1980s revealed that there was a serious morale crisis in the civil service and that members of the Senior Executive Service (SES) were leaving at an alarmingly high rate.[93] The 1989 report of the Volcker Commission, *Leadership for America: Rebuilding the Public Service*, left little doubt that Reagan was leaving behind a badly demoralized and uncertain civil service. It reported that "it is evident that the public service is neither as attractive as it once was nor as effective in meeting perceived needs." It added that "only 13 percent of the senior executives recently interviewed by the General Accounting Office would recommend that young people start their careers in government, while several recent surveys show that less than half the senior career civil servants would recommend a job in government to their own children."[94]

10

Revisiting the Underpinnings

The reforms that Thatcher, Reagan, and Mulroney introduced were wide-ranging and ambitious. Some—such as improved cash management practices—had little to do with the constitutional conventions of the civil service. But others did. Several features of managerialism raise fundamental questions about how government operations now square with long-established practices of public administration and some constitutional conventions.

It is important to look back to see how the reforms of the 1980s correspond with some of the major essays on public administration. When Thatcher, Reagan, and Mulroney embraced the politics-administration dichotomy and sought to introduce the business-management model to government operations, they were going down a well-traveled road. Seminal studies—some going back a hundred years—are at the root of these ideas. It is hardly possible to overstate the importance of accountability in government operations, where it is much more pronounced than in the private sector. The democratic machinery in both the parliamentary and congressional forms of government lays down a set of rules to hold elected and nonelected officials to account for their actions, and these rules permeate the work of civil servants at every level. It is important at some point to reconcile the management model, in particular the notion of empowerment, with the requirements for accountability in government operations.

THE POLITICS-ADMINISTRATION DICHOTOMY

Scholars everywhere have debunked the politics-administration dichotomy. Frederick Mosher wrote in the 1960s,

> The developments in recent decades in the real world of government have brought to the politics-administration dichotomy

strains which have grown almost beyond the point of toleration. In fact, on the theoretical plane, the finding of a viable substitute may well be the number one problem of public administration today.[1]

We are still searching. The only difference today is that we now call it the major problem in public management rather than in public administration.

In the absence of a new foundation, the politics-administration dichotomy lives on. It lives on in the literature—some recent studies attempt to modernize the concept by breaking it down into different stages.[2] The concept also lives on in government—politicians find it convenient to refer to when making the case that they, and not civil servants, should make policy. It also allows them to introduce new measures designed to strengthen their own hands in the field of policy, which Thatcher, Reagan, and Mulroney all did. The U.S. practice by which a new president brings in his own cadre of policy advisors is, of course, more akin to the politics-administration dichotomy than is the experience in either Britain or Canada. Reagan sought to entrench the tradition further, while Thatcher and Mulroney sought to move toward the American model.[3] The objectives were the same in the three countries: to leave policy decisions to politicians and their trusted partisan advisors and to see to it that the permanent civil service learns how to manage better.

The politics-administration-dichotomy-turned-politics-management-dichotomy concept held a number of advantages for Thatcher, Reagan, and Mulroney in their attempts to reform the civil service. For one thing, it drove the career bureaucrats with their thinly disguised policy agendas back to their proper place. For another, the concept squared with the leaders' concentration on managerialism, their bottom-up market-oriented approach to management, and the establishment of an empowered managerial class. Their goal was to set the course toward less government while at the same time energizing those bureaucrats who remained, and to empower the clients.

Aside from the bureaucrat-bashing, the rhetoric of Thatcher, Reagan, and Mulroney spoke to deregulating government operations and, once again, to letting the managers manage. The goal was to streamline and simplify government decision making. This goal, taken at face value, meant nothing short of replacing public administration with public management. The difference between the two is much less subtle than one might assume. It means a new mind-set. It means separating policy and administration. It also means rejecting traditional public-administration concerns with accountability and control, and giving way to the business-management emphasis on productivity, performance, and service to clients. The new focus is on the organizational unit, the manager, and the individual employee, and away from the civil service as an institution. The executive agencies in Britain and the SOAs in Canada are both rooted in the politics-management dichotomy, as are direct funding, or vouchering (much talked about in the 1980s, particularly by the Reaganites), and contracting out. Reports coming out of the British Treasury on contracting out made direct reference to a more businesslike approach and to the need to distinguish the roles of policy formulation and service delivery.

Government officials are ambivalent about the politics-management dichotomy.[4] They know intuitively that the concept is hopelessly dated and that it is no longer applicable, even to apparently routine matters. One Canadian official used the country's unemployment insurance program to make the point:

> The idea that processing a claim is purely an administrative matter is wrong. The clerk who makes the decision that the claimant has quit his or her work voluntarily, which means that the claimant can be disenfranchised from insurance benefits for 12, 6, 2 weeks or not at all, is making a policy decision. Do not think that politicians are uninterested in that decision.[5]

Yet, most officials are not prepared to reject the concept out of hand. They will argue that, of course, it is the politicians who make policy and that it is they, the officials, who carry it out. Although they recognize that a clear demarcation line can never be drawn, their years of experience have taught them to discern quickly what belongs to the realm of the politicians and what does not. They add that the inability of business executives to do this and to know what is "doable" in government explains why so many of them do not do so well in the civil service. To be sure, the politics-administration dichotomy has in the past served both politicians and career officials well. It has enabled politicians to claim that their policy initiatives were full of promise but that bureaucracy or the administration was unable to deliver. Similarly, it has enabled officials to dig in their heels to stop politicians from meddling too deeply in their operations.[6]

The work of Max Weber is also still being felt today in government operations. Yet, Weber's theories have also been discredited and many of his specific claims have been disproved. No sooner was Weber's work translated than scholars began to point out the lacunae when applied to many countries—in particular, those with a parliamentary form of government. In addition, government in Weber's Germany played a far different role from the role modern governments now play. We no longer have small governments performing mostly regulatory functions and staffed largely by clerks. Government is now so complex and so vast that neither senior politicians nor legislation can operate except at a high level of generalization. This effectively means that the administrative side of government no longer resembles what it was in Weber's time. Where a case could be made for something like bureaucracy in a Weberian sense is with the delivery of services, or with what James Q. Wilson labels "production organizations," whose work is predictable and whose goals often can be precisely specified and measured.[7] But many government agencies no longer fit this description.

Again, government officials know intuitively that the Weberian idea of bureaucracy is no longer sufficient to explain what it is they do and how they do it. Yet Weber, like the politics-administration dichotomy, still haunts many government bureaus. A cursory look at Weber's central characteristic of bureaucracy (see chapter 2) reveals that several characteristics remain in today's bureaucracy. Despite Weber's short-comings, however, we have yet to come up with a new, more fitting model. Hierarchy is under attack everywhere, including inside government. In lacking proper anchors or underpinnings, the work of bureaucracy can be subjected to the latest fad or fashion, to the quick fix from the snake oil salesman.

The great majority of career officials I consulted believe that few people outside government appreciate the nature of civil servants' work, the constraints they constantly contend with, and the forces at play that shape what they do and why. I asked them, particularly the managers, how for example Luther Gulick's PODSCRB explained their work or helped shape their approach to management. While most of them were not aware of this work, those who were familiar with the studies (and those who were not, after I explained the broad outlines to them) argued that an entirely new literature is required. When I asked them to describe what this new literature would encompass, they suggested a strong emphasis on the role of the political process and institutions, on the traditional values of the public service, and on reconciling the best management practices with the requirements of government, including notions of equity, fairness, and probity, as well as improved techniques to formulate and evaluate public policy. The literature would also investigate interdepartmental conflicts, different or conflicting program objectives, how one deals with Congress or with committees of Parliament, how central agencies influence the work of line departments and agencies, and so on.[8]

These are the most important issues facing government officials. Managerialism as defined by Thatcher, Reagan, and Mulroney would not figure as prominently in their search for a new literature as I had first assumed it would. Certainly, the disbelief culture is important here, but it does not tell the whole story. The great majority of officials consulted insist that managerialism will, in the end, accomplish precious little. One career official in Washington summed up the view of many officials in the United States and Canada when he remarked, "Reform 88 came up with a lot of dry holes."[9] To many, the concept of managerialism is naive, it belittles the noble side of their profession, and it ignores the realities of their work—although officials in Britain are less dismissive of managerialism than their Washington- and Ottawa-based counterparts.

All in all, many officials report that the politics-administration dichotomy, Weber's theory of hierarchy, and the reforms—most notably the merit principle, which flowed out of the Northcote-Trevelyan report in Britain and the reform movements in the United States and Canada at the turn of the century—have had a lasting impact, however discredited in the literature today, because they constituted solid underpinnings for civil service and government operations. As one Canadian official explained, "They may be incomplete, but they remain very helpful, particularly when you have little else to work from."[10]

AN APPROACH: LOOKING FOR UNDERPINNINGS

As we have seen, Thatcher, Reagan, and Mulroney set out to introduce business-management practices to government operations. Although they were not the first to attempt this, they were the first to try to introduce the "ethos" of the private sector to government to accompany the techniques. They spoke of "market forces" deciding the level and quality of public service; of empowering clients; of new measures to enhance productivity and performance; and of assessing the impact of these measures. They also, however, ignored numerous cautions that there are fundamental differences between the management of private firms and government operations.[11] They were in no mood to listen to naysayers.

In this study I have shown how the business-management model or bias was introduced to government. The great majority of Reagan appointees had a business background. Although it worked closely with the Heritage Foundation and the American Enterprise Institute (AEI), the Reagan administration, to staff political positions, did not rely on the advice of academics, think tanks, or other levels of government to the same extent that Carter, Kennedy, and even Nixon had done. Reagan established the Grace Commission, set two thousand business people to roam around inside government, and set up several blue-ribbon business panels to look at various management issues. His administration was often willing to listen to and act on the management advice of large businesses, as in the instance of TQM. Thatcher had Raynerism, Mulroney had Nielsen, and both sought to bring business executives into government through various schemes, most notably through exchange programs.

The vocabulary of the 1980s had a clear business-management bias. This began with the political leadership and in time was adopted by senior civil servants, at least when they spoke publicly about their operations. Several new and high-profile management-development courses, with hardly a trace of the public-administration vocabulary, were established in the 1980s to promote the management bias and to teach management skills to government employees.

The management vocabulary held an obvious appeal for the politicians. The word *management* itself implies a decisiveness, a dynamic mind-set, and a bias for action that contrasts sharply with the traditional public-administration language that conjures up images of rules, regulations, and lethargic decision-making processes. Management also held the promise that some tough-minded decisions would be made, if only to shake up the status quo and what was perceived as too-comfortable working arrangements designed to perpetuate large bureaucracy rather than to getting the public's business done.[12]

Managerialism, at least on the face of things, challenged a number of widely accepted notions and practices in government. First, it challenged the emphasis on functionalism associated with the classical writings of Weber and Frederick Taylor. Functionalism, along with hierarchy, was felt to inhibit flexibility, responsiveness, quality of services to clients, and quick decisions, all a part of the new public management ethos. Functionalism, or functional specialization, leads to procedural rigidity, which in turn entails time-consuming and costly lateral coordination and fragmentation of responsibility. The government system, the argument goes, begins to feed on itself and little gets done.[13]

Second, managerialism also challenged the top-down approach to decision making commonly found in government operations. The new vocabulary spoke frequently about "bottom-up" decision making and empowerment, which, much like in the private sector, was felt to hold promise both for the organization and the individual. Quicker and better decisions would be made by the people on the front line than by faceless bureaucrats in faraway London, Washington, and Ottawa. Red tape would be eliminated, as would be management layers. In the long run, all this would make for a less costly government. Empowerment also serves to motivate individuals and to make them more productive. This can only lead to job enrichment, to better morale within the organization, and more self-confidence in problem solving. In brief, "motivation through pressure from outside goes together with low job satisfaction. Motivation from within goes together with higher job satisfaction."[14]

Empowerment is the key to making managerialism work. This, combined with other features, would lead to a new culture in government, a culture that would stress "management by design" instead of "management by direction." The compliant, reactive style of the latter goes to the heart of public administration. Aaron Wildavsky put it best:

> The question must be faced: can we denigrate hierarchy from which bureaucracy derives while still honouring public service? Can there be an effective bureaucracy without respect for authority? . . . What is left for administration, we may ask, if its hierar-

chical form of organization and its search for efficiency are rejected? Why does one hear so little now about the virtues (as well
as the vices) of hierarchy—stability, continuity, predictability—
with enthusiasm and pride?[15]

Third, managerialism also challenges the merits of the "neutral
competence" of the civil service, and to some extent—although never
openly—the merit principle. The political leaders quite openly admitted that they were out to challenge the notion of neutral competence.
Thatcher and Reagan, in particular, and Mulroney, to a lesser extent,
had little time for policy advice that "purported" to be above the
political fray. One former senior Reagan appointee explained, "No
question, we were out to challenge the idea of neutral competence.
You know neutral competence really means that you are handed a car
that's in neutral. What do you do with that? What you do is put an end
to the charade and you get on with the job."[16] Mulroney's decision to
appoint a chief of staff in each ministerial office similarly served notice
that neutral competence had its limits in the Canadian setting also.

The merit principle is not easily challenged. Politicians playing fast
and loose here can be called to order by the media and civil service
associations. Congress in the United States and opposition parties in
Britain and Canada are also bound to challenge anyone tampering with
the merit principle in staffing government positions. There is always
the fear in some quarters that if you compromise the merit principle,
you run the risk of returning to the evils of the spoils system, routed by
Northcote-Trevelyan and the Pendleton Act. A keen student of American government has written that the merit principle gave rise to an
ideology in the United States that serves to underpin the system of
government. "The people of the United States built an ideology which
related the public service to their indigenous concept of democracy in
a unique but basically coherent fashion. . . . A neutral, efficient civil
service was viewed as not merely desirable; it was essential to democracy itself."[17]

The merit principle nevertheless began to lose some of its appeal in
the 1960s. By the 1980s, the political leadership was looking for ways
to circumvent it, at least on occasion. For one thing, the merit principle does not easily square with the business-management model, or
indeed with empowerment. To many, it is a code for indisputable job
security for bureaucrats, implying paperwork and individual job own-

ership. It means that appointments, transfers, promotions, and demotions and release for incompetency are tied up in statutes and centrally prescribed rules and regulations. The merit principle and all that it entails absolves line managers of any real responsibility by putting personnel management on a kind of automatic pilot. Its purpose and its only value, the argument goes, is still to stop bad things from happening. Even some career government officials began in the 1980s to question the merit principle, mostly in the hope of promoting empowerment. A former chairman of the Canadian Civil Service Commission wrote that

> merit in the public service, except in the negative sense of being the opposite of patronage, has never been and never can be defined in any absolute, universal fashion. . . . At times, the merit principle has favored veterans, veterans' widows. At other times, it has discriminated against married women and immigrants and more subtly against francophones and native people.

His solution is to empower managers or "those who are concerned with getting the job done" to make decisions and to hold them accountable, not only to the government but also to employees through audits.[18]

The political leadership and their partisan advisors were convinced that the merit principle had simply replaced political patronage with bureaucratic patronage. This, they insisted, had led to the kind of inbreeding commonly seen in government bureaucracies—that is, an overreliance on seniority and on promotions from within. They have a point. For example, some 94 percent of new career appointees to the U.S. Senior Executive Service in the 1980s came from inside government. About 88 percent came from within the agency itself. In Britain and Canada, about 90 percent of new appointees to management positions also come from within the government, although there appears to be more mobility between government departments and agencies than in the United States. In Britain and Canada, some 80 percent of new appointees came from within their own department or agency.[19]

Thatcher, Reagan, and Mulroney circumvented the merit principle in many ways. Thatcher, and occasionally Mulroney, took a strong personal interest in senior appointments. Mulroney and especially Thatcher also promoted government-business exchange programs.

Both strengthened the policy capacity of their own offices and that of their ministers with partisan appointments. Reagan's administration had as one of its key strategies the staffing of "top positions in the civil service." Observers also became critical of the Merit Systems Protection Board under Reagan for failing to protect federal employees from "merit system abuses."[20]

Although not the first to try it, Thatcher, Reagan, and Mulroney also put considerable emphasis on developing performance pay for managers as a means to strengthen managerialism. They increased the pay of their top managers. Some efforts were made to make pension plans more portable and to encourage "out mobility" for government employees. It was felt that reforming pension schemes to lessen their "holding power" would get at the "job-for-life" ethos of the civil service.[21]

I have also reported on a number of measures that were designed to promote a more aggressive and independent style of management. Again, the business world provided the model. The establishment of executive agencies and SOAs in Britain and Canada are two examples. Reagan advisors report that they also pondered establishing new presidential corporations to deliver government services.[22] They did not do so, because a number of agencies already enjoyed autonomy, possessing their own distinct organizational cultures, and because they suspected that Congress would never go along with such a new concept (examples include, among others, the FBI, the CIA, the Forest Service, and the National Park Service). Some elements of Reform 88 and TQM were clearly borrowed from the private sector. The Reagan administration also launched pilot projects, notably the American Navy's China Lake and San Diego facilities, which sought to empower employees and deregulate decision making. It prepared at one point a government-wide civil-service-simplification plan to deregulate decision making. Similar schemes, in one form or another, took hold in Canada, including TQM and IMAA. Thatcher boasted that many of her reform initiatives were borrowed from business practices. Derek Rayner also believed in the superiority of the business-management model and used the phrase "Whitehall culture" in order "to draw attention to the inbuilt limitations of the civil service to think about management." The scrutinies, FMI, and executive agencies were designed to instill a more managerial culture in government operations—but from the top down. Gilles Loiselle, a senior Mulroney minister and president of the Treasury Board, spoke Rayner's language when he argued "We need a massive cultural change. We need less time reporting to head office and more time helping people solve their problems."[23]

Despite the rhetoric, the Thatcher, Reagan, and Mulroney governments did not fully embrace private-management techniques. All three (and the Reagan administration in particular) sent out contradictory signals on this front. At the same time that Reagan appointees were talking about the need for empowerment and were planning Reform 88, they were also waging "war on the bureaucracy." Stockman at OMB and Devine at OPM were anything but proponents of a bottom-up or empowered approach to management. The great majority of observers insist that both these men actually damaged the civil service instead of modernizing it or giving it a new sense of confidence. Stockman and Devine were not alone in sending out mixed signals. Terry Culler, associate director of OPM, argued publicly that the government "should be content to hire competent people, not the best and most talented."[24] The objective was to have qualified personnel to meet minimum and routine requirements. The argument here is that the best and brightest should work in the private sector where wealth is created.

I asked a former senior Reagan advisor to explain the contradictory messages. He responded,

> You can argue that we were not consistent. But I argue that we were. What we wanted was a more businesslike government. That is what Reform 88 is all about. You are talking about changing a deeply ingrained bureaucratic culture to a more businesslike culture. You can't do that overnight. Yes, we did things that ran counter to a businesslike approach. Had you seen what we saw when we came in you would have done the same thing. As a simple example, there were all kinds of different accounting and financial systems that did not add up. Sure, you need to empower employees, but only after you have been able to establish some order and successfully promoted a new culture. Empowerment without a new business culture firmly in place would have meant trusting the ones who had broken into the candy store. We were not prepared to do that.

I also asked whether there were some central ideas or themes under-pinning measures such as Reform 88, and he responded:

> Yes, there was certainly one. We wanted to turn the bureaucracy upside down. We wanted to make bureaucracy less bureaucratic, less costly. We wanted bureaucracy to stop looking at itself and begin looking outward and to challenge what it does and how it does it. Again, we wanted bureaucracy to look at how business gets things done. There is nothing complicated about how business works, it does not procrastinate, it does not ask one hundred questions before doing things, it is continually looking at ways to cut cost and to increase productivity, it does not have time for petty bureaucratic fights, and it is willing to make tough decisions. Businessmen who are not willing to do this do not survive. We wanted to introduce this discipline to government.[25]

Publicly, a number of senior government officials in the three countries were enthusiastic about managerialism and some reported that they were, indeed, looking to the private sector for new ideas. Peter Kemp, who joined the British civil service from the private sector, explains that his work consisted of applying

> broad public sector rules with a private sector approach to running businesses because that's what many Civil Service activities are—businesses—and there's not that much difference between a chain of nationwide building society offices and social security offices. Over an enormous range of things we are like the private sector. We want efficiency, value for money and a better service for our customers.[26]

J. L. Manion, former secretary to the Treasury Board and principal of the newly created Centre for Management Development, wrote a widely read "management model" for government operations in the late 1980s. Manion admits that he borrowed heavily from the private sector.[27] He set out to modernize government operations "by bringing them in tune" with the business-management emphasis on productivity and performance. The model took

> more than a page from recent private sector companies that turned around productivity by focusing on employees as their most important resource. Themes such as individual motivation,

leadership and communication dominate and human relations management principles are seen as the key to unleashing creativity and commitment in a responsive competitive and efficient public bureaucracy.[28]

Not all civil servants are happy about managerialism, in particular the practice of importing private sector practices into government. Privately, many expressed deep concern that managerialism could ultimately make matters worst. Gérard Veilleux, former secretary to the Treasury Board, spoke to this issue in a meeting with senior government officials:

> We are not the private sector and we should not try to measure our success by their yardstick. Because we are looking here and there for solutions, we seem to be floundering and giving the appearance that we are no longer certain of who we are and even what we should be doing. In short, we are losing our sense of pride in what we—as an institution—do.[29]

A former U.S. National Security Council staff member spoke to distinct public service values when he declared, "I will break and enter for my country, but I am not going to do it for K-mart or Citicorp."[30]

In my consultations, some officials reported that a selection of business-management concepts and practices could apply to government. The majority, however, argued that adopting the business-management model amounted to little more than taking a walk on the wrong road. A large number of officials in London, Washington, and Ottawa expressed strong frustrations that so many people outside government and so many politicians could think it possible to transfer business-management practices to government. One official in Washington remarked,

> How anyone can come to Washington even for only a few days and not see that you do not run government operations like you run a business is beyond me. Yet, many do. They arrive with simple bottom-line solutions. During the Reagan years, it felt like a bad virus that would not go away. They were everywhere and they were singing from the same private sector hymn book.[31]

Some officials I consulted even questioned Wallace Sayre's assertion that public and private management are fundamentally alike in all unimportant ways. They insist that the context, the issues, the values, the goals (if ever defined), the setting, and the ways of doing things are vastly different on virtually every front. An American official made this point:

> You would think, for example, that something like collective bargaining would be basically similar between the public and private sectors. It is not. The bargaining is different and the issues are different. If you look carefully at the main issues in labour-management relations in the private sector, they very often relate to charges that management is discriminating because of labour affiliation. There are never such charges in the public sector. Here, the issues revolve around unfair management practices like deciding to open an office at eight rather than eight-thirty without providing sufficient advance notice.

A Canadian official claimed that

> there are countless examples staring in the face of politicians and business people, but they don't see them. One is what politicians say about us. When the prime minister speaks to public servants—his employees—it is a media event. In fact, most public servants pick up what the prime minister and ministers say to them through the media and after that from their neighbours. Bureaucrat bashing often resonates for a while before it dies down. By contrast, when a chief executive officer of a large private firm talks to his employees, only he and the employees are aware of what is being said. It is a private matter. I could list countless such examples.[32]

Virtually to a person the career officials I consulted in all three countries wanted to discuss at some length, at times with no urging on my part, how the business community and many elected politicians have little or no appreciation of the backdrop of rules and regulations they must contend with in their work, nor of the kind of political context they must operate in. They stressed how the constantly changing political environment plays havoc with virtually every long-term planning exercise they ever engage in; how goals in government agencies are often vague; how past experience tells them it is more important to follow prescribed rules than to dart off in an uncharted direction, even though it may well hold considerable promise; how there are always many "bosses" in government; and how those at the top of the hierarchy are constantly managing crisis situations.[33] All of this suggests that government managers are in the business of "coping," not managing in a private sector sense. It is not so much that Gulick's PODSCRB is irrelevant to managing in government bureaucracies, but that it is not very helpful. It only speaks to what government managers should be doing and not to the circumstances under which they actually must work. In short, management in government is more about managing relationships with Parliament, Congress, politicians, other departments, interest groups, and the public, than it is about managing in the business sense.

A typical government manager will find James Q. Wilson's advice on how government departments and agencies can minimize the number of rivals and constraints more relevant—and his description of life in government bureaucracies more accurate and a great deal more helpful—than any generic management book.[34] Therein lies the rub. Managerialism suggests that senior government managers should look down to their employees, to their clients, and to the bottom line of their budgets. My study suggests, however, that in fact they must first look up to the political level and then sideways to interdepartmental conflicts and policy issues. They do this in part because of a deeply ingrained corporate culture, but also because politicians prefer it that way. Seasoned officials know that, although politicians will speak of empowering employees and serving clients better, what matters most to them is how to diffuse a political crisis (of which there is never a shortage) or how to pilot a new policy or program through the government approval process and then how to package it for public consumption. Senior officials, including those in Washington, are valued for their ability to read the political significance of emerging issues and to get a politician's pet project through the various hoops. The general policy-advisory role of officials, however, is a different matter. In the 1980s, this role suffered from benign neglect and in certain instances met with a distinctly cool reception from the political leadership. Despite the decline of the policy-advisory role, officials insist that there are still very few rewards for being known as a good manager.[35] Management in government still commands low prestige, and politicians are the first to regard its tasks as inferior.[36] It came as no surprise to long-serving officials to see management issues the first to be brushed off the overloaded agenda in favor of dealing with a current or emerging crisis.

It also came as no surprise to see such concepts as empowerment run up against the old paradigm of punishment for errors and the requirements of hierarchical discipline. I was given a number of specific examples. One from Canada illustrates the point. An employee in the large Department of Supply and Services took both empowerment and the need to focus on the bottom line at face value. He contacted a municipal government and offered to sell office supplies and services at a better price than could local distributors. He saw it as a win-win situation. His department would realize a small profit and the municipality a saving. The local business community, however, did not see it that way. It accused the federal government of moving in on its turf and argued that it could never compete successfully against an "institution with a bottomless wallet." Local business leaders met with their member of Parliament, who happily championed their cause before the minister. The result was that the empowered front-line employee was instructed not to try that again.[37]

Officials also report that the unsuccessful attempts to implement performance-pay schemes for managers brings home the point that public sector and private sector managements are vastly different, although the three governments are still trying to make performance-pay schemes work. The U.S. government, for example, has recently put out an array of papers trying to identify what has gone wrong and how things could be improved.[38] In addition, the promise that the SES group would identify and then weed out the nonperformers has not lived up to expectations in that no one evaluated ever receives an unsatisfactory appraisal. In figure 1 we can see that the majority receive outstanding appraisals (58 percent of career officers and 71 percent of noncareer SES received the highest appraisal level). It remains a rare occasion indeed to see a government manager released or even demoted for nonperformance, in the United States or, for that matter, in Britain and Canada. In Britain, after a number of false starts, a new performance-pay system was introduced in April 1991. To receive a performance pay, the Treasury suggests that "an individual should have demonstrated effective management and successful achievement." In Canada, the performance-pay scheme has been modified in light of criticism coming from managers themselves. A 1986 survey of

FIGURE 1. SES Performance Appraisals

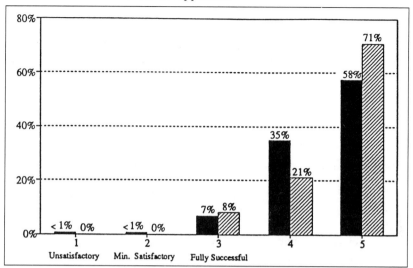

Source: Office of Personnel Management, April 1992.

Notes: Appraisal period ending in FY 1990. Agencies with only three levels were excluded. Solid coloring denotes Career SES; oblique shading denotes non-career SES.

managers revealed "widespread dissatisfaction" with merit bonuses. The changes now mean that funds allocated to the bonus pool is spread out among 95 percent of the managers rather than about 30 percent, as was previously the case.[39]

The reason for problems with the various performance-pay schemes is that it is not easy to assess the performance of government managers. There are too many variables playing on the success of a program or a government operation, and there are rarely any clear-cut criteria to determine who is a top performer. The SES group, for example, judge competency by the following criteria: the integration of internal and external program and policy issues; organizational representation and liaison; direction and guidance of programs, projects, or policy development; acquisition and administration of resources; utilization of human resources; and review of implementation and results. Because circumstances differ in almost every case, it is extremely difficult, if not impossible, to arrive at widely accepted common measurements. The problem is the same in Britain and Canada. Because you cannot properly assess the quality of the work or identify what can be considered success and who precisely is responsible for it, you end up measuring what one British official calls "meaningless things, like whether reports come in on time or if you did not make life miserable for your superiors."[40] Frequently, it is the perception of success that counts in the end, and officials and politicians have very different perceptions of what constitutes a success story.

Government officials in all three countries readily admit it is very difficult, if possible at all, to establish work objectives and individual performance standards. Many have asked fundamental questions to which we simply have no answers. For example, one observer wrote,

> Firstly, whose performance are you assessing—the minister's or the secretary's? Can a central public service agency really distinguish who is responsible for a policy failure—particularly if the minister is supportive and so is the secretary and neither acknowledges that it, in fact, is a failure?[41]

The same questions apply—if not more so—in a congressional form of government.

The pursuit of means to measure efficiency in bureaucracy continues, despite successive efforts at their discovery seeming only to make them more elusive. Managerialism is based largely on the premise that such measures do exist or can be developed. It looks to "output measures" as a necessary replacement for "profit" in assessing how well the job is getting done. Moreover, in keeping with its general preoccupation with productivity, managerialism favors efficiency measures based on outputs. Several points should be made here. First, any approach to evaluating effectiveness and efficiency in government will have to involve different kinds of measures that are tailored to particular types of government activity. Further, not all public service activity lends itself to this criterion. For example, it is very difficult to measure output in many if not most of the central agencies, such as the Cabinet Office, the Treasury, the Office of Management and Budget, the State Department, and the Department of Defense. Even within line departments some activities are more amenable to quantitative output measures than others. For example, what output measure would one expect of a regulatory agency concerned with the protection of public health and safety? In short, far from there being a universal approach to evaluating efficiency and effectiveness in the public service, such measures, if at all possible, will have to be identified on a case-by-case basis in relation to the particular type of activity pursued.

The success of government programs cannot be determined in isolation from the accountability relationship between the public service and the government. Discussions of organizational efficiency and effectiveness too often do not give sufficient consideration to the broad goals or mission of an organization, instead focusing on specific activities that lend themselves more easily to scientific evaluation. The goals and missions of public bureaucracies are set by politicians and often involve deliberate trade-offs between considerations such as efficiency and equity, or effectiveness and flexibility. Even in an area like "service to the public" which might at first blush seem amenable to evaluation based on output, questions relating to quality cannot be separated from policy questions relating to standards or levels of service or to how many resources will be allocated to a particular activity. These are essentially political decisions that set the parameters within which is set the program for service delivery. The point is as simple as it is uncontentious—in the public sector the science of evaluation must be married to the art of governing.

Career officials are convinced that Thatcher, Reagan, and Mulroney had no design or coherent framework to reform their civil services. One Washington official who was at OMB throughout the Reagan years insists that there were "plenty of prejudices, lots of ideology, a great deal of show-and-tell stuff, but very little substance." Other career officials I consulted in Washington, to a person, reported similar observations. One who worked directly on Reform 88 said, "Don't look for underpinnings of the kind you are talking about. There are none. What you have is a variety of initiatives, some complementary, some not." Another reports that, if there were any underlying agenda,

it stemmed from a profound conviction that the civil service was the problem, not the solution. At times, I honestly believed that the agenda was to make the civil service look so inept that Americans would have little choice but to agree that the country needs less government. The rhetoric, the talk about privatization and contracting out and the obvious attempts by some Reaganites like Devine at OPM to make life impossible for civil servants, certainly suggest such an agenda.[42]

Career officials report that the Reform 88 package was put together in some haste. The exercise was led by Joe Wright, a senior Reagan appointee at OMB, with the assistance of a handful of appointed and career officials. "The underpinnings" one career official explained,

> were four cases of beer and a brainstorming session one evening. We heard a lot about how the private sector would go about it and then we tossed a number of ideas around. These ideas eventually became Reform 88. Joe packaged everything in a slide show and went before Cabinet where he got the go-ahead. He came back to tell us that after his presentation, President Reagan said to Cabinet: "what you have heard is the very reason we all came to Washington. Let's do it." As simple and superficial as it may sound, that is what Reform 88 was all about.[43]

Career officials also report that the politics of Reform 88 spoke volumes about the Reagan administration itself in that the great majority of appointees to OMB and even to the management side of the office were consultants from the private sector rather than seasoned business managers. Their strength was in making first-rate presentations to clients—and Reagan and his cabinet became their clients. They played to the administration's conservative ideology and views on government inefficiencies. These had brought the Reaganites to power, and once in office, politics dominated their agenda or, as David Stockman put it, "Reality happened once a day on the evening news." On the whole, career officials in OMB and OPM were convinced that Reagan advisors understood "little about management and even less about how government works."[44]

Career officials also report that Reform 88 produced heated turf wars between Reaganites. Stockman saw little merit in management measures or, for that matter, for much of what Grace had to say. Ed Meese and senior appointees at OMB saw Stockman as a key stumbling block to new management measures they wished to promote. Meetings were called to review the issues, but often, one side or the other did not show up. Meanwhile, Stockman issued directives to some senior OMB staff to ignore management-development efforts. Things improved when Stockman left government, which was about the same time that Reform 88 came to life. Still, the irony was not lost on career officials. One explained,

The Reaganites held the civil service in contempt. They regarded civil servants as little people preoccupied with fighting turf and protecting their agencies with little regard for taxpayers' money. Well, at OMB we could have learned a thing or two about fighting over turf from some senior Reagan appointees.[45]

British officials confirm the literature's contention that Thatcher came to office with no grand design in hand to reform government operations. Like Reagan, she tried some "this" and a little bit of "that."[46] The difference is that she had more scope than Reagan had to roll back the state, she proved to be much more determined, she took a hands-on approach, and she had more impact. Thatcher also held strong views on the shortcomings of the civil service and she believed firmly in the superiority of private sector management practices. But there was little of substance to set against her preconceived prejudices.

In time, Thatcher muted her direct criticism of the civil service, fearing to make an already serious morale problem worse. She continued, however, "to extol the virtues of the private sector over the public sector."[47] Officials report that her belief in the business-management model influenced or shaped virtually every management measure she introduced. Raynerism, FMI, new development programs for government managers, her emphasis on management rather than on policy as being the correct function of government operations and executive agencies, all "bear the stamp of the business-management model."[48]

Officials reveal that Thatcher tried "this" and "that" because there were simply no alternatives. They admit that they had little to offer to help her achieve the overhaul of the civil service when she first arrived in office. They also admit that they underestimated Thatcher's determination. They insist, however, that there is no magic formula to fix what politicians perceive to be wrong with the civil service. Still, they report that, on the whole, civil servants were willing to adopt the government's initiatives directed at reforming the civil service and that a good number of civil servants played a key role in implementing them. This is true for all Thatcher reforms, from Rayner's scrutinies to the new executive agencies. If nothing else, they insist, the 1980s proved to Thatcher and many of her colleagues that they were wrong to argue that civil servants have a dogged resistance to change. One senior official put it this way: "We demonstrated that we were just as eager as anyone in the private sector to pick up every management fashion." However, a former official, Lord Bancroft, argues that things went too far and that civil servants became too eager to pick up every "management nostrum." He wrote, "We were stunningly good at re-inventing the wheel. We put too much effort into devising new systems and new initiatives in response to passing fads and fancies."[49]

In short, then, underpinning Thatcher's managerialism was a strong belief that a private sector discipline could be introduced to government operations, that political control of policy could be strengthened, that government budgets could be trimmed, and that a more business-like organizational model—executive agencies—could be introduced to flush out the natural inefficiencies of bureaucracy.[50] Meanwhile, civil servants—anxious to prove that the bureaucracy is not consistently resistant to change and also because many senior officials regard it as their duty to implement the government's agenda—were willing to experiment with new management approaches, some of which may well have served to compromise the underpinnings that had given rise to a modern civil service.

Managerialism calls for an autonomous and aggressive management style similar to that employed in the private sector. But political and administrative traditions in parliamentary forms of government do not provide much autonomy to civil servants who are expected to operate within the confines of rules established by acts of Parliament and subject to the control of ministers.[51] The executive agencies were established to resolve that dilemma, and the jury is still out on whether they will be successful. Successful or not, the agencies could in time undermine the idea of a single, unified civil service that Northcote-Trevelyan first promoted. The agencies are moving toward having their own career- and personnel-development programs. With something like half of the British civil service now in executive agencies, each with its own pay and classification system, and all sharing a natural tendency to develop staff from within or through exchanges with the private sector, there will probably in future be very limited mobility between agencies or between agencies and the core civil service. It is also unlikely that permanent secretaries will emerge from the agencies. Thus, if the agencies truly foster management abilities, the most capable will probably not rise to the top of the civil service. By the time these high fliers reach senior positions and achieve some visibility, they will have put in some twenty years in only one agency and will have had no exposure to the broader issues of government.

Officials in Canada are, if anything, more adamant than their American and British counterparts that the political leadership had no underlying framework in its attempt to reform the civil service. One senior official claimed that there "are no underpinnings to much of what Mulroney tried to do to reform the public service." Another argued that Mulroney's approach to the civil service is a "bundle" of contradictions. Mulroney, he reported, wanted "to bring in business management practices to government to empower employees and managers, yet he also wanted an error-free bureaucracy. He ridiculed public servants in public speeches and in private, yet he expected complete loyalty from public servants."[52]

Mulroney's initiatives were inspired by a variety of forces. His SOAs were inspired by Thatcher's executive agencies. His government's espousal of TQM followed Reagan's adoption of the concept. His PS 2000—with its emphasis on service to the public, empowerment, and the delayering of management levels—came on the heels of similar developments in the business community. The IMAA initiative flowed out of commitments made during the 1984 election campaign but was put together by officials in the Treasury Board secretariat.

PUBLIC CHOICE LITERATURE

If there was one body of literature that influenced Thatcher, Reagan, and Mulroney, it was the literature coming out of the public choice school. Thatcher urged her permanent officials to read public choice literature, and some Reagan advisors spoke its language verbatim. David Stockman, for example, argued,

> Do you want to understand why government officials behave the way they do? All you need to know is that they are trying to maximize the budgets of their agencies. Do you want to understand what drives politicians? All you need to know is that they want to be re-elected. Do you want to understand legislation? Just see it as a sale of the coercive power of government to the highest bidder, like a cattle auction.[53]

In Canada, Mulroney's own senior policy advisors and some chiefs of staff, in defining their agenda, also pointed to public choice theory as the single most influential body of literature. Discussion with these officials reveals that their enthusiasm for public choice literature was based more on its repeated support of the neoconservative agenda than because they had a deep understanding of its theory. However, they were sufficiently familiar with it to know that it labeled bureaucrats "budget maximizers."[54]

In some ways, the public choice literature captured the right-of-center political parties in the 1980s as Keynesian economics had captured the government treasuries in the 1930s and 1940s. There were important differences, however. For one thing, Keynesian economics did not have to confront entrenched programs and bureaucracies. Indeed, Keynesian economics offered opportunities to those who wanted to expand the role of the state and their own programs. For another, Keynesian economics is much more prescriptive about what should be done, and how, than is the public choice literature.

One can make the case that public choice promotes a decentralist, consumer-oriented bias. A central theme of managerialism is to decentralize, to empower employees, and to stress service to the public. In a similar way, public choice theorists would applaud any move to privatize or contract out government activities—and Thatcher, Reagan, and Mulroney did both. Public choice literature also squares with many of the features of Reagan's "supply-side management approach."[55] To be sure, the public choice school is conservative in nature and its aim is to minimize the role of the state. Its prescriptions would see new limits on the discretionary power of politicians and curb the functions of government departments and agencies. But the school is not very helpful about how to improve those functions that remain in government, and this is a failing that may explain why the political leadership had to resort to trying "this" and "that" and the consequent numerous contradictory messages.

ACCOUNTABILITY

Of all the things that make public sector management different from the private sector management, none is more important than how managers and employers are held accountable. The question of how politicians and officials exercise power and how they share power and activities is very important. Hugh Heclo goes so far as to suggest that "the problem of the higher civil service is not, fundamentally, a problem of personnel policy. It is a constitutional issue."[56]

There is no denying that there are important basic differences between the ways elected and nonelected officials and business executives are held accountable for their activities. Albert Hirschman spoke to the issue when he wrote that, in the business world, "the customer who, dissatisfied with the product of one firm, shifts to that of another, uses the market to defend his welfare and to improve his position." This is neat, tidy, impersonal, effective, and quiet. It easily lends itself to quantifying success and failure. With government, however, the customer uses "voice" to express dissatisfaction. Voice is, of course, much more messy than a quiet exit, since it can range "all the way from faint grumbling to violent protest; it implies articulation of one's critical opinions rather than a private secret vote in the anonymity of a supermarket; and finally, it is direct and straightforward rather than roundabout."[57] Public opinion surveys now capture voice on a monthly basis, or even more frequently if political parties desire it and are prepared to pay. The great majority of politicians react to the voice expressed in public opinion surveys, and government operations are often in their direct line of attack as they seek to introduce corrective measures.

Business executives are also accountable for their activities, but the success of a business executive is much easier to assess than that of a government manager. There is also much less fuss over due process in the private sector than in government, if only because of the differences involved in managing private and public monies. In the business community, the bottom line and the ability to position the firm on a more competitive footing often tells all. A chief executive officer of a large firm meets with his board of directors for a day, or perhaps even less, several times a year. If the firm is turning a profit, he usually gets what he wants. The board will very seldom intervene directly in the day-to-day business operations, and senior executives are usually free to hire and fire at will.[58]

It is never that simple in government. Senior government managers deal with politicians almost on a daily basis. Success cannot always be easily measured (when it can, there are usually a number of variables responsible), and checks and balances are purposely designed to restrict freedom of action in government. Goals are rarely clear, and it is not often that all actors, both political and bureaucratic, can agree to pursue even a limited number of objectives and push in the same direction.

The sharp differences in how the democratic machinery in congressional and parliamentary systems work are well known. The congressional system is basically one of checks and balances, in which the three branches of government—the executive, the legislative, and the judicial—hold certain powers exclusively. In a parliamentary form of government, the judiciary is separate but the executive and legislative are joined. Not only does the legislature support the executive, but recruitment to the executive is drawn from the legislature.

Nevil Johnson summed up the difference by pointing out that in the congressional system bargains are struck in the legislature, while in the parliamentary system the government almost alone, particularly when it has a majority mandate, drives public policy and public spending. There are advantages and drawbacks to both. A majority government operating in a parliamentary system can run the risk of embarking on a "single direction foolishness." A bargaining system in a congressional form can "become ungovernable and run the risk of falling apart."[59] It is ironic that reform-minded people in the United States are suggesting that the president should be asked to defend his policies directly in both houses of Congress, that new ways should be found to integrate the work of the administration and Congress more effectively, and that more posts in the bureaucracy should be reserved for career officials than for political appointees. In contrast, reform-minded people in parliamentary systems are looking for ways to strengthen the involvement of backbenchers without limiting the power or responsibility of the government to Parliament.[60] They are also seeking to bring the relations between senior officials and ministers more into the open.

The various management initiatives introduced in the 1980s did not address the accountability issue or the requirements of political institutions. Some simply dismissed such requirements, while others sought to accommodate them, however uneasily. Still others chose conveniently to overlook the fact that politicians are very seldom inhibited by purely management requirements. They will inevitably draw action closer to themselves whenever it becomes politically sensitive. No matter how dated constitutional conventions and requirements may be to some, they constitute formidable obstacles to the application of managerialism.

Grace carried out his work with little reference to Congress and made the point that politicians and, in particular, Congress have no place in the day-to-day running of a "private business and the same rule should apply to government." It is relatively easy to sit down and prepare a menu of what ought to be cut and what ought to be rearranged in isolation of those who ultimately are responsible for making the decisions. Congress is not just the legislative branch that oversees the work of the executive. It approves the budget and, by extension, government programs. Experience tells us that Congress has a mind of its own and shows no hesitation to rip apart the administration's budget. Congress very rarely cedes its power to the executive. In addition, it is no longer possible to view Congress as a single entity. With its powerful committees, it has become "a multiplicity of sometimes overlapping entities."[61]

For someone reared on the parliamentary form of government, looking at the checks and balances of the American political system is akin to a baseball player's trying to play cricket with no knowledge of the rules. The notion that power is controlled more by being limited—by having its operations curtailed through checks and balances rather than through accountability to the legislative branch—holds obvious implications for how civil servants carry out their responsibilities. Some observers suggest that the constitutional order in the United States provides the civil service a legitimate title in its own right. The argument here is that only the people are sovereign, and the popular will can never reside solely in elected officials. The civil service, much like the judiciary, has a legitimate constitutional title and so there is no need for it to cower before either Congress or the administration.

That may make for a fine constitutional argument but reality reveals that Congress has an "awesome arsenal" of weapons that it can use against government agencies.[62] It has even been suggested that Congress is the "architect" of the bureaucracy. Congress can decide how much money an agency may spend, including on personnel; it can intervene whenever it learns that an agency is sinning by "omission or commission"; and it can also establish the structural conditions under which an agency must operate. The many weapons it has to direct the work of an agency and hold it accountable include "legislation, appropriations, hearings, investigations, personal interventions, and friendly advice that is ignored at executive peril."[63]

We also know that Congress is increasingly getting involved in "micromanaging" government agencies. Again, it has a number of weapons at its disposal to do this, including its right to authorize programs, budget levels, confirm presidential appointees, and carry out investigations. Committees of Congress have also secured more staff in recent years and enlarged their fields of activity and influence. Congress can, whenever it wishes to do so, turn a simple management or administrative matter into a question of policy. Committees or sub-committees now table reports to serve as "guidance" for agencies, but these in effect often contain specific instructions about how money should be spent or law interpreted.[64]

Still, the president is the head of government and directs the work of the civil service. He can also look to the constitution, which directs him to "take care that the laws be faithfully executed" and make the case that government agencies should be accountable to him. He also commands a vast bureaucracy to direct and control the work of the permanent bureaucracy and has the power to propose the establishment of new agencies. The civil service, meanwhile, sits in the middle and is expected to deal with two masters. Both masters have built up their own large bureaucracies to keep each other in check and to oversee the work of the permanent civil service. These developments have added new constraints on management in government rather than attenuating existing ones.

In my consultations, I asked whether the reform of the 1980s had taken account of these developments and if they had made any difference. The answer was no. Officials are quick to explain, however, that in all fairness to the Reagan presidency, there would have been little chance of success even if there had been a sustained effort to reform that part of the machinery of government. Congress and committees of Congress, they insist, are far too sensitive to any sign of executive encroachment on their turf to allow any president, however popular and determined, to make headway on this front.

I also asked career officials whom they felt accountable to, given that they must continually answer to two political masters and in some instances to the Constitution. To a person, they responded that they were accountable to the president, no matter who the incumbent.[65] I probed to see if during the Reagan years, given his antibureaucratic rhetoric, there were any discerning shifts of loyalty toward Congress. The answer was that some senior officials—albeit not many—had begun to look to Congress for leadership. The officials I spoke with insisted, however, that on the whole senior career officials remained loyal to the presidency. Several did reveal that they detected a shift of loyalty toward Congress in the lower levels of the bureaucracy during the Reagan years.

I then put the question of loyalty to middle- and lower-level officials. The response was markedly different from that of the senior officials. Their sense of loyalty and accountability was not at all clear. Indeed, there appears to be a general fault line that separates the senior-level bureaucracy and the middle- and lower-level ones on the issue of accountability. In the United States, the middle- and lower-level officials reported that they were accountable to a variety of actors. Many said that, beyond their immediate manager, they were at one and the same time accountable to the administration, to Congress, to relevant committees of Congress, to the courts, and to their clients. They did not, however, think that, because of its open hostility to some programs, the Reagan administration effected a great deal of change on this front, other than perhaps strengthening somewhat the ties between "program bureaucrats" and what they called "committee staffers on the hill."[66]

Some observers argue that managerialism is having an impact on accountability of government officials in the United States. They argue that the growing complexity of budgetary problems, the shift toward a more consumer-oriented perspective in the provision of public services, and the notion of empowerment is leading government managers to request greater freedom in the search for new revenues. Similarly, managers are also asking for more autonomy from line-item budget controls so as to be more effective and efficient in managing dwindling resources. Public accountability of government spending has always looked to input costs if only because performance based on the bottom line has been difficult, if not impossible, to measure. Carl Bellone and Frederick Goerl argue that "in the name of revenue generation, programs and projects are set in motion that threaten to change drastically the character of . . . the authority relationships between professional public administrators and the citizenry." They add that revenue generating measures under the control of government managers "can be seen as measures to avoid voter approval and thereby increase the autonomy of public officials and public administrators . . . and make public accountability more difficult."[67]

Looking to citizens as customers also conveys an important symbolic message: the citizen's relationship with government is primarily an economic one. The citizen is transformed into a consumer who seeks value for money in his exchange with government. Over time, the citizen could lose interest in being an active participant in the governing process or in the wider public interest.

Managerialism is having a more direct impact on accountability in Britain and Canada. The notion of empowerment and the establishment of the executive agencies in Britain and the SOAs in Canada are raising fundamental questions about the principle of ministerial responsibility, which underpins the relations between senior officials and ministers, and in turn relations between ministers and Parliament. The principle has been challenged of late from a number of quarters, however (see chapter 2). Some observers insist that the principle is hopelessly dated and that it has now become a myth. They argue that ministers no longer resign even when a serious departmental error is committed, nor should they. One keen observer of the parliamentary form of government makes the point that the principle was established in Britain in the nineteenth century at a time when the largest central government department, the Board of Trade, employed only a handful of people.[68]

Constitutional purists, however, argue that the issue of whether a minister should resign over a major departmental error misses the point. They ask, If ministers are not accountable to Parliament for some actions of their officials, then who is? If officials are to be held directly accountable for their actions, then they need ways to defend themselves publicly when accused of incompetence. The purists also ask, If the concept of ministerial responsibility is so outmoded, why is it that no one has come forward with even "an initial draft of a new version more appropriate to modern times?"[69] They insist that the principle exists so that a minister becomes the "constitutional mouthpiece through which departmental actions will be defended or repudiated and from whom information is to be sought." Here, again, anything can become policy, depending on events and interests. This is especially so in light of the fact that, by nature, the House of Commons exerts a negative rather than a positive control. The principle of ministerial responsibility makes the minister "blamable" for both policy and administration, and the minister in turn can reach into the bureaucracy, organized as it is along clear hierarchical lines, and secure an explanation for why things have gone wrong as well as how to make things right. The civil service, meanwhile, has "no constitutional personality or responsibility separate from the duly elected Government of the day." The point, as Herman Finer explained in his classic essay, is that the views and advice of civil servants are to be private and their actions anonymous, so that "Only the Minister has views and takes actions. If this convention is not obeyed, then civil servants may be publicly attacked by one party and praised by another and that must lead to a weakening of the principle of impartiality."[70]

It is important to stress once again that the principle of ministerial responsibility has come under attack in recent years not just from those who argue that the notion that ministers should resign over departmental errors is outdated. Derek Rayner, for example, called it "an absurd convention." Conservatives argue that the principle of ministerial responsibility has encouraged the growth of government. They maintain that it has given the public a false sense of security. They think that one can hold a minister personally responsible for all new government activities. Others have challenged the principle on the basis that it hobbles a new government from introducing changes and that it masks true accountability. Hugh Segal, Mulroney's chief of staff, argues that a new government is often elected on the basis of being able "to clean out the rascals." The principle of ministerial responsibility inhibits the ability of any government to clean out the rascals and to engage in "blunt and frank" talk about who is responsible for what. Segal maintains that it ought to be a matter of "both personal honour and self-respect that those who advise a Cabinet and whose advice may be taken, should not themselves be insulated from the effects of that advice if it is wrong, particularly when those who took the advice may find themselves out of work as a result."[71] His solution is to make civil servants more open and directly accountable for both policy advice and administration.

Thatcher and Mulroney's brand of managerialism was designed to attenuate as much as possible centralized controls and standardized systems. After all, it was these controls and rules that inhibited solid management and the empowerment of managers and front-line service deliverers. Yet, it is also these controls and rules that underpin the principle of ministerial responsibility.

Managerialism can clash with the principle of ministerial responsibility on a number of fronts, particularly in its attempt to separate policy and administration. It has become clear, from this study, that managerialism calls for ministers to decide policy priorities and for officials to become professional managers carrying out the policies to maximize efficiency. Another central theme of managerialism is that officials must be "encouraged, and even forced to accept what is called *personal responsibility* for their actions in administration."[72] Thatcher and Mulroney's decisions—to empower civil servants, to stress service to clients, to delayer managerial levels, and to hive off to nondepartmental agencies the responsibility and accountability for specific program functions—are designed to force personal responsibility for administrative actions on officials and to ensure their political accountability.

Managerialism has never dealt squarely with the issue of accountability. Sir Robert Armstrong, then secretary to the cabinet and head of the Home Civil Service, tabled a memorandum on "The Duties and Responsibilities of Civil Servants in Relation to Ministers" on 2 December 1987. Thatcher made it clear in the Commons that the note was tabled with her consent. The memorandum essentially restates the principle of ministerial responsibility and makes the case for the status quo. It is striking to note, however, that the Armstrong memorandum barely acknowledges the long-term significance of Thatcher's management-reform measures. It is true that the Next Steps initiative was not then in place, but Thatcher's firm direction to introduce a more active managerial style and such measures as the financial-management initiative were.[73]

An attempt was made in Canada, and a more serious attempt was made in Britain, to deal with accountability by introducing executive and operating agencies. The Canadian government essentially restated the status quo, although it argues that accountability has now been enhanced, since everything is spelled out in the framework document and the business plan, both of which detail the agency's area of activities, its powers, its reporting requirements, and its mode of operations. The government explains, however, that ministers are still accountable for the actions of the agencies in Parliament and the heads of agencies remain accountable to the deputy ministers.[74]

In Britain, the Office of the Minister for the Civil Service is playing a leading role in assisting agencies to define their relations with Parliament, ministers, and parent companies. The underlying premise of Next Steps is that the nature of ministerial and parliamentary accountability will remain unchanged.[75] The British government also maintains that the agencies will serve to enhance accountability to Parliament through

> its requirement for Agencies to publish their framework documents, annual targets, annual reports and accounts and, where appropriate, their corporate and business plans. Agency Chief Executives are accounting officers and, as such, are answerable to the Public Accounts Committee for the use of resources allocated to them.[76]

Thatcher, and perhaps Mulroney, may get more than they bargained for in establishing the agencies. The move is nothing short of constitutional tinkering and experience tells us that tinkering does not always produce the desired results. It assumes that the politics-management dichotomy is less fluid than it actually is. Recent events also suggest that managerialism has not had much of an impact on this front. For example, when the Iranian embassy in Ottawa was ransacked, opposition parties wanted the responsible minister to explain why "his" security agents did not dial the police emergency number earlier to ask for help. The question got full airtime on the television news and prominence in the print media the next day.[77] What was the minister to do? Answer that with the advent of managerialism, he was no longer responsible for fielding such questions in Parliament? This would hardly have satisfied the opposition parties, the media, or the general public. There have been numerous examples of similar questions being raised in Parliament, on administrative matters such as the purchase of computers and airline tickets or faulty security systems, all subsequently widely reported in the media.[78] Managerialism requires not only a commitment on the part of permanent officials to make it work, it also requires ministers and members of Parliament to be equally entrepreneurial, ready to take risks, tolerant of errors, and conscious of management issues. It requires that they put aside the opportunity to score quick political points in Question Period in the name of better management of government operations. There is no evidence to suggest that much has changed on this front in the last twelve years or so.

The establishment of executive and operating agencies could well force officials more into the open on management issues. As the agencies evolve, it is likely that the traditional accountability structure of ministers and officials will become blurred. The British government applauded the position of Parliament's all-party Treasury and Civil Service Select Committee, that the establishment of the agencies did not mean the principle of ministerial accountability would be abandoned, but rather, that it would be modified so that the heads of the agencies who had actually taken management decisions could explain them in the first instance rather than through their ministers. The committee argued, "In the last resort, the Minister will bear the responsibility if things go badly wrong and Parliament will expect him or her to put things right, but the process of parliamentary accountability should allow issues to be settled at lower levels whenever possible."[79] The government has made clear that ministers will answer questions concerning policy or will answer members of Parliament who specifically request a ministerial reply. The heads of agencies will answer on issues concerning the day-to-day operations of the agency. There is, of course, no model that can discern which issues will be floated up to ministers and which will be pushed down to the agency heads, nor can there ever be.

Heads of executive agencies are now expected to testify in front of parliamentary committees, together with the permanent secretary, who remains the accounting officer for the department and agencies. If agencies gain a degree of autonomy and if their heads are to be held accountable for management and operations, they will require some elbowroom to explain their success or failure. Quite apart from the likelihood that both ministers and agency heads may well have different answers to similar questions, agency personnel will insist that if they are to be accountable for management, they will need to be given the power to make decisions, to call a spade a spade, and to have the proper funding levels to carry out the tasks. If they cannot secure this, then they should not be held accountable. The Treasury plays a major role in setting up framework agreements and in deciding the funding levels of the agencies. Thus, it is difficult to imagine how the Treasury will escape at least partial responsibility for the performance of the agencies and any potential cost problems. The question that jumps to mind is, How will the Treasury be able to share such accountability in public?

Managerialism, and in particular the agencies, will invariably bring officials under a more direct form of public scrutiny.[80] Peter Aucoin suggests that

> the days of the anonymous bureaucrat are numbered. If sanctions against managers are found to have any teeth, managers will increasingly want to defend themselves publicly and personally against negative evaluations which in their view are unjustified or misplaced. More than just the most senior agency or department, executives will be required to engage in accountability exercises, including those in public fora.[81]

The heads of the agencies, at least those in Britain, are chosen by open competition. Some of them come from outside government and so have little experience in dealing with Parliament. They are not imbued with the civil service culture that places a premium on anonymity. They will become publicly visible, if only to point to the success of their agencies or to explain the reasons for the failures. Constitutional conventions do not provide for an official to engage in a public debate, either challenging the government or individual ministers or, for that matter, applauding government policy. There is certainly no convention to deal with a situation in which officials might "eclipse" their ministers in a public forum. Ministers may well have been taking for granted the benefits of being served by anonymous bureaucrats. They have not had to fear a public challenge from government officials with an intimate knowledge of circumstances and facts. Since the days of the Northcote-Trevelyan reforms and the advent of a nonpartisan civil service, a good part of the work of the service has been anonymous to those outside government, and advice has been put forward under the cloak of secrecy.

Managerialism and SOAs in Canada do not yet raise similar questions. The SOAs have much less autonomy and still operate largely within the accountability structure. In addition, Canada has a demanding Financial Administration Act to guide the work of both departments and agencies. Officials in operating agencies are well aware of the conditions under which executive agencies operate in Britain, however, and they are already clamoring publicly for similar treatment. They argue that if the concept is to work, they need the same conditions as operate in Britain.[82] Yet, at the same time, some Canadian politicians are expressing concern that current reforms may have already gone too far. Jean Robert Gauthier, chairman of the House's Public Accounts Committee, opened a meeting by stating, "over two years after tabling the PS 2000 report, no one is answering how, henceforth, we hold people in government accountable. This is an exceedingly important issue."[83]

The officials I consulted in both Britain and Canada expressed concern over developments in the "accountability structure." Some felt that the developments were manageable, but the majority suggested it was much too early yet to tell how developments would eventually play themselves out.[84] A good number also made the point that the accountability structure is affected by more than just the establishment of new agencies. Managerialism, in general, and empowerment and the emphasis on services to the public, in particular, are having an influence on how officials view their work and how they feel accountable for it. Some, in both Ottawa and London, spoke about a subtle shift of power taking place, whereby managers in the field are gaining a public profile and are being increasingly expected to deal directly with problems, including those at the community level.

Senior officials in London and Ottawa still firmly believe themselves to be accountable to ministers and cabinet for their work. As one goes down the hierarchy, however, this view is much less apparent: the line-program people, especially those operating outside London and Ottawa, are looking increasingly to the public for a sense of accountability. Senior officials report that front-line employees have always had one eye on the hierarchy and another on the clients. They maintain, however, that eyes in recent years are becoming more focused on clients and less on the hierarchy, the department, and the minister. One senior Canadian official in a large department reported, in a seminar held to review the progress of PS 2000, that his department had carried an

informal questioning of both head office and field people to determine to whom they felt accountable. The answer at the regional
level was—we are accountable to the public for what we do. When
we asked the question in Ottawa, people understood much more
directly that they were accountable to ministers.[85]

Thus, the fault line that exists in the accountability structure in
Washington is becoming more evident in the parliamentary form of
government also. Officials in both Britain and Canada explain that this
is the result of mixed signals, stemming from the call to increase the
quality of service to the public. In reviewing Sir Robert Armstrong's
memorandum on the principle of ministerial responsibility, the Treasury and civil subcommittee put a series of questions to all the witnesses who appeared before it, including, What are a department's
obligations to its clients? Can a civil servant's responsibilities to clients
ever override his duty to ministers? Most of the expert witnesses made
the point that, since the civil service had no constitutional personality
or authority in its own right, civil servants are there to serve the
government of the day and to support its members in performing all
the functions for which they are liable to answer to Parliament.[86] The
point here is that the duties of civil servants are to execute their ministers' policies toward the departments' clients. Accordingly, a department's obligation to clients is to administer the legislation and the
government policy as the clients would expect the minister to do it, if
he were present making all the decisions. This speaks to the presence
of detailed rules and controls, designed to specify for officials the
guidance that ministers have or should have approved.[87] All this is clear
to experts on British constitutional conventions. It is much less clear to
British and Canadian officials down the line, delivering programs. One
senior Canadian official observed,

> Funny thing about public servants. You tell them that they are not
> very competent or valued, as Mulroney and many of his ministers
> did, and then you wonder why you have a major morale problem
> on your hands. You then tell them that the way ahead is empow-
> erment and to focus on clients and you repeat that message over
> and over again, as we have during the past several years. You also
> explain that the inside of government operations is not very
> healthy—it is full of red tape, rules and controls. Now we wonder

why our people are looking mostly out to clients and to the public and less and less to within the government.[88]

In short, the conventions of ministerial responsibility and of civil service neutrality and anonymity are in a state of flux. It is no longer clear that the sign of a good civil servant is his ability to "eat salt." Managerialism has let the genie out of the bottle and the long-term implications are not at all clear. It could lead in time to a redefinition of the relationship between officials and politicians, to the perception of a partisan civil service, or to at least some officials' being identified publicly with a particular policy stance or program—rougher justice for some, with different rules and decisions applying in similar circumstances.

11

Deciding What to Fix

ALTHOUGH NONE of them arrived in office with a coherent plan to reform the civil service, and none of them developed one subsequently, Thatcher, Reagan, and Mulroney all believed that they knew exactly what needed to be fixed.[1] What they wanted was to diminish the role of the state in social and economic affairs, to reduce the influence of permanent officials on policy and the policy process, and to make government managers emulate the private sector. They all shared the conviction that most of the perceived inefficiencies in government operations were simply a function of poor management.[2] Privatization, deregulation, and cutbacks of government programs constituted the key instruments to roll back the presence of the state in economic and social affairs. Reducing the influence of permanent officials on policy was also thought to be a relatively straightforward matter—you need only to import your own partisan policy advisors. What was less straightforward was how to get at poor management, and it is on this that they concentrated their efforts. My argument is that by focusing on fixing the boiler room, they may have created new problems, which now need fixing, and overlooked others that required attention. In addition, there are important new forces now at play that call for approaches that go beyond what managerialism has to offer.

FIXING THE BOILER ROOM

Fixing the boiler room involved looking to the private sector for inspiration and to what Christopher Pollitt labels neo-Taylorism. The approach combined a blend of financial controls and business-management techniques.[3] There are remarkable similarities in the approaches tried in the three countries, despite their different institutional structures and public service cultures, and the degree of similarity means one can now make the case that globalization is having as much impact on the public sector as it has on the economy.[4] Management techniques move from one country to another with great speed, as if there were no jurisdictional boundaries. In my last round of consultations in Britain, for example, Treasury officials reported they had a small unit looking at TQM and that it had influenced the development of the Citizen's Charter concept.[5] Pollitt points to some of the more important similarities "in the assumption of public sector inefficiency, the recourse to private sector expertise, the stubborn belief in the usefulness of merit pay and the tremendous emphasis on new accounting procedures."[6] All three countries also tried to distinguish the role of policy formulation from the role of management and to upgrade the importance of management.

Two questions jump to mind: Is the management of government operations now better? and Was the political leadership right in focusing on management as the culprit? My study makes the point that it is extremely difficult, if not impossible, to measure qualitative performance in government operations and, thus, scarcely possible to reach firm conclusions about the state of government management. In any event, it is too early to consider some of the more recent measures (and perhaps, in the longer run, the more important ones) such as the executive and the operating agencies.

It is possible, however, to present some broad observations on the impact of managerialism and to comment on some of the measures that have been in place for some time. I asked officials in both central agencies and line departments, in all three countries, for their views on the success and usefulness of the new financial information system. Officials in Ottawa do not sing the praises of IMAA. Fewer than half of the departments have signed on, and those that have report that the information they must produce to satisfy Treasury Board requirements under IMAA hardly makes it worthwhile.

Officials in Washington readily accept that OMB's directive to upgrade their accounting systems and to bring them into line with a centrally prescribed standardized system made sense. They see some merit in the office's 1986 executive order, in which all agencies were asked to prepare a productivity improvement program.[7] They report, however, that neither measure has had more than a marginal impact on management. New standardized accounting systems and new productivity plans have been implemented, but by and large life goes on much as before. One official made a telling point:

> We now have in place solid accounting and financial reporting systems. The problem is that they are all well dressed and have nowhere to go. The systems produce excellent quarterly reports but they are hardly read. Congress staffers don't read them. They are kept busy chasing after current issues. OMB people do not read them. Why would they? They have little to do with actually making decisions. Very few agencies are putting them to good use. The well managed agencies have been well managed for some time and no one really needs to tell them how to do things. Poorly managed agencies have been poorly managed for some time and it will take more than an executive order to turn that around.[8]

The implementation of the FMI in Britain has been, in the words of a Treasury official, "a picture of patchiness." It appears, however, that it has been more successful than comparable initiatives in the United States and Canada. FMI has, in certain instances, permitted a further decentralization of authority down the line. But it has not made any appreciable impact on how Treasury allocates financial resources to departments, and Treasury officials admit as much. One explained,

> If you were to sit at a meeting between us and departments, you would wonder why we do not talk more about performance and outputs than we actually do. Output measures have fallen on stony ground. The bulk of our discussions is still about inputs. FMI has given us a greater appreciation of case loads and we are now a bit more conscious of output and performance. But that is all.[9]

Much as in the United States, some departments in Britain have been more successful than others in implementing FMI—hence the "picture of patchiness." Again (much as in the United States), the departments that have made the greatest use of FMI are the ones that have been well administered for some time, like the Inland Revenue Office, while those considered poorly managed, like the Foreign Office, have not been very successful in reaping benefits from FMI. It is no coincidence that the successful departments in this respect are those whose work is easily understood, whose work offers limited discretion in decision making, and in which the work load can be measured. An example is the Revenue Department, a machinelike organization that processes huge numbers of claims and forms.[10] Such organizations have a clear mandate, limited policy work, and provide little opportunity for politicians to intervene in their day-to-day work. It is also operations such as these that have been identified as candidates for executive or operating agency status. Where measures like FMI have been less successful is in organizations that have many goals and activities and a medium to high policy content in their work (the British Home Office, for example). Officials in line departments in turn argue that the Treasury's commitment to FMI is also "patchy," that is, some Treasury officials are committed to FMI while others are considerably less so. One department official remarked, "one senses that when it comes to FMI there are a lot of pressed men over in the Treasury."[11]

One of the first departments in the government of Canada to sign on to the IMAA initiative was Customs and Excise. Others that followed suit have similarly been productionlike organizations. In addition, those people who sought to identify "best management practices" or "best performing organizations" have most frequently looked to what James Q. Wilson and Henry Mintzberg have named "production or machine-type organizations" rather than to departments with a high policy content.[12]

This raises the question whether Thatcher, Reagan, and Mulroney set out to fix the one thing in government that was not broken. I argue that they did. They fell into the very trap that had caught many reformers before, particularly those in the 1960s and 1970s. They adopted government-wide measures and sought to introduce them from the top down. They stubbornly believed that the performance of programs and government managers could be measured (much as the architects of PPBS and PAR had once believed), and that such measurements would benefit politicians in their allocation of financial resources. On this front, however, very little has changed. When a performance or output-based system points to an increased work load or to success stories, the officials will trumpet them before the Treasury and OMB. They continue, however, to hide the "horror stories."[13] Experience tells us that horror stories and sloppy administration have been more prevalent in the government organizations with a higher degree of discretion in their spending plans, those that are expected to come up with new measures to promote employment or economic development, that have a relatively high policy content in their work, and that have no easily measured work loads.

The executive and operating agencies are largely machine- or productionlike organizations. One wonders how much more efficiency can be squeezed out of the Land Registry Office, Her Majesty's Stationery Office, the Inland Revenue, or the Passport Office. These agencies have not reduced staff and continually claim that they have insufficient financial resources to meet client expectations. One also wonders why governments have targeted for reform the organizations that appear to be the better administered, rather than the units that have remained in the sponsoring departments. The recommendation of the prime minister's own efficiency unit—that sponsoring departments should cut by 25 percent the staff working in administration, personnel, and financial services—speaks to this point.[14]

When Prime Minister Major said that the need to release "the well-spring of talent and energy in our public service" was a major reason for introducing his Citizen's Charter initiative in 1991, he in effect was also speaking to the limited impact managerialism has had in Britain.[15] He made his observation after some twelve years of Thatcher's managerialism, which as we know was designed precisely to release talent and energy in the civil service.

In the rush to improve "the business of government" (an expression often employed by Derek Rayner and Peter Grace), reformers tended to overlook a few important matters. The very things that we want from government—equality, fairness, and due process—these are precisely what produce some of the bureaucratic dysfunctions that we all complain about. There is a price to pay to ensure that our case before government is considered fairly, equally, and deliberately. There is nothing new in this argument; it is as old as the field of public administration itself. However, it is a fact that it is still overlooked by well-intentioned business people and their sponsoring politicians in their efforts to reform the civil service.

Some of the administrative controls are no doubt stultifying for civil servants and frustrating for the public. Yet they still apply, despite waves of reforms, because they have proved to be beneficial. There are probably only 25 nations out of 175 that have a modern, transparent civil service approaching those found in Britain, the United States, and Canada. What Charles H. Levine wrote about the United States in

1986 applies equally to Britain and Canada. He pointed out that "compared to other countries and to other times, the federal government today is remarkably honest and relatively free of corruption."[16]

I do not mean here that I support the status quo or to argue that all is well in government. Even allowing for some inefficiency resulting from the requirements of due process, all is not well by a long shot and there is room for improvement on many fronts. There are some deep-seated problems. The inherent dysfunction of bureaucracy has been recognized for a long time.[17] Studies abound on organizations that have become overly bureaucratic so that "dynamic action is replaced by dynamic inaction."[18] The charge that government bureaucracies favor the status quo, lack imagination, and harbor mediocrity more willingly than other organizations rings true.

My study points to a number of questions concerning civil servants and the administration of government. One of the most telling is the way the three leaders were welcomed to office. Although the new political leadership was criticizing the size of civil service institutions, the briefing books prepared by civil servants suggested that departments and agencies were stretched to the limit and that new positions were required. Yet, the size of the civil service was reduced in the three countries (albeit temporarily in the case of the United States and Canada), and it still functions and delivers the services expected of it. Had the political leadership listened to the advice of their civil servants, the civil service would have grown still more.

I asked officials why this was so and if it did not suggest that we could not trust the civil service to regulate its own size? There was a remarkable similarity in the answers from the three countries' officials. First, they pointed out that civil servants do not regulate the size of their institution (Thatcher's ability to cut the size of the British civil service is a case in point).[19] They did acknowledge, however, that they can exert considerable influence through the advice they put forward to politicians and that self-interest is often a factor. They also said that unless politicians are told where cuts in staff can be made, they will turn to across-the-board cuts, after picking out targets from nowhere. They reported that the advice put forward to Thatcher, Reagan, and Mulroney was based on their demonstrably increased work load and on a rough calculation of the cost of the goals the incoming political leadership said it wanted to achieve while in office. They did acknowledge, however, that their advice was not based on a thorough review that examined what the existing staff was doing to see if some personnel could not be cut or reassigned. With hindsight, some officials suggested this should have been done. Most, however, insisted that such a review would have been difficult, particularly at the time. For one thing, the full impact of Mulroney, Thatcher, and Reagan had not yet been felt. For another, those in an ideal position to report on where cuts could be made—the managers and employees themselves—had no incentive to report that their positions could be cut. The treasurers and OMB staff could hardly be expected to sit in their offices and pick out which areas (other than programs) could be cut or reduced. In most instances, they had no concrete information on where to recommend cuts. The only areas where outputs can be measured, the production or machine-type organizations, in many instances pointed to an increased work load.

There are important lessons to be learned (or, in some instances, relearned) from the experience of Thatcher, Reagan, and Mulroney. The first one, which by now should be self-evident, is to beware of fashions and fads in the management field. Management gurus have become modern-day witch doctors. One long-term observer of government reform put it this way: "administrative restructuring, technological fixes or gadgets, and soft-headed sloganeering about total quality or client-orientation are not capable of providing an adequate answer."[20] These options are attractive because they offer the prospect for a quick and painless solution. Another observer of government put it well, albeit provocatively, when he observed that solutions of this nature invariably become "today's novelty, tomorrow's orthodoxy and next year's basket case. Yesterday's management gurus are even more pathetic than washed up politicians."[21]

Ambitious government-wide reforms are also not the answer. The literature is replete with cautions that they are largely ineffective and often hold unintended negative consequences. Guy Peters was not being cynical when he wrote, "Reading evaluations of major public reform efforts from a number of national settings appear to indicate that a finding of no significant results is often the indicator of a reform 'success' while a 'failure' often is characterized by serious negative side effects."[22] Still, what is often overlooked in such government-wide reforms is the amount of time and energy officials must invest in implementing them and in trying to make them work. When I asked a Treasury official in London about the kind of policy work being done in certain areas in recent years, he replied that officials at the center and in departments have been largely preoccupied with "setting up executive agencies over the past two or three years and have not had much time to concentrate on other matters."[23]

What works? Political will works. More than anything else, political will works in reforming the civil service. Thatcher had it, Reagan had some at least early on, and Mulroney had not much. It is not enough to have political will in fits and starts. Thatcher demonstrated a strong and lasting commitment in her dealings with the civil service and succeeded in challenging the long-accepted view that the government of the day does not interfere in promotions, postings, and the internal management of the civil service. During her stay in office, the civil service could no longer claim to be the "autonomous, self-regulating body, insulated from politicians in its internal management" as it had claimed before Thatcher and probably could again to some extent today.[24] She ignored the advice of her officials and insisted on substantial cuts in the civil service.

Having the political will to challenge the status quo is not as simple as it may appear at first blush. There is not much of a political constituency in support of administrative improvements. Bureaucrat-bashing may be fun for the public, but measures to improve administration are boring. Beyond making cuts in the size of the civil service—which requires courage inside government but not outside, where it is often applauded—the general public has little interest in changes to government administration, since they have no appreciable direct impact on the public and, in any event, are often regarded as much too complex to understand.[25]

Officials are the first to recognize that civil service reforms will never receive much support from the public and, by ricochet effect, from politicians. This theme came up time and again in my consultations. Officials promoting PS 2000 in Canada reported that they first tried to secure public support and, failing that, public interest of any kind. The clerk of the Privy Council and head of the civil service toured the country to meet with the editorial boards of Canada's leading daily newspapers. The PS 2000 secretariat followed this up by sending special briefing material to all the dailies and to sixteen thousand weekly newspapers. Only a few dailies ran a story on PS 2000 following the clerk's visit, and these were brief and tucked away inside the paper. Not one of the weeklies ran an article on PS 2000.[26]

Officials in the three countries reported that they respect political will even when it calls for cuts in the civil service and that on the whole they will support it. British officials insisted that they are not getting the credit they deserve for the loyalty they showed to Thatcher and the support they gave to her agenda. Some even reported that privately many welcomed Thatcher and her strong convictions. "Without the kind of support we gave her," they claimed, "the government would never have achieved the kind of cuts in the civil service that were realized, particularly between 1979 and 1984." They added that Thatcher had no basis for deciding on the size of the cuts: "She simply came up with the number and said, 'right, now go and do it' and we did." Surprisingly, they did not argue that it was a foolhardy way to make decisions but said instead that there is no foolproof way to decide how large cuts should be. One official explained that Thatcher's targets

> gave us the marching orders and we got on with it. Some of us thought that she was going too far, particularly when she announced her second round of cuts. We also knew that the quality of service and the quality of advice would suffer at some point. We also worried very deeply about morale in the service. But we marched ahead, and looking back, it was probably the only way to proceed to cut back the size of the civil service to the extent we did.[27]

Career officials in Washington made similar observations. In addition, the literature reports that the U.S. civil service in the early 1980s proceeded to make the Reagan cuts, as directed. Irene Rubin, for example, wrote,

> Managers were involved in deciding how to dismantle programs. The overriding belief that the bureaucrats' job is to carry out the president's policy clashed with pride in program accomplishments. Few managers protested the reductions in force. Only the unions and some employees who had been fired openly criticized what was happening.[28]

In Canada, on the advice of senior officials, the Mulroney government did not pursue to the end its pledge to cut the size of the civil service by fifteen thousand person-years. To be sure, there was a sense of relief on the part of many civil servants that no further damage would be made to their institution. The head of the Canadian civil service had the protection of the civil service as one of his key objectives in planning the Mulroney transition. However, Canadian officials reported that they were looking to Britain and the United States in 1984 when Mulroney came to office and expected deeper cuts in the service. I heard a good number of them describe Mulroney as having little real interest in reforming the public service.

The point is that government officials respect firm leadership and many welcome it. Politicians should not expect career civil servants to come forward either with targets for cutting the size of the civil service or with suggestions as to where cuts can be made. About all they can expect is for officials to recommend program cuts, which may well entail reductions in the number of government positions. A lesson learned, it appears, is that when it comes to general cuts in the civil service, politicians have to set their own targets (albeit with a minimum of information), have to stick to their position, and have to insist on the implementation of their aims.[29] Experience also tells us that the most effective way to restrain public spending or growth in the size of the civil service is to have a firm hand—hence, political will. Nevil Johnson made this argument when he wrote that the imposing of firm spending limits is "the only constraint analogous in its effects to the private business's needs to balance its books and secure a return on capital."[30] Attempts in governments to devise output measurements in the budget process through value-for-money indicators of one kind or another to replace "profit" have never lived up to expectations.

Another lesson learned from the 1980s is that the bulk of improvements in efficiency in government operations comes from a number of modest tactical reforms, rather than from grandiose schemes.[31] In Britain, for example, productivity growth in government operations is explained by budget and personnel cuts, not by new management practices like FMI.

The scrutinies introduced by Derek Rayner also worked. The scrutinies involved a few outsiders (with no vested interest in the status quo) working closely with civil servants to carry out high-powered studies to uncover waste. The independently minded National Audit

Office reviewed the results of the first 155 scrutinies and reported potential savings of £450 million, with actual savings of £260 million realized.[32] By mid 1991, the government was claiming that over 350 scrutinies had been carried out with total savings of about £1 billion.[33] The fact that confidence was shown in civil servants by letting them play a lead role in the scrutinies in their departments is important. They were freed from day-to-day operations and permitted to step back to look at their departments with a view to improved efficiency. The scrutinies process revealed that when officials are given such an opportunity, they will uncover things that should be corrected. A good number reported that the scrutinies met with success in many instances, and that they were effective because they constituted a "blunt instrument," operating on the basis of a "few simple and basic rules."[34] It is likely that, without the scrutinies, the research lab in Reading would still be raising £30 rats, rather than purchasing them for £2. What scrutinies cannot do is get at the reason a government bureau ever produced £30 rats in the first place. Still, the idea that civil servants can themselves seek out inefficiencies, with the participation of some outside people, holds far more promise than bringing in any outsider, who knows little about government operations and who usually arrives with many prejudices and simplistic solutions and often does not know even where to begin to look.[35]

The idea of looking at government operations from a viewpoint that encourages different assessments for different kinds of activities also holds promise. Such a framework could distinguish: (a) developmental agencies, which design or create changes, or advise on them; (b) clerical delivery agencies, whose operating employees require relatively little training in providing certain services; (c) professional delivery agencies, which provide governmental services of a more skilled nature; and (d) control agencies, which act in some kind of control capacity, vis-à-vis segments of the population (regulation, for example), the population at large (army, police, and so on), or government itself (the Treasury Board, for example). In addition, new agencies in their start-up years should be distinguished from long-established ones.

Each of these agencies could use a different kind of structure to make it more effective and efficient. Developmental agencies seem to function best with "adhocracy-type" structures, which must be highly flexible and decentralized and must provide relatively quick access to senior officials and to political authority. Professional delivery agencies, as well as many control agencies, tend to require a "professional-bureaucracy" structure that should be decentralized. Neither of these structures, however, lends itself to performance measures. Clerical delivery agencies appropriately rely on the traditional structure of "machine bureaucracy," which is centralized in power and formalized in procedure.[36]

HEAL THYSELF

All too often politicians lose sight of the fact that democratic governmental institutions (including the civil service) are in the first instance organizations intended to foster democratic representation and accountability as an end in itself. They can never be merely means to promote other ends. Indeed, the main reasons for the pervasiveness of bureaucracy in modern life has more to do with administration in a representative democracy than with simple efficiency. Bureaucracy is designed to administer the laws and policies set by elected politicians, and as a result, authority delegated to career officials must be handled bureaucratically in order to accept direction.[37] It is for this reason that due process, fairness, and the keeping of records are all important in government operations. Politicians can very quickly, as experience tells us, provide citizens a focus for grievance. These are the realities of representative democracy, and they do not easily square with the nature of the management reforms introduced in the 1980s, including the concept of empowerment and the underlying objective of running government operations like a business. The U.S. president, the British and Canadian prime ministers, Congress, Parliament, and cabinets stand at the apex of authority. Thinking it was possible to reform the civil service and government operations fundamentally while leaving political institutions virtually intact was shortsighted.

Thatcher, Reagan, and Mulroney taught, as a good number of politicians did before them, that one could replace "profit" with "output measures" in assessing how well the job is getting done. But governments in the 1980s could no more measure the success of government programs and operations in a meaningful way than they could in the 1960s and 1970s. For reasons already discussed (not the least of which is the way politicians and political institutions operate), the majority of government programs and operations do not lend themselves to a cost-benefit evaluation. It is not for want of trying, either, for governments have over the years put in place a costly and elaborate evaluation machinery.

When politicians set out in the 1980s to make the civil service more efficient, they also did not spend much time looking to their own behavior and how they influence government operations. Yet, it is the political goals that drive government and government operations, and there is inevitably a mine field of political constraints when you introduce change in government operations. Key decisions on budgets and even on government organizations are taken by politicians, not by government managers.

There was a certain degree of muddle, even in Thatcher's case, concerning the kind of civil service politicians wanted. There was a general sense that they wanted a smaller, more managerial civil service, but beyond that, little was clear. The best defense politicians can have against what they may perceive as an entrenched and perhaps hostile bureaucracy is a clearly articulated plan, not just broad principles. Thatcher had plenty of political will, but no grand strategy. Reagan's approach was laden with contradictions. Mulroney kept sending out confusing messages and appeared unwilling to take a keen interest in reform measures once they were announced. His unwillingness to follow through is startling in light of his back-to-back majority mandates.[38]

But that is only one part of the problem. It is no longer acceptable for politicians to insist that civil servants improve the efficiency of government operations while they themselves remain above the fray. Their presence in virtually all government activities looms large, and if there is a problem, then they must look at their own roles. In a parliamentary form of government, most new ministers have little appreciation of the requirements involved in directing a large government department. This romantic idea—that a kind of independent amateur, unprepared and untutored, can wander in and overnight become a kind of chief executive officer to a large government department employing tens of thousands of people—needs to be reviewed.[39] To make matters worse, ministers are often shuffled around to other departments after a year or two. In both Britain and Canada, for example, some large departments, such as Industry, had at least six different senior ministers each during Thatcher's and Mulroney's terms in office. My point here is that politicians are probably in greater need of courses on governance and on how to assume their roles and responsibilities than career officials are in need of management-development courses.

The U.S. practice of appointing a cadre of politically partisan officials at the most senior levels may hold merit in promoting a presidential policy agenda inside the civil service, but it hardly makes for efficiency. The average length of service for presidential appointees during the Reagan years was about eighteen months, almost half what it was in the 1950s. Those who support the business-management model will immediately see that this is hardly effective personnel management. It takes several months for even the most competent individuals to get a feel for a new position and the system within which they will be working. The machinery of government in Washington remains complex for long-serving career officials, and one can only imagine what it is for the temporary help. Presidential appointees can also shield the president and his advisors from getting at the information and advice from career officials—the very people who are the most familiar with government operations. Elliot Richardson went to the heart of the matter when he observed,

> A White House personnel assistant sees the position of deputy assistant secretary as a fourth-echelon slot. In his eyes that makes it an ideal reward for a fourth-echelon political type—a campaign advance man, or a regional political organizer. For a senior civil servant, it's irksome to see a position one has spent 20 or 30 years preparing for preempted by an outsider who doesn't know the difference between an audit exception and an authorizing bill.[40]

If greater efficiency in government operations is the overarching objective, then it is time to rethink how politicians and political appointees prepare themselves to serve in government. Political leaders have become quite effective at blaming the civil service for inefficiencies in government operations, and in deflecting attention from their own shortcomings. One British official I interviewed, remarked,

> It is ironic, isn't it, that we would ask the most competent permanent officials who have spent between 15 to 25 years in the service of the government to sign up on a top management course to

become better managers. Ministers, some with no managerial or government experience whatsoever, can be handed the responsibility for very large government departments quite unprepared for the task.[41]

Officials' message to politicians to "heal thyself" also applies to political institutions, whose strengths lie in their capacity to give voice and access to various viewpoints and whose purpose is to bring into the open different perspectives, to give transparency to public policy and public administration, and to hold politicians accountable. Understandably, there is not much reward in these institutions for accumulated knowledge or for efficiency in their own operations. The British and Canadian cabinets and the U.S. Congress have a great capacity to put in place distributive legislation and programs. They are much less adroit when it comes to retrenchment, to cutting programs, or to insisting on efficient administration.

Some officials have suggested that our political institutions are ideally structured for an expanding state in an expanding economy. Now that growth is uncertain and the three countries face heavy public borrowing, the political institutions appear less confident that they have the right tools and the proper structure to do the job.

Public confidence in national political institutions and in politicians is on the wane. Indeed, one senses more and more that political institutions, rather than public bureaucracies, will be the new whipping boy of the 1990s. One is tempted to turn Stephen Skowronek's claim on its head and argue that "the political attack on all-consuming bureaucracies has been replaced by a political attack on all-consuming political institutions"—particularly the U.S. Congress.[42]

There was hardly a day, for example, throughout the spring of 1992 when the *Washington Post* did not run a story on disenchanted members of Congress who decided not to run again because "the system has broken down" or because of the crises facing the presidency and Congress. By 13 May 1992, sixty-two sitting members of the House decided that they would not be back in January. Forty-two of these decided to retire, a post–1945 record. Some high-profile senators, including Senator Rudman, co-author of the Gramm-Rudman laws, decided not to run because of the "pork-barrel politics" in Congress and the inability of the Senate, in particular, to stop "mutual back-scratching" and zero in on the expenditure budget.[43] Stefan Halper, a former official in the Reagan administration, explains that

> At the centre of the problem lies the demand for accountability. And in this context, some ask if a parliamentary system that selects the president from the majority party in Congress wouldn't ensure that someone was responsible for the success or failure of national policy.[44]

It is interesting to note that the work of the Citizens Against Government Waste, the offspring of the Grace Commission, is now mainly concerned with the inability of Congress to keep spending in check. The great majority of their recommendations center around reforming the working of the political institutions rather than that of the bureaucracy. Their work has called for such measures as a line-item veto for the president in the expenditure budget and new statutory limits on spending.[45]

Yet, the parliamentary form of government is also being challenged. Few in Britain or Canada are calling for a U.S.–Congress style of government, but many are calling for reform, a central theme of which is the need to give citizens a greater say in politics than simply the opportunity to vote for their local member of Parliament every four years or so. This is part of the new forces at play in liberal democracies, and it suggests a decline in the deference of citizens for their political leaders and institutions.[46] In Canada, some observers are expressing alarm at the depth to which the reputations of both houses of Parliament have fallen in recent years.[47] In Britain, Prime Minister Major is responding to pressure for formal legislation for freedom of information by pledging to open up the workings of Parliament and the government system. Ferdinand Mount, an influential Conservative party advisor and former policy advisor at No. 10 Downing Street, recently wrote a book on constitutional and parliamentary reform in which he presents a "pluralist" vision that calls for fixed-term parliaments, in addition to a Bill of Rights and a Supreme Court charged with its interpretation.[48]

There are other forces at play that are challenging not just political institutions but the civil service as well. Some consider these forces to be so powerful and the need to rethink the relationship between politicians and officials so crucial that we should now be formulating new theories and constructing new administrative structures, rather than simply undertaking a marginal updating of the existing ones.[49] Although it is beyond the scope of this study to meet such an ambitious challenge, it is possible to consider some of these forces and to suggest what parts of the government machinery truly need fixing.

GOVERNANCE: NEW CHALLENGES

Doug Williams argues that the tradition of Western political thought has looked to a world of more or less "stable regularities about which easy generalizations could readily be advanced."[50] That tradition no longer holds. Modern political theory and our traditions of governance have been built on a number of ideas, which include a view of the nation-state's existing in relative isolation from other states, except in war, diplomatic affairs, and some trade issues; a mechanistic understanding of problem solving; and a relatively clear understanding of the boundaries separating the roles and responsibilities of the rulers and the citizens.

These ideas no longer hold in the post-Marxist, postindustrial, postpositivist, and postbehavioralist world. It has become trite to write that the pace of change is breathtaking and that we are more confident about what has gone before than about what lies ahead.[51]

David Bell wrote that the "nation-state is becoming too small for the big problems of life and too big for the small problems of life."[52] Globalization is eating away at the nation-state. The globalization of finance, trade, investment—as well as of key economic sectors such as transportation and telecommunication—are imposing a new discipline on national governments. National income and its distribution, levels of employment, mortgage rates, and the rate of economic growth are now profoundly affected by the increasingly integrated international economy. Nation-states no longer exercise complete control within their own borders over the major levers of economic and political life. Trade policies are designed with an eye on international agreements and international retaliation. There is now scarcely one area of government jurisdiction that is not influenced by the wider global environment. The global economy is leaving in its wake problems of capital flow, far-reaching sectoral adjustments, and constantly shifting labor markets—but no international policy mechanisms to deal with them.

If there is any consensus on the way ahead, it is that a competitive economy is the key to economic prosperity. Large multinational firms, once thought the pillar of stability in society, are now adjusting to the global economy by shedding jobs and even plants and, as a result, ringing alarm bells in communities and regions. Meanwhile, national governments are not permitted to sit on the sidelines. Calls for assistance from the affected communities and regions are made, as expected. Fiscal, economic, and investment policies are also drawn up with a keen eye on what the competition is doing, and national governments are expected to contribute more than their bit to make national economies competitive.[53] They are invariably being asked by the private sector to trim costs and to lower taxes and borrowing requirements so that, in turn, the private sector can operate on a more competitive footing. Reagan's 1981 tax cuts, for example, arguably initiated a worldwide shift to lower corporate and income taxes. Yet, nation-states are also being asked to lead the way and to identify areas where the country can be competitive and to bring about more collaboration between business, labor, and "civil society."[54]

The global economy is not the only challenge facing nation-states. In much of the world, particularly in liberal democracies but also in Eastern Europe, there is a marked decline in the deference of citizens for their political leaders and government. Canada has joined the United States in becoming a "rights oriented society."[55] There is also a push in Britain to make people symbolically and practically more "citizens" than "subjects" of the realm. John Major's Citizen's Charter and the call for a Bill of Rights are evidence of this. Citizens are more demanding on governments than are subjects, and those who put forward claims under a bill or charter of rights do so under the "most powerful of all moral considerations" and are in no mood to negotiate.[56]

This is happening at a time when historically marginalized groups, such as women and visible minorities, are gaining prominence on the political agenda. We are also seeing an "explosion of ethnicity," together with a "politically-focused cultural pluralism" in many advanced industrial countries, most notably in the three countries surveyed in this study.[57] This, in turn, has given rise to a radically different type of cleavage in society, putting new pressures on the structures of government.

The information revolution is also having far-reaching implications for the nation-state. In the past, the near monopoly government held over the information it generated served to strengthen its dealings considerably with interest groups and the public. This is no longer true. Harland C. Cleveland wrote that the nation-state "is leaking away at the edges."[58] New communications technology and easier access to government information provide to outside groups and individuals a capacity to develop positions on a whole range of policy issues and to challenge government policy.

The breathtaking speed of modern communications, especially television, is putting enormous pressure on government to make decisions quickly for fear of appearing indecisive and not in control. Television gave its viewers a ringside seat during the Gulf War, for example. The modern media is global, increasingly critical, and widely accessible, even to the illiterate class.[59] Within minutes, it can zero in on any issue anywhere in the world and compare virtually any given situation in one country to a similar one in another. Above all, the media has a capacity to intrude into the political arena and into the operations of government and to inform the public quickly, visually, and with considerable impact about what is not working.

Globalization and the modern media are changing the art of governing. The postwar years provided reconstruction, strong economic growth, and a tremendous expansion of government spending. They were also quiet and stable years; countries were relatively free to shape domestic policy in isolation of even neighboring countries. The media was not nearly so critical of government, especially in the pre-Watergate days. It might have been an environment ideally suited to the Sir Humphreys of the world, but this is no longer the case. The world depicted in George Orwell's novel *1984* has been turned upside down. It is not a government elite that uses advanced technology to control the behavior of citizens. Rather, politicians and (albeit to a lesser extent) government agencies are continually "watched, even hounded, as they attempt to go about their daily affairs."[60]

To sum up, the world of relatively isolated national economies, linearity, discrete variables—and even common sense—inhabited by government officials is giving way to a new world. The new order is much more challenging, and less deferential. It requires a strong capacity to adapt to change and to deal with a more probing and better-informed media, policy communities or interest groups, and the public. Yet, at the same time, some of the old challenges have still not been met. Large annual deficits and the cost of servicing the accumulated debt—problems which in large part served to fuel the rhetoric of the new right—are still with us. In addition, there is no convincing evidence yet that the civil service culture has been fundamentally altered. The British civil service is smaller and somewhat more responsive to managerial concerns.[61] But the U.S. and Canadian civil services are not.

LOOKING AHEAD

One theme that surfaced time and again in my consultations, in particular with senior career officials and with recently retired senior civil servants, was the uncertain state of the civil service. Some have gone on to write about it. They are not alone. A number of students of government in Britain, the United States, and Canada have also written about a morale problem and the crisis in confidence in their civil service.[62] A good many officials I consulted addressed this crisis in confidence—they spoke about an "institution having lost its values, its sense of purpose" and "lacking both a rudder and legitimacy." A senior Canadian official sought to sum up the situation by writing that "the sense of unity, of purpose, of professional camaraderie, of basic values that anchor our work is waning."[63]

The majority of career officials point to two reasons to explain the crisis. At the top of most people's list is the rhetoric of the political leadership of the 1980s. They, like the Volcker Commission and other studies on the civil service carried out at the end of the 1980s, stress the "long-term cost of *bureaucrat bashing*."[64]

Others, however, argue that the civil service suffers from overload—the same problem that plagues politicians in power. They argue that government is expected to deal with too many issues and that its organization has grown too big to be innovative or to challenge the status quo. The pressure from above remains as strong as ever and "success" in government is still largely defined in terms of meeting the needs of politicians. One official wrote,

> What it really amounts to is a demand overload on government at
> a time when the gap between what government is expected to do

and what it can do has widened. . . . Fifteen years ago, we felt more in control and more capable of achieving our policy objectives—today, a lot of that confidence has been shaken.[65]

Managerialism has not helped matters. I argue that it missed the mark. Its target was the productionlike parts of the machinery of government such as the Internal Revenue Service and the Motor Vehicle Licensing Authority. These organizations were not broken. Their products and outputs are more easily measured than other government units and their operations are constantly under review by auditors. Indeed, they are the types of operations easily audited from the perspective of cost and in some instances of efficiency. There is no evidence to suggest that such agencies are more efficient today than they were fifteen years ago or that they are more capable of challenging the status quo of what they do and how they do it.[66]

The strong emphasis placed on managerialism left unattended the new challenges confronting government. Indeed, it did not even have much impact in the one area where expectations for it were high—making government more efficient. Managerialism does not question whether a program should continue or whether a government unit should be abolished. Rayner, Grace, and Nielsen all sought to do this, with varying degrees of success, but only Rayner's scrutinies became an ongoing exercise. More important, however, is that managerialism pushed aside policy concerns and did not look at how to strengthen the policy formulation and advisory capacity in government.

The political leadership in the 1980s insisted, as had many others before, that bureaucracy with its "inherent quality of inertia" was uncreative and favored the status quo. In one important sense, government managers are no different from private sector managers—they will not volunteer cuts in their organizations. Lee Iacocca, who has had some firsthand experience of pruning an organization, argued, "If you wait for a manager to *volunteer* a cut in his budget, you're going to be an old man before it happens."[67] Managerialism—again, with the exception of the scrutinies—did not challenge managers to question their programs or the size of their operations. Politicians, of course, do not know where to cut government operations. They need to be told, but that advice is not always forthcoming. Managerialism, with its focus on efficiency and service to the public, is much too narrow in scope to be a guide.

Managerialism was able to challenge the status quo through privatization and contracting out. Improved financial and accounting systems report on what is being spent, can allow the decentralization of some decision-making authority, and attempt to define quantifiable objectives and measure performance indicators. These developments have been, however, markedly unsuccessful in challenging the status quo.

Managerialism stressed the managerial role of the civil servants and not the role of policy advisors. Indeed, Thatcher, Reagan, and Mulroney deliberately set out to undermine the policy role of officials and to check their influence. It is ironic that the politicians and political advisors I consulted for this study now report that the big hole in government organization has more to do with policy than with administration.[68] A senior Mulroney Cabinet minister claimed,

> the biggest letdown in government was the lack of creativity and clear thinking on the part of permanent officials. I imagined while in opposition that it was the Trudeau Cabinet that was stifling the public servants in their attempts to come forward with new ideas and new solutions. I was wrong. . . . Officials in departments will urge us to stick with the status quo and those in central agencies will simply give us twenty reasons why we can't pursue something.[69]

Another senior Mulroney minister explained, "Every time I ask for something that is more than a few pages long or that breaks out of the narrow operating mode of the department, officials always tell me that they have to go to an outside consultant for the work. We have a pretty stale bunch in government."[70]

Politicians in Britain and the United States have been leveling similar charges at their civil service for years. Harold Wilson, Edward Heath, and some of their senior ministers have argued that the British civil service has let them down on policy, insisting that it has not been sufficiently creative. The same is true of the United States, going back to the 1930s. Franklin Roosevelt "arrived in Washington with a vision of profound social change, but found himself confronted by a federal bureaucracy inhospitable to innovation and frankly incapable of meeting the President's demands for redirection."[71] Roosevelt's response was to centralize policy-making in the White House.

Things have changed little since Roosevelt. Kennedy and Johnson resorted to presidential task forces as an instrument of policy innovation, to overcome the "legendary resistance of bureaucracy to innovations." We also know that their successors "Presidents Nixon, Ford and Carter resorted to much the same strategy."[72] Thomas Wolavin explains:

> When the federal bureaucracy cannot do a job, the stage is set for calling upon a commission. In specifics, the bureaucracy is often unable to be innovative or self- critical, to engage in basic reformulation or re-evaluation of its goals, or to reorganize itself, and it often lacks credibility or clout as an advocate.[73]

Warren Bennis argues that the rise of "throw away organizations" in policy formulation is the result of bureaucratic rigidity. He explains that bureaucracy was ideally suited for the routine tasks of economic development in the nineteenth and early twentieth centuries, such as building railroads. Bureaucracy, however, can no longer cope with complex, rapidly changing problems and circumstances.[74] Obviously, bureaucracy is still capable of performing routine work efficiently and ensuring that due process applies in delivering services and in considering cases. Managerialism merely reinforced this capability.

Bureaucracy is less capable of being innovative and of adapting quickly to a changing policy environment that became even more complex for nation-states in the 1980s. The fear of strengthening the policy role of officials prevented the political leadership from reforming the government machinery for policy formulation, coordination, and evaluation. The processing of policy is an expensive part of the machinery, with officials in all three countries suggesting that, all told, it accounts for anywhere between 5 percent to one-third of the total personnel costs in government.[75] Yet, other than introducing some cuts in staff in the case of Britain, managerialism did not touch on this part of the machinery.

With some minor exceptions (the Department of Industry and Trade in Britain has recognized its policy units on a horizontal rather than a sectoral basis, for example), the policy machinery in government looks exactly as it did in 1980. Virtually all government departments and agencies have specialized units responsible for policy formulation and coordination and for policy and program evaluation. These units must compete with the program side of the department for the attention of senior career officials or appointed officials and politicians. These units are expected to challenge the program side of the department or agency and to be at the leading edge of new developments in their sectors. In practice, however, it rarely works out like this. It is a daunting challenge for the policy- and program-evaluation units to push their work up the hierarchical ladder, unhampered, and perhaps calling in question existing programs or important chunks of the departmental organization. It is much more problematic to tell specialists in policy- and program-evaluation units how to do their work than it is to tell clerks how to do theirs. Yet, managerialism sidestepped this issue and concentrated instead on machine-type organizations.

There is also the ongoing bureaucratic dilemma by which the urgent drives out the important. Policy fire fighting is the norm in policy units. Their criteria for success is how well senior officials and politicians are being served on the policy front. The problem here, of course, is that senior officials and politicians are rarely in a position to compare the work of their policy units with others across the street. Standards can change whenever there are changes in senior personnel or in politicians. In addition, in a collegial system, the expectations include securing the respect of other units in the department or other government departments. This is hardly conducive to developing a capacity to be creative or to challenge the status quo. Officials in "policy shops" readily admit a reluctance to tackle "big" issues for fear of challenging the operational side of the department. One British official explained that his policy shop had "become irrelevant by attempting to be relevant and supportive of the operational side of the department." A Canadian official reported that an inordinate amount of time was spent "keeping fingers in all areas to ensure that our side is protected in the interdepartmental game."[76] There were precious few efforts throughout the 1980s to encourage departments to look at policy issues from a government-wide perspective or to strengthen the policy advisory function inside government.

Yet, there was arguably far more evidence in 1979 that the policy side of government and the ability of bureaucracy to be innovative and self-questioning needed more fixing than did the machine- or productionlike agencies. The bulk of the literature critical of public bureaucracies has zeroed in on their lack of creativity, on their inability to be self-critical and to challenge the status quo, and on their being inordinately slow in defining policy proposals.[77]

Officials working in policy units were well aware of the political leadership's focus on management. They saw efforts to remove "administrative shackles" but to leave "policy shackles" intact. The politicians had made it clear, time and again, that they wanted doers, not thinkers. By embracing the politics-management dichotomy, the politicians sent out messages that they and their partisan policy advisors had the policy answers. Officials, with their well-honed capacity to read political signals, understood the message clearly. Confidence and morale plummeted. Officials in all three countries report that there was a tendency to recommend safe policy options and what "politicians would wear."[78] They insist that no "challenging" policy work was carried out on "big ticket programs" and that there was an unwillingness to "say 'No Minister' or at least 'Be Careful Minister.'"[79] There was a reluctance to explain why things must be so, to provide objective or nonpartisan advice to the powerful, and to explain what kind of trade-offs were required if a certain decision was taken, and so on.

Officials in line departments and on the operational side readily acknowledge that the 1980s were more difficult for central agencies and policy units than for themselves. They report that politicians wanted to see position papers that supported their "prejudices" and that they did not have "a favourable view of neutrality—or neutral competence as they used to." One official explained in a seminar that "I see advice going to ministers which is suppressing arguments because it is known that ministers will not want them, and that for me is the betrayal of the civil service." The atmosphere was reflected in the philosophy "Don't tell me why I shouldn't do it but how I can do it."[80] Program officials also report that officials in central agencies and policy units became increasingly "insecure" and indulged in behavior that was damaging to the organization. They became more "aloof, gave the appearance of being very busy, engaged in petty insistence on turf and became increasingly resistant to change." If anything, they sought to concentrate even more than in the past on the role of "disembarrasser" of politicians and less on genuine policy work.[81]

To be sure, there was also considerably less movement of people in and out of policy units in the 1980s. The problem with policy units in the 1960s and 1970s was that "bright" people did not stay long enough to gain a thorough understanding of the sectors or the department. The situation in the 1980s was very different. "Have policy, will travel" took policy analysts to promotions in other departments or in a central agency throughout the 1960s and 1970s. In the 1980s, however, policy people stayed in the same unit and in the same job for several years or longer.[82] This did not appear to concern Thatcher, Mulroney, and Reagan. They sought to encourage a greater exchange of "managers" with the private sector, rather than encourage mobility between government policy units, the universities' research centers, or even other governments.

Managerialism in all its facets did not encourage officials to sit back, to think, to read, to reflect, and to come up with proposals for change, to meet the new challenges confronting the nation-state. It did not attempt to get at the reason bureaucracies are uncreative and unable to be self-critical. Program managers, or "doers," are too busy to be of much help on this front. And yet, if there were a side of government that needed fixing to get at the "deadly sins" of public administration, it was the policy side.[83] Thatcher, Reagan, and Mulroney chose to ignore this, thinking that they needed little help from their civil service to arrive at policy answers, or to restructure the policy-advisory function to prepare government to meet the new challenges.

Indeed, the number of policy shops and their staffs in line departments and agencies were cut back. The role of central agencies was downgraded. In eschewing a planning-and-priorities style of leadership, the three leaders effectively told officials in central agencies that their help in challenging units to come up with imaginative and cross-cutting policy alternatives was hardly required. This meant that there was only limited demand for central agencies to bring together various policy alternatives in a comprehensive strategy. Presidential commissions, ministerial task forces, and partisan policy advisors were more and more called upon to investigate policy issues and to recommend new courses of action.

The three leaders themselves may well have paid a price by weakening the policy side of government. The civil service, a former Reagan advisor explained, requires "a huge wrench of the wheel to transform it and to make it capable of being more innovative."[84] Thatcher gave the wheel a solid jerk through sheer political will and determination, but that was all. Any hope of a huge wrench of the wheel having any lasting impact required reforming the policy formulation and advisory functions of government. It also required a fundamental review of the relationship between central agencies and departments. Above all, it required strengthening the capacity of those who were in an ideal position to assist political leaders in giving "a huge wrench of the wheel," notably central agencies and policy units.

A huge wrench of the wheel would also have required a fundamental review of the merits of advising on policy from a sectoral or departmental perspective. The current machinery of government tends to compartmentalize thinking in government. It was no doubt appropriate at the turn of the century to establish vertical sectoral lines and to deal with problems in agriculture, transportation, and industry in relative isolation. Issues and challenges confronting nation-states now increasingly cross departmental lines, however. If key policy issues are more horizontal, then the bureaucratic policy formulation and advisory structures must become horizontal as well. Civil servants will have to bring a far broader and more informed perspective to bear on their work since issues are now so much more complicated and interrelated.

Another legacy of the Thatcher, Reagan, and Mulroney era is that program delivery is now more diffused. This is true because of contracting out, which has resulted in the private sector's delivering programs and activities and because of the establishment of new, more independent agencies. This development requires civil servants to have a strong capacity to draw up broad policy lines, to bring together alliances of groups who can get things done, to be creative, and to abandon activities quickly. In short, it requires an increased emphasis on policy over program delivery.

The challenges ahead are clear. Governments need a stronger capacity to develop policy, to react to fast-changing circumstances, and to bring together groups to get things done. Bureaucracies also need a stronger capacity to challenge their own operations and to be self-critical. This requires new ways for government organizations to be born, or put to death. The challenge is to tackle institutional sclerosis, and it is a challenge the reforms of the 1980s did not meet.

NOTES
INDEX

Notes

Chapter 1. Introduction

1. Charles H. Levine makes the same point for the American public service in "The Federal Government in the Year 2000: Administrative Legacies of the Reagan Years," in *Public Administration Review*, vol. 46, no. 3 (May–June 1986), p. 195.

2. It was this largely negative perception that led Charles T. Goodsell to write a book in defense of public bureaucracies, a book, as the author readily acknowledged, that was a polemic in response to widespread bureaucrat-bashing. See Charles T. Goodsell, *The Case for Bureaucracy: A Public Administration Polemic* (Chatham, N.J.: Chatham House, 1983).

3. Quoted in Derek Bok, "A Daring and Complicated Strategy," *Harvard Magazine* (May–June 1989), p. 49.

4. Quoted in Peter Hennessy, *Whitehall* (London: Fontana 1989), p. 590.

5. Quoted in Sheldon Ehrenworth, "A Better Public Service Needs Freedom to Manage Its People," *Globe and Mail* (Toronto), 15 April 1989, p. B21.

6. Canada, Royal Commission on the Economic Union and Development Prospects for Canada, *Report* (Ottawa: Minister of Supply and Services, 1985), 3:148.

7. Alan Cairns, "The Nature of the Administrative State," *University of Toronto Law Journal*, no. 40 (1990), p. 345.

8. Quoted in Bok, "A Daring and Complicated Strategy," p. 49.

9. Quoted in David Zussman, "Walking the Tightrope: The Mulroney Government and the Public Service," in Michael J. Prince, ed., *How Ottawa Spends: 1986–87* (Toronto: Methuen, 1986), p. 255.

10. Galbraith quoted in *Dimension* (Winter 1986), p. 13.

11. Christopher Pollitt, *Managerialism and the Public Services: The Anglo-American Experience* (Oxford: Basil Blackwell, 1988), p. 97.

12. Tony Benn, "Manifestors and Mandates," in *Policy and Practice: The Experience of Government* (London: Royal Institute of Public Administration, 1980), p. 62.

13. Shirley Williams, "The Decision Makers," ibid., p. 81.

14. Ferrel Heady, *Public Administration: A Comparative Perspective* (New York: Marcel Dekker, 1904), p. 48.

15. B. Guy Peters, *Comparing Public Bureaucracies: Problems of Theory and Method* (London: University of Alabama Press, 1988), pp. xiii, 182.

16. Robert A. Dahl, "The Science of Public Administration: Three Problems," *Public Administration Review*, vol. 7, no. 1 (1948), p. 10; Lee Sigelman, "In Search of Comparative Administration," ibid., vol. 36, no. 6 (1976), p. 623.

17. Notwithstanding many criticisms directed at the comparative public ad-

ministration field, there is some progress being realized. The work of Guy Peters is one example. Another is the valuable new journal recently launched, *Governance: An International Journal of Policy Administration.*

18. See, among many others, Ronald Inglehart, "Changing Paradigms in Comparative Political Behavior," in Ada W. Finifer, ed., *Political Science: The State of the Discipline* (Washington, D.C.: American Political Science Association, 1983), pp. 429–69, and Ronald H. Chilcate, *Theories of Comparative Politics: The Search for a Paradigm* (Boulder, Colo.: Westview Press, 1981).

19. Peter Savage, "Optimism and Pessimism in Comparative Administration," *Public Administration Review,* vol. 36, no. 4 (1976), p. 417.

20. Sigelman quoted in Dahl, "The Science of Public Administration," pp. 623–24.

21. James Q. Wilson, *Bureaucracy: What Government Agencies Do and Why They Do It* (New York: Basic Books, 1989), p. xi.

22. See, among others, Carol H. Weiss, "Efforts at Bureaucratic Reform," in Carol H. Weiss and Allan H. Barton, eds., *Making Bureaucracies Work* (Beverley Hills, Calif.: Sage Publications, 1980), p. 11.

23. See B. W. Hogwood and B. G. Peters, *Policy Dynamics: The Policy Succession Process* (New York: St. Martins, 1982).

24. Colin Campbell, *Governments Under Stress: Political Executives and Key Bureaucrats in Washington, London, and Ottawa* (Toronto: University of Toronto Press, 1983), p. 1.

25. Joel D. Aberbach and Bert A. Rockman, "Political and Bureaucratic Roles in Public Service Reorganization," in Colin Campbell and B. Guy Peters, eds., *Organizing Governance: Governing Organizations* (Pittsburgh: University of Pittsburgh Press, 1988), pp. 80, 91.

26. Campbell, *Governments Under Stress,* pp. 22, 30.

27. Quoted in John Naisbitt and Patricia Aburdene, *The New Directions for the 1990s: Megatrends 2000* (New York: William Marrow, 1990), p. 155.

28. Desmond King, *The New Right* (London: Macmillan, 1987).

29. See, among others, E. J. Dionne, Jr., *Why Americans Hate Politics* (New York: Simon and Schuster, 1991), p. 284.

30. See Terrel H. Bell, *The Thirteenth Man: A Reagan Cabinet Memoir* (New York: Free Press, 1988), and Walter Williams, *Mismanaging America: The Rise of the Anti-Analytic Presidency* (Kansas: University Press of Kansas, 1990), p. 13.

31. Williams, *Mismanaging America,* p.13.

32. See, for example, Donald J. Savoie, *The Politics of Public Spending in Canada* (Toronto: University of Toronto Press, 1990).

33. Consultation with former senior advisors to prime ministers Thatcher and Mulroney and President Reagan, various dates.

34. See, among others, James N. Rosenau and Ernest-Otto Czempiel, *Governance Without Government: Order and Change in World Politics* (Cambridge: Cambridge University Press, 1992).

35. See Les Metcalfe and Sue Richards, *Improving Public Management* (London: Sage Publications, 1987), pp. 2–3.

36. Both quotations are from Gerald E. Caiden, "Postcript: Public Administration and Administrative Reform," in Gerald E. Caiden and Heinrich Siedentopf, eds., *Strategies for Administrative Reform* (Lexington, Mass.: Lexington Books, 1982), p. 221.

37. See, for example, Colin Campbell, *Managing the Presidency: Carter, Reagan and the Search for Executive Harmony* (Pittsburgh: University of Pittsburgh Press, 1986), pp. 245–46.

38. I also consulted with the staff of some policy groups and research institutes in London, Washington, and Ottawa that had shown an interest in issues of governance and civil service reforms. The purpose was to verify some facts and to solicit their views on the reforms introduced in the 1980s.

Chapter 2. The Underpinnings

1. Robert B. Denhardt, *Theories of Public Organization* (Monterey, Calif.: Books Cole Publishing, 1984), p. 178.

2. See observations made by public servants in Savoie, *Public Spending*, chapter 1.

3. Denhardt, *Public Organization*, p. 186.

4. See, among many others, Denhardt, *Public Organization*, p. 34, and J. D. Williams, *Public Administration: The People's Business* (Boston: Little, Brown, 1980).

5. Woodrow Wilson, "The Study of Administration," *Political Science Quarterly*, vol. 2, no. 2 (June 1887), p. 198.

6. Ibid., pp. 201, 204.

7. See, for example, Dwight Waldo, "Development of a Theory of Democratic Administration," *American Political Service Review*, vol. 47, no. 1 (March 1952), p. 86.

8. Wilson, "The Study of Administration," pp. 213–14, 209.

9. Frank J. Goodnow, *Politics and Administration* (New York: Macmillan Press, 1900).

10. Waldo, "Development of Theory," p. 86.

11. Dwight Waldo, *The Administrative State* (New York: Ronald Press, 1940), p. 200.

12. Howard McCurdy, *Public Administration: A Synthesis* (Mexlo Park, Calif.: Cummings, 1977), p. 19.

13. Dwight Waldo, "Politics and Administration: On Thinking About a Complex Relationship," in Ralph Clark Chandler, ed., *A Centennial History of the American Administrative State* (New York: Free Press, 1987), p. 93.

14. Luther Gulick, "Politics, Administration, and the New Deal," *Annals of the American Academy of Political and Social Science* (September 1933), pp. 61–62.

15. Paul H. Appleby, *Policy and Administration* (Tuscaloosa: University of Alabama Press, 1949), pp. 7, 170.

16. David M. Levitan, "Political Ends and Administrative Means," *Public Administration Review*, vol. 3 (Autumn 1943), p. 356; Edward C. Page, *Political Authority and Bureaucratic Power: A Comparative Analysis* (Knoxville: University of Tennessee Press, 1985), p. 3.

17. Kenneth Kernaghan and John W. Langford, *The Responsible Public Servant* (Halifax: Institute for Research on Public Policy, 1990), p. 56. They do, however, go on to attenuate the division between politics and administration.

18. Denhardt, *Public Organization*, p. 50.

19. See Joel D. Aberbach, Robert A. Putnam, and Bert A. Rockman, *Bureaucrats and Politicians in Western Democracies* (Cambridge: Harvard University Press, 1981).

20. Colin Campbell and B. Guy Peters, "The Politics-Administration Dichotomy: Death or Merely Change?" in *Governance*, vol. 1, no. 1 (January 1988), p. 80.

21. Max Weber, *The Theory of Social and Economic Organization* (New York: Oxford University Press, 1947), pp. 333–34, 337 (first published in Germany in 1922). Nevil Johnson believes that the Weberian theory of bureaucracy is "highly qualified" in Britain mainly because the country lacks the structure of public law that formed the basis for Weber's analyses. See Nevil Johnson, "Management in Government," in Michael J. Earl, ed., *Perspectives on Management: A Multidisciplinary Analysis* (Oxford: Oxford University Press, 1983), pp. 170–96.

22. Max Weber, "Politics as a Vocation," in *From Max Weber: Essays in Sociology*, ed. and trans. H. H. Gerth and C. Wright Mills (New York: Oxford University Press, 1958), p. 91.

23. Weber, *Social and Economic Organization*, p. 337.

24. Quoted in Peter Self, *Political Theories of Modern Government: Its Role and Reform* (London: George Allen and Unwin, 1985), p. 19.

25. Michael M. Harmon and Richard T. Mayer, *Organization Theory for Public Administration* (Boston: Little, Brown, 1986), p. 69.

26. Weber, *Social and Economic Organization*, p. 337.

27. Quoted in Harmon and Mayer, *Organization Theory*, p. 72.

28. Weber cited in Gunther Roth and Claus Wittich, *Economy and Society* (New York: Bedminster Press, 1968), p. 173.

29. Weber cited in ibid., p. 222.

30. Weber, "Politics as a Vocation," p. 127.

31. Roth and Wittich, *Economy and Society*, p. 224.

32. Ibid., p. 316.

33. Self, *Modern Government*, p. 148.

34. Anthony Downs, *Inside Bureaucracy* (Boston: Little, Brown, 1966), p. 59.

35. Denhardt, *Public Organization*, pp. 142–43.

36. Dennis L. Mueller, "Public Choice: A Survey," *Journal of Economic Literature*, vol. 14, no. 2 (1976), p. 395.

37. Vincent Ostrom, *The Intellectual Crisis in American Public Administration* (Tuscaloosa: University of Alabama Press, 1974), p. 55.

38. Ibid., p. 64.

39. Lawrence H. Silkerman, "Policy Analysis: Boom or Curse for Politicians?" in Robert A. Goodwin, ed., *Bureaucrats, Policy Analysts, Statesmen: Who Leads?* (Washington, D.C.: American Enterprise Institute for Public Policy Research, 1980), p. 37.

40. Norton Long, *The Policy* (Chicago: Rand McNally, 1974), p. 804.

41. I borrowed this colorful description from V. Seymour Wilson in his *Canadian Public Policy and Administration: Theory and Environment* (Toronto: McGraw-Hill, 1981), p. 428.

42. Graham T. Allison, "Public and Private Management: Are They Fundamentally Alike in All Unimportant Respects?" in J. M. Shafritz and A. C. Hyde, eds., *Classics of Public Administration* (Illinois: Dorsey, 1987), p. 525.

43. Ibid, p. 511.

44. See, among many others, Hal G. Rainey, R. W. Backoff, and C. H. Levine, "Comparing Public and Private Organizations," *Public Administration Review*, vol. 36, no. 2 (March–April 1976), pp. 233–44.

45. Canada, *Submissions to the Royal Commission on Financial Management and Accountability* (Privy Council Office, March 1979), pp. 1–2, 7, 11.

46. Quoted in Great Britain, *Committee on Political Activities of Civil Servants* (London: Her Majesty's Stationery Office, January 1970), p. B6.

47. William Plowden, "What Prospects for the Civil Service?" *Public Administration*, vol. 63, no. 4 (Winter 1985), p. 395.

48. Gordon Robertson, "The Deputies' Anonymous Duty," *Policy Options* (July 1983), p. 13.

49. Sharon L. Sutherland, "Responsible Government and Ministerial Responsibility: Every Reform Is Its Own Problem," *Canadian Journal of Political Science*, vol. 24, no. 1 (March 1991), p. 100.

50. Ibid., p. 91.

51. Canada, *Report of the Special Committee on Reform of the House of Commons: Third Report* (Ottawa: Queen's Printer, June 1985), p. 20.

52. See Canada, *Submissions to the Royal Commission on Financial Management and Accountability* (Ottawa: Privy Council Office, March 1979), pp. 1–36.

53. Helen V. Smookler, "Accountability of Public Officials in the United States," in Joseph G. Jabbra and O. P. Dwivedi, eds., *Public Service Accountability: A Comparative Perspective* (West Hartford, Conn.: Kermarian Press, 1988), p. 40.

54. United States, *Constitution*, article 1, section 8.

55. Quoted in Peter Kellner and Lord Crowther-Hunt, *The Civil Service: An Inquiry Into Britain's Ruling Class* (London: MacDonald General Books, 1980), p. 45.

56. Canada, *Report of the Special Committee on Reform of the House of Commons*, p. 20.

57. V. Subramoniam, "Public Accountability: Context, Career and Confusions of a Concept," *Indian Journal of Public Administration*, vol. 24, no. 3 (Autumn 1983), p. 449.

58. Morton R. Davies, "Public Accountability in the United Kingdom," in Jabbra and Dwivedi, *Public Service Accountability*, p. 75.

59. Gerald E. Caiden, "Ensuring the Accountability of Public Officials," in Jabbra and Dwivedi, *Public Service Accountability*, p. 25.

60. Subramoniam, "Public Accountability," p. 453.

61. Davies, "Public Accountability in the United Kingdom," p. 80.

62. Campbell, *Managing the Presidency*, p. 9.

63. See, among others, Campbell, *Governments Under Stress*.

64. See, for example, Richard E. Newstadt, *Presidential Power: The Politics of Leadership With Reflections of Johnson and Nixon* (New York: Wiley, 1976).

65. See, among others, Jeffrey Simpson, *Discipline of Power* (Toronto: Personal Library Publishers, 1980).

66. See, for example, Wallace Oates, *Fiscal Federalism* (New York: Harcourt Brace Jovanovich, 1972).

67. See Newstadt, *Presidential Power*.

68. James David Barber, *The Presidential Character: Predicting Performance in the White House*, 2d ed. (Englewood Cliffs, N.J.: Prentice Hall, 1977). Barber presents four personality types: active-positive, active-negative, passive-positive, and passive-negative.

69. Adapted from Campbell, *Government Under Stress*, pp. 23–24.

70. Ibid., p. 72.

71. Ibid., p. 44.

72. Bert A. Rockman, "An Imprint but Not a Revolution," in B. B. Kymlicka and Jean V. Matthews, eds., *The Reagan Revolution?* (Chicago: Dorsey Press, 1988), p. 203.

73. Peter Aucoin, "Organizational Change in the Machinery of Canadian Government: From Rational Management to Brokerage Politics," *Canadian Journal of Political Science*, vol. 19, no. 1 (March 1986), pp. 4, 11–27 (11–12).

74. Todd Laporte, "The Recovery of Relevance in the Study of Public Organization," in Frank Marini, ed., *Toward a New Public Administration: The Minnowbrook Perspective* (Scranton, Pa.: Chandler, 1971), p. 21.

75. It is, of course, impossible to do justice to both Minnowbrook conferences in a few short paragraphs. There is, however, important literature on both conferences. See, among many others, Marini, *Toward a New Public Administration*.

76. See "Minnowbrook II: Changing Epochs of Public Administration," *Public Administration Review*, vol. 49, no. 2, special issue (March–April 1989).

77. Curtis Ventriss, "Toward a Public Philosophy of Public Administration: A Civic Perspective of the Public," *Public Administration Review*, vol. 49, no. 2, special issue (March–April 1989), p. 174.

78. Aaron Wildavsky, "Introduction: Administration Without Hierarchy? Bureaucracy Without Authority," in Naomi B. Lynn and Aaron Wildavsky, eds., *Public Administration: The State of the Discipline* (Chatham, N.J.: Chatham House, 1990), p. xiii.

79. See Bernard Rosen, "Crisis in the U.S. Civil Service," *Public Administration Review*, vol. 46, no. 3 (May–June 1986), p. 213.

80. See, among others, David Zussman and Jak Jabes, *The Vertical Solitude: Managing in the Public Sector* (Halifax: Institute for Research on Public Policy, 1989).

Chapter 3. Getting There

1. Hennessy, *Whitehall*, p. 19.

2. Examples include the introduction of Program Planning and Budgeting System (PPBS) in the United States, which was also later attempted in Canada and to some extent in Britain.

3. Quoted in Hennessy, *Whitehall*, p. 39.

4. Quoted in Kellner and Crowther-Hunt, *The Civil Service*, p. 105. See also E. N. Gladden, *Civil Service of the United Kingdom 1857–1970* (London: Frank Cass, 1967).

5. Quoted in H. C. G. Matthew, *Gladstone 1809–1874* (Oxford: Clarendon Press, 1986), p. 85.

6. Kellner and Crowther-Hunt, *The Civil Service*, p. 105. See also Gladden, *Civil Service*.

7. See, for example, Sir Edward Bridges, *Portrait of a Profession: The Civil Service Tradition* (Cambridge: Cambridge University Press, 1953), p. 9; quotations from Richard A. Chapman and J. R. Greenaway, *The Dynamics of Administrative Reform* (London: Croom Helm, 1980), p. 40.

8. Hennessy, *Whitehall*, p. 40.

9. Bridges, *Portrait of a Profession*, p. 10; Thomas Balogh, "The Apotheosis of the Dilettante: The Establishment of the Manadarins," in Hugh Thomas, ed., *The Establishment* (London: Anthony Bond, 1959), p. 84.

10. Nevil Johnson, "Change in the Civil Service: Retrospect and Prospect," *Public Administration*, vol. 63, no. 4 (Winter 1985), p. 416. Geoffrey K. Fry, *The Changing Civil Service* (London: George Allen and Unwin, 1985), chapter 1.

11. See, for example, Bridges, *Portrait of a Profession*, p. 13.

12. Great Britain, *The Civil Service*, vol. 1, *Report of the Committee 1966–68* (London: Her Majesty's Stationery Office, June 1968), p. 9.

13. Hennessy, *Whitehall*, pp. 40, 31.

14. Frederick C. Mosher, *Democracy and the Public Sector* (New York: Oxford University Press, 1968), p. 39.

15. *Reforming Bureaucracy: The Politics of Institutional Choice* (Englewood Cliffs, N.J.: Prentice Hall, 1987), pp. 5, 58; Frederick W. Taylor, *Scientific Management* (New York: Harper and Row, 1923), p. 64.

16. Paul P. Van Riper, "The Pendleton Act: A Centennial Eulogy," *American Review of Public Administration*, vol. 17, no. 1 (Spring 1983), p. 11.

17. Ibid, p.96. Van Riper argues, however, that "It is not at all well known that everything really began with the early nineteenth century British reformers' envy

of our own federalist and Jeffersonian civil service of relative competence, permanence and incorruptibility. This led to British reform between 1850 and 1870 which our civil service reformers, in turn, brought back again across the Atlantic after the Civil War."

18. Paul P. Van Riper, *History of the United States Civil Service* (Evanston, Ill.: Row Peterson, 1958), pp. 85, 83; Lionel Murphy, "The First Federal Civil Service Commission: 1871–1875," *Public Personnel Review* (October 1942), p. 319.

19. Van Riper, *United States Civil Service*, p. 101.

20. Ibid., p. 105.

21. See Paul P. Van Riper, "The American Administrative State: Wilson and the Founders," in Chandler, *A Centennial History*, p. 19; S. M. Milkis, "The New Deal, Administrative Reform, and the Transcendence of Partisan Politics," *Administration and Society*, vol. 18 (1987), pp. 433–72; also Van Riper, *United States Civil Service*, p. 96.

22. See Mosher, *Democracy and the Public Sector*, p. 70.

23. J. A. Corry and J. E. Hodgetts, *Democratic Government and Politics* (Toronto: University of Toronto Press, 1946), p. 501.

24. R. MacGregor Dawson, *The Government of Canada* (Toronto: University of Toronto Press, 1973), p. 251.

25. O. D. Skelton, *Life and Letters of Sir Wilfred Laurier* (Toronto: University of Toronto Press, 1921), p. 270.

26. Dawson, *Government of Canada*, p. 252.

27. J. E. Hodgetts, *The Canadian Public Service: A Physiology of Government 1867–1970* (Toronto: University of Toronto Press, 1973), p. 265.

28. Skelton, *Sir Wilfred Laurier*, p. 503.

29. Hodgetts, *Canadian Public Service*, p. 268.

30. Quoted in Aaron Wildavsky, *How to Limit Government Spending, or . . .* (Berkeley: University of California Press, 1979), p.173.

31. Ibid.; Ronald C. Moe, "A New Hoover Commission: A Timely Idea or Misdirected Nostalgia?" *Public Administration Review*, vol. 42, no. 3 (May–June 1982), p. 271.

32. Jack H. Knott and Gary J. Miller, *Reforming Bureaucracy: The Politics of Institutional Choice* (Englewood Cliffs, N.J.: Prentice Hall, 1987), p. 86.

33. *Report of the President's Committee on Administrative Management* (Washington, D.C., 1937), pp. 16–18.

34. Knott and Miller, *Reforming Bureaucracy*, p. 88.

35. Ibid., p. 89. See also Peri E. Arnold, "Herbert Hoover and the Continuity of American Public Policy," *Public Policy*, vol. 20 (1972), pp. 526–44.

36. Quoted in William R. Divine, "The Second Hoover Commission Reports: An Analysis," *Public Administration Review*, vol. 15, no. 4 (Autumn 1955), p. 264.

37. Moe, "A New Hoover Commission," p. 271; Hoover quoted in Divine, "Second Hoover Commission Reports," p. 264; Moe, "A New Hoover Commission," p. 272.

38. United States, Commission on Organization of the Executive Branch of the

Government, *General Management of the Executive Branch* (Washington: U.S. Government Printing Office, 1949), p. viii.

39. Ibid., p. 8.

40. Ibid.

41. Peri Arnold, "The First Hoover Commission and the Managerial Presidency," *Journal of Politics*, vol. 38, no. 1 (February 1976), pp. 49–50.

42. United States Senate, Committee on Government Operations, *Establishment of Commission on Organization of the Executive Branch of the Government*, Dept. 216, 83d Cong., 1st sess. (1953), p. 4.

43. Ronald C. Moe, *The Hoover Commissions Revisited* (Boulder, Colo.: Westview Press, 1982), p. 104.

44. Ibid., p. 105.

45. See, among others, Peter C. Newman, *Renegade in Power: The Diefenbaker Years* (Toronto: McClelland and Stewart, 1963).

46. Canada, *The Royal Commission on Government Organization*, vol. 1 (Ottawa: Queen's Printer, 1962), p. 1.

47. Hodgetts, *Canadian Public Service*, p. 127. See also, for example, Walter Baker, "Administrative Reform in the Federal Public Service: The First Faltering Steps," *Canadian Public Administration*, vol. 16, no. 3 (Fall 1973), pp. 381–98.

48. Canada, *The Royal Commission on Government Organization*, vol. 1 (Ottawa: Queen's Printer, 1962), p. 255.

49. Ibid., p. 91.

50. Ibid., p. 154.

51. Hodgetts, *Canadian Public Service*, p. 281.

52. Canada, *Royal Commission on Government Organization*, p. 156.

53. See, for example, Hodgetts, *Canadian Public Service*, p. 260.

54. E. J. Benson, "The New Dynamism," notes for an address to the Canadian Bar Association, 29 March 1967, Winnipeg, Manitoba (mimeo), p. 14.

55. Quotations are from Balogh, "Apotheosis," pp. 109–10, 25. See also Hennessy, *Whitehall*, chapter 5 (Peter Hennessy goes on to argue that Balogh viewed the civil service as an "essentially Victorian model of a 'Mandarin's paradise' . . . outdated by Armistice Day 1919," p. 172).

56. Quotations from Hennessy, *Whitehall*, pp. 173–74, 192. See also Kellner and Crowther-Hunt, *The Civil Service*, chapter 2.

57. See *Sunday Times* (London), 5 September 1965, p. 16.

58. House of Commons, *Debates* (London), 8 February 1966, vol. 210, p. 13.

59. Kellner and Crowther-Hunt, *The Civil Service*, p. 27, and also chapter 2.

60. Ibid.

61. This definition was provided by the Staff Association of the Administrative Class in its submission to the Fulton Committee. See Great Britain, *The Civil Service*, vol. 5, no. 1 (London: Her Majesty's Stationery Office, 1968), p. 106.

62. Ibid., p. 18.

63. Ibid., pp. 173–74, 44, 43. See also Kellner and Crowther-Hunt, *The Civil Service*, p. 39.

64. Great Britain, *The Civil Service*, vol. 1, *Report of the Committee 1966–68* (London: Her Majesty's Stationery Office, June 1968), p. 71.

65. Ibid., pp. 84, 105.

66. Ibid., p. 82.

67. Ibid., p. 106.

68. Kellner and Crowther-Hunt, *The Civil Service*, pp. 55, 56.

69. United States, *The Budget of the United States Government—1968* (Washington: Government Printing Office, 1968), p. 36.

70. Barry Bozeman, *Public Management and Policy Analysis* (New York: St. Martin's Press, 1979), p. 233. For the workings of PPBS, see, among many others, Joan Chien Doh, *The Planning Program Budgeting System in Three Federal Agencies* (New York: Praeger Special Studies, 1971), and Allen Schick, "The Road to PPB: The Stages of Budget Reform," *Public Administration Review*, vol. 26, no. 4 (December 1966), pp. 243–58.

71. Edgar Benson, "The New Budget Process," *Canadian Tax Journal* (May 1968), p. 161; Al Johnson, "Planning, Programming and Budgeting in Canada," *Public Administration Review*, vol. 33, no. 1, p. 24; Al Johnson, "PPB and Decision Making in the Government of Canada," *Cost and Management* (March–April 1971), p. 16.

72. Hugh Heclo and Aaron Wildavsky, *The Private Government of Public Money* (London: MacMillan Press, 1981), p. 268, and chapter 6 for a more in-depth review. See also Campbell, *Governments Under Stress*.

73. Heclo and Wildavsky, *Public Money*, p. 271.

74. Ibid., pp. 279–80.

75. Ibid., p. 290.

76. *Evening Standard* (London), 1 June 1972, p. 6.

77. Quoted in Heclo and Wildavsky, *Public Money*, p. 302.

78. Moe, *Hoover Commissions Revisited*, p. 127.

79. Harold Seidman, *Politics, Position and Power* (New York: Oxford University Press, 1980), p. 328.

80. Quoted in Savoie, *Public Spending*, p. 127.

81. Canada, *Report of the Auditor General to the House of Commons for Fiscal Year Ended 31 March, 1976* (Ottawa: Supply and Services, 1976), p. 10; J. R. Mallory, "The Lambert Report: Central Roles and Responsibilities," *Canadian Public Administration*, vol. 22, no. 4 (1979), p. 517. See also Savoie, *Public Spending*, chapter 6.

82. Canada, Treasury Board, "Statement by the Honourable Robert Andras, President of the Treasury Board, on the Royal Commission of Inquiry on Financial Organization and Accountability in the Government of Canada," 22 November 1976, p. 4. See, among others, Savoie, *Public Spending*, chapter 6.

83. Great Britain, *The Civil Service: Government Observations on the Eleventh Report from the Expenditure Committee* (Her Majesty's Stationery Office, 1978), para. 2. See also Hennessy, *Whitehall*, p. 204.

84. See, among others, Donald J. Savoie, "Public Management Development:

A Comparative Perspective," *International Journal of Public Sector Management*, vol. 3, no. 3 (1990), pp. 40–52.

85. Fulton, Wilson, and Heath cited in Kellner and Crowther-Hunt, *The Civil Service*, pp. 61, 62. See also, among others, John Greenwood and David Wilson, *Public Administration in Britain Today* (London: Unwin and Hyman, 1984), chapter 7.

86. Both senior civil servants quoted in "Whitehall's Loyal Executors of Ordained Error," *The Times* (London), 28 July 1975, p. 8; Hennessy, *Whitehall*, p. 205; Kellner and Crowther-Hunt, *The Civil Service*, p. 66.

87. See Robert F. Adie and Paul G. Thomas, *Canadian Public Administration: Problematical Perspectives* (Scarborough, Ont.: Prentice Hall, 1982), p. 141.

88. Aaron Wildavsky, *The Politics of the Budgetary Process* (Toronto: Little, Brown, 1984), p. 184.

89. Quoted in Savoie, *Public Spending*, p. 60.

90. Hennessy, *Whitehall*, p. 235; Andrew Gray and William Jenkins, "Policy Analysis in British Central Government: The Experience of PAR," *Public Administration*, vol. 60, no. 1 (Winter 1982), p. 429.

91. Heclo and Wildavsky, *Public Money*, p. 294.

92. See Gray and Jenkins, "Policy Analysis," p. 442; Heclo and Wildavsky, *Public Money*, p. 288; Hennessy, *Whitehall*, p. 596.

93. Richard Crossman, *The Diaries of a Cabinet Minister*, vol. 1 (London: Hamilton and Cape, 1975), p. 90.

94. Benn, "Manifestors and Mandates," p. 62; Peter Hennessy, "Demystifying Whitehall: The Great British Civil Service Debate, 1980s Style," in Campbell and Peters, *Organizing Governance*, p. 198; David Lipsey, ed., *Making Government Work* (London: Fabian Society, 1982), p. 37.

95. Wilson, *Bureaucracy*, p. 235; Knott and Miller, *Reforming Bureaucracy*, p. 245.

96. Flora MacDonald, "The Minister and the Mandarins," in *Policy Options*, vol. 1, no. 3 (September–October 1980), pp. 29–31; Simpson, *Discipline of Power*, pp. 119–20.

97. See, for example, Savoie, *Public Spending*, chapter 9.

98. Peter Drucker, "The Sickness of Government," *Public Interest*, vol. 3, no. 3 (Winter 1969), pp. 1–23.

Chapter 4. Rhetoric and Reality

1. See, among others, S. H. Barnes et al., *Political Action: Mass Participation in Five Western Democracies* (London: Sage, 1979), and Aaron Wildavsky, *How to Limit Government Spending*, pp. 147–48.

2. An excellent example here is John K. Galbraith. See *Dimension* (Winter 1986), p. 13.

3. Weiss, "Efforts at Bureaucratic Reform," p. 10; Stephen Michelson, "The Working Bureaucrat and the Working Bureaucracy," in Weiss and Barton, *Mak-*

ing Bureaucracy Work, p. 175; Herbert Kaufman, "Fear of Bureaucracy: A Raging Pandemic," *Public Administration Review*, vol. 59, no. 3 (1981), p. 1.

4. See Gerald M. Pomper, *The Election of 1980: Reports and Interpretations* (Chatham, N.J.: Chatham House, 1981).

5. See, among others, A. Mitchell, *Four Years in the Death of the Labour Party* (London: Methuen, 1983).

6. Carl M. Brauer, *Presidential Transitions: Eisenhower Through Reagan* (New York: Oxford University Press, 1986), p. 220.

7. See, among others, Greg Weston, *Reign of Error* (Toronto: McGraw-Hill Ryerson, 1988).

8. See, among others, Dennis Kavanagh, *Thatcherism and British Politics: The End of Consensus?* (Oxford: Oxford University Press, 1987). See also Barry Cooper, Allan Kornberg, and William Mishler, eds., *The Resurgence of Conservatism in Anglo-American Democracies* (Durham: Duke University Press, 1988).

9. Brian Mulroney, *Where I Stand* (Toronto: McClelland and Stewart, 1983).

10. William Schneider, "The November 4 Vote for President: What Did It Mean?" in A. Ranney, ed., *The American Elections of 1980*, p. 248.

11. Joseph A. Schumpeter, *Capitalism, Socialism and Democracy* (London: Unwin, 1943), p. 295.

12. Kavanagh, *Thatcherism*, p. 315; Patrick Cosgrave, *Thatcher: The First Term* (London: Bodley Head, 1985), p. 169.

13. Hennessy, *Whitehall*, p. 592.

14. See Lester M. Salamon and Allan J. Abramsen, "The Politics of Retrenchment," in John L. Palmer and Isabel V. Sawhill, eds., *The Reagan Record: An Assessment of America's Changing Domestic Priorities* (Cambridge, Mass.: Ballinger Publishing, 1984), pp. 39, 40.

15. See, for example, Pollitt, *Managerialism and the Public Services*, p. 45.

16. See Brian Mulroney's speech to the Progressive Conservative Leadership Convention, 10 June 1983, Ottawa, p. 4.

17. See Progressive Conservative Party, "Background Notes for an Address by Brian Mulroney," 28 August 1984, Toronto. See also Progressive Conservative Party, *On the Issues: Brian Mulroney and the Progressive Conservative Agenda* (Ottawa: July 1984).

18. Hennessy, *Whitehall*, p. 632; memorandum submitted by Professor F. F. Ridley with Mr. Alan Doig to the Treasury and Civil Service Subcommittee (London: Her Majesty's Stationery Office, 29 January 1986), p. 153; Hennessy, *Whitehall*, p. 628.

19. Quoted in A. Dunshire et al., *Whitehall in Retrenchment: Who Got Less, When, How, 1976–83* (Brussels: International Institute of Administrative Sciences, Working Paper No. 9, May 1987), p. 4.

20. Ibid.

21. Quoted in *Management of the United States Government, Executive Office of the President—Office of Management and Budget—Fiscal Year* 1986 (Washington, D.C.: Government Printing Office, 1986), p. 1.

22. Lester M. Salamon and Michael S. Lund, "Governance in the Reagan Era: An Overview," in Lester M. Salamon and Michael S. Lund, eds., *The Reagan Presidency and the Governing of America* (Washington: Urban Institute Press, 1984), p. 14.

23. See E. S. Savas, *How to Shrink Government: Privatizing the Public Sector* (Chatham, N.J.: Chatham House, 1982), pp. 1, 2.

24. See F. C. Mosher, W. D. Clinton, and D. G. Lang, *Presidential Transitions and Foreign Affairs* (Baton Rouge: Louisiana University State Press, 1987), p. 60, and J. P. Pfiffner, *The Strategic Presidency: Hitting the Ground Running* (Pacific Grove, Calif.: Brooks-Cole, 1988), p. 164.

25. Quotations from Brauer, *Presidential Transitions*, p. 225.

26. Chester A. Newland, "Executive Office Policy Apparatus: Enforcing the Reagan Agenda" in Salamon and Lund, *The Reagan Presidency*, p. 143.

27. Consultation with a senior advisor to The Right Honourable Brian Mulroney, Ottawa.

28. See Savoie, *Public Spending*, p. 132.

29. Canada, *A New Direction for Canada: An Agenda for Economic Renewal* (Ottawa: Department of Finance, November 1984), p. 23.

30. Canada, *Expenditure and Program Review* (Ottawa: Treasury Board, November 1984), p. 9.

31. Kavanagh, *Thatcherism*, p. 314.

32. See the Introduction in Donald J. Savoie, ed., *Transition: Taking Power* (Toronto: Institute of Public Administration of Canada, 1993).

33. See Stephen Hess, *Organizing the Presidency* (Washington, D.C.: The Brookings Institution, 1988), p. 12.

34. Ibid., p. 17.

35. Hennessy, *Whitehall*, p. 630. See also, among others, Kavanagh, *Thatcherism*, pp. 195–96. Margaret Thatcher also served as parliamentary under secretary of pensions and national insurance in the Harold Macmillan government.

36. Hugo Young, *One of Us: A Biography of Margaret Thatcher* (London: Macmillan, 1989), p. 48.

37. Ibid., p. 153.

38. See, among others, Kavanagh, *Thatcherism*, p. 289.

39. Lord Rayner interviewed for the TV documentary "All the Prime Minister's Men," 21 May 1986.

40. Hennessy, *Whitehall*, p. 238; Hugo Young, *The Iron Lady: A Biography of Margaret Thatcher* (New York: Farrar Straus Giroux, 1989), p. 158.

41. Young, *The Iron Lady*, pp. 230, 231, 166.

42. Brauer, *Presidential Transitions*, p. 221.

43. Ibid., pp. 222, 224.

44. Ibid., pp. 233, 231, 234.

45. Ibid., p. 235.

46. David A. Stockman, *The Triumph of Politics: Why the Reagan Revolution Failed* (New York: Harper and Row, 1986), p. 2.

47. Ibid., p. 89.

48. Ibid., p. 102.

49. See John L. Manion and Cynthia Williams, "Transitions in the Canadian Government," in Savoie, *Transition.*

50. Office of the Leader of the Opposition, Notes for an Address by Brian Mulroney to the National Newspaper Awards Dinner, 5 May 1984, Toronto, pp. 2, 8, 3, 5.

51. Ibid., pp. 3, 5.

52. See Manion and Williams, "Transitions in the Canadian Government," pp. 32, 37.

53. Ibid., p. 30.

54. Jacques Bourgault and Stéphane Dion, *L'Evolution du profil des sous-ministres fédéraux 1867–1988* (Ottawa: Canadian Centre for Management Development, July 1991—A Working Paper).

55. This is not to suggest that the chief-of-staff concept has been successfully implemented. See, for example, Micheline Plasse, *Les Chefs de cabinets de ministres du gouvernement fédéral en 1990: Profils, recrutement, fonctions et relations avec la haute fonction publique* (Ottawa: Canadian Centre for Management Development, March 1992—A Working Paper).

56. Quoted in Hennessy, *Whitehall,* p. 39.

57. Francis E. Rourke and Paul R. Schulman, "Adhocracy in Policy Development," *Social Science Journal,* vol. 26, no. 2 (1989), p. 140. See also, among many others, Weiss and Barton, *Making Bureaucracies Work,* and William S. Peirce, *Bureaucratic Failure and Public Expenditure* (New York: Academic Press, 1981).

58. Goodsell, *The Case for Bureaucracy.*

59. Quoted in Hugo Young and Anne Sloman, *No, Minister: An Inquiry Into the Civil Service* (London: British Broadcasting Corporation, 1982), p. 19.

60. Norton E. Long, "Power and Administration," *Public Administration Review,* vol. 9, no. 3 (Autumn 1949), p. 257; Weber quoted in H. H. Gerth and C. Wright Mills, *From Max Weber* (New York: Oxford University Press, 1946), pp. 228, 232.

61. James Q. Wilson, "The Rise of the Bureaucratic State," in Francis E. Rourke, *Bureaucratic Power in National Policy Making* (Toronto: Little, Brown, 1986), p. 127. See also, among others, Herman Finer, "Administrative Responsibility in Democratic Government," *Public Administration Review,* vol. 1 (1941), pp. 335–50.

62. Edward Heath, *The Keeling Lecture,* Royal Institute of Public Administration, 7 May 1980, London, p. 4.

63. Quoted in Young and Sloman, *No, Minister,* p. 26.

64. Knott and Miller, *Reforming Bureaucracy,* p. 118. Some prominent Canadian politicians who have been recently critical of the federal bureaucracy and the power it wields include former deputy prime minister Allan J. MacEachen and former minister of Transportation Lloyd Axworthy, from the Liberal party, and

former prime minister Joe Clark and current prime minister Brian Mulroney, of the Progressive Conservative party.

65. See, for example, Knott and Miller, *Reforming Bureaucracy*, p. 167.

66. Caiden and Siedentopf, *Strategies for Administrative Reform*, p. 231.

67. Greenwood and Wilson, *Public Administration in Britain Today*, p. 122.

68. B. Guy Peters, "Government Reorganization: A Theoretical Analysis," a paper prepared for presentation at 1991 meeting of the Canadian Political Science Association, June 1991, Kingston, Ontario, p. 1 (forthcoming in *International Political Science Review*).

69. See, for example, Metcalfe and Richards, *Improving Public Management*, chapter 1.

70. Goodsell, *The Case for Bureaucracy*, p. 75.

71. Plowden, "What Prospects for the Civil Service?" p. 406.

72. Quoted in David Dilks, *The Cadogan Diaries* (London: Cassell, 1971), p. 22.

73. Julian Critchley, member of Parliament, quoted in *The Times* (London), 21 June 1982, p. 6.

74. This was true of Margaret Thatcher (see Hennessy, *Whitehall*, chapter 11) and Brian Mulroney (see Savoie, *Transition*, and Stockman, *The Triumph of Politics*, p. 2).

75. Quotations from Plowden, "What Prospects for the Civil Service?" p. 397.

76. Savoie, *Public Spending*, p. 239, 214.

77. Wilson, "The Study of Administration," p. 204.

Chapter 5. Looking to the Private Sector

1. See Marc Bendick, Jr., and Phyllis M. Levinson, "Private Sector Initiatives or Public/Private Partnerships," in Salamon and Lund, *The Reagan Presidency*, p. 452.

2. For a discussion of the application of turnaround management on government, see Irene S. Rubin, *Shrinking the Federal Government: The Effect of Cutbacks on Five Federal Agencies* (New York: Longman, 1985), chapter 8.

3. Metcalfe and Richards, *Improving Public Management*, p. 3.

4. See Geoffrey Fry et al., "Symposium on Improving Management in Government," *Public Administration*, vol. 66, no. 1 (Winter 1988), p. 437, and H. W. Williams, "In Search of Bureaucratic Excellence," *The Bureaucrat*, vol. 15, no. 1 (Spring 1986), pp. 16–21.

5. B. Guy Peters, "Government Reform and Reorganization in an Era of Retrenchment and Conviction Politics," paper prepared for presentation at the annual meeting of the American Political Science Association, 31 August–3 September 1989, Atlanta, Georgia, p. 9.

6. Quoted in Hennessy, *Whitehall*, p. 633.

7. See Geoffrey Fry, "The Development of the Thatcher Government's Grand Strategy for the Civil Service: A Public Policy Perspective," *Public Administration*, vol. 62, no. 4 (Fall 1984), p. 326.

8. Consultations with officials in Washington, London, and Ottawa. See also,

among others, Edie N. Goldenberg, "The Permanent Government in an Era of Retrenchment and Redirection," in Salamon and Lund, *The Reagan Presidency*, p. 398.

9. See Guy Peters, "Administrative Change and the Grace Commission" in Charles H. Levine, ed., *The Unfinished Agenda for Civil Service Reform: Implications of the Grace Commission Report* (Washington: The Brookings Institution, 1985), p. 19.

10. Bartley W. Hildreth and Rodger P. Hildreth, "The Business of Public Management," *Public Productivity Review*, vol. 12, no. 3 (Spring 1989), p. 309.

11. Lord Derek Rayner, "The Unfinished Agenda, Stamp Memorial Lecture," given at the University of London in November 1984 (London: Atlone Press, 1984), p. 4.

12. Andrew Gray and William Jenkins, *Administrative Politics in British Government* (Sussex: Wheatsheaf Books, 1985), p. 116.

13. Hennessy, *Whitehall*, p. 595.

14. Lord Derek Rayner, "The Scrutiny Programme: A Note of Guidance" (London), p. 2; P. M. Jackson, "Management Techniques in the United Kingdom Public Sector," *International Review of Administrative Sciences*, vol. 54 (1988), p. 249.

15. Norman Warner, "Raynerism in Practice: Anatomy of a Rayner Scrutiny," *Public Administration*, vol. 2, no. 2 (Spring 1984), p. 8.

16. See *Efficiency Scrutinies: Guidance for Ministers and Officials Handling Scrutinies*, document made available by government officials (London: December 1991).

17. Sir Peter Carey, "Management in the Civil Service," *Management in Government*, vol. 39, no. 2 (May 1984), p. 85; Lord Hunt interviewed for *All the Prime Minister's Men*, 29 May 1987.

18. See, among others, Andrew Gray and William Jenkins with Andrew Flynn and Brian Rutherford, "The Management of Change in Whitehall: The Experience of the FMI," *Public Administration*, vol. 69, no. 2 (Spring 1991), pp. 41–60.

19. Sir Frank Cooper interviewed for *All the Prime Minister's Men*, 29 May 1987.

20. See *A Force for Improvements in the UK Civil Service* (London: Office of the Minister for the Civil Service, 1991), p. 12.

21. Metcalfe and Richards, *Improving Public Management*, p. 190.

22. Hennessy, *Whitehall*, p. 60.

23. Metcalfe and Richards, *Improving Public Management*, p. 155.

24. See D. Beeton, "Performance Measurement: The State of the Art," *Public Money and Management*, vol. 8, no. 2 (Spring 1988), pp. 99–101.

25. Reagan quoted in Pollitt, *Managerialism and the Public Services*, p. 7.

26. See Charles T. Goodsell, "The Grace Commission: Seeking Efficiency for the Whole People?" *Public Administration Review*, vol. 44, no. 3 (May–June 1984), pp. 196–204.

27. Gerald E. Caiden, *Administrative Reform Comes of Age* (Berlin: Walter de Gruyter, 1991), p. 216.

28. See Steven Kelman, "The Grace Commission: How Much Waste in Government?" *The Public Interest*, no. 78 (Winter 1985), p. 62.

29. See Goodsell, "The Grace Commission," p. 197.

30. *A Report to the President*, vol. 1 (Washington, D.C.: PPSSCC, 1983), p. 6.

31. Caiden, *Administrative Reform*, p. 216.

32. B. Guy Peter makes this point in his "Government Reform and Reorganization in an Era of Retrenchment and Conviction Politics," a paper prepared for presentation at the annual meeting of the American Political Science Association, 31 August–3 September 1980, Atlanta, Georgia (mimeo), p. 24.

33. E. N. Goldenberg, "The Grace Commission and Civil Service Reform: Seeking a Common Understanding," in Levine, *The Unfinished Agenda*, pp. 87–88.

34. Goodsell, "The Grace Commission," p. 199; Robert M. Hayes, "The President's Private Sector Survey on Cost Control: An Opinion Essay on the Grace Commission Report," *Government Information Quarterly*, vol. 3, no. 1 (1986), p. 81. See also Kelman, "The Grace Commission," pp. 62–82.

35. See U.S. General Accounting Office, Washington, D.C., Statement of Charles A. Bowsher, Comptroller General of the United States Before the Committee on the Budget, U.S. Senate on the Grace Commission Major Proposals to Control Federal Costs, 28 February 1984 (mimeo). See also U.S. Congressional Budget Office, Washington, D.C., Statement of Rudolph G. Penner, Director Congressional Budget Office Before the Committee on the Budget, U.S. Senate, 28 February 1984 (mimeo).

36. Levine, *The Unfinished Agenda*, p. 10; Caiden, *Administrative Reform*, p. 217.

37. Canada, Office of the Prime Minister, *Press Release*, 18 September 1984, p. 1.

38. Savoie, *Public Spending*, p. 133.

39. Quoted in Canada, Task Force on Program Review, *Introduction to the Process of Program Review* (Ottawa: Supply and Services Canada, 1986), p. 1.

40. Erik Nielsen, *The House Is Not a Home: An Autobiography* (Toronto: MacMillan of Canada, 1989), p. 228.

41. See Canada, Task Force on Program Review Private Sector Advisory Committee, *News Release*, 11 March 1986, Ottawa.

42. Canada, *New Management Initiatives: Initial Results From the Ministerial Task Force on Program Review* (Ottawa: Department of Finance, May 1985), pp. 100–104.

43. Ibid., p. 2.

44. See, for example, Savoie, *Public Spending*, p. 136.

45. Vince S. Wilson, "What Legacy? The Nielsen Task Force Program Review" in Katherine A. Graham, ed., *How Ottawa Spends 1988/89: The Conservatives Heading Into the Stretch* (Ottawa: Carleton University Press, 1988), p. 36.

46. Consultation with a former senior public servant with the government of Canada, Ottawa.

47. Savoie, *Public Spending*, pp. 132–42, 290–318.

48. Consultation with a senior public servant with the government of Canada, Ottawa.

49. Quoted in F. F. Ridley, "Administrative Theory and Administrative Reform," in Caiden and Siedentopf, *Strategies for Administrative Reform*, p. 7.

50. See Metcalfe and Richards, *Improving Public Management*, p. 63.

51. The clerk of the Privy Council and secretary to the cabinet at the time, Gordon Osbaldeston, reported that he recommended the Nielsen exercise. Some senior political and even permanent officials insist that he made the recommendation after being told that such an exercise would take place. Saying publicly that he recommended it would, he hoped, encourage public servants to support the exercise. Consultations with officials, including one cabinet minister, with the government of Canada, Ottawa.

52. See, among others, Walter Williams, *Washington, Westminster and Whitehall* (Cambridge: Cambridge University Press, 1988), p. 58.

53. See, among many others, Allison, "Public and Private Management," pp. 510–29.

54. Consultation with a senior official with the government of Canada.

55. Wilson, *Bureaucracy*, pp. 197, 155. Blumenthal quoted on p. 155.

56. Wilson makes that point very well in ibid., chapters 7 and 11.

57. Ibid., p. 115.

58. Consultations with a senior official with the government of Canada, Ottawa.

59. See Henry Mintzberg, *Mintzberg on Management: Inside Our Strange World of Organizations* (New York: Free Press, 1989), pp. 106–7, and chapters 8 and 9; Wilson, *Bureaucracy*, chapters 2, 7, 10, and 12.

60. See, for example, "The Public Service: Looking to the Future," a document prepared by the Government Consulting Group of the Department of Supply and Services, Government of Canada, December 1991 (mimeo).

61. In the United States, if a political executive wishes to demote or dismiss a career employee, the employee is entitled to (1) a written notice stating reasons, at least thirty days before the proposed action; (2) representation by an attorney or union agent; (3) the opportunity to answer orally and in writing within a reasonable time; (4) a written decision by an administrative level higher than the one initiating the action; and (5) the final agency decision within thirty days after the end of the notice period. After the termination decision is made, the affected employee may also appeal the agency decision to the Merit Systems Protection Board (MSPB) and, if he claims discrimination, to the Equal Employment Opportunity Commission (EEOC). See O. Glenn Stahl, *Public Personnel Administration*, 8th ed. (New York: Harper and Row, 1983), p. 302.

62. Quotations are from Johnson, "Management in Government," pp. 185, 188.

63. Wilson, *Bureaucracy*, p. 217.

64. Ibid., pp. 189–92.

65. Consultations with government officials in London, Washington, and Ottawa.

66. The concept of the civil service as a village is explained in Heclo and Wildavsky, *Public Money.* Time and again in my various consultations with government officials, the point was made that, by and large, business executives are ill equipped to come into government for a short duration and make any substantial contribution to improving government operations.

67. See Johnson, "Management in Government," p. 187.

68. Consultations with government officials in Ottawa, Washington, and London.

69. See Savoie, *Public Spending,* chapter 6.

70. Charles Goodsell reports that he was not able to recruit civil servants to contribute papers on the findings of the Grace Commission, not because of a lack of interest or time but because of fear. The White House made it clear, he reports, that anyone in government "informed enough to write about the Grace Commission would also be smart enough not to do so." See Goodsell, "The Grace Commission," p. 196.

71. Quoted in Metcalfe and Richards, *Improving Public Management,* pp. 18–19.

72. Ibid., p. 10.

73. See Rayner, "Unfinished Agenda," pp. 7–8.

74. Ibid. See also Ridley, "Administrative Theory," p. 10.

75. Kate Jenkins et al., "Making Things Happen: A Report on the Implementation of Government Efficiency Scrutinies" (London: Her Majesty's Stationery Office, October 1985), p. 1.

76. See, among others, David Falcon, "Public Service Reform," a paper presented to an Armchair Discussion, the Canadian Centre for Management Development, 4 September 1991, Ottawa.

77. Quoted in Jenkins et al., "Making Things Happen," p. 3.

78. See Gray et al., "The Management of Change in Whitehall," pp. 49.

79. Quoted in Hennessy, *Whitehall,* p. 603.

80. See, for example, Michael G. Hansen and Charles H. Levine, "The Tug-of-War in the New Executive Branch," in Campbell and Peters, *Organizing Governance,* p. 268.

81. Pollitt, *Managerialism and the Public Services,* p. 93.

82. *Management of the United States Government, Executive Office of the President—Office of Management and Budget—Fiscal Year* 1990 (Washington, D.C.: Government Printing Office, 1990), App. 1, pp. 5:1–11.

83. Consultation with a government official in Washington.

84. Consultation with a career official with the U.S. government, Washington.

85. Quotation in "Whitehall's Loyal Executors of Ordained Error," *The Times* (London), 28 July 1975, p. 8.

86. Savoie, *Public Spending,* p. 136.

87. Consultation with a senior official with the government of Canada, Ottawa.

88. See Rayner, "Unfinished Agenda," pp. 7–8, and also Johnson, "Management in Government," p. 187.

89. Quotation from Hennessy, *Whitehall*, p. 603. See Savoie, *Public Spending*, chapter 13.

90. See, among many others, Wilson, *Bureaucracy*, chapter 11.

91. Erik Nielsen had a long career in Ottawa as member of Parliament for the Yukon when he was appointed deputy prime minister after the 1984 election victory of the Progressive Conservative party. He had never, however, served in government.

92. Ridley, "Administrative Theory," p. 7.

93. See Rayner, "Unfinished Agenda," p. 4.

94. Quoted in ibid., p. 5. Charles H. Levine, for example, argues that Grace overestimated the similarities between the public and private sectors and that this inhibited the commission's impact. See the "Introduction" in Levine, *The Unfinished Agenda*, p. 5.

95. Rayner, "Unfinished Agenda," p. 4.

Chapter 6. Turning to the Private Sector

1. See, among others, Madsen Pirie, *Privatization* (London: Wildwood House, 1988), p. 3.

2. Quoted in John D. Donahue, *The Privatization Decision: Public Ends, Private Means* (New York: Basic Books, 1989), p. 4.

3. Norman Macrae, "A Future History of Privatization 1992–2022," *The Economist* (London), 21 December 1991–3 January 1992, p. 16.

4. Pirie, *Privatization*, p. 9.

5. See, for example, Jeffrey R. Henig, Chris Hammett, and Harvey B. Feigengaum, "The Politics of Privatization: A Comparative Perspective," *Governance*, vol. 1, no. 4 (October 1988), p. 443.

6. See, for example, Stuart M. Butler, *Privatizing Federal Spending: A Strategy to Eliminate the Deficit* (New York: Universe Books, 1985), p. 36.

7. Henig et al., "Politics of Privatization," p. 445.

8. Donahue, *The Privatization Decision*, p. 5.

9. See G. Bruce Doern and John Atherton, "The Tories and the Crowns: Restraining and Privatizing in a Political Minefield," in Michael J. Prince, ed., *How Ottawa Spends 1987–88: Restraining the State* (Toronto: Methuen, 1982), p. 130.

10. Charles Wolf, Jr., *Markets or Governments: Choosing Between Imperfect Alternatives* (Cambridge, Mass.: MIT Press, 1988), p. 2.

11. See Milton Friedman, *Tyranny of the Status Quo* (New York: Harcourt Brace Jovanovich, 1984).

12. See Thomas E. Boprcherding, Werner W. Pommerchne, and Friedrich Schneider, *Comparing the Efficiency of Private and Public Production: The Evidence From Five Countries* (Zurich: Institute for Empirical Research in Economics, 1982), pp. 130–33.

13. See, among others, K. Ascher, *The Politics of Privatization: Contracting Out in the NHS and Local Authorities* (London: Macmillan, 1986), chapter 3.

14. Patrick Dunleavy, "Explaining the Privatization Boom: Public Choice Versus Radical Approaches," *Public Administration*, vol. 64, no. 1 (Spring 1986), p. 14.

15. Ibid., pp. 13, 17, 32.

16. Quoted in Butler, *Privatizing Federal Spending*, p. 35.

17. Rosabeth Moss Kanter, *When Giants Learn to Dance* (New York: Simon and Schuster, 1989), p. 96. See also, among others, David Heald, *Public Expenditure* (Oxford: Martin Robertson, 1983).

18. See M. Forsyth, *The Myths of Privatization* (London: Adam Smith Institute, 1983), and Metcalfe and Richards, *Improving Public Management*, chapter 8.

19. See Savas, *How to Shrink Government*, p. 118.

20. Ibid., p. 120.

21. Reagan quoted from "Remarks at the Annual Meeting of the National Alliance of Business, 5 October 1981" in *Public Papers of the President of the United States: Ronald Reagan* (Washington, D.C.: Government Printing Office, 1981), p. 885, and from "Remarks at the New York City Partnership Luncheon in New York, 14 January 1982" in *Public Papers of the President of the United States: Ronald Reagan* (Washington, D.C.: Government Printing Office, 1982), p. 29.

22. See Renée A. Berger, "Private Sector Initiatives in the Reagan Era: New Actors Rework on Old Theme," in Salamon and Lund, *The Reagan Presidency*, pp. 181–211, and Marc Bendick, Jr., "Vouchers Versus Income Versus Services: An American Experiment in Housing Policy," *Journal of Social Policy*, vol. 11, no. 3 (July 1982), pp. 365–77.

23. Wolf, *Markets or Governments*, p. 8.

24. David R. Beam, "New Federalism, Old Realities: The Reagan Administration and Intergovernmental Reform," in Salamon and Lund, *The Reagan Presidency*, pp. 415–42.

25. *Management of the United States Government, Executive Office of the President—Office of Management and Budget—Fiscal Year* 1987 (Washington, D.C.: Government Printing Office, 1987), p. 16.

26. Ibid., p. 85. See also *Management of the United States Government, Executive Office of the President—Office of Management and Budget—Fiscal Year* 1988 (Washington, D.C.: Government Printing Office, 1988), p. 76, and *Public Management Developments* (Paris: OECD, 1990), p. 122.

27. *Management of the United States Government—1990*, pp. 3:118–21 (120).

28. Ibid.

29. James D. Carroll, "Public Administration in the Third Century of the Constitution: Supply-Side Management, Privatization, or Public Investment?" *Public Administration Review*, vol. 47, no. 1 (January–February 1987), p. 108.

30. *Management of the United States Government—1990*, p. 3:119. See also Goldenberg, "The Permanent Government," p. 398.

31. *Management of the United States Government—1990*, p. 3:119.

32. Ibid.

33. Government of Canada, Treasury Board Secretariat, *Make or Buy: An Update Report* (Ottawa, 1988), p. 10.

34. See "Montreal Company Says Mapping Deal Not Yet Concluded," *Globe and Mail* (Toronto), 10 March 1987, p. A5. See also "Privatization Scares EMR Staff," *The Citizen* (Ottawa), 29 December 1988, p. A4.

35. See Savoie, *Public Spending*, chapter 9. In addition, consultations with a minister of the Mulroney cabinet, 10 February 1992, Ottawa.

36. Consultation with a senior government of Canada official, Ottawa.

37. Ibid.

38. Ibid.

39. See, for example, Kavanagh, *Thatcherism*, p. 223.

40. Consultation with a former official of the British government, Ottawa.

41. See, for example, Metcalfe and Richards, *Improving Public Management*, pp. 166–69.

42. See *Public Management Developments*, pp. 31–36, 112–24.

43. David Marsh, "Privatization Under Mrs. Thatcher: A Review of the Literature," *Public Administration*, vol. 69, no. 4 (Winter 1991), p. 464.

44. See, among others, Savoie, *Public Spending*, chapter 13.

45. See, for example, S. Brittain, "The Politics and Economics of Privatization," *Political Quarterly*, vol. 55, no. 2 (1984), pp. 109–27; Marsh, "Privatization Under Mrs. Thatcher," p. 462; Brittain, "Politics and Economics of Privatization," p. 109.

46. See Savas, *How to Shrink Government*, and Henig et al., "Politics of Privatization," p. 447.

47. See Canada, *Public Accounts of Canada*, vol. 3, various dates. The president of the Treasury Board, annual report to Parliament on crown corporations and other corporate interests of Canada.

48. "Up for Grabs," *Time*, 8 April 1991, p. 41.

49. Macrae, "A Future History of Privatization," p. 17; "Up for Grabs," p. 41.

50. Henig et al., "Politics of Privatization," p. 459. See Savoie, *Public Spending*, chapter 10.

51. See, for example, Hershel Hardin, *The Privatization Putsch* (Halifax: Institute for Research on Public Policy, 1989), p. 9. All in all, twenty-nine major businesses were privatized, and around eight hundred thousand jobs were transferred to the private sector. See *Public Management Developments*, p. 113.

52. Pirie, *Privatization*, p. 10.

53. J. Vickers and G. Yarrow, *Privatization: An Economic Analysis* (London: MIT Press, 1988).

54. Metcalfe and Richards, *Improving Public Management*, p. 171; Pirie, *Privatization*, p. 10.

55. See, for example, *Bargaining in Privatized Companies* (London: Trade Union Congress, 1988).

56. Macmillan quoted in Hardin, *Privatization Putsch*, p. 7; "Can You Hear Us?" *The Economist* (London), 5 September 1987, p. 51.

57. See, among others, Pirie, *Privatization*, chapter 26.

58. Hennessy, *Whitehall*, p. 323; Pirie, *Privatization*, p. 255.

59. See, for example, Dunleavy, "Explaining the Privatization Boom," p. 14.

60. See A. Heath, R. Jowell, and J. Curtice, *How Britain Votes* (Oxford: Pergamon, 1985), p. 132; Marsh, "Privatization Under Mrs. Thatcher," p. 461.

61. Butler, *Privatizing Federal Spending*, pp. 37–39.

62. Ibid., p. 37.

63. Henig et al., "Politics of Privatization," pp. 453, 454.

64. Consultation with a former official of the British Cabinet Office, Ottawa.

65. Carroll, "Public Administration in the Third Century of the Constitution," p. 108.

66. Quotations from Henig et al., "Politics of Privatization," p. 447, and *Management of the United States Government—1988*, p. 70.

67. Donahue, *The Privatization Decision*, p. 5. See, for example, *Management of the United States Government—1990*, pp. 3:106, 107.

68. Ibid., pp. 3:452–53.

69. *Management of the United States Government—1990*, pp. 3:105–10.

70. See Canada, Department of Finance, *Securing Economic Renewal: Budget Papers*, 23 May 1985, pp. 26–27. Dissolved corporations included Loto Canada, Canagrex, and Canadian Sports Pool Corporation.

71. Quoted in Jeanne Kirk Laux and Maureen Appal Molot, *State Capitalism: Public Enterprise in Canada* (Ithaca: Cornell University Press, 1988), p. 194.

72. See Savoie, *Public Spending*, p. 261.

73. See "Crown Self Decisions Harder to Get," *Financial Post* (Toronto), 28 December 1987, p. 4.

74. See Savoie, *Public Spending*, p. 264.

75. Quotations from Doern and Atherton, "The Tories and the Crowns," p. 136, and Savoie, *Public Spending*, p. 261.

76. Savoie, *Public Spending*, p. 264; "Petrocan Share Deal Latest Tory Sell-Off," *Toronto Star*, 19 May 1991, p. F1.

77. See, for example, Peter Curwen, *Public Enterprise: A Modern Approach* (Brighton: Wheatsherf Books, 1986). Macrae, "A Future History of Privatization," p. 16.

78. Consultation with a senior government official, Ottawa.

79. Robin Butler, "Public Management: New Challenges or Familiar Prescriptions," *Public Administration*, vol. 69, no. 3 (Autumn 1991), p. 363.

80. Marsh, "Privatization Under Mrs. Thatcher," p. 470.

81. See, among many others, Kavanagh, *Thatcherism*, chapters 3, 4, and 5.

82. See Dunleavy, "Explaining the Privatization Boom," p. 17.

83. Ibid.

84. Ibid.

Chapter 7. Looking to Management

1. See Ralph P. Hummel, "Toward a New Administrative Doctrine: Governance and Management for the 1990s," *American Review of Public Administration*, vol. 19, no. 3 (September 1989), p. 184.

2. One of the most widely read books on marketing speaks directly to this point. See Al Ries and Jack Trout, *Bottom-Up Marketing* (New York: McGraw-Hill, 1989).

3. See, among others, Johnson, "Management in Government," pp. 172, 173.

4. Ibid., and Pollitt, *Managerialism and the Public Services*, p. vi.

5. Pollitt, *Managerialism and the Public Services*, p. vii.

6. Campbell and Peters, "The Politics-Administration Dichotomy," p. 96; Sharon L. Sutherland, "The Al-Mashat Affair: Administrative Accountability in Parliamentary Institutions," *Canadian Public Administration*, vol. 34, no. 4 (Winter 1991), p. 583; Christopher Hood, "De-Sir Humphreyfying the Westminster Model of Bureaucracy: A New Style of Governance," *Governance*, vol. 3, no. 2 (April 1990), p. 206.

7. Campbell and Peters, "The Politics-Administration Dichotomy," p. 96; Rubin, *Shrinking the Federal Government*, p. 28.

8. Goldenberg, "The Permanent Government," p. 384.

9. Lord Rayner, "The Unfinished Agenda," pp. 2, 9.

10. Williams, *Washington, Westminster and Whitehall*, p. 62.

11. Butler, "Public Management," p. 364. Two public servants report on the importance of the micro level in their work and argue that "governments have never had more policy advice. . . . It has been recognized that one major reason why government programs are frequently not successful is that insufficient attention has been given to their implementation." See Michael Keating and Malcolm Holmes, "Reply to Aucoin and Hood," *Governance*, vol. 3, no. 2 (April 1990), pp. 217-18.

12. Paul Tellier, "Public Service 2000: The Renewal of the Public Service," *Canadian Public Administration*, vol. 33, no. 2 (Summer 1990), pp. 123-32.

13. *Revitalizing Federal Management: Managers and Their Overburdened Systems* (Washington, D.C.: National Academy of Public Administration, 1983), p. 1. The academy is a not-for-profit independent organization consisting of civil servants and academics. Its purpose is to promote excellence in public administration.

14. See Graham T. Allison, *Setting the Public Management Research Agenda* (Washington, D.C.: Government Printing Office, document 127-53-1, 1980); James L. Perry and Kenneth L. Kraemer, eds., *Public Management: Public and Private Perspectives* (Palo Alto, Calif.: Mayfield, 1983); Donald J. Savoie, "Studying Public Administration," *Canadian Public Administration*, vol. 33, no. 3 (Fall 1990), pp. 389-413; Lawrence E. Lynn, Jr., *Managing the Public's Business: The Job of the Government Executive* (New York: Basic Books, 1981).

15. See, for example, Butler, "Public Management," pp. 363-72.

16. Greenwood and Wilson, *Public Administration in Britain Today*, p. 129. See also p. 15.

17. See, for example, Great Britain, *Efficiency and Effectiveness in the Civil Service, Third Report of the Treasury and Civil Service Select Committee* (London: Her Majesty's Stationery Office, 8 March 1982), p. 236.

18. See, among others, Williams, *Washington, Westminster and Whitehall*, p. 11.

19. Henry Mintzberg, *The Structuring of Organizations* (Englewood Cliffs, N.J.: Prentice Hall, 1979); Thomas J. Peters and Robert H. Waterman, Jr., *In Search of Excellence: Lessons From America's Best-Run Companies* (New York: Harper and Row, 1982), chapters 5, 6, 7, 11; Peter Block, *The Empowered Manager: Positive Political Skills at Work* (New York: Jossey-Bass, 1988), p. 75.

20. See Pollitt, *Managerialism and the Public Services*, p. 55; Salamon and Lund, *The Reagan Presidency*, chapter 1; and Canada, *Public Service 2000: The Renewal of the Public Service of Canada* (Ottawa: Minister of Supply and Services, 1990).

21. Canada, "Empowerment and Risk Under PS 2000" (Ottawa: Conference of Senior Financial Officers, PS 2000 Secretariat, November 1990), p. 4; Canada, *Public Service 2000*, p. 52

22. Canada, *Service to the Public Task Force* (Ottawa: PS 2000 Secretariat, October 1990), pp. 51–52.

23. Hummel, "Toward a New Administrative Doctrine," p. 188.

24. See, among others, Metcalfe and Richards, *Improving Public Management*, chapters 1, 2, 4, 10 (quotation is from p. 218).

25. *Management of the United States Government—1986*, pp. 5, 7.

26. Pollitt, *Managerialism and the Public Services*, p. 117.

27. *Management of the United States Government—1986*, pp. 30–33; part 1, sections C and E; "Overview" section, p. 4; part 2, sections C, D, and G; p. 53.

28. Canada, Department of Finance, *The Fiscal Plan* (Ottawa, February 1986), p. 26; Canada, Treasury Board Secretariat, *Notes for an Address to the Financial Management Institute*, 18 November 1986, p. 7; Canada, Treasury Board Secretariat, *Increased Ministerial Authority and Accountability: Introduction and Progress Report*, 1988, p. 2.

29. Savoie, *Public Spending*, p. 118.

30. Canada, *Increased Ministerial Authority and Accountability*, pp. 2, 6.

31. Caiden, *Administrative Reform*, p. 83.

32. Quoted in B. Guy Peters, "Burning the Village: The Civil Service Under Thatcher and Reagan," *Parliamentary Affairs* (Oxford University Press, 1986), p. 9.

33. See, for example, Williams, *Washington, Westminster and Whitehall*, p. 122.

34. Consultation with a former official with the British government, London.

35. See, for example, Butler, *Privatizing Federal Spending*, p. 32; Richard Nathan, *The Administrative Presidency* (New York: Wiley, 1983); Rubin, *Shrinking the Federal Government*, p. 26.

36. Jacques Bourgault and Stéphane Dion, "Governments Come and Go, but What of Senior Civil Servants? Canadian Deputy Ministers and Transitions in Power, 1867–1987," *Governance*, vol. 2, no. 1 (1987), pp. 124–51.

37. *Administration as Service: The Public as Client* (Paris: OECD, 1987), pp. 9, 126–27.

38. See, among others, Hummel, "Toward a New Administrative Doctrine," p. 178; Pollitt, *Managerialism and the Public Services*, pp. 183–84.

39. Presentation made by *Officials of the Cabinet Office to the XIth International Congress on the Training of Senior Civil Servants: Report of the United Kingdom Delegation* (London: Cabinet Office, July 1990), p. 2.

40. Canada, *Public Service 2000*, p. 51.

41. Ibid., p. 52.

42. See Henry Mintzberg, *Power In and Around Organizations* (Englewood Cliffs, N.J.: Prentice Hall, 1983), pp. 264, 286.

43. See Rosebeth Moss Kenter, *When Giants Learn to Dance* (New York: Simon and Schuster, 1985); D. Quinn Mills, *Rebirth of the Corporation* (New York: John Wiley and Sons, 1991), p. 110; John Reichert, chief executive officer of Brunswick Corporation, quoted in Frank Swift, "Management Concepts and Prescriptions" (Ottawa: Canadian Centre for Management Development—Research Report, 1991), p. 6.

44. Mills, *Rebirth of the Corporation*, chapter 12; Swift, "Management Concepts and Prescriptions," p. 6.

45. Metcalfe and Richards, *Improving Public Management*, p. 40.

46. See, for example, J. L Granatstein, *The Ottawa Men: The Civil Service Mandarins 1935–57* (Toronto: Oxford University Press, 1982), p. 3, and, among others, Zussman and Jabes, *The Vertical Solitude*, p. 203.

47. Peter Aucoin, "Administrative Reform in Public Management: Paradigms, Principles, Paradoxes and Pendulums," *Governance*, vol. 3, no. 2 (April 1990), pp. 118, 120.

48. Ibid., p. 115.

49. *Revitalizing Federal Management*, p. 1.

50. This was stressed by the U.S. delegate to the OECD panel meeting on managing an internal management consultancy service. See *Internal Consultancy in Government: Responding to the Challenges of Public Sector Reform* (Paris: OECD, 1991).

51. See Goldenberg, "The Permanent Government," p. 412, and Chester A. Newland, "A Midterm Appraisal—The Reagan Presidency: Limited Government and Political Administration," *Public Administration Review*, vol. 43, no. 1 (January–February 1983), p. 21.

52. Rubin, *Shrinking the Federal Government*, p. 16; Newland, "A Midterm Appraisal," p. 14; Brady quoted in William T. Gormley, Jr., *Taming the Bureaucracy: Muscles, Prayers and Other Strategies* (Princeton: Princeton University Press, 1989), p. 123.

53. Reagan reported that, from 1981 to 1986, the budget authority for departmental inspectors general increased by about 34 percent and for staff increased by 23 percent. See *Management of the United States Government—1986*, p. 11.

54. Ibid., p. 12.

55. By 1987, Reagan reported that his Council on Integrity and Efficiency had

reported over $63 billion in improved use of funds. See *Management of the United States Government—1987*, p. 7.

56. Robert Mingie, *Total Quality Management: The Experience of IBM Canada* (Ottawa: Canadian Centre for Management Development, 1991), pp. 1, 3–6.

57. See *Management of the United States Government, Executive Office of the President—Office of Management and Budget—Fiscal Year* 1989 (Washington, D.C.: Government Printing Office, 1989), pp. 51–53, 56, 57.

58. See *Management of the United States Government—1986*, pp. 34–36 (35).

59. See Canada, Treasury Board, "Federal Government Cash Management—News Release," 7 March 1988.

60. Christopher Hood, "A Public Management For All Seasons?" *Public Administration*, vol. 69, no. 1 (Spring 1991), pp. 11–12.

61. Quoted in Caiden, *Administrative Reform*, p. 83.

62. See Donald J. Savoie, "Evaluating the Evaluators," *International Journal of Public Sector Management* 5, no. 1 (Winter 1992), and Savoie, "Public Management Development."

63. See, for example, Geoffrey J. Gammon, "The British Higher Civil Service: Recruitment and Training," a paper prepared for presentation at the Fourteenth World Congress of the International Political Science Association, 28 August–1 September 1988, p. 13.

64. *Management Development Programmes in the Civil Service, Cabinet Office—Office of the Minister for the Civil Service* (London, 1988).

65. Ibid.

66. Ibid.

67. Ibid, and consultation with Bob Wright at the OECD meeting, 26–28 June 1989, Paris.

68. See presentation made by *Officials of the Cabinet Office*, p. 2.

69. See, for example, "Rebuilding a Flagship for Executives," *Washington Post*, 17 October 1987, p. A17.

70. "Meeting the Challenge," Federal Executive Institute (Charlottesville, Va.: October 1988–September 1989).

71. *Management of the United States Government—1989*, pp. 52–61 (61).

72. Ibid., p. 67. Information in this paragraph also comes from consultation with an official with the Office of Personnel Management, Washington, D.C.

73. Government of Canada, Office of the Prime Minister, *Release: New Centre for Management Studies Announced*, Ottawa, 14 April 1988.

74. See Government of Canada, *The Canadian Centre for Management Development—Proposed Program Structure and Organization*, Ottawa, undated, pp. 11–16. Quotation is from "A New Commitment to Public Sector Management," notes for an address by the Honourable Don Mazankowski to the Public Policy Forum, 14 April 1988, Toronto, p. 7.

75. See Canadian Centre for Management Development, pp. 11–16; and, among others, Jim Armstrong, "Birth of an Institution," *Dialogue*, vol. 13, no. 3 (June 1989), pp. 12–14.

76. Armstrong, "Birth of an Institution," pp.12–14; see also Savoie, "Public Management Development."

77. See Gray et al., "The Management of Change in Whitehall," p. 52.

78. Metcalfe and Richards, *Improving Public Management*, p. 18.

79. Ibid., p. 169; also consultations with career government officials in Ottawa, Washington, and London.

80. Consultations with career government officials in Ottawa, Washington, and London; and with a deputy minister with the government of Canada, Ottawa.

81. One British official employed this expression to describe the work of senior officials in London. He saw little promise for "managerialism," insisting that the intellectual challenge for senior officials is to work with ministers to sort out problems. These officials, he argued, "don't give a toss about what some middle-level official in Glasgow is doing."

82. Mills, *Rebirth of the Corporation*, p. 41.

83. For Reagan, see Gormley, *Taming the Bureaucracy*, chapters 6, 7, 9; for Mulroney, see *Policy Guidelines for Public Servants: Communications With the Media*, release from the Office of the Prime Minister, 23 November 1984.

84. An excellent case in point is the Al-Mashat affair in Canada, when Iraq's former ambassador to the United States entered Canada as a landed immigrant and the Mulroney government conveniently pinned the blame directly on the bureaucrats. See Sutherland, "The Al-Mashat Affair," pp. 573–603.

85. Consultations with career government officials in Ottawa, Washington, and London.

86. For FMI, see, for example, Hennessy, *Whitehall*, p. 620. By the end of fiscal year 1990–1991, only ten departments had entered into MOUs with the Treasury Board. See Canada, Treasury Board Secretariat, *1991–92 Estimates*, part 3, pp. 2–14.

87. Consultation with officials with the government of Canada, Ottawa.

Chapter 8. Restructuring the Machinery

1. See, among others, Campbell, *Managing the Presidency*; Campbell, *Governments Under Stress*; Hennessy, *Whitehall*; and Savoie, *Public Spending*.

2. An excellent case in point here is Brian Mulroney's decision to abolish the Department of Regional Industrial Expansion and to establish new economic development agencies and offices for Atlantic Canada, western Canada, and northern Ontario. See Donald J. Savoie, *Regional Economic Development: Canada's Search for Solutions*, 2d ed. (Toronto: University of Toronto Press, 1992).

3. Fry, "The Development of the Thatcher Government 'Guard Strategy,'" p. 325; Campbell, *Managing the Presidency*, p. 189.

4. Campbell, *Managing the Presidency*, p. 189; quotation from Hennessy, *Whitehall*, p. 603.

5. Pollitt, *Managerialism and the Public Services*, p. 53; Hennessy, *Whitehall*, p. 604.

6. Great Britain, *The Reorganization of Central Government* (London: Her Majesty's Stationery Office, 1970); quotation from Douglas Hurd, *An End to Promises: Sketch of a Government 1970–74* (London: Collins, 1979), p. 39; Hennessy, *Whitehall*, pp. 228–29.

7. Hennessy, *Whitehall*, p. 245; Harold Wilson, *The Governance of Britain* (London: Weidenfeld and Michael Joseph, 1976), p. 95. CPRS's review of overseas representation projects proved controversial and hardly a success story. See Hennessy, *Whitehall*, pp. 266–71; also, among others, Christopher Pollitt, "The Central Policy Review Staff," *Public Administration*, vol. 55, no. 4 (1974), pp. 375–92.

8. Quotations from Pollitt, "The Central Policy Review Staff," p. 381; and Professor Ashworth quoted in Hennessy, *Whitehall*, p. 656.

9. See David Willitts, "The Role of the Prime Minister's Policy Unit," *Public Administration*, vol. 65, no. 4 (Winter 1987), p. 445. Professor Ashworth quoted in Hennessy, *Whitehall*, p. 656.

10. Thatcher quoted in Hennessy, *Whitehall*, p. 658; Willitts, "The Role of the Prime Ministers's Policy Unit," pp. 443–55 (448, 449).

11. Consultations with present and former officials of the Cabinet Office and the Treasury, various dates in 1992.

12. See, among others, R. Norton-Taylor, "Whitehall Top Brass Rebel on Pay Plan," *Guardian* (London), 29 April 1985, p. 2.

13. Consultation with a former official with the Cabinet Office, London.

14. Kate Jenkins, Karen Caines, and Andrew Jackson, *Improving Management in Government: The Next Steps* (London: Her Majesty's Stationery Office, 1988), p. 2.

15. Ibid., pp. 3–4, 7.

16. Ibid., pp. 9, 15.

17. Ibid., p. 15, see annex A, p. 1.

18. Ibid., p. 14.

19. "Prime Minister Announces Change in Way Whitehall Delivers Services," *Press Notice* (10 Downing Street, 18 February 1987). See also the section "Notes to Editors."

20. Peter Kemp, "Next Steps for the British Civil Service," *Governance*, vol. 3, no. 2 (April 1990), pp. 196, 194, 196, 195.

21. Consultations with officials with the British government, London.

22. Hansard (London), 18 February 1988, col. 1159.

23. See Geoffrey Fry et al., "Symposium on Improving Management in Government," *Public Administration*, vol. 66, no. 4 (Winter 1988), p. 443.

24. Butler cited in House of Commons, London, *Official Report*, 18 February 1988. See also Hennessy, *Whitehall*, p. 621.

25. Quoted in Fry et al., "Symposium on Improving Management in Government," p. 442.

26. Ibid., p. 441.

27. Quoted in *Next Steps: Some Questions Answered* (London: Office of the Minister for the Civil Service, 1988), p. 3.

28. Quoted in Fry et al., "Symposium on Improving Management in Government," p. 441.

29. Ibid., p. 442.

30. See, for example, Robin Butler, "New Challenges or Familiar Prescriptions," *Public Administration*, vol. 69, no. 3 (Autumn 1991), pp. 363–71. See also Fry et al., "Symposium on Improving Management in Government," p. 442.

31. See Fry et al., "Symposium on Improving Management in Government," p. 442.

32. See, for example, Hood, "De-Sir Humphreyfying the Westminster Model of Bureaucracy," p. 212. Consultation with present and former British officials, various dates in 1992, London and Ottawa.

33. See Fry et al., "Symposium on Improving Management in Government," p. 443. See also Great Britain, *Civil Service Management Reform: The Next Steps*, 8th report of the Treasury and Civil Service Committee, House of Commons (London: Her Majesty's Stationery Office, 1987–88), p. 494–1. This is testimony presented by influential academics and former senior civil servants before the parliamentary committee, and serious students of public administration would find this both fascinating and worthwhile reading.

34. Hennessy, *Whitehall*, p. 624.

35. See Falcon, "Public Service Reform," p. 6.

36. Hennessy, *Whitehall*, p. 622. Quotations from Falcon, "Public Service Reform," pp. 7, 12.

37. Elliot Finer, "The Next Steps Program: Executive Agencies in the United Kingdom," *Optimum*, vol. 22, no. 2, pp. 24–28. See also Peter Kemp, "Next Steps for the British Civil Service," pp. 186–96.

38. Legislation was passed in 1990 to enable agencies to become trading funds. See Finer, "The Next Steps Program," p. 24.

39. See Harold Seidman, "Government Corporations in the United States," *Optimum*, vol. 22, no. 2, p. 40.

40. Quotation from Gormley, *Taming the Bureaucracy*, p. 120. See also Caiden, *Administrative Reform*, p. 212. Consultations with officials with the U.S. government, various dates in March and April 1992, Washington.

41. Levine, "The Federal Government in the Year 2000," p. 198.

42. See Herbert Kaufman, *Are Government Organizations Immortal?* (Washington, D.C.: The Brookings Institution, 1976), p. 21, and Gormley, *Taming the Bureaucracy*, p. 120.

43. This was consistently Reagan's theme in all his reports on *Management of the United States Government*, from 1985 to 1990.

44. See John Kissel, "The Structures of the Reagan White House," *American Journal of Political Science*, vol. 28, no. 2 (May 1984), p. 247, and Caiden, *Administrative Reform*, p. 215.

45. Campbell, *Managing the Presidency*, pp. 188, 171; Terry M. Moe, "The Politicized Presidency," in John E. Chubb and Paul E. Peterson, eds., *The New Direction in American Politics* (Washington, D.C.: The Brookings Institution, 1985),

p. 262; Chester A. Newland, "A Mid-Term Appraisal—The Reagan Presidency: Limited Government and Political Administration," *Public Administration Review*, vol. 43, no. 1 (January–February 1983), p. 14.

46. See President's Council on Integrity and Efficiency, *Addressing Fraud, Waste and Abuse: A Summary of Inspector General's Activities, Fiscal Year 1982, First Six Months* (Washington, D.C.: PCIE, 1982).

47. OMB quoted in Newland, "A Mid-Term Appraisal," p. 14.

48. Caiden, *Administrative Reform*, p. 217.

49. Chester A. Newland, "Executive Office Policy Apparatus: Enforcing the Reagan Agenda," in Salamon and Lund, *The Reagan Presidency*.

50. Caiden, *Administrative Reform*, p. 218.

51. *Management of the United States Government—1989*, p. 26.

52. See, for example, Newland, "Executive Office Policy Apparatus," pp. 153–61, and Campbell, *Managing the Presidency*, pp. 140–52.

53. See, for example, Newland, "Executive Office Policy Apparatus," pp. 153, 151.

54. Moe, "The Politicized Presidency," pp. 261, 262.

55. See, for example, *Management of the United States Government—1986*, p. 54.

56. See, among others, Steven Kelman, *Making Public Policy: A Hopeful View of American Government* (New York: Basic Books, 1987), p. 101; Moe, "The Politicized Presidency," p. 260; see Newland, "A Mid-Term Appraisal," p. 3; the Reagan advisor was Henri Salvatore, quoted in Dom Bonafede, "Reagan and His Kitchen Cabinet Are Bound by Friendship and Ideology," *National Journal*, vol. 13, no. 15 (April 1981), p. 608; Gormley, *Taming the Bureaucracy*, p. 134.

57. It should be noted that since 1990 a recertification process has been in place for career members of the SES. The process can identify executives unfit for continued membership in the group. In such a case, a person not certified must either retreat to the lower levels of the career service or leave government.

58. Goldenberg, "The Permanent Government," p. 394; Bernard Rosen, "Federal Civil Service Reform: A Disaster for Merit," *The Bureaucrat*, vol. 2, no. 1 (Winter 1982–1983), pp. 55–70; Newland, "A Mid-Term Appraisal," p. 15.

59. See, among many others, Rubin, *Shrinking the Federal Government*, p. 187.

60. Levine, "The Federal Government in the Year 2000," p. 203; Goldenberg, "The Permanent Government," p. 396; see also, among others, Rosen, "Crisis in the U.S. Civil Service," pp. 207–14.

61. Gormley, *Taming the Bureaucracy*, p. 133.

62. Rubin, *Shrinking the Federal Government*, p. 177.

63. Quoted in Rosen, "Federal Civil Service Reform," p. 62.

64. For an excellent article on Devine's reconfirmation process, see Rosen, "Crisis in the U.S. Civil Service," pp. 207–14.

65. Progressive Conservative Party of Canada, "Towards Production Management" (background notes, Ottawa, undated), p. 1.

66. See Aucoin, "Organizational Change in the Machinery of Canadian Government," pp. 3–27.

67. See Sutherland, "The Al-Mashat Affair," p. 592. This point was made on numerous occasions in my consultations with senior Canadian public servants.

68. See, for example, Aucoin, "Organizational Change in the Machinery of Canadian Government," p. 19. Consultation with a former senior advisor to the Right Honourable Brian Mulroney, 17 February 1992, Ottawa.

69. Consultation with a federal Cabinet minister, 18 March 1992, Ottawa.

70. Consultation with a deputy minister with the government of Canada, 11 January 1991, Ottawa. See also Sutherland, "The Al-Mashat Affair," p. 592.

71. Quoted in Savoie, *Public Spending*, p. 63.

72. The operation of PEMS has been fully explained in R. Van Loon, "Stop the Music: The Current Policy and Expenditure Management System in Ottawa," *Canadian Public Administration*, vol. 24, no. 2 (1981); also, "The Policy and Expenditure Management System in the Federal Government: The First Three Years," *Canadian Public Administration*, vol. 26, no. 2 (1983); with Richard French in *How Ottawa Decides: Planning and Industrial Policy Making, 1968–84* (Toronto: James Lorimer, 1984), chapter 9; and "Ottawa's Expenditure Process: Four Systems in Search of Co-ordination," in *How Ottawa Spends*, ed. G. B. Doern (Toronto: James Lorimer, 1982), chapter 4. See also R. Dobell, "Pressing the Envelope," *Policy Options*, vol. 2, no. 5 (November–December 1981); Sandford Borins, "Ottawa, Expenditure Envelopes: Workable Rationality at Last," in *How Ottawa Spends*, ed. G. B. Doern (Toronto: James Lorimer, 1982); G. B. Doern and Richard Phidd, *Canadian Public Policy* (Toronto: Methuen, 1983).

73. See Savoie, *Public Spending*, chapter 13.

74. See Canada, Privy Council Office, *Background Paper on the New Cabinet Decision-Making System*, undated. Consultations with officials with the government of Canada, various dates from January to March 1992, Ottawa.

75. Quotations are from Canada, Privy Council Office, *Background Paper on the New Cabinet Decision-Making System*, undated, and from "Mulroney to Crack Down on Government Spending," *Gazette*, 31 January 1989, D1. Officials in the Privy Council Office report that Mulroney also consulted with Australian prime minister Bob Hawkes on new expenditure control measures.

76. Quoted in Savoie, *Public Spending*, p. 351. Consultations with a senior government of Canada official, 17 January 1992, Ottawa.

77. See Kenneth Kernaghan, "Career Public Service 2000: Road to Renewal or Impractical Vision," *Canadian Public Administration*, vol. 34, no. 4 (Winter 1991), pp. 551–72. Task forces were established on resource management and budget controls, on staffing, on staff relations, on the management category, on training and development, on work force adaptiveness, on classification and occupational structures, on service to the public, on compensation and benefits, on administrative policy, and on the role of common service agencies.

78. Chair of the PS 2000 secretariat, John Edwards, *Revitalization of the Canadian Public Service*, notes for a speaking engagement to the Association of Professional Executives, 11 March 1991, Ottawa, p. 131.

79. Paul M. Tellier, "Public Service 2000: The Renewal of the Public Service," *Canadian Public Administration*, vol. 33, no. 2 (Summer 1990), p. 131.

80. See Canada, Treasury Board, "Loiselle Introduces Bill to Support the Overhaul of the Federal Public Service," *News Release*, 18 June 1991, Ottawa; *Highlights of the White Paper on Public Service 2000: The Renewal of the Public Service of Canada* (Ottawa: Government of Canada, 1990), pp. 4, 3.

81. Consultations with senior officials with the government of Canada, various dates from November 1991 to March 1992, Ottawa.

82. I. D. Clark, "Special Operating Agencies: The Challenges of Innovation," *Optimum*, vol. 22, no. 2, p. 13.

83. Consultation with a former senior official with the Treasury Board secretariat, various dates from January to February 1992, Ottawa.

84. Canada, *Speech From the Throne to Open the Third Session, Thirty Fourth Parliament of Canada*, 13 May 1991, p. 4. The Canadian SOAs announced in December 1989 include Passport Office; Government Telecommunications Agency; Training and Development Canada; Canada Communication Group; and Consulting and Audit Canada. Those announced in February 1991 include Intellectual Property Office; Race-Track Supervision Operation; Canadian Grains Commission: Canadian General Standards Board; Transport Canada Training Institute; Indian Oil and Gas Canada; Correctional Service's Occupational Development Programs; Canadian Heritage Information Network; and Canadian Conservation Institute.

85. See David Roth, "Innovation in Government: The Case of Special Operating Agencies," Department of Supply and Services, Consulting and Audit Canada, Ottawa, September 1990, p. 2.

86. Ibid., pp. 2, 3.

87. *The Special Operating Agency* (Ottawa: Treasury Board Secretariat, n.d.), p. 1.

88. See Jim Armstrong, "Special Operating Agencies: Evolution or Revolution?" *Optimum*, vol. 22, no. 2, p. 10.

89. Canada, Treasury Board, *Operating Agencies: An Overview* (Canada, Treasury Board, November 1989), p. 3.

90. Canada, Treasury Board, *Towards a Shared Management Agenda* (Canada, Treasury Board, 25 July 1991).

91. Patrick Dunleavy, "The Architecture of the British Central State, Part I: Framework for Analysis," *Public Administration*, vol. 67, no. 3 (Autumn 1991), p. 367.

92. Robin Butler, "New Challenges or Familiar Prescriptions," p. 367; Finer, "The Next Steps Program," pp. 23–30. Butler makes the last point in this paragraph in his "New Challenges or Familiar Prescriptions?" p. 368, and the point was also made by several present and former British government officials in my consultations.

93. The first observation in this paragraph was made by several present and former British officials in my consultations, various dates from February to May

1992, Ottawa and London. Quotations are from *Executive Agencies: Facts and Trends*, 3d ed. (London: Price Waterhouse, March 1991), p. 9; and "The Next Steps Shuffle," *The Economist* (London), 31 December 1991–3 January 1992, p. 67.

94. Great Britain, *Making the Most of Next Steps: The Management of Ministers' Departments and the Executive Agencies* (London: Her Majesty's Stationery Office, 1991).

95. Consultations with officials with the British government, London.

96. Consultations with present and former officials with the British government, various dates, Ottawa and London; Finer, "The Next Steps Program," p. 29; *Executive Agencies: Facts and Trends*, 4th ed. (London: Price Waterhouse, March 1992), p. 12.

97. See, among others, David Dillman, "Civil Service Reform in Comparative Perspective: The United States and Great Britain," in Patricia Ingraham and Carolyn Ban, eds., *Legislating Bureaucratic Change: The Civil Service Reform Act of 1978* (Albany: State University of New York Press, 1986).

98. Moe, "The Politicized Presidency," p. 235. See among others, Campbell, *Managing the Presidency*, p. 255.

99. See, among others, James D. Carroll, A. Lee Fritschler, and Bruce L. R. Smith, "Supply-Side Management in the Reagan Administration," *Public Administration Review*, vol. 45, no. 6 (November–December 1985), p. 806; Rubin, *Shrinking the Federal Government*, pp. 168–69; Rosen, "Crisis in the U.S. Civil Service," pp. 207–14; Hugh Heclo, "A Government of Enemies," *The Bureaucrat*, vol. 13, no. 12, p. 14.

100. See Campbell and Peters, "The Politics-Administration Dichotomy," p. 94.

101. For a review of Mulroney's reorganization of economic development departments, see Savoie, *Regional Economic Development*, chapter 8. Consultations with a central agency official with the government of Canada, 31 March 1992, Ottawa.

102. Consultations with cabinet ministers in Ottawa, various dates. See also Clark, "Special Operating Agencies," pp. 16–17. Quotations are from Nick Mulder, "Managing Special Operating Agencies: A Practitioner's Perspective," *Optimum*, vol. 22, no. 2, p. 19, and Armstrong, "Special Operating Agencies," p. 7.

103. Mulder, "Managing Special Operating Agencies," pp. 19, 21; Clark, "Special Operating Agencies," p. 17.

104. Clark, "Special Operating Agencies," p. 17.

105. See Fry et al., "Symposium on Improving Management in Government," pp. 10–12.

106. Ibid., p. 11.

107. Consultation with a middle-level officer-level official in an SOA, 6 March 1992, Ottawa.

108. Consultations with one deputy minister, 17 February 1992, Ottawa, and with another deputy minister, 30 March 1992, Ottawa.

109. Daryl Bean of the Public Service Alliance and David Zussman quoted in

Charlotte Gray, "Civil Strife," *Saturday Night* (Toronto), January–February 1991, p. 56; see also pp. 15–17, 56.

110. Consultations with government of Canada officials, various dates, Ottawa; with a deputy minister, 17 February 1992, Ottawa; and with officials with the Treasury Board secretariat, various dates in December 1991 and March 1992, Ottawa.

Chapter 9. Being There

1. See Jeffrey Simpson, "Comforting the Government by Taking Pot Shots at the Troops," *Globe and Mail* (Toronto), 1 April 1992, p. A18.

2. Consultation with a former federal cabinet minister, 16 December 1991, Ottawa. Honourable Allan Blakeney has also reported on many occasions that he did the same in Saskatchewan after the government he was serving in was defeated in the mid 1960s.

3. Weiss and Barton, *Making Bureaucracies Work*, p. 10.

4. See Cooper et al., *The Resurgence of Conservatism*, p. 23. The editors note, however, that in Canada conservatism was "neither as ideologically defined nor as contemptuous of welfare state liberalism," p. 8.

5. *Management Matters* is a joint OMCS (Office for the Minister of the Civil Service) and Treasury magazine in Britain, while the *Manager's Magazine* is produced by the Treasury Board secretariat, government of Canada. The reference is to Hennessy, *Whitehall*, p. 19.

6. Caiden, *Administrative Reform*, p. 210. Consultation with an official with the U.S. government, 17 January 1992, Washington. The Canadian official made this observation at the seminar I attended on the implementation of PS 2000, 17 January 1992, Ottawa.

7. Gray et al., "The Management of Change in Whitehall," p. 56.

8. Williams, *Washington, Westminster and Whitehall*, p. 9; S. E. Finer, "Thatcherism and British Political History," in Kenneth Minogue and Richard Biddiss, eds., *Thatcherism: Personality and Politics* (London: Macmillan, 1987), p. 140; Kavanagh, *Thatcherism*, p. 255.

9. Geoffrey K. Fry, "The Development of the Thatcher Government's Grand Strategy for the Civil Service: A Public Policy Perspective," *Public Administration*, vol. 62, no. 3 (Autumn 1984), p. 325.

10. Consultations with officials in the British government, various dates, 1992. See also Geoffrey K. Fry, "The Thatcher Government, the Financial Management Initiative and the New Civil Service," *Public Administration*, vol. 66, no. 2 (Spring 1988), p. 7.

11. London, *House of Commons*, pp. 711–12, also app. 1, pp. 170–72.

12. Jenkins et al., *Improving Management in Government*, p. 24. This last point is based on information provided by British government officials, March 1992.

13. Information provided by British government officials, March 1992.

14. See *Reports on Manpower Reductions 1980–81, 1982–83, 1983–84 to the Trea-*

sury and Civil Service Committee (London: Management and Personnel Office, n.d.).

15. Fry, "The Thatcher Government," p. 5.

16. *Public Management Development—Survey 1990* (Paris: OECD, 1990), p. 114; Jenkins et al., *Improving Management in Government*, p. 23.

17. Martin Burch, "Mrs. Thatcher's Approach to Leadership in Government: 1979 to June 1983," *Parliamentary Affairs* (London), (Autumn 1983), p. 410. See also Williams, *Washington, Westminster and Whitehall*, p. 122.

18. Williams, *Washington, Westminster and Whitehall*, p. 123.

19. Civil servants and ministers, London, Cmmd. 9841, par. 28. See, among others, Fry, "The Thatcher Government," pp. 1–20. Consultations with present and former officials of the British government, various dates between February and April 1992, Ottawa and London.

20. Consultations with officials with the British government, London.

21. See Fry, "The Thatcher Government," p. 333.

22. Walter Williams, for example, wrote that "FMI has been a horse of a different color," in Williams, *Washington, Westminster and Whitehall*, p. 120.

23. Consultations with officials of the British government, various dates from January to April 1992, Ottawa and London.

24. Donald Schon, *Beyond the Stable State* (London: Maurice Temple Smith, 1971), pp. 120–24; see *Executive Agencies, Facts and Trends Survey Report*, 3d ed. (London: Price Waterhouse, March 1991), pp. 4, 12.

25. See Kavanagh, *Thatcherism*, p. 315.

26. Consultation with a former senior official with the British government, 9 April 1992, London; Johnson, "Change in the Civil Service," p. 422.

27. Fry, "The Thatcher Government," p. 9; Jenkins et al., *Improving Management in Government*, p. 23.

28. For an excellent case in point, see Al Johnson, *What Is Public Management: An Autobiographical View* (Ottawa: Canadian Centre for Management Development, 1991). Mr. Johnson is a widely respected former senior official of the government of Canada. He served as secretary to the Treasury Board in the early 1970s, deputy minister of Health and Welfare in the mid 1970s, and subsequently president of Canadian Broadcasting Corporation.

29. Williams, *Washington, Westminster and Whitehall*, p. 125; "The Next Steps Shuffle," *The Economist* (London), 31 December 1991–3 January 1992, p. 66.

30. "In Pantoland," *The Economist* (London), 9 November 1991, p. 72.

31. Quoted in Hennessy, *Whitehall*, p. 628.

32. See, for example, Johnson, "Change in the Civil Service," p. 433.

33. See, among others, Williams, *Washington, Westminster and Whitehall*, p. 100.

34. See Rubin, *Shrinking the Federal Government*, p. 49.

35. Campbell, *Managing the Presidency*, p. 67.

36. Stockman, *The Triumph of Politics*, pp. 111, 101.

37. Carroll et al., "Supply-Side Management in the Reagan Administration," p. 806.

38. See Rubin, *Shrinking the Federal Government,* p. 31.

39. Stockman, *The Triumph of Politics,* p. 159.

40. John L. Palmer and Isabel V. Sawhill, "Overview," in Palmer and Sawhill, *The Reagan Record,* p. 5. The authors also explain that "reconciliation is a complicated feature of the 1974 Congressional Budget Act originally intended to enable the congressional budget committees to enforce spending targets at the final stages of the appropriations process. The administration succeeded in moving a binding reconciliation measure to the beginning of the process, thereby wrapping the entire administration budget and program reform package into one massive piece of legislation. Otherwise, its proposals would have had to be dealt with in thirteen separate appropriation bills and numerous authorizing committees, as usual" (ibid., p. 5).

41. See Jeff Fishel, *Presidents and Promises* (Washington, D.C.: Congressional Quarterly Press, 1985), chapter 5.

42. Stockman, *The Triumph of Politics,* p. 136.

43. William Greiter, "The Education of David Stockman," *Atlantic Monthly,* 1 December 1981, p. 47. See, among others, Chester Newland, "A Mid-Term Appraisal: The Reagan Presidency: Limited Government and Political Administration," *Public Administration Review,* vol. 43, no. 1 (January–February 1975), p. 12.

44. Palmer and Sawhill, *The Reagan Record,* p. 4.

45. Pollitt, *Managerialism and the Public Services,* p. 91.

46. See, among many others, Stockman, *The Triumph of Politics,* p. 159; Salamon and Lund, *The Reagan Presidency;* and Rubin, *Shrinking the Federal Government,* p. 31.

47. Stockman, *The Triumph of Politics,* p. 9.

48. Pollitt, *Managerialism and the Public Services,* p. 117.

49. See Ralph P. Hummel, "Toward a New Administrative Doctrine: Governance and Management for the 1990s," *American Review of Public Administration,* vol. 19, no. 3 (September 1989), pp. 182–83.

50. Consultations with Office of Personal Management officials, various dates, Washington. See also Charles H. Levine, "Human Resource Erosion and the Uncertain Future of the U.S. Civil Service: From Policy Gridlock to Structured Fragmentation," *Governance,* vol. 1, no. 2 (April 1988), p. 118.

51. Goldenberg, "The Permanent Government," pp. 396–97, 402; Levine, "The Federal Government in the Year 2000," p. 201; Williams, *Mismanaging America,* pp. 98–100.

52. *Public Management Developments,* pp. 120–24; Levine, "The Federal Government in the Year 2000," p. 200.

53. See, for example, Hugh Heclo and Rudolph Penner, *National Journal,* 23 January 1982, p. 8., and Levine, "The Federal Government in the Year 2000," p. 12.

54. Consultation with federal Cabinet ministers, various dates, Ottawa.

55. Canada, Department of Finance, *The Budget Speech,* 23 May 1985, p. 11. See also Canada, *Annual Report 1984* (Ottawa: Civil Service Commission, 1985), p. 60.

56. See Savoie, *Public Spending*, p. 174. See also Canada, *Annual Report 1990* (Ottawa: Civil Service Commission, 1991), p. 39.

57. Consultation with officials of the Treasury Board secretariat, various dates, Ottawa.

58. Savoie, *Public Spending*, p. 174.

59. *Public Management Developments*, p. 31. See also Canada, *Annual Report 1990*, p. 58. The numbers for both 1984 and 1990 are from the "Treasury Board Universe" and adjusted to take into account changes to the universe made between 1984 and 1990.

60. Canada, *Annual Report 1990*. See also *Managing Government Expenditures* (Ottawa: Minister of Supply and Services, 1990), p. 20.

61. See Canada, Department of Finance, *The Budget Speech*, various dates from 1985 to 1992.

62. See Canada, Department of Finance, *The Budget Speech*, 23 May 1985. Examples where Mulroney played a key role include the new regional development agencies and aid to western grain farmers. See also Savoie, *Public Spending*, chapter 11.

63. Consultation with a senior member of the cabinet in the Canadian government, 8 April 1992, Ottawa.

64. See J. L. Manion, *Notes for a Presentation to the Dalhousie Conference on Career Public Service* (Ottawa: Canadian Centre for Management Development, 5 October 1990), pp. 18–20; Jim Armstrong, "Special Operating Agencies: Evolution or Revolution?" *Optimum*, vol. 22, no. 2, pp. 5–12; consultations with officials with the Treasury Board secretariat, various dates, Ottawa.

65. Consultations with Canadian government officials, various dates, Ottawa. The quotations are from Canada, *Public Service 2000*, p. 35, and Manion, *Dalhousie Conference on Career Public Service*, p. 16.

66. John Edwards, "Public Service Reform Bill" (Ottawa: PS 2000 Secretariat, June 1991), p. 2.

67. John Edwards, head of PS 2000 made these observations at a joint CCMD-ENAP (Ecole Nationale Administration Publique) seminar held on 8 May 1992 in Montreal, Canada.

68. Consultation with a senior official of a line department, 9 April 1992, Ottawa.

69. Ibid.

70. Consultation with a senior member of the Canadian cabinet, 8 April 1992, Ottawa.

71. Consultation with a former senior central-agency official, 17 February 1992, Ottawa.

72. Canada, Treasury Board Secretariat, "Collective Bargaining in the Public Service of Canada," statement by the Honourable Gilles Loiselle, 19 June 1991, p. 4.

73. See Canada, *Annual Report* (Civil Service Commission), various dates. During the spring of 1992, only one deputy minister came to the position directly from

the private sector. Canada, *Annual Report 1990*, p. 23, and also various dates from 1970 to 1984.

74. Quotation is from a consultation with a senior minister with the Canadian cabinet, 8 April 1992, Ottawa; Frank Swift, *Deputies and Executives Succession*, a paper prepared for the Canadian Centre for Management Development (Ottawa, January 1992), pp. 14–20.

75. Armstrong, "Special Operating Agencies," p. 11.

76. Consultations with government of Canada officials, various dates, Ottawa. See also three articles on SOAs by senior federal government officials, *Optimum*, vol. 22, no. 2, pp. 5–22.

77. Quotations are from Peters, "Burning the Village," p. 79, and consultation with a career official with the U.S. government, Washington.

78. Salamon and Lund, "Governance in the Reagan Era," p. 14.

79. Consultation with a senior cabinet minister of the government of Canada, 2 March 1992, Ottawa.

80. My consultations in London, Washington, and Ottawa clearly support this view. In addition, a number of students of government have also made similar observations. See, among others, Gray et al., "The Management of Change in Whitehall," p. 51.

81. Les Metcalfe and Sue Richards employ the term *impoverished* in "The Impact of the Efficiency Strategy: Political Clout or Cultural Change?" *Public Administration*, vol. 67, no. 4 (Winter 1983), pp. 439–54. Quotation is from Pollitt, *Managerialism and the Public Services*, p. 55.

82. See Aucoin, "Administrative Reform in Public Management," p. 120.

83. It is true that by the early 1990s a group of a few chief executive officers of large firms—most notably John Ackers, chairman of IBM—began to question publicly the competence of some of their managers. But it remains a very "small club," and "management experts" were quick to counsel publicly against making such comments public. They argued that such comments would bring "a drop in morale just when a company needs to energize its troops." See "Walking a Risky Morale Line," *Globe and Mail* (Toronto), 20 March 1992, p. B1.

84. Consultations with officials with the U.S. government, various dates, Washington. Quotation is from D. Quinn Mills, *Rebirth of the Corporation* (New York: John Wiley and Sons, 1991), p. 253.

85. *Executive Agencies—Facts and Trends—Survey Report*, 4th ed. (London: Price Waterhouse, March 1992).

86. Michael Beer, Russell A. Eisenstat, and Bert Spector, "Why Change Programs Don't Produce Change," *Harvard Business Review*, no. 90601 (November–December 1990), p. 158. See also Williams, *Washington, Westminster and Whitehall*, chapter 5.

87. Consultation with a senior official with the Ministry of Transport, 16 March 1992, Ottawa.

88. See, among many others, Carroll et al., "Supply-Side Management in the Reagan Administration," pp. 805–14.

89. See, among others, Williams, *Washington, Westminster and Whitehall*; Hennessy, *Whitehall*; and Great Britain, *Civil Servants and Ministers: Duties and Responsibilities*, government response to the seventh report from the Treasury and Civil Service Committee (London: Her Majesty's Stationery Office, July 1986), p. 11.

90. Manion, *Dalhousie Conference on Career Public Service*, pp. 10–11.

91. Zussman and Jabes, *The Vertical Solitude*, p. 196.

92. Daryl Copeland, *Foreign Service in the Nineties: Problems and Prospects* (Ottawa: Professional Association of Foreign Service Officials, 1990), p. 27.

93. See among others Levine, "The Federal Government in the Year 2000," pp. 195–206 (201).

94. *Leadership for America: Rebuilding the Public Service*, Report of the National Commission on the Public Service (Washington, D.C.: 1989), p. 3.

Chapter 10. Revisiting the Underpinnings

1. Mosher, *Democracy and the Public Service*, p. 6.

2. See, for example, Campbell and Peters, "The Politics-Administration Dichotomy," p. 80.

3. Two students of American government suggest that it constitutes the American "myth" rather than "model." See Aberbach and Rockman, "Political and Bureaucratic Roles in Public Service Reorganization," p. 83.

4. See, for example, Plowden, "What Prospects for the Civil Service?" p. 395.

5. Comments made by a senior official with the government of Canada at a seminar on PS 2000, 10 January 1992, Ottawa.

6. Consultations with government officials, London, Washington, and Ottawa. See Campbell and Peters, "The Politics-Administration Dichotomy," p. 81.

7. Wilson, *Bureaucracy*, pp. 1, 11.

8. Government officials would undoubtedly find much more relevant the work of Aaron Wildavsky, James Q. Wilson, Hugh Heclo, Colin Campbell, Guy Peters, Geoffrey Fry, Peter Hennessy, Nevil Johnson, and others who write about traditional concerns of public administration and the machinery of government. Indeed, the above names came up at one point or another in my consultations.

9. Consultation with an official with the U.S. government, Washington.

10. Consultation with an official with the government of Canada, Ottawa.

11. Guy Peters, "Government Reform and Reorganization in an Era of Retrenchment and Conviction Politics," paper presented to the 1989 annual meeting of the American Political Science Association, 31 August–3 September 1991, Atlanta, Georgia, p. 27. See also, among others, Allison, "Public and Private Management," and Rainey et al., "Comparing Public and Private Organizations," pp. 325–44.

12. See Carroll et al., "Supply-Side Management in the Reagan Administration," p. 812.

13. See, for example, Metcalfe and Richards, *Improving Public Management*, p. 187.

14. Ibid., p. 180.

15. Ibid., p. 225; Aaron Wildavsky, "Introduction," in Lynn and Wildavsky, *Public Administration,* pp. xiv–xviii.

16. Consultations with an official with the government of Great Britain, London, and with a former official with the U.S. government, New York.

17. Mosher, *Democracy and the Public Service,* p. 202.

18. See, among others, ibid., chapter 7. Quotations are from John Carson, "Merit System in Public Service Has Little Merit," *The Citizen* (Ottawa), 2 February 1989, p. 8.

19. Information for the United States was made available by the Office of Personnel Management (OPM), April 1992, Washington; for Canada, by the Public Service Commission; and for Britain, by the Office of the Minister for the Civil Service.

20. Charles H. Levine with the assistance of Rosslyn S. Kleeman, *The Quiet Crisis of the Civil Service: The Federal Personnel System at the Crossroads* (Washington: National Academy of Public Administration, 1986), p. 29. See also, among others, Rosen, "Federal Civil Service Reform," pp. 55–70.

21. Levine with Kleeman, *The Quiet Crisis of the Civil Service,* p. 3.

22. Consultations with former appointed officials in the Reagan administration, Washington and New York.

23. See, among others, Williams, *Washington, Westminster and Whitehall,* chapter 5. Rayner quoted in Metcalfe and Richards, *Improving Public Management,* p. 16. Loiselle quoted in "Diplomat Negotiates Treasury Board Minefield," *The Star* (Toronto), 29 November 1990, p. A23.

24. Levine with Kleeman, *The Quiet Crisis of the Civil Service,* p. 5; Terrey W. Culler, "Most Federal Workers Need Only Be Competent," *Wall Street Journal* (New York), 21 May 1986, p. 33.

25. Consultation with a former official with the U.S. government, New York.

26. Peter Kemp, quoted in Hennessy, *Whitehall,* p. 624.

27. See J. L. Manion, *A Management Model* (Ottawa: Canadian Centre for Management Development, 1989).

28. Cynthia Williams, "Public Management in the 1990s: A Canadian Perspective," a paper prepared for the 1990 annual conference of the American Society for Public Administration, Los Angeles, California, p. 7.

29. Gérard Veilleux, Treasury Board Secretariat, "Notes for an Address to the APEX Symposium," 19 January 1989, Ottawa, p. 5.

30. Quoted in "Government," *Business Week* (Hightstown, N.J.), 14 October 1991, p. 100.

31. Consultation with government officials in London, Washington, and Ottawa.

32. Consultation with an official with the U.S. government in Washington, and with an official with the government of Canada, Ottawa.

33. Gordon Osbaldeston, a former clerk of the Privy Council in the government of Canada, made a similar observation in his study: "Deputy Ministers

become accountable for following rules rather than finding the best solution using their own judgement." Gordon F. Osbaldeston, *Keeping Deputy Ministers Accountable* (Toronto: McGraw-Hill Ryerson, 1989), p. 154.

34. See Wilson, *Bureaucracy*, pp. 190–91.

35. Ibid., p. 217.

36. See, among others, Plowden, "What Prospects for the Civil Service?" pp. 393–414.

37. Consultations with officials of the government of Canada, Ottawa.

38. See, among many others, *To Meet the Needs of the Nations: Staffing the U.S. Civil Service and the Public Service of Canada* (Washington: U.S. Merit Systems Protection Board, 1992). The OPM also produced a number of reports from 1991 to 1992 on ways to improve the SES performance pay initiative.

39. Andrey Hede, "Trends in the Higher Civil Service of Anglo-American Systems," *Governance*, vol. 4, no. 4 (October 1991), pp. 499, 495; consultations with senior officials with the government of Canada, Ottawa; Hede, "Trends in the Higher Civil Service," p. 496.

40. Consultation with an official of the British government, London.

41. R. D. Beale, "Strategies for Management in the Commonwealth Public Service," New South Wales Institute of Technology, Australia, 27 August 1985 (mimeo), p. 20.

42. Consultation with career officials with the U.S. government, Washington.

43. Ibid.

44. Stockman, *The Triumph of Politics*, p. 5; consultation with a long-serving career official in OMB, Washington.

45. Consultation with a long-serving career official in OMB, Washington.

46. Consultations with officials of the British government, London.

47. See Williams, *Washington, Westminster and Whitehall*, p. 100.

48. Consultations with officials of the British government, London.

49. Consultations with officials of the British government, London; Lord Bancroft, "Whitehall and Management: A Retrospect," paper delivered to the Royal Society, 30 January 1984, London, p. 3.

50. Consultations with officials of the British government, London. See also Pollitt, *Managerialism and the Public Services*, p. 49.

51. See, for example, Johnson, "Management in Government," p. 191.

52. Consultation with a senior official with the government of Canada, Ottawa; Veilleux, "Notes for an Address to the APEX Symposium," p. 5.

53. Quoted in Steven Kelman, "Public Choice and Public Spirit," *Public Interest*, no. 87 (1987), p. 81.

54. Consultation with senior government officials with the government of Canada, Ottawa.

55. See Hood, "De-Sir Humphreyfying the Westminster Model of Bureaucracy," p. 212, and Carroll et al., "Supply-Side Management in the Reagan Administration," pp. 805–14.

56. Hugh Heclo, "A Comment on the Future U.S. Civil Service," in Bruce

L. R. Smith, ed., *The Higher Civil Service in Europe and Canada* (Washington, D.C.: The Brookings Institution, 1984), p. 104.

57. Albert O. Hirschman, *Exit, Voice and Loyalty: Responses to Decline in Firms, Organizations and States* (Cambridge, Mass.: Harvard University Press, 1970), pp. 15, 16.

58. See Wilson, *Bureaucracy*, chapter 3.

59. Nevil Johnson, *In Search of the Constitution: Reflections on State and Society in Britain* (Oxford: Pergamon Press, 1977), p. 74.

60. This point was made by Sharon Sutherland at a seminar sponsored by the Canadian Centre for Management Development, May 1990, Ottawa.

61. Quotations from Pollitt, *Managerialism and the Public Services*, p. 93, and Aberbach and Rockman, "Political and Bureaucratic Roles in Public Service Reorganization," p. 92.

62. See Herbert Kaufman, *The Administrative Behavior of Federal Bureau Chiefs* (Washington, D.C.: The Brookings Institution, 1981), p. 164.

63. See Wilson, *Bureaucracy*, pp. 236–38 (236).

64. Ibid., p. 243.

65. Consultations with officials with the U.S. government, Washington.

66. Ibid.

67. Carl J. Bellone and Frederick Goerl, "Reconciling Public Entrepreneurship and Democracy," *Public Administration Review*, vol 52, no 2 (March–April 1992), p. 131.

68. This observation was made by Peter Hennessy at a seminar on PS 2000, 10 January 1992, Ottawa.

69. See "Symposium on Ministerial Responsibility," *Public Administration*, vol. 65, no. 1 (Spring 1987), pp. 61–91 (88).

70. Quotations are from Geoffrey Marshall and Graeme Moodie, *Some Problems of the Constitution* (London: Hutchinson University Library, 1971), p. 55; Sir Robert Armstrong, "Duties and Responsibilities of Civil Servants in Relation to Ministers. Note by the Head of the Home Civil Service," *Cabinet Office*, 25 February 1985, London; Herman Finer, *The British Civil Service* (London: Allen and Unwin, 1937), p. 196.

71. Rayner quoted in "Symposium on Ministerial Responsibility," p. 65; Johnson, *In Search of the Constitution*, p. 42; Hugh Segal, "The Accountability of Public Servants," *Policy Options*, vol. 2, no. 5 (November–December 1981), pp. 11, 12.

72. Sutherland, "The Al-Mashat Affair," p. 583.

73. I strongly encourage the reader to consult Great Britain, *Minutes of Evidence Taken Before the Treasury and Civil Service Sub-Committee on the Armstrong Memorandum* (London: Her Majesty's Stationery Office, 1986). The material makes for a fascinating read with some of the leading political and academic thinkers in Britain presenting their views on the principle of ministerial responsibility.

74. See the special issue of *Optimum*, vol. 22, no. 2, on SOAs in Canada.

75. The Treasury and Civil Service Select Committee report concluded in 1990 that the establishment of agencies does not diminish ministerial accountability.

76. *Next Steps—Brief Notes* (London: Office of the Minister for the Civil Service, 26 March 1992), p. 3.

77. See, for example, "CSIS Agents Filmed Attack, MP Says," *Globe and Mail* (Toronto), 11 April 1991, p. A4.

78. See, among many others, "Faulty Security System Cost Ottawa $140 Million," *Sunday Star* (Toronto), 22 September 1991, p. 1.

79. Quoted in *Setting Up Next Steps* (London: Her Majesty's Stationery Office, May 1991), pp. 17–18.

80. See, for example, Geoffrey K. Fry, "The Development of the Thatcher Government's Grand Strategy for the Civil Service: A Public Policy Perspective," *Public Administration*, vol. 62, no. 4 (1984), pp. 322–35.

81. Peter Aucoin, "Comment: Assessing Managerial Reforms," *Governance*, vol. 3, no. 2 (April 1990), p. 203.

82. See special issue of *Optimum*, vol. 22, no. 2.

83. Mr. Gauthier made this statement in opening the Public Accounts Committee, 14 May 1992, Ottawa.

84. Consultations with permanent officials with the governments of Great Britain and Canada, London and Ottawa.

85. Quoted in "Nuggets of Wisdom" from the PS 2000 Government Consulting Group seminar held by the Department of Supply and Services, 10 January 1992, at the Chateau Laurier.

86. See presentation made by Nevil Johnson to the Treasury and Civil Service subcommittee, 29 January 1986 (London: Her Majesty's Stationery Office), pp. 170–71.

87. See presentation by the Right Honourable Patrick Jenkin to the Treasury and Civil Service subcommittee, 29 January 1986 (London: Her Majesty's Stationery Office), pp. 170–71.

88. Consultation with a senior official with the government of Canada, Ottawa.

Chapter 11. Deciding What to Fix

1. This was true even for Margaret Thatcher. See, among others, Johnson, "Change in the Civil Service," p. 427.

2. See Metcalfe and Richards, *Improving Public Management*, and Kelman, "The Grace Commission," pp. 33–42.

3. Pollitt, *Managerialism and the Public Services*, chapters 6 and 7.

4. Peter Aucoin makes a similar observation in his "Administrative Reform in Public Management," p. 134.

5. See *The Citizen's Charter*, presented to Parliament by the prime minister (London: Her Majesty's Stationery Office, July 1991).

6. Pollitt, *Managerialism and the Public Services*, p. 181.

7. Executive Order 12552 directed productivity plans be prepared and called on OMB to review the plans.

8. Consultation with an official with the U.S. government, Washington.

9. Consultation with an official with the British government, London.

10. See, for example, Wilson, *Bureaucracy*, chapter 2.

11. Consultation with an official with the British government, London.

12. I am thinking here of the work of Otto Brodtrick for the Office of the Auditor General of Canada. See *Annual Report* (Ottawa: Office of the Auditor General, 1988).

13. Consultations with officials with the British government, London.

14. See *Making the Most of Next Steps: The Management of Ministers: Departments and the Executive* (London: Her Majesty's Stationery Office, 1991).

15. *The Citizen's Charter*, p. 4.

16. Levine, "The Federal Government in the Year 2000," p. 199.

17. See, among others, Gerald E. Caiden, "What Really Is Public Misadministration?" *Indian Journal of Public Administration*, vol. 37, no. 1, pp. 1–16.

18. James Boren, *Have Your Way With Bureaucrats* (Radnor, Pa.: Chilton Books, 1975), p. 7.

19. Consultations with government officials, London, Washington, and Ottawa.

20. Gilles Paquet, "Betting on Moral Contracts," *Optimum*, vol. 23, no. 3, p. 45.

21. Comments made by Peter Hennessy at a seminar on PS 2000, 17 January 1992, Ottawa. TQM also appears to be under attack in the private sector. See "The Cracks in Quality," *The Economist* (London), 18 April 1992, p. 67. See also Alexander Ross, "The Long View of Leadership," *Canadian Business* (Toronto, May 1992), pp. 46–51.

22. Guy Peters, "Government Reform and Reorganization in an Era of Retrenchment and Conviction Politics," paper presented to the 1989 annual meeting of the American Political Science Association, 31 August–3 September 1989, Atlanta, Georgia, p. 1.

23. Consultation with an official with the British government, London.

24. See testimony by Professor F. F. Ridley with Mr. Alan Doig to the Treasury and Civil Service subcommittee (London: Her Majesty's Stationery Office, 29 January 1986), p. 155.

25. See Levine, "The Federal Government in the Year 2000," p. 199.

26. John Edwards, head of the PS 2000 secretariat, made these observations at a joint CCMD-ENAP seminar on civil service reforms held on 8 May 1992 in Montreal.

27. Consultation with a former official with the British government, London.

28. Rubin, *Shrinking the Federal Government*, p. 205.

29. Not everyone will agree with this argument. See Gormley, *Taming the Bureaucracy*.

30. Johnson, "Management in Government."

31. See also George W. Downs and Patrick D. Larkey, *The Search for Govern-*

ment Efficiency: From Hubris to Helplessness (Philadelphia: Temple University Press, 1983), p. 259.

32. Consultations with officials with the National Audit Office, London. They also reported that, on the whole, scrutinies proved effective, if only because they forced departments to reexamine what they do and how they do it.

33. See *A Force for Improvement in the UK Civil Service* (London: Office of the Minister for the Civil Service, 1991), p. 13.

34. Consultations with officials with the British government, London.

35. Gormley, *Taming the Bureaucracy*, p. 124.

36. See J. Q. Wilson, *Bureaucracy and Mintzberg: Power in and Around Organizations* (Englewood Cliffs, N.J.: Prentice Hall, 1983) for a further elaboration on these and other models.

37. See, among many others, J. A. R. Marriott, *English Political Institutions*, 4th ed. (Oxford: Clarendon Press, 1938).

38. See, among others, Savoie, *Public Spending*.

39. Hugh Faulkner, a former minister in the Trudeau government, makes this point in his "Looking to Public Management," in Donald J. Savoie, ed., *Innovations and Trends in Management Development* (Toronto: IPAC, 1990), pp. 383–88.

40. See, among others, *Leadership for America: Rebuilding the Public Service* (Washington: Report of the National Commission of the Public Service, 1989), pp. 15–18 (17).

41. Consultation with an official with the British government, London.

42. Stephen Skowronek, *Building a New American State: The Expansion of National Administrative Capacities 1877–1920* (Cambridge: Cambridge University Press, 1982), pp. 290–91.

43. See, among others, "Hill Pressure to Outlaw Deficits Builds," *Washington Post*, 30 April 1992, p. A1, and "Throw the Bums Out, Part Two," *The Economist* (London), 16 May 1992, pp. 27–28.

44. Stefan Halper, "Making a Mockery of Washington," *Globe and Mail* (Toronto), 4 May 1992, p. A19.

45. See *Government Waste Watch* (Washington: Citizens Against Government Waste, 1992) and *Taxpayers Reform Program for the 1990s* (Washington: Citizens Against Government Waste, 1991), pp. 22–37.

46. See, among others, Doug Williams, *Problems of Governance: Political Participation and Administration of Justice in an Information Society* (Ottawa: Department of Justice, 1991), pp. 10–19, and Max Kaase, "The Challenge of the Participatory Revolution in Pluralist Democracies," *International Political Science Review*, vol. 5, no. 3, pp. 243–59.

47. This was a recurring theme in the work of Canada's leading political columnist Jeffrey Simpson. See the *Globe and Mail* (Toronto), p. A7, various dates from November 1991 to April 1992.

48. For Prime Minister Major, see "Lifting the Lid on a Pandora's Box," *Financial Times* (London), 14 May 1992, p. 19; Ferdinand Mount, *The British Constitution Now* (London: Heinemann, 1992).

49. See, among others, Johan P. Olsen, "Administrative Reform and Theories of Organization," in Campbell and Peters, *Organizing Governance*, p. 234.

50. Williams, *Problems of Governance*, p. 6.

51. Ibid., pp. 6, 9.

52. David Bell, "The World and the United States in 2013," *Daedalus*, vol. 116, no. 3, p. 22.

53. See, for example, Faulkner, "Looking to Public Management."

54. Gilles Paquet, "Betting on Moral Contracts," *Optimum*, vol. 23, no. 3, p. 52.

55. See Alan C. Cairns, *Charter Versus Federalism* (Montreal: McGill-Queen's University Press, 1992).

56. Tom Parklington, "Against Inflating Human Rights," *The Windsor Yearbook of Access to Justice* (Windsor, Ont.: University of Windsor, 1982), p. 85.

57. Williams, *Problems of Governance*, p. 19.

58. Harland Cleveland, "The Twilight of Hierarchy: Speculations on the Global Information Society," *Public Administration Review*, vol. 45, no. 1 (January–February 1985), p. 195.

59. See David Taras, *The Newsmakers: The Media's Influence on Canadian Politics* (Scarborough: Nelson Canada, 1990), and Joshua Meyrowitz, *No Sense of Place* (New York: Oxford University Press, 1985).

60. Pollitt, *Managerialism and the Public Services*, p. 178. See also Williams, *Problems of Governance*, p. 29.

61. I asked officials in the National Audit Office in London, the Auditor General in Canada, and the U.S. General Accounting Office to comment on evidence that machine- or productionlike agencies, including executive agencies and operating agencies, are more efficient. In Britain and Canada, officials made the point that it was too early to try to determine if agencies are more efficient today than when they were integral parts of the host departments. No one, however, suggested that managerialism, particularly new financial and accounting systems, led to lower costs in government operations.

62. See, among many others, Gerry Stoner, "Public Service Needs Good Dose of the Vision Thing," *The Citizen* (Ottawa), 6 April 1992, p. A8; Levine with Kleeman, *The Quiet Crisis of the Civil Service*; Williams, *Washington, Westminster and Whitehall*; and Zussman and Jabes, *The Vertical Solitude*.

63. Consultations with present and former government officials, London, Washington, and Ottawa; Gérard Veilleux, "The Federal Public Service: Standing at the Crossroads," notes for a speech to the Association of Professional Executives, May 1988, Ottawa.

64. *Leadership for America: Rebuilding the Public Service* (Washington: Report of the National Commission on the Public Service, 1989), p. 9.

65. Marcel Massé, "Managing the Policy Process—Some Research Priorities," speaking notes to a meeting of the Research Advisory Committee of the Canadian Centre for Management Development, 22 April 1991, Ottawa, p. 2.

66. See, among others, Pollitt, *Managerialism and the Public Services*, chapters 6 and 7.

67. Quotations are from Heath, *Keeling Lecture*, p. 2, and Lee Iacocca, "The Fine Art of Compromise," *Newsweek*, 23 December 1985, p. 10.

68. Consultation with present and former government officials in London, Washington, and Ottawa.

69. Quoted in Savoie, *Public Spending*, p. 216.

70. Ibid.

71. Robert Rector and Michael Sanera, "The Reagan Presidency and Policy Change," in Robert Rector and Michael Sanera, eds., *Steering the Elephant* (New York: Universe Books, 1987), p. 330.

72. Rourke and Schulman, "Adhocracy in Policy Development," pp. 135, 132.

73. Thomas R. Wolavin, *Presidential Advisory Commissions* (Madison: University of Wisconsin Press, 1972), p. 54.

74. Quoted in Rourke and Schulman, "Adhocracy in Policy Development," p. 134.

75. Consultations with government officials in London, Washington, and Ottawa. These figures include individuals working in central agencies; people working in liaison, coordination, and policy formulation units; and people charged with defining new projects within open-ended programs. They also include individuals engaged in policy fire fighting, in briefing ministers, and in research and development units.

76. Consultation with government officials in London, Washington, and Ottawa.

77. Rourke and Schulman, for example, argued that "bureaucratic think tank comes close to being an oxymoron." See Rourke and Schulman, "Adhocracy in Policy Development," p. 133. See also, among many others, Michael J. Prince and John A. Chenier, "The Rise and Fall of Policy Planning and Research Units: An Organizational Perspective," *Canadian Public Administration*, vol. 33, no. 4 (1980), pp. 535–46; Aberbach et al., *Bureaucrats and Politicians in Western Democracies*; and Rourke, *Bureaucratic Power in National Policy Making*.

78. See, among others, *Minutes of Evidence, Treasury and Civil Service Committee—Civil Servants and Ministers: Duties and Responsibilities* (London: Her Majesty's Stationery Office, 29 January 1986), p. 182.

79. See, among others, Stoner, "Public Service Needs Good Dose of the Vision Thing," p. A8.

80. Quotations are from *Minutes of Evidence, Treasury and Civil Service Committee—Civil Servants and Ministers*, p. 176; Ann Robinson, Rob Shepherd, F. F. Ridley, and G. W. Jones, "Symposium on Ministerial Responsibility," *Public Administration*, vol. 65, no. 1 (Spring 1987), p. 73; "The Growing Unease and Timidity in External Affairs," *Hill Times* (Ottawa), 3 January 1992, p. 5.

81. Consultation with government officials in London, Washington, and Ottawa. See Gerald Caiden, "Getting at the Essence of the Administrative State," *Indian Journal of Public Administration*, vol. 37, no 2 (April–June 1991), pp. 147–61.

82. Caiden, "Getting at the Essence of the Administrative State," pp. 147–61.

83. See Peter F. Drucker, "The Deadly Sins of Public Administration," *Public Administration Review*, vol. 26, no. 2 (March–April 1980), pp. 103–6.

84. Consultations with government officials in London, Washington, and Ottawa.

Index

Macmillan, Harold, 162, 361*n35*
Major, John, 256, 323, 334, 336
Make-or-buy policy, 64, 129, 130, 154–57
Making the Most of Next Steps: The Management of Ministers' Departments and the Executive Agencies (Fraser), 236
Management, 14, 30–32, 58, 116, 150; vs. administration, 12–13, 172–73; functions of, 31 (table); macro level, 118; by ministers, 120–21; vs. policy-making, 173–76, 197–98, 339–45; in private and public sectors compared, 30, 32, 136–38, 172, 282; teaching of, 191–96, 206; turnaround, 116, 139. *See also* Financial Management Initiative; Managerialism; Personnel management
Management and Personnel Office (MPO) (Great Britain), 122, 201, 204, 235
Management charter initiative, 193
Management-development training, 191–96, 206
Management Initiatives (Nielsen), 129–30
Management Matters, 246
Management of the United States Government (Reagan), 142, 189, 219
Managerialism, 172–77, 282, 285–87; and accountability of British civil service, 310–12, 313, 314–15, 316–17; and account-ability of Canadian civil service, 310, 313–14, 315–16, 317–18; and accountability of United States civil service, 306–10; civil service attitude toward, 196–99, 275–79, 292–96; and efficiency, 177, 186–91, 298–99, 395*n61*;

impact in Canada, 303, 322; impact in Great Britain, 255–56, 301–03, 321–22, 323; impact in United States, 188–91, 263–65, 290–91, 299–301, 320–21; and merit system, 288–90; and performance pay schemes, 290, 296–98; and policy role of officials, 173–76, 197–98, 339–45; and political appointments, 181–82, 276, 332; and public choice theory, 184, 304; and service to clients, 177, 183–86; Thatcher, Reagan and Mulroney approaches compared, 275–79, 290–92; and training, 191–96; and variety of measures under Mulroney, 268–72. *See also* Empowerment; *Reform 88*; Total Quality Management
Manager's Magazine, 246
Manion, John L., 195, 292
Market mechanisms, 11, 116, 148, 152, 286
Marks and Spencer, 118, 138
Masterman Committee, 34
Media, 337
Meese, Edwin, 216, 300
Merit system, 285, 288–90; in Canada, 53–55, 230, 289–90; in Great Britain, 48, 289–90; in United States, 51–53, 56, 220–22, 288, 289–90
Merit Systems Protection Board (MSPB), 221, 223, 290, 366*n61*
Metcalfe, Les, 122, 138, 197
Middleton, Peter, 209
Ministerial responsibility, 32–37, 108, 207, 211, 233, 310–14
Ministerial Task Force (MTF) (Canada). *See* Nielsen task force
Ministers: as managers, 120–21; overload of, 205; and senior officials, 376*n81*